SUSTAINABLE COMMUNITY DEVELOPMENT SERIES

Chris Maser, Editor

Resolving Environmental Conflict:
Towards Sustainable Community Development

Sustainable Community Development:
Principles and Concepts

Setting the Stage for Sustainability:
A Citizen's Handbook

Vision and Leadership in Sustainable Development

*Reuniting Ecology and Economy in
Sustainable Development*

*Ecological Diversity in Sustainable Development:
The Vital and Forgotten Dimension*

SUSTAINABLE COMMUNITY DEVELOPMENT SERIES

ECOLOGICAL DIVERSITY
in Sustainable Development

The Vital and Forgotten Dimension

Chris Maser

LEWIS PUBLISHERS

Boca Raton London New York Washington, D.C.

Library of Congress Cataloging-in-Publication Data

Catalog information may be obtained from the Library of Congress.

© 1999 by CRC Press LLC
Lewis Publishers is an imprint of CRC Press LLC

No claim to original U.S. Government works
International Standard Book Number 1-56670-377-8
Printed in the United States of America 1 2 3 4 5 6 7 8 9 0
Printed on acid-free paper

To the memory of E. Wayne Hammer, who for many years taught me how to read the tiny, subtle signs of diversity in forest, field, and fen. And to Sandy Pearlman, my friend and editor, who with patience, wit, and wisdom helps me struggle toward my ever-elusive horizon of excellence in writing.

How do all the energies of the universe originate? Through struggle, contest, conflict! Supposing all the particles of matter were continuously in equilibrium; would there then be any creative process at all?

Vivekananda

To the poet, to the philosopher, to the saint all things are friendly and sacred, all events profitable, all days holy, all people divine. For the eye is fastened on the life, and slights the circumstance. Every chemical substance, every plant, every animal in its growth teaches the unity of cause, the variety of appearance.

Ralph Waldo Emerson

TABLE OF CONTENTS

EDITOR'S NOTE

The book you are holding is part of a series on the various aspects of sustainable community development, where "community" focuses on the primacy and quality of relationships among people sharing a particular place and between people and their environment. "Development" means personal and social transformation to a higher level of consciousness and a greater responsibility to be one another's keepers, and "sustainability" is the act whereby one generation saves options by passing them to the next generation, which saves options by passing them to the next, and so on.

This series came about because, during the 25 years I was in scientific research, I discovered disturbing patterns of human thought and behavior that continually squelch sustainable community development. These patterns are as follows:

1. While physicists have found a greater voice for the spiritual underpinnings of physics, the biological sciences have all but lost their spiritual foundation, casting us adrift on a sea of arrogance and increasing spiritual, emotional, and intellectual isolation.

2. There is a continuing attempt to force specialization into ever-narrowing mental boxes, thereby so fragmenting our view of the world that we continually disarticulate the very processes that produce and maintain the viability of the ecosystems on which we, as individuals and societies, depend for survival.

3. People point outside themselves to the cause of environmental problems without understanding that all such problems arise within ourselves, with our thinking. Before we can heal the environment, we must learn to heal ourselves emotionally and spiritually.

4. We are asking science to answer questions concerning social values, which science is not designed to do. Social questions require social answers.

5. One who has the courage to ask questions outside the accepted norm of scientific inquiry is ostracized because, as English philosopher John Locke said, "New opinions are always suspected, and usually opposed, without any other reason...[than] they are not already common."

This series of books on the various facets of sustainable community development is thus a forum in which those who dare to seek harmony and wholeness can struggle to integrate disciplines and balance the material world with the spiritual, the scientific with the social, and in so doing expose their vulnerabilities, human frailties, and hope, as well as their visions for a sustainable future.

The decision to contribute to this series of books necessarily entails the willingness to risk, as author Scott Nearing noted many years ago when he wrote on a small card, "The majority will always be for caution, hesitation, and the status quo—always against creation and innovation. The innovator—he [or she] who leaves the beaten track—must therefore always be a minoritarian—always be an object of opposition, scorn, hatred. It is part of the price he [or she] must pay for the ecstasy that accompanies creative thinking and acting."

As the title of this book implies, ecological diversity, including the human component, is one of the critically important but often overlooked dimensions of social–environmental sustainability. Yet it is the integrity of the relationships among the diverse elements in any system that not only defines the system through its functional processes but also confers stability to the system in its functioning. *Ecological Diversity in Sustainable Development: The Vital and Forgotten Dimension* examines this notion in terms of Nature, culture, and sustainable community development.

Chris Maser
Series Editor

FOREWORD

In his usual well-written, entertaining, and clear style, Chris Maser once again has produced a writing likely to generate considerable dialogue among all "stakeholders" of our global natural resources. From industry, environmental, and political leaders to researchers, entrepreneurs, and community activists—Maser provides no escape for any of us in our responsibilities to acknowledge and work toward achieving long-term ecological diversity.

If the author's cited case studies are any example, achieving ecological diversity is not only a hugely daunting task but one for which humans, especially in Western civilization, have little *talent* (versus skill). We concentrate far too much on *product* versus *process,* on *abundance* versus *balance,* on *science* versus *nature,* on *machine* versus *man.* Our vision tends toward the myopic, and our focus in thought and action is (all too often) short term.

I, for one, am less critical of Western civilization on these matters. And while there will always be exceptions throughout time, I believe we as humans will always strive to make the right choices—to do the right thing—not only for ourselves but for our future civilizations. I also believe that in order to make those right choices, we must consistently and persuasively be reminded of the *consequences* and the *what ifs*—as they have unfolded in the past, as they will occur again in the future, without our due diligence. It is this that Maser does so well.

Do not expect to feel comfortable about the issues and examples raised in Maser's work. You will not. Do not expect to find solutions neatly spelled out for you. They are not there. Rather, expect to be challenged, to struggle, to debate, to create. *Ecological Diversity in Sustainable Development: The Vital and Forgotten Dimension* is a book you will remember.

Catherine M. Mater, Vice President
Mater Engineering, Ltd.
Corvallis, Oregon

PREFACE

I used to study tiger beetles, which are in the family Cicindelidae and are cosmopolitan in geographical distribution. One of the things that I found fascinating about them is that they are devoid of pigment and yet are arrayed in brilliant metallic hues. But how can that be, one might ask. Rather than pigment, the colors exhibited by tiger beetles are created by light refracted off the minute structural topography of their wing covers and external skeletons. The day I first noticed this, I was examining an Oregon tiger beetle, *Cicindela oregona*, under a binocular scope. Although the background color of the beetle appeared dull brown to my naked eye, under the scope, every color of the rainbow dazzled my view as I turned the beetle this way and that in awe of its brilliance. Its beauty was to me breathtaking.

Like the background color of the Oregon tiger beetle, our world is filled with unseen wonders, one of the most phenomenal of which is the often hidden beauty of the diversity that surrounds us. Apart from the beauty it affords our lives, however, there is the functional aspect of diversity that is absolutely necessary to the sustainability of life itself.

It is the functional aspect of diversity that is the wealth of each and every village, town, city, and nation. It is the functional aspect of diversity that is the soil in which the taproot of social–environmental sustainability grows. It is the functional aspect of diversity that causes us to plumb the depths of our imaginations, where, enshrouded in that holy place we call ignorance, bubbles the mystery we try so hard through science to unveil that we might understand its significance to our lives.

There is more to diversity, however, than just the physical dimension with which we are so often preoccupied in the biological sciences. There also is a human dimension, which extends beyond the physical to include the realms of perception and spirituality. "We don't see things as they are," wrote American author Anaïs Nin. "We see things as we are." To this, American clergyman Henry Emerson Fosdick might have added, "I would rather live in a world where my life is surrounded by mystery than live in a world so small that my mind could comprehend it." I am of like mind.

In dealing with diversity, as best I understand it anyway, I find it to be the currency of social–environmental sustainability, both locally and globally, because it both adds and subtracts pieces of a living system in such a way that manipulation of those pieces causes a chain of events to occur that in effect becomes continually directed change, often of unknown magnitude. In turn, every change is beneficial to some organisms and detrimental to others. Whether a particular chain of events is thus beneficial or detrimental to humanity depends on how the outcome in time and space either adds to or subtracts from the necessities of human survival and the potentialities of human values.

The dimension of time is important because an outcome that is apparently beneficial in the short term can prove detrimental in the long term, well after the decision makers are deceased. On the other hand, the dimension of space is critical because a decision that is seemingly beneficial in a local area can, and often does, have detrimental effects many miles away, unbeknownst to the decision makers. In either case, the outcome affects the social–environmental sustainability of human communities at the local level—often without recourse to rectify negative impacts, even life-threatening ones.

I have elected to write about the various dimensions of diversity because I am firmly convinced that the importance of diversity—and our relationship to it in time and space, both materially and spiritually—are little understood in the social realm, where decisions are made that affect all of society for generations to come. In so doing, I have summed up knowledge gleaned from more than two decades as a research scientist, knowledge I found out of balance with my spiritual knowing, which lies beyond such knowledge.

I recognize that the problems communities and their collective society are facing—an uncertain future because of the growing losses of biological, genetic, and functional diversity; because of growing pollution of air, water, and soil; because of depletion of the ozone layer and potential global warming; because of crumbling families and loss of community trust—cannot be mended with scientific Band-Aids and technological quick fixes. Nevertheless, out of the current growing social chaos can come a society with a better balance between the scientific and the social, the materialistic and the spiritual, the masculine and the feminine, the intellectual and the intuitive, the unconscious and the conscious, the present and the future, and the local and the global. To achieve that better balance, however, we must view the world and society differently, including the varied dimensions of diversity.

Humanity has taken for granted the world as designed by Nature and has exploited it in such a way and to such an extent that human society cannot long endure with any sense of well-being and dignity on its present course. People within a community compete with one another for the goods and services of Nature. In turn, each community competes with every other community within a society and each society competes with every other society for the same goods and services. In that competition, each community within a society—and therefore the society itself—has become so needy and so specialized in the materialistic sense that today we live in a global collection of competing societies, which stands like a house of cards. If one major society falls, the ripples of collapse are felt throughout the world, at times with stunning rapidity.

The day must therefore arrive when the citizens of this planet come to understand that if local communities and their societies are to survive, we must set aside our historic, exploitive, environmental competition and begin instead to cooperate and to coordinate with one another. Only then will we be able to bring our various cultures into social–environmental harmony so there will be room for all planetary citizens, both human and nonhuman. Only then will planet Earth be adaptable to changes wrought by the hand of humanity and be at least benign to humanity, within the physical–biological guidelines established by Nature for this grand experiment called "life."

Clearly, as a single human being with a single perceptive lens, I write this book in accord with my own perception of the world and how *I think* it might work. I can do nothing else, as it were, but tell it *as I see it* because neither I nor anyone else *knows* how it is. As I chronicle what I perceive to be the passing events of my time, I add a pinch of the historian to the scientist I was trained to be.

In so doing, I hark to the beautifully penned words of British historian Arnold Toynbee, who said, "There are many angles of vision from which human minds peer at the universe. My view of history is [thus] itself a tiny piece of history; and this mainly other people's history and not my own....If my individual view of history is to be made at all illuminating, or indeed intelligible, it must be presented in its origin, growth, and social and personal setting."* I have done my best to follow Toynbee's lead,

---

* Arnold Toynbee. 1958. *Civilization on Trial and the World and the West,* Meridian Books, New York.

recognizing, of course, that history, like everything else in the world, is a revolving doorway of perception that can no more stand still than science, art, or even life itself. History is the continual reexamination and reinterpretation of who we humans think we are in the present collective mind based on the collective recollection of our ancestors' past behavior.

Although I have in my past writings briefly examined a few facets of diversity, I have never before put in one place the full extent of my often daunting struggle to grasp the dimensions of diversity as they apply to sustainable community development, the very foundation of which is creative novelty that in turn leads to diversity. Diversity, after all, is the outcome of relationships, and all we as humans do in life is practice relationship. Therefore, if we, you and I, want to change anything for the better, we must work constructively and purposefully with other people at our respective local levels because that is where we have our most intimate living relationships with one another and our environment.

To this end, understanding and dealing with diversity in contemporary life not only is a mammoth social problem but also has two sides, one ecological and the other cultural. My purpose in writing this book is to set up the ecological framework into which culture must fit if it is to survive the 21st century in any semblance of the way in which we know it. Thus, when I speak about the "long term," it must be understood that I do so in the modern social sense, not in the geological sense.

To write this book required that I become knowledgeable enough about a geographical area, such as the state of Oregon, to piece together the principles and concepts of how ecosystems function. These principles and concepts are generally applicable worldwide, but the landforms and species involved in any given area are unique. It is my hope that you, the reader, can understand the principles and concepts as they apply to your specific locale.

As you read this book, you may find that the overarching problems we all face as a society appear to be overwhelming and depressing, but keep in mind that we have not arrived at our current world circumstances overnight and we will not cure them overnight. With this in mind, I have scattered throughout the book solutions to the problems faced by society. They come in four guises. Raising a question to which people must respond is potentially the most powerful way to present a solution be-cause in answering the question people discover their own empowerment to change. Using suggestions given as quotes by other people is the second way solutions are presented. A third way is through stories that have different ways of thinking embedded within them. Finally, presenting my own experience and ideas based on many years of research and travel is the fourth way solutions are incorporated into the text.

I write this book with hope for the future because choice equals hope, and choice and hope equal dignity. Recognizing that we are where we are by the collective of our individual choices is to recognize that we can change by choice. If we err in the process of choosing our thoughts and actions, we can always choose to choose again because we are not locked into any circumstances except by our individual choices taken in the collective. The choice is yours, mine, and ours collectively.

This book is divided into three parts. Part I looks at diversity as we inherited it from Nature. Part II considers culture as it affects diversity through its evolution, and Part III examines the diversity of Nature through the eyes of culture in an attempt to guide culture toward social–environmental sustainability. As we begin our journey into the labyrinth of diversity, it would be wise to ponder the counsel of Henry David Thoreau, who wrote that "the frontiers are not east or west, north or south, but wherever a…[person] fronts a fact [or idea, such as diversity]."

ACKNOWLEDGMENTS

I t is with genuine pleasure that I thank the following people, listed in alphabetical order, for reviewing the manuscript with care and diligence: Rob Bonnichsen (director of the Center for the Study of First Americans, Oregon State University, Corvallis), Jane Lubchenco (distinguished professor of zoology, Oregon State University, Corvallis, and past president of the American Association for the Advancement of Science), and Joyce Pytkowicz (environmental assistant to Oregon State Representative Barbara Ross, Corvallis).

I thank my friend and editor, Sandy Pearlman, for her usual marvelous job of clarifying my writing for the reader's benefit. It is Sandy's editing that constantly nudges my writing toward the excellence I have for so long sought.

To my ever-loving wife, Zane, I offer special thanks for her patience with my many hours of working on this book, but especially for proofreading the entire manuscript.

AUTHOR

C hris Maser spent over 20 years as a research scientist in natural history and ecology in forest, shrub steppe, subarctic, desert, and coastal settings. Trained primarily as a vertebrate zoologist, he was a research mammalogist in Nubia, Egypt (1963–64) with the Yale University Peabody Museum Prehistoric Expedition and was a research mammalogist in Nepal (1966–67) for the U.S. Naval Medical Research Unit #3 based in Cairo, Egypt, where he participated in a study of tick-borne diseases. He conducted a three-year (1970–73) ecological survey of the Oregon coast for the University of Puget Sound, Tacoma, Washington. He was a research ecologist with the U.S. Department of the Interior, Bureau of Land Management, for 12 years (1975–87), the last 8 years studying old-growth forests in western Oregon, and a landscape ecologist with the Environmental Protection Agency for a year (1990–91).

Today he is an independent author as well as an international lecturer and a facilitator in resolving environmental disputes, vision statements, and sustainable community development. He is also an international consultant in forest ecology and sustainable forestry practices.

He has written over 260 publications, including the following books: *Mammals of the Pacific Northwest: From the Coast to the High Cascades* (1988), *Forest Primeval: The Natural History of an Ancient Forest* (1989, listed in the *School Library Journal* as best science and technical book of 1989), *Global Imperative: Harmonizing Culture and Nature* (1992), *Sustainable Forestry: Philosophy, Science, and Economics* (1994), *From the Forest to the Sea: The Ecology of Wood in Streams, Rivers, Estuaries, and Oceans* (1994, with James R. Sedell), *Resolving Environmental Conflict: Towards Sustainable Community Development* (1996), *Sustainable Community Development: Principles and Concepts* (1997), *Setting the Stage for Sustainability: A Citizen's Handbook* (1998, with Russ Beaton and Kevin

Smith), *Vision and Leadership in Sustainable Development* (1999), and *Reuniting Economy and Ecology in Sustainable Development* (1999, with Russ Beaton). Although he has worked in Canada, Egypt, France, Germany, Japan, Malaysia, Nepal, Slovakia, and Switzerland, he calls Corvallis, Oregon, home.

PART I

DIVERSITY AS
A PART OF NATURE

*Scholars in our century have forgotten
that theory owes its existence to practice
and that Nature existed before there were rules.*

Eckartshausen

SURVIVAL, ECONOMICS, AND DIVERSITY

W e are born. We grow. We learn. We grow. We change. We destroy. We create. We destroy. But what endures? Chocolate? Perhaps not even that!

THE CHOCOLATE CRISIS

Chocoholics of the world may soon be in crisis, unless an alliance of candy manufacturers and environmental groups can prevent a disaster of gigantic proportions—a shortage of chocolate.[1] While the world's appetite for chocolate grows ever-more voracious (led by the United States and Germany, wherein 629,000 and 286,000 tons of chocolate, respectively, were consumed annually from 1990 to 1994), cocoa farms around the world are under siege and failing because of attacks by fungal and viral diseases and insects.

For decades, cocoa farmers have escaped such problems as diseases and insects by moving to new areas of tropical forest, or even new countries or continents, where growers found more of the rain forest in which cocoa trees thrive. The forest was then cut down and cocoa plantations were created in its place. But of late, the number of tropical forests to replace with cocoa plantations is dwindling, and researchers predict a shortage of cocoa beans, the raw material from which chocolate is made, in as little as five to ten years.

"We're running out of places in the world" to plant cocoa trees, said Dr. Carol Knight, vice president of scientific affairs at the American Cocoa

3

Research Institute, a nonprofit group that tracks the supply of cocoa. "We have to figure out how to grow it sustainably. Nobody wants to lose chocolate." Therefore, in April 1998, representatives from the Mars, Cadbury, Nestlé, and Hershey companies met at the Smithsonian Tropical Research Institute in Panama with conservation groups to talk about strategies for farming cocoa trees sustainably, and the Mars Company paid the bill.

Sustainability, researchers say, will require a shift *away* from the traditional large plantations carved out of the rain forest that are open to the sun and thus heavily depend on pesticides, fungicides, and fertilizers and which are simply abandoned when the cost of maintenance becomes prohibitive. Sustainability, they say, will require a shift *toward* small farms, where cocoa trees are grown in the shade of larger trees, and cocoa trees are replanted as needed, rather than abandoning the farm. A shift toward small cocoa farms not only will help reduce the cost of growing cocoa beans but also will help save rain forests and many of the species of plants and animals that appear to flourish in a cocoa grove that approaches its more natural setting.

The task of ecologically designing a small-scale cocoa farm is daunting because little is known about the best way to grow cocoa trees, which evolved in the tropical rain forests of the New World, where they grow in the shade under taller trees. After six years or so, these slow-growing trees produce pods about the size and shape of a football; each pod contains about 40 cocoa beans about the size of a lima bean. The cocoa beans can be roasted, finely ground, and mixed with sugar and milk to produce chocolate.

But the cocoa tree is particularly vulnerable to disease for reasons researchers do not understand. For example, Dr. Jim Gockowski, an agricultural economist at the International Institute of Tropical Agriculture in Cameroon, said, "There are diseases in South America that are threatening to wipe out the industry there, as well as the rest of the world if they spread." Tony Lass, an expert on the cultivation of cocoa trees at Cadbury Ltd., the British chocolate maker, pointed out that a new species of black pod disease, a disease of West Africa that is a cousin of the potato blight, has evolved and quickly spread to the border of the Ivory Coast, the world's largest producer of cocoa. "It's now sitting on the frontier," said Lass, "where a million tons of cocoa a year is under threat," because once disease strikes a cocoa tree, it produces not only fewer beans but also beans that, according to some people, are of less reliable quality and poorer flavor.

Dr. Alison Power and her colleague, Dr. Alex Flecker, both ecologists at Cornell University in New York, have been working in the Dominican

Republic, where cocoa trees are grown under what may be the most natural conditions, in the shade of tall trees that remain from the original tropical forest. By comparing patches of habitat within relatively undisturbed forest with patches of habitat within cocoa farms, they have found that both habitats support similar levels of diversity in species of birds, lizards, and insects. However, while Dr. Power noted that the diversity of species found on cocoa farms is different from that in undisturbed forest, compared with the sterility of plantations of bananas or oil palms, the small, naturally shaded cocoa farms are havens of biodiversity.

Researchers suspect that the diversity of species living in these farmed forests is helping the cocoa trees to fare better against diseases than they do in large monocultural plantations, where there is nothing but cocoa trees for hundreds of acres. "The closer it can be grown to a more or less natural state with some natural predators," contends Dr. Gockowski, "that's when you're going to really talk about a sustainable system."

Dr. Allen M. Young, a tropical biologist at the Milwaukee Public Museum in Milwaukee, Wisconsin, is conducting an experiment in Costa Rica to test these ideas. His early findings indicate that the closer the growing environment of the cocoa tree is to its indigenous old-growth forest, the better it fares against fungal diseases and insects. Conversely, the more plantation-like the growing environment of the cocoa tree is, the more rampant are the pests that plague it. But clearly, it is not just for cocoa beans that people compete with one another in ways that are environmentally destructive. The root of such destructive competition is a misguided sense of personal survival.

THE RIGHT OF PERSONAL SURVIVAL

Author Bill McKibben, writing in *The Atlantic Monthly*, puts an interesting and little considered spin on the root of destructive environmental competition.[2] Since agriculture began, 10,000 years ago, says McKibben, human endeavor has flowed in one direction—toward *more of everything*, which we have made synonymous with social progress. At first, the momentum toward more was gradual, almost imperceptible, checked by wars, the Dark Ages, plagues, and taboos, but it has accelerated in recent centuries, its curves on every graph becoming ever steeper.

"The *increase* in human population in the 1990s has exceeded the *total* population in 1600," writes McKibben. "The population has grown more since 1950 than it did during the previous four million years." The reason seems clearly to have been the revolution in public health since World

War II, including the nonindustrialized countries. Vaccines and antibiotics burst onto the scene, and right behind them exploded the human population. If, however, people in the United States had died throughout this century at the same rate as they did at its beginning, instead of being saved by the revolution in public health, the population of the United States would be 140 million rather than 270 million.

According to McKibben, William Catton, a sociologist at Washington State University in Pullman, once tried to calculate the amount of energy people used daily. In the time when people hunted and gathered, they used about 2,500 calories, all of it in food, which is the daily intake of energy by a common dolphin. A modern person uses 31,000 calories a day, mostly from fossil fuel, which is the intake of a pilot whale. An average citizen of the United States, on the other hand, uses six times that, or 186,000 calories per day—an amount equivalent to that of a sperm whale.

We are, continues McKibben, different people than our ancestors in that we have gotten bigger. I remember, for example, going into a museum in a town in southern Japan some years ago. I was stunned when I looked at the armor worn by the fabled Samurai warriors in centuries past because they were fitted for men who might have reached five feet in height had they stood on their tiptoes. Today, however, we cast a much bigger shadow, as do the younger generations of Japanese, not only in stature but also in material appetites.

For instance, scientists in Vancouver, British Columbia, Canada, trying to calculate the shadow cast by modern humans, found that while 1.7 million people lived on 1 million acres surrounding the city of Vancouver, those same people required 21.5 million acres of land to support them. This 21.5 million acres included such things as wheat fields in Alberta; oxygen from tropical forests in Central and South America, Africa, and Asia; fish from the eastern Pacific Ocean; oil from deposits in Saudi Arabia; bananas from South America; and vegetables from fields in California. In essence, says McKibben, "people in Manhattan [New York] are as dependent on faraway resources as people on the Mir space station."

Our collective shadows have grown so much in the past 20 to 30 years, according to McKibben, that we are even changing those places we do not inhabit—changing the way in which weather works, changing the way in which plants and animals live and relate to one another from the Arctic to the deep jungle. "Of all the remarkable and unexpected things we've ever done as a species, this," contends McKibben, "may be the biggest."

As more people crowd onto this tiny planet spinning in space, each person's share of the land area to support him or her shrinks, which means that more people want their "fair share" of resources from supplies that are either finite, already dwindling, or unavailable because of the social injustice of allocation based on material wealth and political power. Destructive environmental competition is thus born out of a perceived threat to a person's "right of survival," however that is defined.

The perceived security of our right to survive is measured against the number of choices we think are available to us as individuals and our ability to control those choices. The greater the supply of a particular resource, the greater the freedom of choice an individual has with respect to that resource. Conversely, the smaller the supply, the narrower the range of choices unless, of course, we steal choices from other people—in the present and/or the future—to augment our own. And scarcity, real or perceived, is the breeding ground of environmental injustice, which rears its ugly head each time someone steals from another rather than taking responsibility for his or her own behavior and sharing equally. Thus, as long as one party in a competitive battle over resources thinks it can win agreement with its stance, which means to defend its perceived choices, that party will neither compromise nor change its position.

Perceived choices are ultimately affected by the real supply and demand for natural resources, the source of energy required by all life in one form or another. Perhaps with this in mind, former Soviet leader Mikhail Gorbachev asked: "If we're going to protect the planet's ecology, we're going to need to find alternatives to the consumerist dream that is attracting the world. Otherwise, how will we conserve our resources, and how will we avoid setting people against each other when resources are depleted?"[3]

Gorbachev's question calls to mind a line from a song popular some years ago: "Freedom's just another word for nothing left to lose"; in a peculiar way, it speaks of an apparent human truth. When one is unconscious of a material value, one is free of its psychological grip. But the instant one perceives a material value and anticipates possible material gain, one also perceives the psychological pain of potential loss.

The larger and more immediate the prospects for material gain, the greater the political power used to ensure and expedite exploitation, because not to exploit is perceived as losing an opportunity to someone else. And it is this notion of loss that one fights so hard to avoid. In this sense, it is more appropriate to think of resources as managing humans than of humans as managing resources.[4]

Historically, then, any newly identified resource is inevitably overexploited, often to the point of collapse or extinction. Its overexploitation is based, first, on the perceived rights or entitlement of the discoverer–exploiter to get his or her share before someone else does and, second, on the right or entitlement to protect his or her economic investment from loss, real or perceived. There is more to it than this, however, because the concept of a healthy capitalistic system is one that is ever growing, ever expanding, but such a system is not biologically sustainable. With renewable natural resources, such nonsustainable exploitation is based on a "ratchet effect," where to ratchet means to constantly, albeit unevenly, increase the rate of exploitation of a resource—but not decrease it.

The ratchet effect works as follows: During periods of relative economic stability, the rate of cut or capture of a given renewable resource, say timber or salmon, tends to stabilize at a level that economic theory predicts can be *sustained* through some scale of time. Such levels, however, are almost always excessive, because economists take existing unknown and unpredictable ecological variables and convert them, in theory at least, into known and predictable economic constants in order to better calculate the expected return on a given investment from a sustained harvest. Here, it must be noted that a sustain*ed* harvest is not a sustain*able* harvest.

Then comes a sequence of good years in the market or in the availability of the resource, or both, and additional capital investments in harvesting and processing are encouraged because competitive economic growth is the root of capitalism. When conditions return to normal or even below normal, however, the industry, having overinvested, appeals to the government for help because substantial economic capital is at stake. The government typically responds with direct or indirect subsidies, justifying the expenditure of taxpayer dollars by the intention of saving jobs. But however well intentioned the subsidies are, they only encourage continual overharvesting.

The ratchet effect is thus caused by unrestrained economic investment to increase short-term yields in good times and strong opposition to losing those yields in bad times. This opposition to losing yields means there is great resistance to using a resource in a biologically sustainable manner because there is no predictability in yields and no guarantee of yield increases in the foreseeable future. In addition, our linear economic models of ever-increasing yield are built on the assumption that we can in fact have an economically sustained yield, but this contrived concept fails in the face of the *biological sustainability* of that yield.

Then, because there is no mechanism in our linear economic models of ever-increasing yield that allows for the uncertainties of ecological cycles and variability or for the inevitable decreases in yield during bad times, the long-term outcome is a heavily subsidized industry. Such an industry continually overharvests the resource on an artificially created, sustained-yield basis that is not biologically sustainable, as exemplified by the white abalone, a marine snail.[5]

Biologists have long assumed that the oceans are too vast and their inhabitants too diverse, too widespread, too numerous, and too prolific for humans to ever extinguish a marine species—a thought once held about the great herds of buffalo, the countless flocks of passenger pigeons, and the old-growth forests. Finally, the notion of limitless resources in the oceans of the world is crumbling, as it continues to do so for terrestrial ecosystems.

Thirty years ago, as a graduate student, Ted Tutschulte, a former marine ecologist, took a deep breath, dove into the shallow ocean off California's Catalina Island, and scooped up as many white abalone as he could hold. Later, as part of his doctoral dissertation, he estimated that an area of 2.5 acres harbored up to 10,000 of these large, flattened marine snails. But now Tutschulte has learned that a recent census in his old study area turned up just three white abalone, and scientists are predicting that the species will soon be extinct in the wild. "It just doesn't seem possible," he said.

Tutschulte is not alone in his thinking. People, including biologists, have for centuries doubted that humans could ever extinguish the white abalone—or any other species that spends its entire life at sea. Even the most persecuted marine creatures, biologists said, would find refuge somewhere in the vastness of the seas, which they would eventually repopulate. But the population of white abalone plummeted because regulators overlooked a critical factor concerning the snail's reproductive biology.

To breed successfully, the white abalone had to be close enough together, within three feet of each other, so that the eggs and sperm released into the water could mix and find one another for fertilization to take place. Data show that since 1969, probably the last successful breeding season, the continual harvest has reduced the population below its critical density, and the snails have been dying faster than they can reproduce, although some state biologists and commercial divers disagree, claiming that remnant populations remain in deep water. "Even if the species is not biologically extinct," says Paul Dayton of the Scripps Institute of Oceanography in La Jolla, California, "its population has been reduced so low that it cannot exert its former ecological role." In other words, the white abalone is functionally extinct within the ocean.

But when the notion of sustainability arises in a conflict over destructive competition for resources, the parties marshal all scientific data favorable to their respective sides as "good" science and discount all unfavorable data as "bad" science. Destructive environmental conflict over the rights of economic competition is thus the stage on which science is politicized, largely obfuscating its service to society.

Because the availability of choices dictates the amount of control we feel we have with respect to our sense of security, a potential loss of money is the breeding ground for environmental injustice. This is the kind of environmental injustice in which the present generation steals from all future generations by overexploiting a resource rather than facing the uncertainty of giving up potential income. The current differences of opinion over whether North Atlantic swordfish should be sold in American restaurants is a case in point.[6]

Two environmental groups, Sea-Web and the Natural Resources Defense Council, contend that the numbers of North Atlantic swordfish are being depleted by a new fishing technique that catches them when they are too young to reproduce. This contention is based on the fact that until the middle of this century, North Atlantic swordfish were captured by harpooning, so that only the largest (those weighing between 200 and 1,200 pounds) ended up in the marketplace. Today, however, the new technique, which uses lines with hundreds of baited hooks attached, catches far more fish, but they average only about 90 pounds.

Lisa Speer, a spokeswoman for the Natural Resources Defense Council, stated that the population of North Atlantic swordfish has declined by more than half since 1978 and that U.S. fishermen account for about a third of the catch worldwide. The threat of overexploiting the North Atlantic swordfish led the U.S. government in 1991 to place restrictions on the size and quantity that can be caught. Even stricter quotas were adopted in 1997.

Because of the warning that the population of North Atlantic swordfish is declining at an alarming rate, 27 chefs at some of the finest U.S. restaurants are eliminating it from their menus for at least a year, in what is being called the "Give Swordfish a Break" campaign. "We depend on the continued supply of the fish," said Rick Moonen, executive chef–partner at the restaurant Oceana, "and [we] have a clear responsibility to ensure that it continues."

The "Give Swordfish a Break" campaign is not a boycott, says Speer. "We just want to give the fish a break so that future generations can enjoy them." But not everyone agrees with this stand.

Some chefs, particularly those who use large quantities of swordfish, say they will not join the campaign and remove the fish from their menus. Stanley Kramer, executive chef at Docks Oyster Bar in New York, is of the opinion that only an international effort would be effective in saving the swordfish. He is quoted as saying, "Why should we punish American fishermen [by joining the campaign] while Spanish and Japanese fishermen continue to fish for North Atlantic swordfish of all sizes and sell them?"

There are important lessons in all of this for anyone concerned about biological and genetic diversity. First, history suggests that a biologically sustainable use of any resource has never been achieved without first overexploiting it, despite historical warnings and contemporary data. If history is correct, resource problems are not environmental problems but rather human ones that we have created many times, in many places, under a wide variety of social, political, and economic systems.

Second, the fundamental issues involving resources, the environment, and people are complex and process driven. An integrated knowledge of multiple disciplines is required to understand them. These underlying complexities of the physical and biological systems preclude a simplistic approach to both management and conflict resolution. In addition, the wide natural variability and the compounding, cumulative influence of continual human activity mask the results of overexploitation until they are severe and often irreversible.

Third, as long as the uncertainty of continual change is considered a condition to be avoided, nothing will be resolved and the biological sustainability of our renewable natural resources will suffer to the increasing impoverishment of future generations. However, once the uncertainty of change is accepted as an inevitable, open-ended, creative life process, most decision making is simply common sense. For example, common sense dictates that one would favor actions that have the greatest potential for reversibility, as opposed to those with little or none. Such reversibility can be ascertained by monitoring results of actions and modifying those actions and policy accordingly.

Having said this, it is clear to me that Western industrialized society—and we in the United States in particular—have no moral right to continue with the self-centered attitude that all the world's resources exist to bathe our generation in material comforts, such as the American propensity for large, gas-guzzling utility and sport vehicles, without regard for those whose lands we are depleting of sustainability by destroying their biological and genetic diversity. Nor, I submit, do we have the moral right to steal from those who must follow, those whom *we* have brought into the world—the children. I also understand, however, that some of our adult attitudes are governed largely by ignorance and fear, which together add up to greed.

Although I can do nothing directly about the fear that is so pervasive in the world today, I can do something about the ignorance, which is the purpose of this book. If one's ignorance can be lifted to some extent, then, perhaps, so can one's fear. Ignorance is nothing to be ashamed of; we all have our own share. But ignorance can be lifted if we are willing to see ourselves as one another's keepers, which means we must individually change our thinking so that our collective social behavior can change.

Consider the following story: A man is given permission to see both heaven and hell while he is still alive. He chooses to visit hell first. To his surprise, he finds an enormous gathering of people at a feast. They are seated at a long table covered with every imaginable delicacy. Yet the people, all lamenting loudly, are slowly starving to death.

As the man studies this strange scene more closely, he observes that the handles of their eating utensils are so long that they are unable to bring the food to their own mouths. The man leaves with sorrow in his heart and goes to visit heaven.

In heaven he finds an almost identical scene: the same eating utensils with handles much too long for the people to reach their own mouths. But the people of heaven are laughing and rejoicing, because rather than choosing to try to feed themselves, as did those in hell, the people in heaven are choosing to feed one another.

In the final analysis, the choice of our behavior is ours. We must therefore accept that by our thoughts, which we put into actions, we can maintain our old destructive ways of doing things or we can create new ways based on mutual caring and social–environmental harmony. If we keep our old ways of self-centered, environmentally destructive competition and conflict, like the people in hell, we will be the authors of our own increasing misery and that of our children and grandchildren and beyond. On the other hand, we can choose to create a new way of living through other-centered cooperation and coordination, like the people in heaven feeding one another, and so offer our children and grandchildren an unconditional gift of life with dignity.

Such an unconditional gift must be given with the understanding that both the quality of human life and the health of our human economy depend on the services performed "free of charge" by ecosystems, services that are worth many trillions of dollars annually. Economic activities that destroy habitats and impair services performed by ecosystems will create costs to humanity over the long term that will undoubtedly exceed in great measure the perceived short-term economic profits. Yet because most of these services, and the benefits they provide, are not traded in economic markets, they carry no visible price tags that would alert society to their relative value, changes in their supply, or deterioration of the underlying ecological systems that generate them.[7]

These ecological costs are usually hidden from traditional economic accounting, but are nevertheless real and borne by society at large—especially the children. Tragically, a short-term economic focus in current decisions concerning land use often sets in motion great costs that, again, are bequeathed by myopic adults not only to their own children but also to all the children of the future.[7] Unfortunately, humanity, as history shows, finds the real value of something taken for granted only when that something is lost; real value of common things is too often found only in hindsight.

This is but saying that we can design our world in such a way that culture both creates its own harmony and is in harmony with Nature. To do this, however, we must understand the dimensions of diversity and consciously, purposefully protect those that govern the biological sustainability of our home planet for the benefit of all generations.

THE UNIVERSE IS BORN   2

Before time, the Universe was naught, and, according to the Bible, "the earth was without form, and void; and darkness was upon the face of the deep."[8] Then, according to current scientific thought, arose a great cataclysm, the "big bang," which created a supremely harmonious and logical process as a foundation for the evolution of matter, and the Universe was born. So began the impartial process of evolution, which proceeds from the simple to the complex, from the general to the specific, and from the strongly bound to the more weakly bound.

Although I suspect many people have at least some familiarity with the concept that evolution moves from the simple toward the complex and from the general toward the specific, I doubt as many people are familiar with the notion of moving from the strongly bound toward the weakly bound. To understand the latter, consider an extended family. The strongest bond is between a husband and wife, then between the parents and their children. As the family grows, the bonds between the children and their various aunts and uncles and their first, second, and third cousins become progressively weaker as relationships become more distant with the increasing size of the family, not to mention the continual inclusion of marriage partners from heretofore unrelated families.

Taking this notion of the strength of a bond one step further, consider a community. There is a definite limit to the number of people that can live together with a sense of community. This limit is brought about by the necessity of having frequent face-to-face contact as a continuing bond of recognition. The more a community loosens in the center, such as the downtown area where people congregate, the more it goes off in different directions and gradually disintegrates into neighborhoods that often compete with one another for resources based on special interests.

15

To understand the creation of the Universe, it is necessary to examine its basic building blocks and the way they evolved into organized systems. The big bang created particles of an extremely high state of concentration bound together by almost unimaginably strong forces. From these original microunits, quarks and electrons were formed. (Scientists propose the term "quark" as the fundamental unit of matter.) Quarks combined to form protons and neutrons; protons and neutrons formed atomic nuclei, which were complemented by shells of electrons. Atoms of various weights and complexities could, in some parts of the Universe, combine into chains of molecules and, on suitable planetary surfaces, give birth to life. On Earth, for example, living organisms became ecological systems, within which arose human communities with the remarkable features of language, consciousness, and free choice, which aggregated over time into societies with distinctive cultures.

In this giant process of evolution, relationships among things are changing continually as complex systems rise from subatomic and atomic particles. In each higher level of complexity and organization, we find an increase in the size of the system and a corresponding decrease in the energies holding it together. Thus, as evolution proceeds, the forces that hold together the evolving systems, from a molecule to a human society, weaken as the size of the systems increases.

Earth has been exposed for billions of years to a constant flow of energy streaming from the sun and radiating back into space. On Earth, this flow of energy produces the vast variety of living systems from the simple, such as an individual cell, to the complex, such as a human society. Each system uses the sun's energy to fuel its own internal processes, and each in turn provides fuel to others.

During its evolution, every system must develop the ability to constantly balance the energy it uses to function with the energies available in its environment. Ecosystems and social systems, like organisms, constantly bring in, break down, and use energy not only for repair but also for regeneration and to adapt to changing environmental conditions.

Keep in mind that we live in a world where everything seems to have its exact opposite, such as love/hate, black/white, life/death. The relationship of cause/effect seems also to be one of opposites. Consider that the first relationship between two things, whatever gave birth to cause, also gave birth to effect. But rather than being discrete opposites, cause and effect are part of a process of both creation and extinction.

Creation was the initial cause of extinction when the world was formed, and since that instant, extinction has been the continual cause of creation.

Thus, in effect, the act of creation also becomes the act of extinction, and the act of extinction becomes the act of creation, as Roman statesman Marcus Aurelius intimated when he wrote: "Time is a...river of passing events, and strong is its current. No sooner is a thing brought to sight then it is swept by and another takes its place, and this too will be swept away." This river of passing events, of cause and effect, of creation and extinction, is the continual, fluid motion of change, which gives rise to diversity.

Change, which includes both creation and extinction, is thus a linear process of everything constantly becoming something else, which is the basis of the world around us. As such, change is the catalyst of diversity.

DIVERSITY IS THE QUALITY OF BEING DIFFERENT

Diversity is not only the quality of being different but also is the richness of the world and our experience of it. Diversity means variety. Diversity comes in many forms, each of which is a relationship that fits precisely into every other relationship in the Universe and is constantly changing, constantly becoming something else (Figure 1).

Nature crafted the world inherited by human beings through the principle of cause and effect, which gave rise to the diversity of nonliving matter. When the first living cell came into being, diversity not only became limitless but also was responsible for the possibility of the extinction of life. What we as human beings must understand, accept, and remember is that we live between two spheres, the atmosphere (air) and the lithosphere (soil), and if we destroy either one, we will be the creators of our own extinction.

We humans are already causing the exponential loss of diversity (genetic, biological, and functional diversity) worldwide. Functional diversity refers to the notion that the more different kinds of pieces a system has that can interact among themselves, the more varied functions the system can produce. Conversely, the fewer kinds of interactive parts a system has, the less diverse are its possible functions. Thus we need to have some notion of diversity itself, because genetic, biological, and functional diversity are in many ways the cumulative effect of diversity in all its various dimensions.

FIGURE 1   First there was the lava rock with a crack in it. Then the seed of a lodgepole pine fell in the crack and germinated. Now a seedling pine grows in the crack. Should the seedling become a tree, it will widen the crack and perhaps split the rock. Should the seedling die, there will be the rock—alone until some other seed falls in the crack and germinates. (Photograph by author.)

DIVERSITY AS A MATTER OF DIMENSION

Diversity is partly a matter of dimension. Dimension, in a general sense, is a measure of spatial extent, such as height, width, or length. It also is a physical property, often mass, length, time, or some combination of those characteristics. Speed, for example, has the dimensions of length divided by time.

Scale: From the Microscope to Infinity

We also see diversity in scale, from the infinitesimal through the electron microscope to the infinity of space. The dimension of scale is important, because it adds greatly not only to our perception of diversity in the landscape but also to our perception of the way one part of the landscape relates to another. And both perceptions are necessary for us to make the wisest possible decisions concerning the best use of such things as our backyard gardens and our national forests.

Scale is a progressive classification in size, amount, importance, rank, or even a relative level or degree. When dealing with diversity, however, we often overlook space or distance as a dimension of diversity.

Space and distance as a scale of diversity is right in our own backyard—and always has been. If, for example, you study a pinch of soil through a high-powered microscope, you will see things that you never imagined to be living in your backyard, but you cannot see the roses or even your house as long as you focus your attention into the microscope.

If you use a ten-power hand lens to look at the same pinch of soil, you cannot see what you saw through the microscope, but you can see more of the way the particles of soil and some of the larger soil organisms relate one to another. But as long as you are looking through the hand lens, you still cannot see the roses or your house.

On the other hand, if you put the pinch of soil back where you got it and stand up straight and look down, you have still a different scale of diversity. Now you see a wider patch of soil, but without the detail. If you climb onto the roof of your house and look down on the patch of soil, you now see even less detail of the soil, but you see the roses growing out of the soil, and you see your house. Imagine, therefore, what you would see if you hovered in a helicopter 100 feet, 1,000 feet, or 10,000 feet above the patch of soil in your backyard. What would you see from a satellite in outer space?

Let's look for a moment at the scale of distance and space in still another way. What would you see in your backyard if you were a microorganism peeking out of the soil from under a grain of sand? What would you see in your backyard if you were an ant, a mouse, a cat, or a dog? Then again, what would you see if you were a sparrow, first feeding on the ground, then suddenly flying into a tree, and then just as suddenly flying to the other end of the neighborhood?

Scale, as we perceive it, is an aspect of diversity in distance and space. Diversity includes every conceivable scale, such as time, viewed from every conceivable place in distance and space simultaneously, from the viewpoint of the ant to the viewpoint of the sparrow and beyond.

Diversity in Time

Time is our invisible creation. Somewhere in the far memory of human evolution, the notion of repetitive cycles, such as the lunar cycle, melded into the intellectual concept of time, which humanity named, learned how to measure, and is now stuck with and in. Because our society is run by the clock, we try to manage our landscapes by that measure. In dealing with our renewable natural resources, for example, we try to rush Nature's processes, because to us in the United States "time is money." To Nature, however, both time and money are nonexistent. We must therefore learn that Nature will never bow to the ticking of society's clock in the sense that time is money, urging Nature to work faster to make us richer in a monetary sense.

In our Western industrialized culture, we often think of time as a nonspatial continuum in which events occur in an apparently irreversible sequence from the past through the present into the future. Time also is thought of as an interval separating two points on this continuum, points we select by centering on a regularly recurring event, such as the sunrise, and counting the number of its occurrences during the interval. And time is represented as numbers, in the form of seconds, minutes, days, weeks, months, years, centuries, millennia, or geological epochs.

In the dimension of time, your backyard may once have been the bottom of an ancient ocean or an ice-age lake, or it could have been a mountaintop, a tropical forest, an ice-age tundra, or a desert. It could have been all of these things. What you perceive your backyard to be today is only an instant in an ever-expanding explosion of diversity, one aspect of which is time.

Consider as a simple example the backyard of my home when I lived in a small town in northeastern Oregon. Behind my house I had a vegetable garden, which I used to rototill every spring. And just as soon as I was finished rototilling the soil, I began picking up squarish nails and clinkers from coal that someone had burned in a forge to heat and shape shoes for mules and horses. Why? Because a hundred years earlier, a blacksmith shop stood where today my garden is.

The acre of ground I used for a garden in 1978 was the same physical acre a hundred years earlier, but the diversity of materials in the soil of that acre was very different from that of my neighbors on either side, both of whom had gardens but neither of whom found any of the artifacts that I did. And today, for all I know, that acre of ground could have a garage built on it. Thus, if we add the dimension of time to all the other forms of diversity, we learn that diversity is really an infinity. It is something we cannot define. We can only crudely and imperfectly characterize it.

Life, The Creator of Infinite Diversity

The most wonderful diversity of all lies in life itself. Just imagine—since that first living cell, nothing has ever again been alone on Earth, because since that first living cell, the diversity of life has literally filled the planet. And the experiment continues.

How exactly that part of creation called life began is a question as old as the first human being to wonder about it. Nevertheless, the first animated cell opened up not only the possibility of life and living diversity but also a whole dimension of diversity beyond our present comprehension—infinite diversity, created out of nonliving substances and living tissue as well as a combination of the living with the nonliving. Think, for example, of the vast array of marine snails, each of which makes its own peculiar shell out of nonliving materials; without the variety of living snails, the variety of shells could not exist.

The wonder of biological diversity is the wonder of its having begun with a single living cell, or maybe even a handful of cells scattered throughout the ancient seas of the world. From that cell, or perhaps those cells, arose the longest known living experiment on Earth—the genetic experiment of life. You could argue that combinations of genetic materials are really no different from the original combinations of chemicals that gave rise to chemical compounds. If you omit the spark of life from this equation, you would be right. But that undefinable spark of life is there, and that changes everything.

When, for example, the sprout of a wild radish early in its growing season becomes breakfast for a caterpillar, the insect's munching induces the radish to produce chemical defenses against another attack.[9] According to scientist Anurag Agrawal of the University of California at Davis, as the munched plant grows, other insects in the area may chew on it also, but do far less damage than they do to plants that have not been previously nibbled. Thus, by the end of the growing season, the plant munched on early in the season not only suffers less damage from subsequent samplings by insects but also produces more seeds than do radish plants that escaped early damage.

Today, therefore, as I meet each living thing that shares the world with me, I see the pinnacle—the culmination—of billions upon billions upon billions of genetic experiments, all of which have taken place over millions of years, all embodied in each butterfly, each rose, each tree, each bird, and each human being. Every individual living thing on Earth is the apex of creation, because every living thing is the result of an unbroken chain of genetic experiments (each individual that ever lived being part of a single experiment) that began with the original living cell that filled the lifeless sea with life.

How Diversity Compounds Itself

Diversity as a dimension of itself may seem like an odd idea. But consider that all the various dimensions of diversity ultimately come together to create diversity in the form of a seascape, a landscape, the Earth, a moonscape, the moon, or even the Universe as a whole. Thus when we alter one thing, we alter everything. That cumulative alteration is the ongoing principle of creation. To see how this principle works, how diversity continually creates itself, we will examine the history of a landscape in the southern Appalachian Mountains at a place where the states of Tennessee, North Carolina, and Georgia meet.[10]

It has been 260 million years since the Appalachian Mountain chain was last affected by significant upward thrusting of the Earth's crust. At mid and high elevations, during the last period in which the glaciers of the Pleistocene epoch reached their maximum development, about 20,000 years ago, the ground surrounding the glaciers was permanently frozen. In addition, the potential area of alpine tundra extended from an elevation of about 5,000 feet to the summits of the highest mountain peaks. (Tundra is a treeless area that has a permanently frozen subsoil and supports such low-growing vegetation as lichens, mosses, and stunted shrubs. Tundra that occurs above the tree line in elevation on high mountains is termed "alpine tundra," as opposed to "arctic tundra," which occurs above the tree line in latitude.)

During this time, sediments of all sizes, ranging from boulders to silt and clay, surrounding the glaciers were frozen in place. With the warming of the climate about 15,000 years ago, both the frequency and the intensity of the cycles of freezing and thawing increased. Finally, the climate warmed sufficiently so that the once frozen materials began to move downslope with the pull of gravity.

With the onset of recent times, about 10,000 years ago, the climate warmed again. This change resulted in the sediments, such as boulders, pebbles, or clay, washing downslope through the force of water, as opposed to moving downslope by the pull of gravity as in colder times.

From the time when the last glacial period was at its height to the present, the major factor in forcing the landscape to change was shifts in climate. Freezing and other ice-related phenomena were the main causes of disturbance in the biological system. The combination of cold temperatures and cycles of freezing and thawing, which churned the soil, resulted in a landscape mosaic of permanent snowfields and alpine tundra above 5,000 feet elevation, while there was a species-rich boreal forest below 1,600 feet. Boreal forest means "northern forest," which today is characterized by the vast, short forest of small trees that occurs across central and northern Canada and throughout interior Alaska.

As the climate warmed, herbaceous species of plants that formerly grew in alpine tundra either died out or were restricted to high-elevation sites kept open by such disturbances as fire, falling rocks, and landslides. In addition, the boreal forest had spread upslope to the summits of the highest mountain peaks, and a deciduous forest had replaced it at mid and low elevations. The forest communities as we know them today have evolved only recently, some within the lifetimes of the oldest living trees.

So the diverse elements of diversity itself, such as the scales of time, space, and temperature and the processes that shape the Earth, as well as the Earth's living organisms—all coordinated by climate, have molded and remolded the landscape into an ever-changing kaleidoscope of mosaics.

Perception: What I See that You Don't

Perception is a composite of one's past experience, present sense of reality, and expectations in the future, which precludes any two people from seeing the same things in the same way. Of perception, poet William Blake wrote: "If the doors of perception were cleansed everything would appear as it is, infinite." But alas, the doors of human perception are not cleansed, and that makes all the difference, as Margaret Shannon points out.

When Margaret Shannon, a professor of natural resource policy and sociology at the State University of New York, said, "the world does not define itself for us; rather we choose to see some parts of the world and not others," she opened for me the door to a whole new way to think about diversity: that of our individual and collective perceptions. Her statement puts us on notice that we do not *see* diversity but rather that we have some perception of diversity—which in itself creates diversity, because my perception is more or less different from yours.

Shannon's observation points out that I am right from my point of view, you are right from your point of view, and others are right from their points of view. Thus we can, if we choose, view the world and one another from the position of I'm right *and you're right* (and different) with respect to our points of view—as opposed to "I'm right so *you have to be wrong*." With this view, negotiating a new relationship with one another and with our home planet would be much easier than constantly fighting the emotional gridlock in which we all too often find ourselves.

Our perceptions can even be thought of in a manner similar to that of an insect's compound eye, because it is through perception that we "see" one another and everything else. The cornea of an insect's compound eye is divided into a number of separate facets, which, depending on the insect, may vary from a few hundred to a few thousand. Each compound eye is formed from a group of separate visual elements, each of which corresponds to a single facet of the cornea. Each facet has what amounts to a single nerve fiber, which sends optical messages to the brain. Seeing with an insect's compound eye would be like seeing with many different points of view simultaneously.

Each human perception is like a facet in the compound eye of an insect, with its independent nerve fiber connecting it to our local community, national society, and collective global society (the brain). Thus each perception, which simultaneously represents an individual's own personal and cultural foundation, expressed as moral limitations, has its unique construct, which determines the possibilities of the individual's understanding. A person who tends to be negative or pessimistic, for example, sees a glass of water as half empty, while a person who tends to be positive or optimistic sees the same glass of water as half full. Regardless of the way it is perceived, the level of water is the same, which illustrates, as Shannon says, that we see what we choose to see. And what we see may have little to do with reality.

It therefore seems reasonable that the freer we are as individuals to change our perceptions without social resistance in the form of ridicule or shame, the freer society (the collective of individual perceptions) is to adapt to change in a healthy, evolutionary way. On the other hand, the more rigidly monitored and controlled "acceptable" perceptions are (i.e., politically and scientifically correct), the more prone a society is to the cracking of its moral foundation and the crumbling of its infrastructure, because nothing can be held long in abeyance, least of all social evolution.

For this reason, I suggest that the perception of an individual human being both adds to and compounds diversity, because an individual's perceptions change with age and with life's experiences. According to yoga philosophy, for example, the human personality is a constant interplay of inertia, energy, and harmony. While all three are ever present, one tends to be dominant at any given time, be it a day, throughout a stage in one's life, or over an entire lifetime. These three characteristics lie along a continuum; just as matter can exist along the continuum of a solid, liquid, or gas (for example, as ice, water, or steam), so our own energy, like matter, moves into and out of inertia, activity, and harmony. Fortunately, all three are states of the same energy, so each state can be changed into another should we so choose, and each choice determines a different facet of our perception, thus creating additional diversity.

Perceptions also change with an individual's degree of focus, centeredness, personal identity, formal education (both secular and religious), and age. And finally, they change with changing social and peer pressures and with the ever-changing relationships of human beings to one another, each of whom has different perceptions, which also are constantly changing.

In this sense, each human being is the sum total of all his or her perceptions of everything in life, and it is the cumulative integration of these perceptions that makes not only each individual unique but also the collective of individuals into a unique society. If, therefore, we could add diversity to diversity, we would find in the end that it is human perception that at once creates, integrates, and recreates diversity in an ever-widening sphere of consciousness. Because we create what we think, and what we think we create, the richness or the poverty of our individual and collective life's experience is our choice, but that choice is to some extent, at least, based on what we inherit from the generations that went before us.

Perception and Reality

An indigenous American hunter discovered a lake high in the Rocky Mountains on a warm, sunny, mid-September afternoon in the year 1000 A.D. The hunter's perception was a snapshot in time—a lake seen in a certain way and felt with a certain emotion, both of which were influenced by the particular set of circumstances that created his mood on that particular afternoon. Although the hunter didn't know it, the peculiar chemistry of the lake's water, a chemistry created through innumerable chemical, physical, and biological interactions over time, added materially to the clarity of the water and to its abundant life. The hunter, for his part, merely observed what to him was a perfect lake.

Centuries passed, and in the year 1829 a fur trapper discovered the lake. As the years unfolded, the lake became known to other trappers and was given a name. Again, to the trappers, who also saw but a snapshot in time, the lake was perfect, its clarity and teeming life a wonder to behold.

Then, on August 5, 1960, personnel of the State Department of Fish and Game analyzed and characterized the chemistry of the lake's water. What the personnel of the department couldn't possibly know was that the water's chemistry was already different from what it had been when the first indigenous hunter discovered the lake in the year 1000 or even when the trapper discovered it in 1829. Neither did the personnel of the department know that airborne industrial pollution had been seriously affecting the lake for the previous 50 years or so.

Be that as it may, from August 5, 1960 on, all future change in the quality of the lake's water will be measured against the standard established by the first chemical analysis, as though on that day the lake was the best it had ever been or the best it would ever be. What is seldom considered, however, is that the lake's chemistry, its thermal dynamics, and its community of plants and animals are interdependent and over the millennia had been changing, albeit gradually and without being perceived by humans, to arrive at the particular condition recorded at the moment of the measurement. Once the water's chemistry has been described, like a snapshot in time, any negatively perceived change from that characterization is likely to cause concern because the quality of the lake's water deviates measurably from our standard of its perceived pristine purity.

By the late 1800s, however, on the eastern seaboard of the United States, the Industrial Revolution had already begun, with all its unintended so-called "side effects" pouring into the air; these effects would later be viewed by many human beings as pollutants belching into the atmosphere. Over the next several decades, the types and amounts of atmospheric pollutants on the eastern seaboard increased. This buildup resulted in more pollutants being borne aloft, to be scrubbed from the air each winter by falling snow, and each winter they accumulated in the snowpack only to be released into the lake with each spring's thaw.

By September 10 in the year 2000, when the lake's waters will be reanalyzed, the chemistry will have been so altered by the human-introduced airborne chemicals that its water may be lifeless or the medium for different life. Thus, 40 years after the water's chemistry was first characterized, not only may the lake's original chemical composition, as measured in 1960, be extinct but also the life it once nurtured.

Here one might ask whether we can rehabilitate the lake and bring it back to its "original" state. No, we cannot, because society, through industrial pollution, has released into the Earth's life-support systems concentrated forms of energy far in excess of Nature's ability to recycle them in the foreseeable future. But if we humans cleaned the world's air—all of it—and kept it free of our human-introduced pollutants, the lake, given enough time, perhaps centuries, may in a relative sense approach a state similar to its "original" state (the state of the water's chemistry on the day it was first characterized).

Somehow, we humans must all become conscious of the fact that in the wink of an eye we can alter irreparably what it took Nature hundreds, thousands, or even millions of years to create. Once we have polluted Nature's purity, we simply cannot undo what we have done or even redo what Nature did originally. Nature alone may be able to do that, and then only in a relative manner. Such a feat takes time, however, far more time than we either have in one life span or are willing to allow beyond our lifetimes.

We thus may drastically alter the lake's chemistry and may unconsciously bring forth a new creation, a new chemistry, one that could in a few years translate into a sterile, lifeless lake—not the creation we wanted. I say this because human society is only now beginning to come to grips with air pollution, amid much informed denial of the problem and foot-dragging from the industrialized nations, especially the United States.

Consider, for example, that controls on emissions will strike at the economic heart of all industrialized nations, which derive their power principally from the combustion of fossil fuels. In the end, therefore, if we continue on our present course with our foot-dragging, our unwillingness to change our thinking, and our unwillingness to control ourselves and to master the greed of our own behavior, we may ultimately so damage both the soils and the waters of the world that we make them uninhabitable for most if not all life—including ourselves. In some places, we already are but a step away from such disaster because we have disregarded the nature of sustainable relationships.

DIVERSITY AS A MATTER OF RELATIONSHIP

Although there are no doubt numerous relationships within the concept of diversity, I will discuss three. When these are added to the various dimensions already discussed—scale, time, life, diversity itself, and perception, diversity becomes an infinite novelty of creation.

Chemical Diversity

Diversity in chemistry is another aspect of diversity in our Universe. Chemical diversity is the diversity of physical things, which are individual elements, such as nitrogen and oxygen, and the compounds produced by combining elements in relationship with one another, such as nitrogen and oxygen to form nitrous oxide or laughing gas, which is used as a mild anesthetic.

If it is true that the first two physical things were chemicals, then the initial relationship between those two chemicals produced the initial chemical reaction, which in turn produced something else. This means that a third thing—a chemical compound—arose out of the initial chemical reaction. That chemical compound simultaneously created the possibility of new relationships and a new definition of relationship. Thus the result of the interaction between the two chemicals—the compound— becomes an integral part of the definition of each parent chemical. At some point, in the classic concept of cause and effect, the growth of possible physical–chemical relationships becomes exponential, which means that one thing's hidden potential to become something else takes it beyond what it seems to be.

When a Chair Is Not a Chair

We perceive objects by means of their obvious structures or functions. Structure is the configuration of elements, parts, or constituents of a thing, be it simple or complex. The structure can be thought of as the organization, arrangement, or makeup of a thing. Function, on the other hand, is what a particular structure either can do or allows to be done to it or with it.

Let's consider a common object, a chair. A chair is a chair because of its structure, which gives it a particular shape. A chair can be characterized as a piece of furniture consisting of a seat, four legs, a back, and often arms; it is an object designed to accommodate a sitting person. Because of the seat, we can sit in a chair, and it is the act of sitting, the functional component allowed by the structure, that makes a chair a chair.

Suppose we remove the seat so that the supporting structure on which we sit no longer exists. Now to sit, we must sit on the ground between the legs of the "chair." By definition, when we remove a chair's seat, we no longer have a chair, because we have altered the structure and therefore also altered its function. Thus, the structure of an object defines its function and the function of an object defines its necessary structure, and both add to the ever-widening ripples of diversity. How might the inter-relationship of structure and function work in Nature?

To maintain ecological functions means that one must maintain the characteristics of the ecosystem in such a way that its processes are sustainable. The characteristics one must be concerned with are (1) composition, (2) structure, (3) function, and (4) Nature's disturbance regimes, which periodically alter an ecosystem's composition, structure, and function.

Nature's disturbance regimes tend to be environmental constraints. True, we can tinker with them, such as the suppression of fire in forests and grasslands, but in the end our tinkering catches up with us and we pay the price.

We can, for example, change the composition of an ecosystem, such as the kinds and arrangement of plants within a forest, which means that composition is malleable to human desire and thus negotiable within the context of cause and effect. In this case, composition is the determiner of the structure and function in that composition is the cause rather than the effect of the structure and function.

Composition determines the structure, and structure determines the function. By negotiating the composition, one simultaneously negotiates both the structure and function. Once the composition is in place, how-ever, the structure and function are set—unless, of course, the composition is altered, at which time both the structure and function are altered accordingly.

The composition or kinds of plants and their age classes within a plant community create a certain structure that is characteristic of the plant community at any given age. It is the structure of the plant community that in turn creates and maintains certain functions. In addition, it is the composition, structure, and function of a plant community that determine what kinds of animals can live there, how many, and for how long.

If one changes the composition of a forest, one changes the structure, and hence the function, and thus affects the animals. The animals in general are thus ultimately constrained by the composition.

If, therefore, a community wants a particular animal or group of animals within its forest, let's say a rich diversity of summering birds to attract tourist dollars from bird-watchers, members of the community would have to work backward by determining what kind of function to create, which means knowing what kind of structure to create, which means knowing what type of composition is necessary to produce the required habitat(s) for the animal(s) the community wants. Once the composition is ensconced, the structure and its attendant functions operate as a unit in terms of the habitat required for the animal(s).

People and Nature are continually changing the structure and function of this ecosystem or that ecosystem by manipulating the composition of its plants, which subsequently changes the composition of the animals dependent on the structure and function of the resultant habitat. By altering the composition of plants within an ecosystem, people and Nature alter its structure, which in turn affects how it functions, which in turn determines not only what kinds of and how many animals can live there but also what uses humans can make from the ecosystem. Fortunately for us, ecosystems have built-in redundancy.

Ecosystems Have Built-in Redundancy

Each ecosystem contains built-in redundancies, which means it contains more than one species that can perform similar functions. Such redundancies give an ecosystem the resilience either to resist change and/or to bounce back after disturbance. Redundancy in the biological functions of various species is an environmental insurance policy built into every ecosystem. To maintain this insurance policy, an ecosystem needs diversity of at least three important kinds: composition, structure, and function, where composition creates structure and structure allows function.

We would be wise, therefore, to think of each of these kinds of diversity as an individual leg of an old-fashioned, three-legged milking stool because it becomes clear that if we lose one leg (one kind of diversity), the stool will fall over. In reality, however, a considerable amount of functional redundancy is built into an ecosystem, which means that more than one species can perform the same or a very similar function. This results in a stabilizing effect similar to having a six-legged milking stool with two legs in each of three locations. If one leg is removed, it makes no difference which one it is; the stool will remain standing. But if a second leg is removed, the location of the removed leg is crucial, because if it is removed from the same place as the first leg, the stool will fall. If a third leg is removed, the location of the removed leg is even more crucial, because removal has now pushed the system to the limits of its stability, and it is courting ecological collapse. The removal of one more piece, no matter how well intentioned, will cause the system to collapse.

When we tinker willy-nilly with an ecosystem's structure to suit our short-term economic desires, we lose species to extinction and thus reduce the ecosystem's biodiversity, and thus its genetic diversity, and finally its functional diversity. With decreased diversity, we lose choices for safely manipulating our environment, which directly affects our lifestyles. The loss of biodiversity may so alter the ecosystem that it can no longer produce that for which we valued it in the first place, be it a specific commodity or a desired lifestyle.

Long-term ecological wholeness and biological richness of the landscape must therefore become the measure of economic health because if we want the land to be able to provide for us, we must do our best to care first and foremost for the land. This matter of caring for the land brings us to the notion of ecosystems as dissipative structures.

Ecosystems as Dissipative Structures

Ecosystems move inevitably toward a critical state in which a minor event sooner or later leads to a catastrophic event, one that alters the ecosystem in some dramatic way. In this sense, ecosystems as portions of landscapes are dissipative structures in that energy is built up through time only to be released in a disturbance of some kind, such as a fire, flood, or landslide, in some scale, ranging from a freshet in a stream to the eruption of a volcano, after which energy begins building again toward the next release of pent-up energy somewhere in time on the landscape.

Such disturbances, as ecologists think of these events, can be long term and chronic, such as large movements of soil that take place over hundreds of years (termed an earth flow), or acute, such as the crescendo of a volcanic eruption that sends a pyroclastic flow speeding down its side. (A pyroclastic flow is a turbulent mixture of hot gas and fragments of rock, such as pumice, that is violently ejected from a fissure and moves with great speed down the side of a volcano. *Pyroclastic* is Greek for "fire-broken.")

Here, you might interject that neither soil nor a volcano is a living system in the sense of a forest. So how is a forest an example of a dissipative structure?

As a young Douglas fir forest grows old, it converts energy from the sun into living tissue, which ultimately dies and accumulates as organic debris on the floor of the forest. There, through decomposition, the organic debris releases the energy stored in its dead tissue. A forest is, therefore, a dissipative system in that energy acquired from the sun is dissipated gradually through decomposition or rapidly through fire.

Of course, rates of decomposition vary. A leaf rots quickly and releases its stored energy rapidly. Woody material, on the other hand, rots much more slowly, often over centuries. As the woody material accumulates, so does the energy stored in its fibers. Before the suppression of fire by such agencies as the U.S. Forest Service, fires burned frequently enough to generally control the amount of energy stored in the accumulating woody debris by burning it up, thus releasing the stored energy, which in turn protected the forest for decades, even centuries, from a catastrophic fire that would kill it.

Over time, however, a forest eventually builds up enough woody debris to fuel a catastrophic fire, such as those experienced over much of the western United States in recent years. Once available, the fuel needs only one or two very dry, hot years with lightning storms to ignite such a fire, which kills the forest and sets it back in succession to the earliest stage of grasses and herbs. From this early stage, a new forest again evolves toward the old-growth stage, again accumulating stored energy in dead wood, again organizing itself toward the next critical state, a catastrophic fire, which starts the cycle over.

After a fire, earthquake, volcanic eruption, flood, or landslide, a biological system may eventually be able to approximate what it was through resilience—the ability of the system to retain the integrity of its basic relationships. But regardless of how closely an ecosystem might approximate its former state following a disturbance, the existence of every ecosystem is a tenuous balancing act because every ecosystem is in a constant state of disequilibrium from the pressure of forces outside it.

Thus, a 700-year-old forest that burned could be replaced by another, albeit different, 700-year-old forest on the same acreage. In this way, despite a series of catastrophic fires, a forest ecosystem can remain a forest ecosystem. In this sense, the old-growth forests of western North America have been evolving from one catastrophic fire to the next, from one critical state to the next.

Because of the dynamic nature of evolving ecosystems and because each system is constantly organizing itself from one critical state to another, we can only manipulate an ecosystem for its possible evolution—not for a sustained yield of products—and hope that we are wise enough to care for the system in a way that may be favorable for us, such as patterns across the landscape.

Patterns Across the Landscape

Spatial patterns we see on landscapes result from complex interactions among physical, biological, and social forces. Most landscapes have also

own disturbances, to which they are adapted and which control their insects and diseases.

The precise mechanisms by which ecosystems cope with stress vary, but one mechanism is tied closely to the genetic selectivity of an ecosystem's species. Thus, as an ecosystem changes and is influenced by increasing magnitudes of stresses, the replacement of a stress-sensitive species with a functionally similar but more stress-resistant species preserves the ecosystem's overall productivity. Such replacements of species—redundancy—can result only from within the existing pool of biodiversity. Nature's redundancy must be protected and encouraged.

Human-introduced disturbances, especially fragmentation of habitat, impose stresses with which an ecosystem is ill-adapted to cope. Not surprisingly, biogeographical studies show that "connectivity" of habitats within the landscape is of prime importance to the persistence of plants and animals in viable numbers in their respective habitats—again, a matter of biodiversity. In this sense, the landscape must be considered a mosaic of interconnected patches of habitats like vegetated fencerows, which act as corridors or routes of travel between patches of farm forest, livestock allotments, or other suitable habitats.

Whether populations of plants and animals survive in a particular landscape depends on the rate of local extinctions from a patch of habitat and the rate with which an organism can move among existing patches of habitat. Those species living in habitats isolated as a result of fragmentation are therefore less likely to persist. Fragmentation of habitat, the most serious threat to biological diversity, is the primary cause of the present global crisis in the rate of biological extinctions. On public lands, much, if not most, of the fragmentation of the habitat is a "side effect" of management policies that stress the short-term production of commodities at the long-term expense of the environment. Actually, there is no such thing as a "side effect"—only an unintentional effect!

Modifying the existing connectivity among patches of habitat strongly influences the abundance of species and their patterns of movement. The size, shape, and diversity of patches also influence the patterns of species abundance, and the shape of a patch may determine which species can use it as habitat. The interaction between the processes of a species' dispersal and the pattern of a landscape determines the temporal dynamics of the species' populations. Local populations of organisms that can disperse great distances may not be as strongly affected by the spatial arrangement of patches of habitat as more sedentary species.

Our responsibility now is to make decisions about patterns across the landscape while considering the consequences of our decisions on the land's potential productive capacity for generations to come. The decisions are up to us, but one thing is clear: although the current trend toward homogenizing the landscape may help maximize short-term monetary profits, it devastates the long-term biological sustainability and adaptability of the land and thus devastates the land's long-term potential productive capacity.

It is not, after all, the relationship of numbers that confers stability on ecosystems; it is the relationship of pattern. Stability flows from the patterns of relationship that have evolved among the various species. A stable, culturally oriented system, even a very diverse one, that fails to support these ecologically coevolved relationships has little chance of being sustainable.

To create viable culturally oriented landscapes, we must begin now to work toward connectivity of habitats because ecological sustainability and adaptability depend on the connectivity of the landscape. We must therefore ground our culturally designed landscapes within Nature's evolved patterns and take advantage of them if we are to have a chance of creating a quality environment that is both ecologically adaptable and pleasing to our cultural senses.

If we are to have adaptable landscapes with desirable productive capacities to pass to our heirs, we must focus on two primary things: (1) caring for and "managing" for a sustainable connectivity and biological richness between such areas as forest clear-cuts, agricultural fields, livestock-grazing allotments, and urban developments within the context of the landscape as a whole and (2) protecting existing biodiversity—including habitats—at any price for the long-term sustainability of the ecological wholeness and the biological richness of the patterns we create across its landscapes. To do this, however, we have to both understand and pay heed to the context of relationship.

Context Affects Relationship

In addition to composition, structure, and function, our universe contains the characteristic of context—the way an object relates to its environment. The context of any object affects the relationship of that feature with its surroundings.

Because the notion of context affecting relationship is so important to an understanding of extinction, we will consider three examples of how this dynamic works. The first example deals with an old-growth forest and human alteration of that forest.

Suppose you have access to a 5,000-acre tract of undisturbed, old-growth forest. Then suppose I put an imaginary boundary around the central 100 acres. That section becomes the feature, and I am going to start clear-cutting the rest of the land surrounding that feature (the central 100 acres), beginning along the outer edge of the 5,000-acre tract. How will clear-cutting affect the relationship of the central 100 acres with the surrounding 4,900 acres? How will clear-cutting affect your relationship with that of the central 100 acres? How will clear-cutting affect your relationship with the surrounding 4,900 acres?

First, noise from road-building and logging equipment will begin to pollute Nature's silence, bird song, and the whispering of the wind in the tops of the trees. With the noise comes a sense of intrusion—a violation— of the millennial, symphonic harmony of Nature's forest. As the clear-cutting draws ever nearer, the noise of the large machinery becomes louder and is now punctuated with the scream of chain saws. Finally, the sense of violation becomes unbearable as the death knell of ancient trees is added to the roar of machinery and the wailing of chain saws each time a forest giant crashes to earth, its life severed by a speeding steel chain of opposing teeth ripping through its fibers.

In the beginning, clear-cutting seems remote from the 100 acres, but on the heels of the mechanical noise comes the first sense that the central portion of the 5,000 acres is becoming an island as the noise comes from various places all around it. Next, the crashing of the falling trees brings a real sense of the forest being cut down, forever altering Nature's evolutionary experiment that is the forest. And suddenly the clear-cutting is close enough that the trees are seen falling. Now there exists a 100-acre patch of old-growth trees in the middle of a sea of stumps and the mangled bodies of plants.

The 100-acre patch of old-growth trees is no longer a forest but an unprotected island, which is too small to support many of the species of vertebrate wildlife that not only once lived there but also require or find their preferred habitat in the old-growth forest. These species will become extinct within the 100 acres because the context of the landscape (unbroken forest as opposed to a vast clear-cut) has changed the relationship of the 100 acres with its surroundings. In turn, the loss of the species will change the ancient forest's functional relationship within itself; although perhaps not visible to the human eye, even within a human lifetime, the forest has been changed nonetheless.

The 100 acres, once protected by the surrounding forest from the drying winds of summer and the freezing winds of winter, is now unprotected and exposed to the whim of the winds. In addition, 100 acres is too small an area for old-growth-dependent species, such as the marten and the pileated woodpecker, to live in, breed in, and survive, and there may be no place else for them to go. The demise of the marten and the pileated woodpecker further changes the relationship of the 100 acres to its surroundings.

The second example of context is a farmer's field in the flatlands of Nebraska. The field is not far from a farming community that is rapidly pumping the stored water out of a millennia-old underground lake for use in people's homes and for irrigating the surrounding farm crops. Over a period of years, far more water is pumped out of the ground than can possibly be replaced, and the farmer under whose field the lake lies begins to notice that his field, instead of being flat, is sinking in the middle.

He notices a bare spot gradually developing in his crop, because cold air drains into the sunken middle of the field and freezes the wheat. Draining the underground lake altered its structure, and that alteration caused the sinking of the field when the water holding up the farmer's field was pumped out, which in turn changed the airflow patterns of the landscape and thus created a different relationship between the field and its aboveground surroundings.

In this case, human society has created the feature, the farmer's field, and has also created the change in context below the field through the massive pumping of underground water. That change in the field's belowground context simultaneously altered its aboveground context by causing it to sink, which shifted the airflow patterns in relationship to the surface of the field and now causes the wheat in the bottom of the sunken area to freeze.

The third and final example of context is the Bonneville Salt Flats in Utah.[12] This desolate white plain, one of Nature's more bizarre geological inventions, is so flat that the curvature of the Earth is visible from the level of the ground.

Geologically speaking, the salt flats are a relatively recent phenomenon. During the Pleistocene epoch, which began about 2.4 million years ago, Lake Bonneville covered a third of Utah as well as parts of Nevada and Idaho, to a depth of nearly a thousand feet. By the end of the Pleistocene epoch about 10,000 years ago, Lake Bonneville was already drying up, depositing its dissolved salts and other minerals in the lowest part of the Great Salt Lake Basin, the area now known as the "salt flats."

Long a magnet for tourists, filmmakers, and daredevils who thunder across the salty, concrete-smooth surface in the world's fastest automobiles, the salt flats are disappearing more than 7,000 years after they formed from the dried-up remnants of Lake Bonneville. Since 1926, when surveyors first mapped the area, the salt flats have shrunk from 96,000 acres to about 25,000 acres. The salt is thus vanishing at a rate of about 1 percent a year—which means that the salt flats could be gone within decades.

Although proof is inconclusive, one of the reasons for the loss of salt is thought to be a nearby mine, which pumps salt-laden groundwater to produce potash, an ingredient in fertilizers. As the water table is lowered by pumping and removing the groundwater, the water, which is replaced by rains, percolates downward through the flats, dissolving the salts and carrying them into the lowering water table from which they are continually removed. On top of this come such events as El Niño, which brings above normal precipitation that aids in the dissolution of the salts.

In addition, construction of the interstate highway may also have modified the hidden movement of water in the shallow aquifers that underlie the plain. By creating yet another "conduit" for the drainage of salt-laden water, the building of the highway has lowered the water table in many directions around the salt flats.

Regardless of the cause or causes, measurements taken since 1960 show that the salt crust of the Bonneville Salt Flats has thinned from seven feet to five feet at its thickest point and to mere inches in some spots. This thinning of the salt crust constitutes an estimated loss of 1.5 million tons of salt per year.

Few places on the surface of the Earth are so well suited to the pursuit of speed as the Bonneville Salt Flats, and it was there in 1970 that the world's land-speed record was set, 622 miles per hour, in a jet-powered automobile. This speed was attainable because the flats, covered with water throughout the winter and spring, are dry as a bone, hard as concrete, and about as smooth by late summer. In recent years, however, cracks, holes, and pressure ridges have begun to appear around the edges of the thinning, weakening flats, which soon may be more mud than salt—a change that will forever alter the context of the salt flats with their surroundings as they dissolve into extinction. As the context of the Bonneville Salt Flats changes through human-caused alterations to its composition, structure, and function, so too the diversity of the entire area changes through the loss of this unique feature and whatever life is adapted specifically to it.

CREATION AND EXTINCTION

4

In discussing diversity, the primordial alphabet soup of living systems, the notion of creation and extinction must be addressed. Creation means something has come into being that heretofore did not exist physically. Where did it come from?

Creation is generally thought of in terms of theology or biological evolution. But think about the destruction or extinction of a habitat. After the change, does it not become another, very different habitat? A swamp, for example, can be drained to create an agricultural pasture. In draining the water, the swamp-dwelling organisms become extinct locally, but the resultant pasture becomes inhabited by pasture-dwelling organisms. This does not mean that the draining of the swamp is either desirable or undesirable. It means only that in some cases we can easily see the creative side of extinction.

Extinction means that something no longer exists in its living form; its spark of life has died out like embers of a dying fire. Extinction is generally thought of only in terms of the disappearance of a living entity. But the concept of extinction goes far beyond living things. The disappearance, the irreparable alteration of the nonliving components of the environment, such as a lake, is linked inseparably to the extinction of living things, and herein lies a critical problem exemplified by extinctions of species in the oceans of the world.[5]

In addition to the white abalone previously discussed, James Carlton, director of the Williams College–Mystic Seaport Maritime Studies Program in Mystic, Connecticut, points out that the demise of even once common creatures can pass unnoticed—and he should know. In 1991, Carlton became the first scientist in modern history to actually document the extinction of a marine invertebrate, the limpet, which is a snail-like organism that once lived along the North Atlantic coast.

The limpet apparently succumbed after a blight killed most of its major source of food, eelgrass, sometime around 1930. "What does it tell us that we didn't notice for 60 years that a once-common species became extinct, literally under the noses of marine biologists?" Carlton asks, noting that the coastline of New England is "dotted with some of the nation's most prestigious marine biological laboratories."

The crux of the issue is not only that many marine creatures have not yet been identified and described by scientists but also that the world's classically trained marine systematists (those who describe new species) and biogeographers (those who decipher the geographical distribution of those same species)—who together would be the first to notice the disappearance of a species—are themselves dying out in a world that increasingly sees less and less value in anything that cannot be immediately converted into money. "Future historians of science may well find a crisis was upon us at the end of the 20th century," wrote Carlton. "[It was] the extinction of the systematist, the extinction of the naturalist, the extinction of the biogeographer—those who could tell the tales of the potential demise of global marine diversity." The same scenario is true, of course, for the dense, tangled tropical forests.

This link is important to appreciate, because by the time a species is documented as extinct, the alterations wrought by humans have caused one or more physical/chemical/structural/functional extinctions in the habitat. It is these "hidden extinctions," the ones of which we are almost always unaware, the ones to which we pay no heed, that cause habitats to change.

As a habitat changes, it in effect becomes extinct not only in a particular place but also to the species living therein. In turn, the species that are adapted to that specific habitat become extinct as their habitat requirements disappear, as happened with the passenger pigeon and the Carolina parakeet.

Creation and extinction can hardly be discussed today without including the influence of humanity as a species. Human social activity is, for example, changing the chemistry of the water in Colorado's high-mountain lakes through the spread of air pollutants. Each winter, the pollutants are scrubbed from the air by falling snow and stored in the snowpack until released with the spring thaw to alter the lakes in a way that kills their living organisms. Human social activity is also rapidly and systematically deforesting Canada, the Pacific Northwest of the United States, and the tropical rain forests of the world. This deforestation eliminates habitats and alters the global climate.

What we are doing to Earth is natural, even though it may be viewed as destructive, because we are one species of animal among the many populating our home planet. But the changes we create are faster, more radical, more thoroughly systematic, and simultaneously more widespread than any changes caused by any single species at any other time in the history of Earth. Humanity, especially through society, is constantly altering the Earth. Such alterations create something "new" at the expense of something already in existence. To understand this notion, let's examine the concept of a "species."

ON SPECIES

A species is thought of as the basic building block of biological diversity, and hence the epitome of the creative process. In fact, the concept of a species is so fantastic in evolutionary terms and so important ecologically that the U.S. Congress passed a public law—the Endangered Species Act—specifically to protect species and subspecies from extinction by an act of human society. Canadian writer Kevin Van Tighem says that "Alberta needed an endangered species act 100 years ago" and that an awful silence has settled across the land, where only a few decades earlier, it had resembled the Serengeti in its wealth of life with its large herds of North American bison.

What Is a Species?

The word "species" has one significance to a student of taxonomy and another to a student of evolution. To the student of taxonomy, the concept of a species is a practical device designed to reduce the almost endless variety of living things to a comprehensible system of classification. To the student of evolution, a species is a passing stage in the stream of evolution. And here the concept of extinction is simple: it is what happens when whatever we call a species disappears.

Before 1935, scientists based most definitions of species on the degree to which they were distinct in form and structure, with little attention to evolutionary relationships. In 1937, scientists revisited the definition and began to emphasize the dynamic aspects of species—their potential for change. Today, species are thought of as groups of natural populations that can or do interbreed and are isolated from other such groups, first in an ecological sense and second in a reproductive sense. To be reproductively isolated means that even if two species were put together, they could not produce fertile offspring in a way that will perpetuate the species.

Examples of such populations are the Oregon and the California red tree voles, which are reddish "mice" that live primarily in Douglas fir trees of western Oregon and northwestern California. These two species meet occasionally in the vicinity of the Smith River just south of the Oregon–California border near the Pacific Ocean. Although voles of the two species may interbreed now and then, hybrid males produced by such a union are sterile, and hybrid females, although fertile, can breed only with males of one species or the other. Because the habitat is not well suited to the tree voles of either species, there are not enough voles to populate the area, which constitutes isolation in the ecological sense. Thus the scarcity of voles, plus the fact that hybrid males are sterile, which constitutes isolation in the reproductive sense, maintains the integrity of the two species.

Where Do Species Come From? Where Do They Go?

To find out where species come from, we need to think about two theories of evolution, beginning with Darwin, who was of the opinion that evolution is both continuous and gradual. His theory says that evolution proceeds by mutation and natural selection. Mutations, which are simply "typing mistakes" in the repetition of the genetic code passed from parent to offspring, are produced by all species at a more or less constant rate. Most individuals with mutations are eliminated through time, because they are "faulty" in some respect and unable to reproduce or adapt as well as "normal" individuals.

Occasionally, however, a mutation arises with a genetic makeup that renders the individual more, rather than less, fit to survive and reproduce. When this happens, the individual is given a chance to pass its mutant genes on to its own offspring, which in turn passes them to its own offspring, and so on until the mutant trait becomes both dominant and "normal" in the population.

Thus, through the combination of random mutations and natural selection, evolution continually adapts species to their environments by weeding out the less fit in favor of the more fit. Here the notion is that species continue to evolve until they at last occupy all available habitats in the biosphere, which keeps changing, so that the species must continually adapt or become extinct.

Darwin probably adopted the two basic but unnecessary assumptions—that evolution is both gradual and continuous—more out of innate conservatism than weighty scientific evidence. Darwin thought that Nature made no great leaps. Sudden leaps in Nature resembled for Darwin the uncomfortable, sudden changes, such as revolutions, that transform human society. The dominant personalities of Darwin's time abhorred the revolutionary process of wholesale transformations. They clung instead to the idea of tiny, continual changes, which gradually adjusted one thing to another. Then, 120 years after Darwin's *Origin of the Species* was first published, Steven Jay Gould and Niles Eldredge, both American paleobiologists, wrote a seminal paper introducing the theory of evolutionary leaps. According to their theory, these leaps, although dramatic, occur relatively infrequently.

Evolutionary stability or plateaus, it appears, are the normal course of events in the persistence of species over long periods of time. Paleontologists have long dismissed this "lack of evolution" as faulty judgments based on "apparent" gaps in the fossil record. The Darwinists believed that such gaps could be explained by the imperfection of the record, which had nothing to do with a lack of ongoing evolution. The fossil record, although perhaps imperfect, does not prove that evolution is a continual process.

In fact, evolution, as it now appears, proceeds through leaps of "speciation" (the sudden appearance, geologically speaking, of new species) rather than through a slow, gradual, continuous adaptation of existing species to fit changing conditions. These periodic leaps of speciation are like major earthquakes, which suddenly relieve the gradually building pressures of the Earth's mantle.

In this new theory of periodic leaps of speciation, evolutionary change, rather than affecting individuals as survivors and reproducers, affects the entire system, which is composed of living organisms as they interact within their environments. Evolution occurs when a dominant species is destabilized within its habitat, when its cycle of dominance is broken by a new species, which may have emerged "haphazardly" at the edge of the cycle of dominance. The dynamic equilibrium is thus broken as the old species is suddenly replaced by the emerging new species in a leap of evolution.

Therefore, according to this most recent theory, new species are selected in sudden bursts of evolution during periods of critical instability within the cycles of dominant species. This sort of change is similar to what happens to an established singer who has long held an uncontested place in the spotlight. Suddenly, from seemingly "out of nowhere," a new, hot star emerges who commands the audience's attention and thereby takes over the spotlight and permanently displaces the old star.

Where do old species go when they become extinct? To find out, we need to visit the coelacanth (pronounced "*seal*-a-canth"), a rare fish that has survived deep in the Earth's seas almost unchanged for 380 million years.[13] The first coelacanth was caught in a deep-water gill net (about 600 feet down) set for sharks off the mouth of the Chalumna River in south-eastern Africa in 1938. This individual, given the generic named *Latimeria* in honor of naturalist Marjorie Courtenay Latimer, represented the only surviving species (*Latimeria chalumna*) of the coelacanths, from a lineage of fishes that originated in the Devonian period, about 380 million years ago, but was thought to have become extinct in the Upper Cretaceous period, some 80 million years ago, which is the date of the youngest fossil. How could this lineage of fishes have survived all that time without leaving a trace of its existence? Since then, however, others have been caught in deep water off the Comoros Islands, which lie between the coast of southeastern Africa and the northwestern tip of Madagascar.

On September 18, 1997, the wife of Mark V. Erdmann, an author of one of the recent articles about coelacanths in Indonesia, saw a coela-canth in Sulawesi (Celebes), Indonesia, being wheeled across a fish market on a cart. Erdmann's wife only had time to photograph the fish before it was sold. Then, on July 30, 1998, Sulawesi fishermen dragged up a $4\frac{1}{2}$-foot-long, 65-pound coelacanth, which they had caught in a gill net set for sharks about 400 feet down off the young volcanic island of Manado Tua, north Sulawesi. Manado Tua is known to have submarine caves at about the same depth as those that occur on the Comoros Islands, 6,000 mile away.

Is it possible that the coelacanth population of Sulawesi is distinct from that of the Comoros Islands? According to Peter Forey, "DNA and protein profiling should provide the unequivocal answer." "Tissue samples," adds Susan L. Jewett, manager of the fish collection at the Smithsonian's National Museum of Natural History, are going to be the key." If, however, the coelacanths from Sulawesi and those from the Comoros Islands prove to be the same species, they could be much more widespread than originally thought. Regardless of the outcome, the Sulawesi fishermen seem to be well acquainted with the fish because they even have a name for it. All this illustrates, once again, how very little we know about our home planet—despite our vast accumulation of knowledge.

Today, humans are threatening this fish through greed, curiosity, superstition, and the pollution of its deep-sea habitat with toxins. The general curiosity value of a living fossil has caused great demand for coelacanths. Given an estimated 500 individuals in the total population around the Comoros Islands, coupled with the species' low rate of reproduction (it bears live young), there is cause for concern. In addition, a team of scientists at the Virginia Institute of Marine Science in Gloucester has found high levels of DDT and PCBs in the tissues of frozen specimens of the coelacanth taken from the population off the Comoros Islands. "It's a very scary situation," said John A. Musick, who headed the study at the institute. "It's even more alarming because if we lose the coelacanths, we're not losing a species, or a genus, or a family. We're losing a superorder—the last member of a species that dominated the world's ecology for millions of years." The loss of a superorder is, to scientists, the loss of a gigantic branch in the tree of life, the tree of evolution.

Some ancient species, such as opossums, are unlikely to become extinct because they meet Nature's criteria for persistence. In addition, they live in environments that vary so much from day to day, month to month, and year to year that they are unlikely to meet anything in the future that they have not already survived in the past. Another category of organisms, however, called living fossils, is in much more severe danger of extinction.

Organisms like the coelacanth are called "living fossils" because they are the only surviving species of a taxonomic group that was once considerably richer. As the last living species in that group, they have not changed in millions of years. This notion of the living fossil has an air of doom about it, as though the coelacanth were living on borrowed time, a holdover from a more aristocratic era. Some "living fossils" are indeed living on borrowed time because they are adapted only to specific habitats threatened with drastic modification, or the species themselves are simply disappearing into extinction.

In the game of survival, the coelacanth has three strikes against it: it is the only surviving species of a taxonomic group that was once considerably richer, it has not changed in millions of years, and it is adapted to a specific habitat that is now threatened by human-caused pollution and exploited by human intrusion.

The continued survival of the coelacanth, after 380 million years of history in the deep sea, is suddenly threatened by major changes in its environment. These changes have been created by an upstart species that has been around for only about five to eight million years. What does it mean if we, the human species, critically destabilize the coelacanth's habitat and its patterns of self-maintenance to the point that it becomes extinct?

In the case of the coelacanth, it means that a whole, major line of evolution will suddenly disappear—forever. It means that all living individuals in the species, each one of which is the culmination of 380 million years of an unbroken chain of genetic experiments, will cease to be. And the loss of these individual genetic experiments amounts to the cumulative loss of the collective individuals that comprise the species.

The loss of the coelacanth after 380 million years because of human-caused disturbance to its habitat shows us something else: the effects of our materialistic form of society are now reaching into the furthermost recesses of the planetary ecosystem. The impending extinction of the coelacanth is a warning that the effects we are having on the environments of our home planet are deleterious to the survival of human society. The coelacanth is perhaps the most ancient living form of the "miner's canary." Yet the greater meaning of our having caused the coelacanth's extinction rests privately in our hearts.

But what about you and me? Each of us is also the culmination of an unbroken chain of genetic experiments reaching back millions of years into antiquity. When you and I depart this Earth, we too, in the earthly sense, are individually extinct, although our genes are passed on if we have living children. But we have disappeared, vanished from the scene, and the play of human speciation goes on without us. The millennial genetic experiment of an individual life is suddenly terminated with a finality that only the bereaved can understand.

Extinction carries two meanings: one local and one global. A local extinction refers to a particular population, such as the red squirrel on Mount Graham, a mountaintop island in the desert of Arizona. A global extinction, on the other hand, refers to an entire species (all the red squirrels everywhere).

Local populations may—and often do—disappear, either temporarily or permanently, without implying extinction or even the near extinction of the species. A species, on the other hand, is composed of the sum of its populations, whether plants or animals, and so the loss of populations will affect the species as a whole and can imply danger to its survival.

Global extinction becomes a certainty when the rate of deaths exceeds the rate of births, with no way to reverse the trend. Suppose, for instance, that a population of whales has been hunted so heavily that at a given moment in time the rate of births and survival to breeding age exactly offsets the rate of deaths. In other words, that population of whales is just holding its own with respect to its survival as a species.

Then the crew aboard a factory ship kills five whales, three of them females. That killing, unbeknownst to the crew, causes the rate of death among all the whales of that species to exceed the possible rate of birth and survival to reproductive age, even under the best of circumstances. At that very moment, the evolutionary fate of the entire species of whales is sealed. Extinction has become an irreversible certainty!

Let's take this discussion one step further and suppose that I have studied this particular species of whale for many years and you are placed in charge of protecting the species from extinction. If you had any inkling that the species might be in trouble from overhunting and were to ask me what size the population of whales must be in order to perpetuate the species, I would have to say that I did not know because their survival as a species depends on so many variables. Having said that, however, I could make an educated guess based on my years of research. Would I be correct? Neither I nor you would probably live long enough to know.

Let's look at a real example, the northern elephant seal.[14] The northern elephant seal was hunted to near extinction in the 1800s in order to procure the prized oil from its blubber. In 1892, a tiny herd of 30 individuals was found on Isla de Guadalupe, off Mexico, but admittedly more individuals may have been at sea. Sadly, even these few survivors were exploited; some were shot to make displays for museums because they were thought to be the last of their kind.

All my years of studying mammals tells me that common sense would dictate that so small a number of so large a mammal would surely be headed irreversibly down the hallway of extinction. And, in this case, I would be wrong because that small number of survivors has multiplied into a rapidly growing population, which is truly remarkable. Why did the northern elephant seal survive, whereas other species with so few remaining individuals would be irretrievable? The most probable answer is simultaneously intriguing and a double-edged sword.

"Despite a lack of genetic variation," says Burney Le Boeuf, a scientist at the University of California, Santa Cruz, "they [northern elephant seals] are one of the fastest-growing pinniped species [seals and sea lions belong to the order Pinnipedia]." Brent Stewart, a scientist at the Hubbs–Sea World Research Institute in San Diego, California, adds that feeding elephant seals are the diving champions of the mammalian world, and therein may lie their secret to survival.

Most dives extend downward from 1,000 to 1,200 feet, but some have been recorded to depths of 5,000 feet. In addition, elephant seals can stay in this sunless abyss for an hour or two while they hunt for squid and fish, which constitute their main foods. Le Boeuf, who has studied elephant seals for 30 years, is of the opinion that "the exponential growth [of the elephant seal population] is probably because they occupy a unique ecological niche, one that just awaited their return." He goes on to say that "it's very difficult for other species, including...[humans], to compete with them for food."

Is their survival thus linked to their specialized adaptations for feeding in the oceanic depths, where they bypass competition from other species in obtaining food? On the other hand, like the coelacanth, does this very specialization to the deep sea make them vulnerable to extinction in the future should humanity irreversibly pollute those depths beyond some point of no return?

There is an inescapable irony in this situation. While the seal's only known enemies are great white sharks and people, only sharks kill them outright for food. People, on the other hand, can actively work to maintain the species on the surface of the ocean by not hunting it and by protecting its shoreline habitats while simultaneously killing it through the hidden menace of generalized pollution in its deep-sea feeding grounds. Therefore, if we humans want the northern elephant seal to remain part of our coastal scenery, we must, in addition to whatever else we do, keep the oceans healthy enough to protect the seal's deep-sea habitat for feeding and the health of its food along with it.

Despite the miraculous survival of the northern elephant seal against seemingly overwhelming odds for so small a number of remaining individuals, the minimum size of a population is critical to its continued survival in the face of change; the smaller the population, the more susceptible it is to extinction from any of various causes. This scenario is exemplified by the extinction of nine populations of the northern leopard frog in the mountainous Red Feather Lakes region of Larimer County, Colorado.[15]

Between 1973 and 1982, the nine populations of frogs failed to reproduce and thus became extinct. Although one area, which had formerly supported a population, was recolonized in 1980, nobody saw any frogs at any of the sites in 1981 or 1982. Six of the populations became extinct because the ponds in which they bred dried up. The remaining three populations were so small that they were susceptible to other events, the nature of which remains unknown.

Even though nine populations of the northern leopard frog have become extinct, the significance of such extinctions to a species with as large a network of populations over as wide a geographical area as the leopard frog is vastly different than it would be to a species with few populations. A species subdivided into a large number of semiautonomous populations that cover a vast geographical area is less susceptible to extinction than a species of only one or two populations.

The salmon is an excellent intermediate example of the way such a dynamic might work. Salmon have discrete populations of adults, often called "strains" or "runs," which breed in particular streams—those in which they originally hatched. Once the young salmon reach a certain size, they swim downstream and mingle in the ocean with individuals of all the other populations. With maturity, however, members of each genetically discrete population leave the ocean and swim up the particular river they originally descended on their way to the ocean as they seek the exact stream in which they were hatched and in which they will spawn.

Someone interested in managing a population of salmon in a particular river must pay close attention to the dynamics of that population, which only becomes apparent when the salmon are actually in the river. On the other hand, when salmon from all of the rivers are massed in the ocean in a "superpopulation," the management of the marine salmon fishery is a vastly different affair.

Today, the Pacific Northwest region of the United States has a number of discrete populations or runs of breeding salmon in particular rivers, such as the Columbia and the Snake, that face extinction because of hydroelectric dams, among other things. The dams not only trap the young fish upstream, preventing most of them from reaching the ocean, but also kill fish passing through the hydroelectric turbines in their efforts to reach the sea. Others die when the impounded waters behind the series of dams are drawn down to accommodate large irrigation projects, because the people who constructed both the dams and the irrigation projects did so without regard to the habitat requirements of the salmon.

Losing a given run of salmon will affect the superpopulation in the ocean through the loss of genetic diversity, a "secret extinction," albeit one hidden in the totality of the superpopulation. Such a loss is hardly noticeable because the superpopulation is a collective of immature salmon from all populations growing in unison to reproductive maturity.

But if you are a fisheries biologist responsible for the health of a particular population of breeding adults once it leaves the ocean and arrives in the river, the secret extinction in the superpopulation is no longer a secret. It is a permanent disaster. The impact of that extinction on the river, which may never again see a salmon, differs significantly from its impact on the ocean, which still sees millions of the same species of salmon, although none from that particular run.

Secret extinction or not, where do species come from? Where do they go? Species arise out of the creative process of evolutionary change, and when their time is over, they disappear back into that process, making way for yet another species.

After all, you and I are but refabrications composed of the atoms borrowed by the earliest invertebrates of the Cambrian period, about 600 million years ago; then passed on to the dinosaurs of the Cretaceous period, about 130 million years ago; then on to the woolly mammoths, dire wolves, saber-toothed tigers, and cave bears of the Pleistocene epoch, about a million years ago; until now, finally, it is our turn to borrow them. When we die, when we become extinct as individuals in this world, where will the atoms go? That is the eternal mystery!

How Species Enrich the World

Why do we need such a variety of species anyway? Would the coelacanth really be so great a loss? What effect does a variety of species have on the world ecosystem?

One marvelous effect they have is increasing the stability of ecosystems by means of feedback loops. Feedback loops are the means by which processes reinforce themselves.

Strong, self-reinforcing feedback loops characterize many interactions in Nature and have long been thought to account for the stability of complex systems. Ecosystems with strong interactions among components, such as those contributed by feedback loops, can be complex, productive, stable, and resilient under the conditions to which they are adapted. When these critical loops are disrupted, such as by the extinction of species, these same systems become fragile and are easily affected by slight changes.

It is the variety of species that create the feedback loops that makes each individual species so valuable. Each species by its very existence has a shape and therefore a structure that in turn allows certain functions to take place, functions that interact with those of other species to create a living system. For example, the hood of a pitcher plant in the Pine Barrens of New Jersey forms a vessel that holds enough water in spring for a particular mosquito to lay its eggs within the protected pool, and the pitcher plant rears the mosquito's young. Another example, perhaps closer to home, might be opening up the center of a rosebush with a pair of snippers to allow the circulation of air by altering the bush's structure and thus its internal microclimate, thereby drying the air and controlling the black spot fungus, which requires a moist environment in which to live. All of this is governed ultimately by the genetic code, which by replicating species' character traits builds a certain amount of redundancy into each ecosystem.

Redundancy, as stated earlier, means that more than one species can perform similar functions. It is a type of ecological insurance policy, which strengthens the ability of the system to retain the integrity of its basic relationships. The insurance of redundancy means that the loss of a species or two is not likely to result in such severe functional disruptions of the ecosystem so as to cause its collapse because other species can make up for the functional loss. But there comes a point, a threshold, when the loss of one or two more species may in fact tip the balance and cause the system to begin an irreversible change. That change may signal a decline in quality or productivity of the very things for which we humans valued the system in the first place. An example might be the loss of indigenous perennial grasses in the Great Basin of the American West due to overgrazing by domestic livestock coupled with the suppression of fire. This combination allowed the takeover of such exotic annuals as cheatgrass brome, which effectively excluded indigenous perennial grasses and thereby created a virtual monoculture of little value as habitat for wildlife or for grazing livestock compared with the habitat diversity and quality of the forage inherent in the indigenous grassland.

Although an ecosystem may be stable and able to respond "positively" to the disturbances in its own environment to which it is adapted, the same system may be exceedingly vulnerable to the introduction of foreign disturbances to which it is not adapted (to be discussed in detail later). We can avoid disrupting ecosystems supported by feedback loops only if we understand and protect the critical interactions that bind the parts of an ecosystem one to another and thus create the system itself.

Diversity of plants and animals therefore plays a seminal role in buffering an ecosystem against disturbances from which it cannot recover, and many of these services to an ecosystem are indirect and thus hidden in their significance. By this I mean that species by themselves may have small, direct effects on a biological process but can simultaneously have large indirect effects on an ecosystem as a whole if they influence the abundance of other species with large direct effects on the ecosystem. A

disperser of seeds or a pollinator that has little direct effect on the processes of a forested ecosystem can thus be essential for the persistence
of a species in the canopy that has greater direct effects on the ecosystem
itself.[16]

Although unknown indirect effects of species on ecosystems are often
cited by ecologists as ample justification for the protection of the diversity
of species, there currently is no theoretical framework within which to
predict the relative importance of such indirect effects.[16] Thus, as we lose
species, we lose not only their diversity of structure and function, be it
direct or indirect, but also their genetic diversity, which sooner or later
results in complex ecosystems becoming so simplified that they will be
unable to sustain us as a society. Here a lesson from Easter Island is
instructive.[17]

Easter Island is a tiny, 43-square-mile piece of land in the South Pacific
2,400 miles off the coast of South America. The oldest pollen dates on the
island go back some 30,000 years, long before the first people, seafaring
Polynesians, arrived. At that time, the island was forested.

The Polynesians settled on the island in about 400 A.D. They began
gradually to clear the land for agriculture, and they cut trees to build
canoes. The land was relatively fertile, the sea teemed with fish, and the
people flourished. Their population rose to about 15,000, and the culture
grew sophisticated enough to carve the giant statues that have since
become famous. The people eventually also cut trees to provide logs for
transporting and erecting those hundreds of eerie statues, or *moai*, some
of which are about 32 feet high and weigh as much as 85 tons.

Unfortunately, when the trees were cut, they did not grow back.
Deforestation began about 1,200 years ago, a few hundred years after the
people arrived, and was almost complete by 800 years ago. The people
of Easter Island also exploited many of the island's other resources, such
as its abundance of birds' eggs. The result was an ecological disaster.

The people had cleared so much of the forest that they were without
trees to build canoes for fishing. They probably also had exploited the
eggs of the sooty tern to the point that the bird no longer nested on the
island. And deforestation led to erosion of the soil and reduced yields of
crops.

The downward spiral of culture on Easter Island had begun. Fewer
fish, eggs, and crops led to a shortage of food. Hunger in turn brought
warfare, even cannibalism, and the whole civilization was pushed to the
brink of collapse. By the time European explorers arrived in the 1700s,
only 4,000 people remained on the island, and the culture that produced
the statues had completely disappeared.

Today, all we can do is marvel at the remains of the culture of Easter Island—statues that once stood erect on specially built platforms, others that lie abandoned between the volcanic quarries of their origin and their planned destinations, and still others that remain unfinished in the quarries.

Clearly, any societal strategy aimed at protecting diversity and its evolution is a critically important step toward ensuring an ecosystem's ability to adapt to change in a way that is compatible with human existence. Diversity counts in all its myriad scales, forms, and functions. To better understand the importance of diversity, we shall enter briefly the world of trees and salmon.

Of Trees and Salmon

Some trees are among the oldest and longest living beings on Earth. As such, they represent safety and a sense of eternity and draw us to them, although we are seldom aware of it.

We commune with trees almost unconsciously by bringing them into our lives. We plant them in our gardens and yards and along our city streets for the shade they give in summer's heat. We plant them for their beauty of flower in spring and their color of leaf in autumn. We select them by their shape of leaf and pattern of branch, by their straightness of trunk and texture of bark. The trees we plant are chosen for the contextual dimension their presence adds to our lives as they grace our soulscapes, gardenscapes, cityscapes, and landscapes.

Their presence, particularly that of deciduous trees, demonstrates for us the seasons of the year even as they remind and instruct us about the inner seasons of our lives. Some trees support within their mighty branches the playhouses of the young, while others become the coffins within which rest those departed. Some trees are planted as memorials to deceased loved ones, where their longevity may somehow counterbalance our brevity. And some trees become the houses in which we live and the paper upon which we write. "A stricken tree," wrote author Edna Ferber, "is, next to man, perhaps the most touching of wounded objects."

In areas where wind blows incessantly, such tall, slender trees as the Lombardi poplar are planted in tight rows as windbreaks to protect homes and crops, which may be other trees bearing fruits and nuts for human consumption. Windbreaks are also used to protect topsoil from being blown away. When these trees die, they may be felled for firewood to keep home and hearth cozy against plummeting temperatures ushered in by winter's winds.

And as if that were not enough, we name towns and cities in honor of trees, such as Buttonwillow and Cottonwood, California; Oakville and Pine, Oregon; Cedar City and Elmwood, Utah; and Aspen and Alder, Colorado.

In light of all this, you might well ask what a tree is. If you were to ask me that question directly, I could not answer it. I don't know what a tree is; I only know what a tree is not. It is not a horse, it is not a mountain, it is not lightning; yet it has something in common with all three. A tree, like a horse, is a living being. Like a mountain, a tree is a historian, recording Earth's history in its annual growth rings as a mountain archives cosmic events in its geological strata. And like the electrical soul of lightning, a tree's impulse to live is transmitted throughout its being by electrical current.

But a tree is much more than this, for a tree travels the world in time, its roots growing out of the same soil in which lies the seed of our human heritage. If I followed my ancestral lineage back some 5,000 years, the life span of one bristlecone pine (Figure 2) that was cut down at Great Basin National Park in the state of Nevada, I would be looking at the history of 100 generations if the average life span of my ancestors was 50 years or 71 generations if the average life span was 70 years.

These generations are a bridge across time within the lineage or ancestral tree of a single human family. As such, the shape of a deciduous tree in winter without leaf is a cosmopolitan motif. Consider, for example, the branching behavior of a tree, be it maple, oak, chestnut, elm, or beech.

As a tree moves from Heaven to Earth collecting into branches, consolidating into trunk, and outflowing into roots, it forms a great repetitive dendritic pattern seen everywhere in the waterways of the world. Dendritic comes from the Greek *dendron*, "tree."

This dendritic pattern appears across the surface of the Earth's landscapes as the arterial system guiding rain and melting snow from mountain and plain to valley and sea. As raindrop and snowflake become trickle, stream, and river, gathering into main stems (trunks) like the Mississippi, the Amazon, and the Nile, they come together in their flowing only to dissipate again over the great deltas where river and sea meet.

Here the waters spread out over the submerged land of the continental shelf and maintain the integrity of their past flowing when the glaciers of ancient times hoarded unto themselves the water and lowered the level of the sea. Today, with the death of the Pleistocene glaciers, these rivers flow in secret, sandwiched between the pulsating sea and the continental

FIGURE 2 Bristlecone pine grows slowly and has wood that is so fine-grained and resinous that it is exceedingly resistant to decay. Instead of rotting, these pines, like the one depicted in the center of the photograph, are bleached by the sun and polished and eroded by wind and, during the storms of winter, by ice crystals. In addition, dead bristlecone pines may stand for thousands of years after death. (Photograph by author.)

shelf, building their deltas, expanding their ever-changing network of channels as each discharges the fresh water of its being into the salty body of the sea.

What is hidden by the great body of salt water, however, can be seen in miniature on its sandy shore as the receding tide leaves its musings in the shape of little trees with their collecting branches, uniting trunks, and outflowing roots (Figures 3 to 6). This dendritic pattern, which unites land and sea, is sculpted by water under the tutelage of gravity. But not

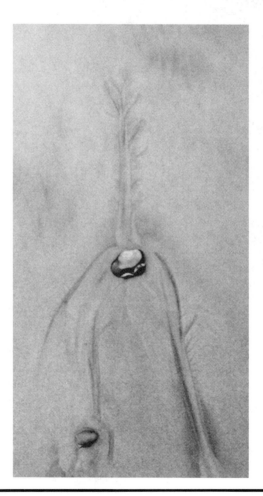

FIGURE 3   Dendritic patterns in the sand along the Oregon coast. (Photograph by author.)

FIGURE 4   Dendritic patterns in the sand along the Oregon coast. (Photograph by author.)

so the tree itself, where its trunk defies gravity's tug and sends skyward its branches to bear leaf, flower, and fruit. The leaves in turn send the sun's energy downward through branch and trunk to feed the hungry roots.

As a cosmopolitan motif, trees represent the spiritual ground out of which the human struggle for consciousness evolves; witness the battle over old-growth trees in the Pacific Northwest or in the tropical rain forest. As the oldest living individual beings on Earth, trees also represent the continuity of life in time and space.

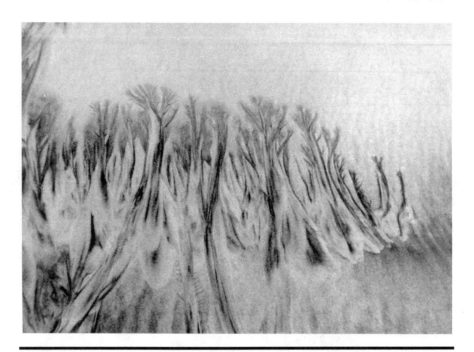

FIGURE 5   Dendritic patterns in the sand along the Oregon coast. (Photograph by author.)

Trees in Time and Space

There are in my garden two trees: one pear, the other apple. Along the southern border of my garden, but outside the fence, stand four Norway maples. It is a curious thing, but when I work with them, harvesting fruit in summer, raking leaves in autumn, and pruning branches in winter, I am often struck with awe when I consider what each tree represents in time and space as it stands rooted in the soil through the decades while reaching daily for the sky.

Trees represent for me the flow and ebb of events as they stretch from the present into the distant past. For example, about 55 miles northeast of Las Vegas, Nevada, is the Valley of Fire, a vivid land of bold cliffs amidst the grandeur of the Mojave Desert, where 150 million years ago, during the age of dinosaurs, a forest of primitive evergreen trees called Araucarian pines grew a few miles outside the valley along the edge of a great sea.[18] (The monkey puzzle tree or Chile pine of the western slopes of the Chilean Andes in South America; the Norfolk Island pine of Norfolk

FIGURE 6 Dendritic patterns in the sand along the Oregon coast. (Photograph by author.)

Island, east of Australia; and the bunya-bunya of Queensland, Australia, are the best-known living species of the genus *Araucaria*.)

Storms and floods carried branches and whole trunks of these trees into the ancient sea. As trees became waterlogged and sank to the sea floor, they were buried by hundreds to thousands of feet of mud and sand. Here, in secret, the woody materials were slowly altered molecule by molecule and replaced by silica, quartz, and other minerals until the trees were turned to stone in an almost exact replica of their original design.

Beginning about 140 million years ago, the sea retreated and mud and sand took over and reigned for nearly 75 million years, during which time the valley's limestones were covered to a depth of about 4,500 feet. Carried by winds from the erosion of distant highlands, masses of lofty, shifting dunes—sometimes thousands of feet high—piled up in the valley. Over time, the grains of sand became cemented together with iron to form "fossil" dunes almost a half-mile thick.

Then, about 100 million years ago, as the seafloor plate that lay beneath the Pacific Ocean to the west of the North American continent moved directly against the continent, the heavy oceanic plate was forced below North America. It created titanic forces as it crashed against North America in its resistance to being pushed under the continent. As the seafloor plate moved beneath the continental plate, it melted and injected its lighter weight components upward into the continent.

The Sierra Nevada mountains of California thus began to form as gigantic intrusions of molten rock forced their way up into the Earth's crust, shoving aside the existing continental rock. The rise of the Sierra Nevadas not only began to trap moisture on the mountains' western slopes, which caused the region east of the mountains to become increasingly arid, but also closed southern Nevada's outlet to the sea some 25 million years ago. Since then, erosion has been the dominant geological activity in the valley.

Today, the grains of sand released from their millennial bondage once again blow across the desert. And here and there scattered about the desert is the multicolored petrified wood, including whole trunks, of the Araucarian pines whose inner spaces have been formed over the millennia into little troves of minute crystals that now dazzle the eye as they lie sparkling in the sun, where they rest among other rocks whose rough gray bodies guard fossil seashells, corals, sponges, and sea lilies from the time when the valley was a warm and watery world teeming with life.

Not all ancient trees are fossils, however. In August of 1994, David Noble, the Parks and Wildlife Service officer in Wollemi National Park in the Blue Mountains near Sydney, Australia, walked into a damp, protected gorge in the park. As he did so, he stepped into a tiny one-acre grove of Jurassic-age pines thought to have been extinct these last 150 million years.[19] Although the Wollemi Pines, as they have been dubbed, once covered vast areas of the world, they were thought to have succumbed to changing climate—that is, all but the 39 individuals now known to be still living. The grove consists of 23 adult trees and 16 juveniles, making the Wollemi pine one of the world's rarest plants.

Its foliage is dense and waxy, and its knobby brown bark gives it the appearance of being coated in bubbly chocolate. The largest tree towers 130 feet into the air and has a 10-foot girth, indicating that it may be at least 150 years old.

Ironically, "wollemi" is an Australian aboriginal word meaning "look around you," which points to the notion that we do not know our own planet very well when such a large tree can go undiscovered for so long in, of all places, an established national park. As such, "wollemi" has encompassed within its symbolism the wonder of these trees that for so long have been enshrouded in the Eternal Mystery. Think for just a moment of the Wollemi pine's incredible journey through the all but trackless sands of time, over 150 million years, the last two centuries or so under the very nose of learned society.

Unfortunately, many people define the things in their environment by their ability to convert them into money, and that includes the newly discovered Wollemi pine. Of the 40 seeds that were taken from the grove, one has germinated. Now the Mount Annan Botanic Garden is hoping to become rich by propagating them. "Let's face it," says Mark Savio, curator of the gardens, "everyone is going to want one of these plants from the age of the dinosaurs."

How can something so ancient in lineage, so venerated in age, so magnificent in structure and function, and so awesome in stature as a mature Wollemi pine, or any number of other trees, be reduced solely to an intellectual definition or a quantifiable monetary value? To me, no tree can be so treated, for trees connect the generations of life not only in time as the oldest beings on Earth but also in space as they travel around the oceans of the world.[20]

Drifting trees, either individually or as wood islands, ferry communities of plants and animals from one geographical location to another as they are carried hither and yon by ocean currents and trade winds. In the North Pacific, for example, drifting trees that escape the inshore oscillations of the tidal currents enter the open ocean, where they may eventually contact the westward transport of the North Pacific gyre, a great circular vortex.

Some drifting trees become waterlogged and sink once they become entrained in the North Pacific vortex. Such trees become islands of food for deep-sea wood-dependent organisms on the floor of the ocean. Other large drifting trees, however, remain afloat for long periods and great distances to come ashore in such exotic places as the Hawaiian Islands, where in fact trees from the Pacific Northwest account for most of the large driftwood on the beaches. Other drifted trees on the beaches of the Hawaiian Islands are indigenous to the Philippines, Japan, or Malaysia.

Anthropological records show that the beached Douglas fir, western red cedar, and coast redwood were even integrated into the customs and rituals of oceanic cultures. Ancient Hawaiians prized these huge trees washed up on their shores because local chiefs preferred them for construction of their large double canoes, a symbol of wealth and power.

Iceland provides another example of traveling trees. According to geologist Sir Charles Lyell,[21] Iceland's ancient forests had already been "improvidently exhausted" by the mid-1800s:

> ...although the Icelander can obtain no timber from the land, he is supplied with it abundantly by the ocean. An immense quantity of thick trunks of pines, firs, and other trees...is thrown upon the northern coast of the island...[sufficient]...for fuel and for constructing boats. The timber is also carried to the shores of Labrador [the mainland part of Newfoundland, Canada] and Greenland; and Crantz assures us that the masses of floating wood thrown by the waves upon the island of John de Mayen often equal the whole of that island in extent. [John de Mayen is now called "Jan Mayen" and is a fairly large island of Norwegian ownership lying north northeast of Iceland and east of Greenland.]
>
> In a similar manner the bays of Spitzbergen [a Norwegian archipelago in the Arctic Ocean between Greenland and Franz Josef Land] are filled with drift-wood...consisting of larch trees, pines, Siberian cedars, firs, and Pernambuco and Campeachy [sic] woods [trees from Pernambuco, a state in northeastern Brazil, and the Campeache or longwood tree, a species indigenous to tropical America and the West Indies].

Considering trees in time and space makes it impossible for me to reduce a tree to a mere intellectual abstraction. I shall therefore endeavor to paint a word portrait of a tree in but a few of its myriad forms. To paint such a portrait, it is necessary to examine the leaves, flowers and fruits, branches, trunk, and roots.

Although I discuss the parts of a tree as separate components, remember that a tree is a living being, an integrated living system in constant motion, and as such is surrounded by and infused in a large system called the biosphere, which includes you and me. This being the case, I shall discuss the tree within the context of itself, beginning with the leaves and progressing to the roots, so that you may gain a small measure of how trees as species enrich the world through their almost unbelievable diversity in form, function, and interaction with their environment.

Leaves

With the advent of each spring, there comes forth a soft green halo on the trees of my garden as the sleeping leaves of winter awaken and grow. I love the leaves of spring, for they are bright and tender with the innocence of a new year. With the passing days, however, the leaves mature in the warmth of the sun and become home and food to insects. And it is while watching a wee caterpillar climb a leaf on my pear tree that I find myself contemplating what a leaf really is.

Leaves come in limitless sizes and shapes, no two of them ever exactly alike. They have many functions, be they the broad leaves of a maple, the needles of a noble fir, or the small leaves and long thorns of a desert acacia. They are, for example, amazingly compact energy converters, which use chlorophyll to harness the sun's energy, to convert carbon dioxide, water, and elemental nutrients from the soil into simple sugars that are in one form or another distributed throughout and among eco-systems, where they are a critical part of the world's food web.

Leaves also transpire water, creating a humid microclimate around their individual surfaces within a tree's crown and within a forest. As they filter the sun's light passing through their bodies, the leaf community of a tree's top creates an ever-moving dapple of lights and shadows on the forest floor in response to the sun's daily passage across the heavens.

A forest spider can find shade from the sun and a roof from the rain under a single leaf. Although considerably larger than a spider, some tropical bats chew partway through certain leaves, causing them to fold over and create an instant shelter in which the bats pass the daylight hours sleeping.

As far as we humans are concerned, however, it takes the combined shadows of many leaves to cast one large enough to protect us from the sun's heat and ultraviolet rays. But in the distant Congo where the Pyg-mies live, there are leaves large enough for these small forest folk to thatch their simple huts with roofs of green.

And leaves create beauty not only in form and function as they grow and mature in spring and summer but also in color as they change hue with their dying in autumn. For it is autumn's warm days and crisp, clear nights that begin calling the leaves back to earth to share the atoms they have so briefly borrowed from the atomic interchange of the ages. As autumn matures and the winds blow colder and harder, the dying leaves break loose their bonds to bump and bounce and float to earth. Others, clinging stubbornly to dormant twigs, rustle in the teasing wind. Each passing day sees more leaves collect beneath trees, forming a brittle, crunchy blanket over the ground.

It is in autumn that I get out my rake and begin collecting the falling leaves of the pear and apple trees in my garden and of the maples just outside the fence. No matter how often I rake under the trees, each warm, blustery, southwesterly wind off the Pacific Ocean and each cold north wind from the Alaskan and Canadian arctic sends more leaves scurrying across the ground I have just cleared. Be that as it may, each time I rake the leaves into piles, I am reminded of my youth.

Autumn was the time in my youth when the fallen oak and maple leaves were raked by hand into long rows on the golf course next to where I lived. The rows of leaves were collected into a trailer pulled behind an old Ford tractor and taken to the traditional burning area, which just happened to be near my house. And it was here in the autumns of the past that I discovered the pure joy of jumping into mammoth piles of leaves and of throwing them into the air and having them rain down around me. As Indian summer drew to a close, however, my leaf-jumping season ended, for this was the time when the leaf mountains were lighted to smolder for days with tiny red, orange, and yellow flames writhing hither and yon in a tortured dance amidst the billowing greenish-gray smoke until all that remained were great piles of ashes.

And then comes winter, the season of leafless trees and bare-limbed shrubs, of withered bygone flowers and dead grasses. It is a time for hibernating, for being snug and sleepy in a cozy nest as wind-driven rain and sleet and snow buffet the outside world. But what about the leaves of next spring and summer? Where are they?

Have you ever looked closely at a leaf bud on a tree in winter? Inside the frozen bud is a miniature leaf just waiting for spring to release it from bondage to begin again the dance of leaves exemplified by the trembling ballet of quaking aspen as they rustle softly in summer's breezes.

Unlike the leaves of maple and oak, of beech and ash, the needles of coniferous trees do not dance in the breezes, for they tend to be narrow and stiff, designed with the rigidity of soldiers clinging to limb and twig in orderly file. Although they do not dance, they sing. And to me, the greatest love song of all time is the wind playing its melody through the orchestra of needles high in the crowns of ponderosa pine. Although the needles of coast redwood trees do not sing like those of pine, they collect precious water.

The great redwood forest of northwestern California would not exist if not for the coastal fogs. Most of the redwoods' summer moisture is gleaned from fog flowing inland a short distance from the Pacific Ocean, where it collects on needle after needle. Here it forms into crystalline mounds that converge into fluid pendants that drip with the persistence of Chinese water torture from lofty crowns to saturate the forest floor, where salamanders depend on it for the breath of life because they absorb oxygen through their skin and must therefore remain moist or they suffocate. Beyond the salamanders, deeper in the soil, wait the thirsty roots of the giant trees that for millennia have gathered their own drinking water from fog condensed along the edge of the sea.

To the north, in western Oregon, lives the small red tree vole, mentioned earlier, a mouse-like denizen of the stately Douglas firs. Building its nest anywhere from 6 to 150 feet above the ground, it depends for life on the needles of Douglas fir and along the coast on western hemlock and Sitka spruce. In addition to eating the needles, however, these little tree-dwelling mammals lick the dew off of them and thus quench their thirst. Their ability to use this source of water allows them to extend their geographical distribution eastward into the hot interior of the land along major rivers, which create their own fog that in turn envelops the Douglas firs growing along their banks to the benefit of these small voles.

Halfway around the world, in the deserts of Egypt, grow acacia trees whose tiny leaves and rapier-like thorns conserve precious moisture as they endure the scorching heat of a relentless sun, the hot breath of desert winds, and the choking clutch of howling sand storms. Yet even here, the leaves must produce the essential sugars from the sun's harvested light if they are to live.

Here, too, lives the shrike or "butcher bird." The butcher bird is so called for its habit of fastening extra food securely to the acacia's thorns by impaling its prey thereon for another day's feast. Thus a thorn, which on some plants is an anatomically modified leaf in Nature's scheme of things, not only conserves moisture and protects its bearer from being eaten by most large herbivores but also serves as a pantry for so deft a hunter as the shrike.

I also remember finding a mummified hawk in the top of a date palm at Kurkur Oasis in the desert west of Aswan, Egypt, on Christmas Day in 1963. On retrieving the bird, which was in a diving position or "stoop," I discovered that it had pierced itself to death on the single blade of one of the palm's fronds and became an instant mystery riveted in time and space.

Clearly, it had been in its eternal dive a long time for its feathers of brown were severely faded. But how long? What had the hawk been so intent on capturing that in its singular focus it had run itself entirely through?

The irony is that the palm frond, which may have shaded the hawk one day from the sun's searing heat and glaring reflection off the desert sand, had the next taken its life. How long would the hawk have remained skewered, bleaching in the sun, had I not happened on the scene to bear witness to one of life's many unexpected twists?

Unlike deciduous trees, which lose their leaves seasonally and stand in naked slumber for part of each year, such conifers as Douglas fir and western hemlock shed about a third of their needles annually. As the needles die and turn yellowish, they loosen from their moorings and spin quietly to the forest floor or ride the gusty winds to their final resting place. There, they serve as food for a host of organisms and through many circuitous routes are eventually incorporated into the forest soil only to rise again in some future microbe, flower, mouse, or tree, each of which in turn completes its cycle and passes on the atoms it borrowed from needle and leaf.

While a deciduous tree or forest annually produces two entirely different habitats, one in full leaf and another following leaf fall, a coniferous tree or forest produces a continuous habitat of relatively similar characteristics throughout the year. In addition, broad leaves decompose rapidly and pass into the soil within a year, which makes them ideal mulch and compost for my garden, whereas coniferous needles may take a decade or more to break down and recycle through the system.

The length of time a leaf adheres to its tree is important to the leaf miners, which are any of a number of insect larvae that live in the thin layer of cells sandwiched between the opposing outer surfaces of leaves. To survive, they must time their life cycles to coincide with those of the leaves in which they dwell.

A leaf miner hollows out its path from egg to adult as it eats its way through the interior of a leaf. The hollowness of the tunnel grows in a width commensurate with the growth of the larva. But a leaf whose internal structure has been weakened by a miner cannot, I have learned, produce the quality of sound needed to be a musical instrument. To be true in melody, a leaf must be structurally sound and carefully chosen.

In May 1967, while taking a rest on the climb to my field camp at the 11,500-foot level on the mountain known as Phulung Ghyang, in Newakot District, Nepal, I watched one of my Tamang porters, a woman, search a small tree with oval leaves three to four inches long, examining leaf after leaf. Finally, with a look of absolute serenity, she selected one. Walking to a medium-sized boulder along the edge of the trail overlooking the vast emptiness of space as it plunged thousands of feet into the valley below, she climbed upon the rock and faced outward into the void.

Holding the leaf horizontally with one hand on each side of her mouth, she blew on its edge, and there came forth the most exquisite melody I have ever heard in my life. The liquid notes of a winter wren or a meadowlark are no match for the mystical quality of the music I heard that day so long ago. In that instant, the woman and the leaf became one, and from their union was born the most intricate, the most delicate praise of life I have ever experienced, or probably ever will experience in my earthly pilgrimage. The soul of all humanity, from its earliest dawning, was called forth to rejoice in the perfection of woman, leaf, music, and the Eternal Mystery that created them all.

From that day into forever, a tree's leaf will for me always be a symbol of the human spirit, perhaps in a way similar to the emblem of the maple leaf on the Canadian flag that represents Canada's national spirit.

However one looks at leaves, they are a graphic symbol of life's cycle and its diversity, from their emergence in spring, through their maturation in summer, to their decline and death in autumn, and their apparent absence in winter. But the leaves of trees are more than that. They are also a barometer of the harmony with which human society coexists within its environment, for they simultaneously produce the oxygen we breathe and monitor our trusteeship of the world's air, soil, and water, which affect the tree's flowers and fruits in my garden as well as in the forests of the world.

Flowers and Fruits

I find in every plant's seed the miracle of its being, because each seed has already present, hidden within its coat, not only the size and shape of the tree but also the size, shape, color, odor, and season of bloom of its flowers, as well as the size, shape, color, odor, flavor, and season of maturation of its fruits. The pear tree in my garden looks like a pear tree and produces only pear blossoms and fruits, and the apple tree likewise produces after its kind, as do the maples. Like all other components of life, there is infinite variety in flowers and fruits.

Some flowers are bright and showy, some drab and secretive; some are large while others are tiny; some transmit from place to place wonderful perfume on the pathways of the air, and others do not. Some flowers are pollinated by wind, some by insects, and others by birds and bats. Brightly colored flowers always cheer me, regardless of circumstances. And some flowers scent the air in such a way that on smelling them I am transported to another world.

Some trees have both male and female flowers on the same individual plant, whereas others have them on separate plants. Some flowers contain both male and female parts in the same blossom; others have separate blossoms. Some flowers are self-fertilizing when cross-pollination fails; others can only be pollinated by blossoms other than themselves.

In addition, some male flowers, through their wind-borne pollen, have left a multimillennial climatic record and through it given society a glimpse into its own evolution before language made recorded history possible. Archived in the sedimentary strata of lake bottoms, peat bogs, and glaciers lie the time-encapsulated secrets of a world before humans even knew how to question its existence. Here is secreted the drama of migrating trees and forests, of great fires and raging floods, of glaciers and drought-ridden deserts. Here, too, resides the ancestral lineage of communities of trees whose pollen chronicled their comings and goings even as their blooms brightened the day with color and tinted the air with odor in their bid to bring forth fruit and seed—the trees of the future.

But most of all, I marvel that so small a cone, so tiny a seed as that of the western red cedar can produce the ancient trees I remember from my youth, when a fallen monarch was so big that I could not climb over it when it blocked the trail as I hiked along the Green River in western Washington State. And the coastal redwoods of northwestern California live even longer and grow larger than the cedar.

The first time I saw a redwood, I pressed my cheek against its bark in an effort to look up the straightness of its trunk to the place where its top and the sky met. I failed, however, because the tip of the redwood's crown was far loftier than I had ever imagined. While I was awed by the sheer size and majesty of this ancient tree, I was comforted by it as well. This redwood, close to 3,000 years old, also arose, like the cedar, from a seed so fragile that I could squash the life out of it between my fingers.

As flowers provide food for such animals as honeybees, butterflies, hummingbirds, sunbirds, and nectar-eating bats, fruits, seeds, and nuts offer food to others, such as squirrels, mice, deer, bear, and fruit bats, some of which have wingspans approaching four feet. The flowers and fruits eaten by animals are not, however, free of service to Nature.

Many species of trees in the tropical rain forests, especially those which germinate in the dark understory, have large seeds that carry enough stored energy to grow leaves and roots without much help from the sun. Such fruits and seeds are often so large that only proportionately sized birds and mammals can swallow or carry them. In Gabon, a republic of west-central Africa, for example, monkeys may disperse 67 percent of the fruits eaten by animals.[22]

Seed-dispersing animals, such as large birds and monkeys, are critical in replacing the large trees and lianas (high-climbing vines) of the tropical forest canopy. By eating the fruits and defecating the seeds some distance from the parent plants, thereby improving the seeds' chances of landing in a favorable place for germination, the birds and monkeys are helping the trees and lianas, as species, to survive. These animals are the first species to disappear, however, when humans hunt for food and, along with elephants, have already been hunted so heavily that they either have been drastically reduced in numbers or eliminated completely over vast areas of the African forest, as well as in the tropical rain forests of Central and South America.

For the most part, foresters have overlooked how the interdependency of plants and animals affects the biodiversity of a plant community. Elephants, for example, disperse the seeds of 37 species of trees in the Ivory Coast, a republic of western Africa. Of those, only seven species have alternate means of dispersal (by birds and monkeys). Of the 201 individual trees in one study area, 83 species were dispersed by elephants. In one forest where humans had eliminated elephants a century earlier, few juvenile trees of the elephant-dispersed species were left, and the two major species had no offspring at all.

Once the large species of birds and mammals are gone, the stunningly rich tropical rain forests will change and gradually lose species of trees, lianas, and other plants. Smaller seeds dispersed by wind will replace large seeds dispersed by large animals. Those species of plants whose seeds grow in the shaded understory will not survive, and the land will gradually be forested by fewer, more common species.

A similar, albeit simpler, phenomenon is taking place in my own garden with scrub jays. Each autumn, the jays bury hazelnuts, filberts (also a nut), and acorns and simply leave them over winter, forgetting where they are. But the jays are back in late spring and early summer searching for seedlings that germinated from their autumn caches. On finding a seedling, a jay digs down to the filbert or acorn, plucks it from the seedling, cracks it open, eats the remains, and flies away. The seedling, meanwhile, is well established and flourishes—until I pluck it out.

Some animal–fruit interactions, however, appear to have little or nothing to do with seed propagation. In mid-February 1972, I was in the canyon along the Crooked River near the town of Prineville in central Oregon. It was a clear, warm, sunny day. The ground was mottled with snow. A light breeze, blowing up the Crooked River, carried with it ever so faint a hint of spring. As I glanced toward the river, I saw a muskrat climb out of the water and search the bank for something to eat. Somewhere a Canadian goose called, then another. It was peaceful with the little sucking noises of the water against the banks and the voices of the animals.

What a perfect day! I was protected from the wind by juniper trees growing along the river and up the slopes to the massive rims of basalt, which capped the canyon's walls. And just across the river, I could see more junipers marching out of sight into the distance. As I stood breathing deeply of the cold, clean winter air, I glanced toward the rim of the canyon, where part way up the slope was an incredible commotion. Birds were plummeting out of the trees for no apparent reason. My curiosity aroused, I found a place to cross the river and started up the slope.

It is common in this country for birds of different species to band together in winter, forming what is called a feeding flock. As I climbed toward the rim, the commotion, which until then had been silent with distance, became an awful din. Mountain bluebirds, evening grosbeaks, cedar waxwings, and robins, with a few birds of other species thrown in, were creating incredible pandemonium. There were hundreds of them, all seeming to squawk at once. In addition, I could see, even from a distance, that some of them were literally falling out of the trees and flopping around on the ground with their heads lolling this way and that, unable to fly. What on earth was going on?

I began walking a little faster, for it was now obvious that something was seriously amiss. I had seen birds act in a similar manner in years past when pesticides had been sprayed in an area. But who would be spraying pesticides in this isolated canyon country at this time of year, and what would they be spraying for? It just didn't make sense.

I was still some distance from the birds, and slightly out of breath from my rapid climb, when I became conscious of just how sweet the juniper berries were that I had been plucking off the trees as I walked by. They had an unmistakable zing to them—the berries were fermenting because they had been frozen and warmed again by the sun only to be refrozen and warmed again.

I suddenly understood, and all I could do was laugh until my stomach and sides ached. The birds were drunk, very drunk, but dangerous mostly to themselves. They were just crashing into things, and once down, they simply could not get up again. No matter what they did, they could not become airborne. And there were hundreds of them, all in various stages of inebriation.

If birds get hangovers, I mused, there would be a bunch of miserable birds in the days ahead. Just then, a bluebird fell off a branch. Well, I thought, if they don't get hangovers, they must certainly get bruises.

Branches

The leaves, flowers, and fruits of a tree are simultaneously nurtured, held for a time securely in place, united, and ultimately allowed to fall from branches. January and February are the months each year during which I must attend to the branches of my fruit trees and, if necessary, those of the maples. It is the time of year when the sleeping trees are ready for pruning, when last year's growth is cut and the trees shaped to keep them under a semblance of control.

When Zane, my wife, and I bought our house, the pear and apple trees were unkempt and in need of attention. Arriving at our new home in late summer, our first harvest needed to be done by climbing into the trees to reach those fruits whose locations were beyond the capacity of my ladder. But over the next three years, I pruned the branches shorter and shorter each winter, and I can now reach almost every pear and apple from a six-foot stepladder.

It is during the activity of pruning that each year I revisit the concept of a branch and how humanity has endowed this portion of a tree with a variety of symbolic meanings. Branches, for example, are like the arms of a tree, the shape of which often conjures its human-envisioned demeanor—a gnarled oak, a weeping willow, or a stately ash.

Beyond space, in the realm of time and human imagination, a tree offers a symbol of Creation and the balance between the spiritual (branch) and material (root) aspects of life in the "tree of life," of the continuing evolution of life's infinite variety in the branching of the "phylogenetic tree," and of the continuity and divergence of personal lineage in the branching of the "family tree."

But what does a spider whose sole intent is to fasten its web from branch to branch or a warbler seeking a suitable location for its nest know of time or human imaginings? To the spider, one branch may be much like another as an anchor for its web, but to the nesting bird or sleeping bat, branches are as varied as the trees themselves.

A Douglas fir, for example, offers many suitable nesting sites for a variety of birds among it horizontal branches and abundant, stiff needles and a secure place for the hoary bat to hang by day; but a western red cedar or Alaska yellow cedar, with its drooping branches and tiny scale-like leaves, has little that a nesting bird or sleepy bat requires. The same is true of a Pacific yew with its zigzaggy branches and often scraggly form, of a western hemlock whose branches are sparsely clothed in lacy needles, or of a tamarack, whose branches are covered with little pegs to which are attached whorls of soft, pliable needles offering little protection from sun, wind, or rain.

But the same limber, downward sweeping branches that are unsuitable for a nesting bird, such as those of a grand fir, can shelter a snowshoe hare. A grand fir's boughs with their flat needles often become weighted down and frozen into snow as it continually piles up around the fir's base during a long mountain winter. In the cavity created and maintained under the fir's bough as it becomes roofed over by snow, a hare is safe and warm, out of the bitter cold wind.

As a boy, I thought branches were made for climbing. But even then, I discerned that there were safe and unsafe branches and that some trees, because of the characteristics of their branches, were easier to climb than others. I learned to "read" a tree's branches, taking none for granted before placing my weight on them or using them to pull myself upward.

Some branches, such as those of the hawthorn, locust, or acacia, are not readily climbable because of their thorns. Some, such as those of the South American monkey puzzle tree, are protected by sharp, scaly leaves that can confound even a monkey. Others, like beech, are smooth and difficult to grasp. Spruce branches are covered by tiny, rough "pegs," whereas rhododendron branches at the timberline on Phulung Ghyang in Nepal have exfoliating bark, which is continually self-peeling. And the branches of the true fir, which grow between 11,000 and 12,000 feet on the same mountain, are strong enough to give the common langur, a large monkey, safe purchase for a good night's sleep because they are simultaneously too limber to support the weight of the heavier clouded leopard, which hunts the monkeys at night for food. But whatever a branch is like, it is somehow synonymous with camp fires.

Fire was my only constant companion in years bygone, as it was that of my boyhood heroes, the American Indian and the mountain man. My first fire was intensely spiritual and private, known only to me and to the silent forest. The wisp of fir smoke, the heat, the tiny licking flame, the crackling branches became part of my spirit. And still are.

Since the days of my youth, fire has warmed me during cold winter nights in interior Alaska and during chilly desert nights in North Africa. Fire has cooked my food in the jungle of northern India and in the Himalayas of Nepal. And it has lifted my spirit on days of seemingly endless rain and shrouding fog in the coastal mountains of western Oregon and Washington.

Each fire is a reflection of the past, of the dawn of humanity, when the first purposefully made fire united humans and branches in a cultural dance the world over, a dance to remove the darkness and its terror, to heat a protective shelter, to cook food, and to alter the landscape for hunting, gathering, agriculture, and war.

Then again, the notion of a branch or branching has found its way through language into our culture. We say, for example, that we are going to open a branch office or that we are branching out into other things. In this sense, a branch is seen as moving away from the trunk, from the collective, to broach the unknown, which is the very essence of the Creative Principle, exploration, and personal growth.

These are some of the things I think about each winter as I prune the fruit trees in my garden. Why do I think about these things? I focus on them because the health of a tree's crown determines in large measure the health of its trunk, which is a great conduit of flowing energy that unites Heaven and Earth through the living being of a tree. And I want to keep my fruit trees and maple trees healthy, and myself along with them.

Trunk

Although there is nothing that I must do with the trunks of the trees in my garden or with those of the maples just outside, except be careful not to injure them, I am reminded while pruning the branches each year that it is the trunk of a tree that has in so many ways influenced humankind. The trunk, in this sense, is the main ascending axis of a tree, a stalk or stem. To me, however, a tree's trunk has always been more than simply the stem of a plant, especially one trunk, that of a giant noble fir on Marys Peak, the highest mountain in the Coast Range of western Oregon, whose campground near the summit is only 25 miles from my hometown of Corvallis.

The campground was at the end of a narrow gravel road that made a short loop through blue-tinted grandparent noble firs that ringed the lower edge of the grassy meadow atop the peak. And it was here, near the last picnic table at the meadow's edge, that in 1943 at age four I discovered the huge trunk of a fallen noble fir.

The trunk, which had already lain on the ground for some decades, was so large that I had a difficult time climbing on top of it. Nevertheless, I never got enough of climbing on it, exploring its nooks and crannies and examining the mosses, lichens, mushrooms, and various insects and centipedes that lived in, on, and around it. And sometimes, if I managed to lie quiet long enough, a Douglas squirrel or Townsend chipmunk would scamper over the top of me as though I was part of the trunk.

I visited the old trunk as the years passed. While I matured in stature, the old trunk became smaller and smaller as it gradually rotted away, returning to the soil from whence it had grown in times before my birth, when it had stood for centuries as a sentinel along the edge of the ancient, powdery-blue forest. In the summer of 1964, when I was 25 years old, I visited the old trunk, sat on it while enjoying the warmth of the sun, and stepped over the top of it as though it were now the child.

I felt a sadness in so doing, however, because the old trunk, now mostly collapsed in on itself, had given me as a child a measure of stability that I could not find in my family. As a child, I could talk to it, confide in it, and be safe with it. I wonder if the sadness I felt was in part a premonition that this was to be my last visit to the old trunk. In any case, it was; a severe early-winter storm blew down that whole portion of the forest and the old trunk all but disappeared under the impact of neighboring trees as they fell on it.

Thinking back to the trunk of that ancient noble fir, I wonder how the first humans might have begun a purposeful relationship with the trunks of trees. Was it the discovery of hollow trunks as shelter or drums? Was it the leaping flames, far-flung light, and long-lasting heat of a trunk burning? Or was it when the first human hollowed a tree's trunk with fire and the canoe was born, and so might have begun the purposeful exploration of the world's waterways?

Consider that without the large trunks of trees, there would have been no cedar bark from which indigenous peoples of the north Pacific coast of North America could make their waterproof capes and hats, no birch bark from which indigenous peoples of northern and eastern Canada could make bowls and canoes, no cork from the cork oak with which to seal bottles of vintage wine, no tannin from the tan oak with which to prepare leather, and no taxol from the Pacific yew with which to treat or cure breast or ovarian cancer in women.

Without the large trunks of trees, there would have been no wood for drums, wheels, ox yokes, houses, ships of olden days, or the first airplanes. And what about one of humanity's greatest triumphs, music.

Over the centuries, music has been committed to paper by great composers and translated into sound through orchestras. An orchestra, in turn, is composed of musical instruments and musicians that together give voice to the mute beauty on paper. A musician's ability to play a musical instrument is dependent not only on human skill but also on the quality of the instrument.

Over the last two centuries, the violins made by Antonio Stradivari (1644–1737) have given to the human ear some of the world's most exquisite melodies. To build a violin of the quality of a Stradivarius, however, one must not only be an expert violin maker but also have available fine-grained wood from the trunk of an ancient tree, such as a Sitka spruce.

Without trees, the peoples of the great continents would still be separated from one another; the oceanic islands, such as Hawaii, New Zealand, and Australia, would be barren of people; and the oceans and the skies of the world would still be unknown. The world and human culture would be very different without the sounds of the Stradivarius and all other musical instruments crafted from the trunks of trees. Without heat from wood, there could be no metal, and the face of the moon would still be without the footprints of humanity. And I, as a boy, would not have had my sacred old-growth Douglas fir to climb on windy days, where near its top, reveling in its supple strength, I could ride with the wind as it blew the ancient tree hither and yon.

But the influence of a tree's trunk reaches far beyond human history into the eons of life's web as it grows, matures, declines, dies, falls, and recycles into the soil. An old Douglas fir tree in its 810th year dies in the mountains of western Oregon and falls to the floor of the forest. The forest grows up around the decomposing giant for 525 years, until its last vestige is incorporated into the soil. Over the decades and centuries, the tree's atoms become parts of bacteria, fungi, earthworms, insects, birds, mammals, and green plants as each in turn has borrowed, used, and given up the atoms of its being to the next in line. Some atoms may go from insect to mother bird to her offspring and be carried away on wings and wind to a distant land, there to enter a different strand in life's web.

Suppose, for instance, that a young warbler matures and dies while overwintering in South America, where it falls into a jungle stream and is eaten by a scavenging fish. The fish is caught by the son of a poor slash-and-burn farmer who builds a small fire and cooks and eats the fish. A year later, the boy leaves the jungle and goes into a city to attend school. After some years of wandering, he goes to sea as a merchant seaman and dies an old man on a far distant shore where the atom of the ancient tree that became part of the insect that became part of the warbler that became part of the fish that became part of the boy now enters yet another strand of life's web.

Thus from seed to soil, the old fir's trunk influenced the site on which it grew and fell for 1,335 years, but its atoms will travel the world forever. As I mentioned earlier, I know of a bristlecone pine in Great Basin National Park that was finally cut down at an age of more than 5,000 years. How long would its trunk have influenced the site on which it grew had it been allowed to fulfill its entire ecological role? Where might its atoms travel if we could follow them through the corridors of time—to the root of another tree?

Speaking of roots, one of the maples just outside my fence has at least one root close enough to the surface of the ground under the concrete walk alongside my house that is large enough to both split the walk and elevate part of it at least an inch. Such is the power of roots.

Roots

Unlike the crowns of my pear and apple trees or those of the maples, which periodically require my attention during any given year, none of the trees' roots make such demands. Although there is nothing I need do directly to or with the roots in the sense of gardening, I must understand something about their relationship to both the soil and the aboveground portion of the trees they support, lest I inadvertently compact the soil and thereby hinder their ability to function.

As a tree's leaves caress the sky and harvest momentarily the sun's energy, so its roots are fastened in the Earth, where they grip the soil while harvesting the sun's energy stored in darkness from millennia past. The soil, where nonliving and living components of the landscape join, is also where past and present flow one into the other and determine a tree's future.

Soil supports the plants and animals that in turn create and maintain the myriad hidden processes that translate into soil productivity. Into this incredibly thin band of seething activity, the very ferment of terrestrial life, a tree thrusts its roots that it may withdraw energy long stored in Nature's warehouse and replace energy derived from the present net worth of its photosynthetic exchange, the leaves of its crown.

But here one might ask, "What is a root?" Most people probably think of a root as the underground portion of a plant that serves as support, draws food and water from the surrounding soil, and stores food, all the while holding the soil together. A root is far more than this simple description, however.

To examine the notion of a root, we will venture into a largely unknown, hidden world with the slightly buried seed of a Douglas fir as our guide. It is spring and the seed begins to swell as it absorbs moisture from the warm soil. The seed's coat splits, and a tiny root begins to penetrate the bosom of the Earth as small, green seed leaves reach toward the sun. Thus the seed of the tree becomes the seedling of the tree in its first spring of life.

As the seedling's roots spread through the soil, the new nonwoody root tip of a tiny feeder root comes in contact with a week-old fecal pellet of a deer mouse. The deer mouse had dined on a truffle (the belowground fruiting body of a fungus) the night before it deposited the pellet. The pellet, packed full of the truffle's spores, is still soft from the moisture in the soil, and the root tip has little difficulty penetrating it.

Inside the pellet, the root tip comes in contact with the spores that have passed unscathed through the mouse's intestinal tract. Meanwhile, the yeast (a fungus) in the pellet is growing and producing a substance called yeast extract that is food for the nitrogen-fixing bacteria. ("Nitrogen fixing" means to capture gaseous nitrogen and convert it into a form usable by the plant.) As the root tip contacts the spores, the yeast helps stimulate the spores to germinate and grow into and around the root tip; the nitrogen-fixing bacteria and yeast become enveloped in the fungal tissues. Once inside the fungal tissue and in the absence of oxygen, the nitrogen-fixing bacteria are nurtured by the extracts of both the yeast and the truffle's nonreproductive tissue. The bacteria in turn fix atmospheric nitrogen that can be used by both the fungi and the host tree.

The nonreproductive tissue of the truffle, called mycelia, forms a mantle around the tree's feeder root; this symbiotic association is called mycorrhiza, which literally means "fungus-root." As the mycelia grow into and around the root tips, they also grow out into the soil where they join billions of miles of gossamer threads from other mycorrhiza-forming fungi. These mycelial threads act as extensions of the seedling's root system as they wend their way through the soil absorbing such things as water, phosphorus, and nitrogen and sending them into the seedling's roots. As the seedling grows, it produces sugars that feed the fungus, which in turn expands through the soil as it is nourished by and nourishes the seedling. The tree is therefore a product of both the sun's light and soil's darkness; the nutrients of darkness feed the tree's top in light and the sugars of light feed the tree's roots and their fungi in darkness.

Although as a young man I knew nothing about this tree/fungal association and doubt that I had ever really considered the functional aspects of a tree's roots, I learned about their tenacity the year I was confronted by an old cottonwood stump on a ranch in northwestern Colorado, where I worked as a ranch hand. This particular cottonwood stump was in a small grove of its kind along the little stream that supplied water to the main ranch house. I forget the reason now, but the old rancher wanted the stump taken out, and removing it fell on my shoulders.

"Well," I thought to myself with the surety of youth, "this will be easy. All I have to do is chop through its roots with my ax, and I can pull it out with a team of horses." That's what I thought until the first day I hacked unceremoniously at the stump and the blade of my ax got so deeply buried in the soft wood that I couldn't get it out no matter how hard I tried.

The upshot is that I had to dig out each root on which I then cut, hacked, and sawed. In addition to my physical assault on its roots, I muttered at that infernal stump for the better part of the summer and autumn until the day came when I thought that I could in fact pull it out with a team of workhorses.

With the team hitched and anchored securely to the stump by a chain, I gave the word and the horses began to pull. I had, over the course of time, dug so far under the stump that I thought it would snap out in a twinkling. The old stump groaned and shivered, rose and fell until the chain broke, but would not release its grip in the soil. It had, I found, a monstrous taproot, which I could see only when the horses were pulling on the stump. I therefore had to dig the hole deeper.

Then came the day in early October when the old stump finally relinquished its hold, and the horses pulled it free of the soil. That was a bittersweet moment because it wasn't just a stump anymore; it had become a stump with a personality. I had unknowingly developed an honest-to-goodness relationship with it, one that challenged not only me but also technology and a team of powerful horses.

But I don't think I really ever conquered it, because I have long had the distinct feeling that at some point in our relationship the old cotton-wood stump decided, for whatever reason, to let me cut it out. That stump, perhaps more than any other, caused me to focus on roots. Yet as I chopped at the old stump's roots, I had no inkling of how vitally important tree roots are to the health of the forest beyond the individual trees.

Decomposing woody roots of tree stumps have distinct functions. Tree roots contribute to the shear strength of the soil, which is a root's ability to hold soil in place. Declining shear strength of decomposing woody roots increases mass soil movement after such disturbances as catastrophic fire and clear-cut logging.

Another related function of decomposing tree stumps and roots is the frequent formation of interconnected, surface-to-bedrock channels that rapidly drain water from heavy rains and melting snow. The collapse and plugging of these channels as roots decay may force more water to drain through the soil matrix, which reduces soil cohesion and increases hy-draulic pressure, which in turn may cause mass soil movement. Because these plumbing systems are necessary to the stability and sustainable productivity of the soil in a forest and cannot be replaced by young trees with their relatively small roots, grandparent trees are necessary to mediate the relationship between water and soil.

Although the pear and apple trees in my garden hardly qualify as a forest, their roots perform similar functions in the soil, many of which I know nothing about. What I do know, however, is that the care I take of my fruit trees aboveground affects directly the health of their roots belowground. In addition, how I choose to participate with the aboveground environment of my garden is a choice, my choice and nothing more. But the consequences of my choices will in many unknown and hidden ways affect not only the trees but also the next person to call this small piece of ground "my garden."

Mark Collins of the World Conservation Monitoring Center says that "forest destruction is the key threat to species worldwide," including 10 percent of the world's species of trees.[23] One-tenth of the known species of trees in the world are in danger of extinction, yet fewer than one in four species benefit from any kind of protection, according to the 650-page report *World List of Threatened Trees*.

According to the study, which was financed by the Dutch government and released in Geneva, Switzerland, on August 25, 1998, 8,753 of the world's estimated 80,000 to 100,000 species of trees are vulnerable. Of these, 1,000 are classified as critically endangered, reduced to less than 100 living individuals. Some of the species threatened with extinction have yet to be investigated scientifically. What will society lose with these secret extinctions?

It is my hope that whoever reads these words will pause for a moment before putting his or her saw or ax to a tree and in that moment pay homage to the being whose life is about to be severed. I say this because it is through the consciousness with which we act, and not the acts themselves, that we honor the Creation of which we are all an inseparable part, including the passage of wood from the forest to the sea.

From the Forest to the Sea and Back Again

I grew up in Oregon and over the years spent considerable time at the ocean. I remember the huge piles of driftwood along the beaches, piles that seemed to grow with each winter storm. In fact, one of the challenges of getting to the sandy shores of the Pacific was having to climb over the jumbled mountains of driftwood. There was so much wood, ranging from small branches to boards to huge whole trees, that one could build shelters from the wind that easily held 15 or more people. Enormous piles of driftwood were simply taken for granted as part of the beach.

Then, when I was grown, suddenly the driftwood mountains were gone. What happened to them? When did they disappear and why? How could the mountains of driftwood I so clearly remember have vanished without my noticing?

Driftwood is floating trees and parts of trees carried by water from the forest to the sea.[20] It is a critically important source of habitat and food for the marine ecosystem, including the deep-sea floor. Even during its seaward journey, driftwood is both habitat and a source of food for a multitude of plants and animals, both aquatic and terrestrial. In addition, some driftwood controls stream velocities, stabilizes stream banks, makes waterfalls and pools, and creates and protects areas where fish spawn. Other driftwood protects vegetation as it encroaches on floodplains and allows forests to expand. In short, driftwood makes a vital contribution to the health of streams, rivers, estuaries, and oceans worldwide.

The Stream-Order Continuum and Driftwood

In thinking about a forested water catchment from which the gift of driftwood comes, one must consider it in terms of the stream-order continuum, which operates on a simple premise: streams are Nature's arterial system of the land. As such, they form a continuum or spectrum of physical environments, with associated aquatic and terrestrial plant and animal communities, as a longitudinally connected part of the ecosystem in which downstream processes are linked to upstream processes.

The idea of the stream-order continuum begins with the smallest stream (a first-order stream) and ends at the ocean. The concept centers around the resources of available food for the animals inhabiting the continuum, which range from invertebrates to fish, amphibians, reptiles, birds, and mammals, including humans.

A first-order stream is the smallest undivided waterway or headwaters. Where two first-order streams join, they enlarge as a second-order stream. Where two second-order streams come together, they enlarge as a third-order stream and so on.

The concept of stream order is based on the size of a stream in terms of the cumulative volume of water, not just on which stream of what order joins with another stream of a given order. For example, a first-order stream can join either with another first-order stream to form a second-order stream or it can enter directly into a second-, third-, fourth-, fifth-, or even larger order stream. The same is true of a second-order stream, a third-order stream, and so on.

A first-order stream and its catchment basin are always a special case because they are not influenced by any other water catchment; in fact, they are probably the only part of the land where the hydrology has ecological integrity. Further, they are the headwaters and therefore control the initial quality of the water for the whole of the larger drainage basin.

A first-order water catchment by definition is unique. A second-order water catchment is unique among second-order water catchments, but is a common denominator, an integrator, of the first-order water catchments that created it. A third-order water catchment is unique among third-order water catchments, but is a common denominator of the first- and second-order water catchments that created it, and so on.

The stream order influences the role played by streamside vegetation in controlling water temperature, stabilizing banks, and producing food. Forest trees adjacent to streams supply wood from their branches, trunks, and rootwads. Erosion also contributes organic material to streams.

Wood in streams increases the diversity of habitats by forming dams and their attendant pools and by protecting backwater areas. Wood also provides nutrients and a variety of foundations for biological activity, and it both dissipates the energy of the water and traps its sediments.

When captured in the stream-order continuum, organic material, such as driftwood, floats downhill from its source to the sea. In so doing, it becomes smaller while the volume of water carrying it becomes larger. Thus small streams feed larger streams and larger streams feed rivers with partially processed organic matter, the amount of which becomes progressively smaller the farther down the continuum of the river system it goes.

Processing the organic debris entering the aquatic system includes digestion by bacteria, fungi, and insects and physical abrasion against such things as the stream bottom and its boulders. In all cases, debris is continually broken into smaller pieces, which makes the particles increasingly susceptible to microbial consumption.

The amount of different kinds of organic matter processed in a reach of stream (the stretch of water visible between two bends in a channel) depends on the quality and the quantity of nutrients in the material and on the stream's capacity to hold fine particles long enough to complete their processing. The debris may be fully utilized by the biotic community within a reach of stream or it may be exported downstream.

Debris moves fastest through the system during high water and is not thoroughly processed at any one spot. The same is true in streams that do not have a sufficient number of instream obstacles to slow the water and act as areas of deposition, sieving the incompletely processed organic material out of the current so its organic breakdown can be completed.

As a stream gets larger, its source of food energy is derived more from aquatic algae and less from organic material of terrestrial origin. The greatest influence of terrestrial vegetation is in first-order streams, but the greatest diversity of incoming organic matter and habitats is found in third- to fifth-order streams and large rivers with floodplains.

Small, first-order, headwater streams largely determine the type and quality of the downstream habitat. They and second-order streams are influenced not only by the configuration of surrounding landforms but also by the live and dead vegetation along their channels. This vegetation is called riparian vegetation and interacts in many ways with the stream.

The canopy of vegetation, when undisturbed, shades the streamside. The physical energy of the flowing water is dissipated by wood in stream channels, slowing erosion and fostering the deposition of inorganic and organic debris.

Because these small streams arise in tiny drainages with a limited capacity to store water, their flow may be scanty or intermittent during late summer and autumn. During periods of high flows in winter and spring, however, they can move prodigious amounts of sediment and organic material. Nevertheless, it is the stream-order continuum that has bestowed upon the oceans of the world the forest's gift of driftwood. And it is the driftwood within the stream-order continuum that forms the vital habitat for the salmon.

The Salmon's Story

A flash of silver, a swirl of bright water—a female salmon flexes her tail against the swift current as she propels herself to a small gravelly bar just under the surface in the headwaters of a Pacific Coast stream. Again a flash of silver, then another, and another as other salmon press against the rush of crystalline water, each seeking the exact spot to which its inner drive to spawn impels it.

Suddenly, from somewhere in the shadow of trees overhanging the tiny, clear stream, there comes a large, magnificent male salmon of metallic luster; he swims alongside the female with powerful undulations of his body. They touch, and the female immediately turns on her side and fans the gravel with strong beats of her tail.

She continues spraying gravel into the current until a shallow depression comes into definition, after which she begins depositing reddish-orange eggs, hundreds of them, as the male squirts milky-white sperm into the water. The cloud of sperm, enveloping the eggs as the current carries it downstream, fertilizes them as they settle into the shallow "nest."

Having spent themselves to ensure the essence of their existence, their offspring, the female covers the nest just as she excavated it, with powerful strokes of her tail against the gravelly bottom of the stream. Now she and her mate, having fulfilled the inner purpose of their lives, swim into deeper water and rest.

Only then, exhausted from their long and difficult journey up river and stream from the Pacific Ocean and from their final passionate act of spawning, are they quiet enough for an observer to see the small patches of white fungus that have already begun to invade their bruised and battered flesh. As the fungus grows into their bodies, the life force, which has for so long served them well, begins to wane. They grow weaker and weaker, until the last cells in their bodies die and their now-spent carcasses are washed against the shore, where they will recycle into the atomic interchange from whence they came.

But in the gravelly stream bottom, an opaque egg is secreted as the salmon develops inside. In time, the baby salmon hatches and struggles out of the gravel into the open water of protected, hidden places in the stream. Here it grows until it is time to leave the stream of its origin and venture forth into life. It can go only one way—downstream to larger and larger streams and rivers until at last it reaches the ocean, all the way beset by increasing numbers of distracting nooks and crannies to explore and dangers to overcome.

Salmon from all of the various streams and rivers mingle in the ocean, where external influences affect them in common, such as ocean currents, in what might be called a pool of commonalty. It is therefore impossible to view salmon in the ocean as discrete populations because they behave as an aggregate individual with no visible affinity to a particular river and stream.

Only after some years at sea will the inner urge of individual salmon dictate that it is their time to spawn. This inner urge will drive the adult salmon along the Pacific Coast to find the precise river they descended years earlier, and in so doing, the aggregate individual will differentiate into identifiable populations, each with its own affinity to a particular river. Once in the river, they will again differentiate as discrete subpopulations, each with its own affinity to a particular stream within the river system.

A salmon can return to the gravel in which it was deposited as a fertilized egg only if it knows where it is going and when it has arrived. Its objective is to reach a particular place in a particular stream within a particular time to deposit either its eggs or sperm, after which it will die.

As each salmon approaches a river, it must make a critical decision. If it selects a river other than the one it descended, it will not reach its destination, regardless of all the other choices it makes. If, however, it swims into the same river it once descended, it is on the correct course— until it comes to the first fork and must choose again.

Regardless of its immediate choice in the lower reaches of the drainage basin, the water is deep, polluted, relatively warm, and its current placid. Here the salmon swims easily, comfortably in the wide river among all the other fishes and river life, where there is much to distract it from its appointed upstream journey.

With time, however, it begins to feel an inner restlessness to go against the current, to seek its home waters. Each time the salmon comes to a fork in its journey, it must make a choice and must accept what the chosen fork has to offer and forego the possibilities in the one not taken. In this sense, each choice is an inescapable consequence of the other choices already made. Each time it chooses the correct fork, the salmon finds that the water, confined within an ever-narrowing channel, is flowing progressively swifter, purer, and colder than from where it has just come.

As the stream's banks become more confining, the salmon finds its focus on its destination becoming sharper and more urgent and the channel less and less crowded as those lacking sufficient determination drop by the wayside. Now the distractions of youth and the obstacles in the streambed, such as large boulders and low, swift waterfalls, are as nothing, so focused has the salmon become, so clear is its determination, so urgent is its inner need to arrive at the particular spot within the designated time. When the salmon reaches this state, its focus is so concentrated that it finds the current's force diminished against the internal power of its life's spirit, its inner drive to reach its place of origin.

Thus in youth the many traveled seaward to become in aggregate the one. Although most died either on that journey or at sea, the rest confronted the external commonalties that helped to shape their lives. Then came the time of maturity, when the compelling inner drive to spawn, to achieve their life's purpose, caused them to separate into smaller groups of like-minded individuals. Many more died on the upstream journey, which reached its climax with the act of spawning, after which all salmon die, returning to the Great Mystery from whence they came.

As the dead salmon washed into the shallow water along the edge of the stream's banks, they entered the atomic interchange, where they represented a biological mechanism through which the elements of their bodies became concentrations of nutrients and energy that subsidized the forest ecosystem from which they originated as fertilized eggs.[24] In the past, even as late as the 1890s, about 27,500 Chinook and 218,750 coho salmon annually migrated up the Siuslaw River of north coastal Oregon to spawn and die.

This massive infusion of dead salmon into the forested stream was a boon to caddis flies, which are aquatic in their larval stages, and other insects that colonized the carcasses and fed on them. Skunks, otters, raccoons, bears, foxes, mice, shrews, eagles, jays, ravens, and wrens came to the banquet. Juvenile salmon, steelhead, and trout also poked around the expired, rotting bodies, eating the eggs left in the females and, eventually, picking off pieces of flesh.

The huge input of nutriments was critical for the young salmon because the rich banquet of dead fish enabled youngsters to double their weight in about six weeks. The added body weight greatly increased the chances that a particular fish would survive to swim the gauntlet from the stream of its origin far out into the North Pacific Ocean and return again years later to spawn in the place it was hatched.

As a carcass decomposed underwater, its dissolved nitrogen and carbon were soaked up by algae and diatoms, which are one-celled plants, that formed a scum on the gravel and rocks, which in turn was grazed by aquatic insects that became food for the salmon hatching the next spring. In addition to the scum on the gravel and rocks, the plants along the stream's banks, including trees, sucked up the nitrogen from the rotting salmon because nitrogen is an element in short supply in the soils of the Pacific Northwest.

Thus, as driftwood travels down the streams and rivers, it carries the carbon and nitrogen of its body to the food chain of the ocean and creates stabilizing instream structures and habitat for young salmon and other fish as it rests here and there along the way. As salmon travel seaward, they too bring elements, such as nitrogen and carbon, from the forest to the sea. Those that die at sea leave their forest-derived elements in the ocean, whereas those salmon that survive to swim the gauntlet back to their stream of origin leave their ocean-derived elements in the streams and vegetation of the forest.

So it is that the natural processes by which driftwood disappears from streams and rivers have positive effects on the ecosystem. Human activities, on the other hand, such as logging to the edge of a stream, salvage logging in riparian zones, cleaning wood out of streams, and cutting firewood, have had negative effects over the last several decades. The consequences of these actions, however, are both little understood and far reaching.

Streams historically replenished annual supplies of driftwood to the lower portions of river basins and out into the sea, where it washed up on beaches. But the banks of lower rivers and estuaries (the riparian corridor) were probably the common source of large driftwood in the bays.

Substantial amounts of driftwood must have been transported to the sea at the time when most riparian zones were dominated by such large coniferous trees as Douglas fir, western red cedar, and Sitka spruce and such deciduous trees as black cottonwood, bigleaf maple, Oregon ash, and red alder. Hundreds of millions of board feet of logs and driftwood have entered Puget Sound and the Georgia Straits from the rivers draining the Cascade Mountains of Washington and the coastal mountains of British Columbia. They were joined by large numbers of "escapees" from log rafts. Over ten billion board feet of logs is annually stored or travels in the estuaries and the lower segments of rivers in the Pacific Northwest. A 1 percent escape rate would allow over 100 million board feet of driftwood to enter the ocean from this source alone.

A conservative estimate is that in days past, as much as two billion board feet of wood per year was transported to the sea. Two billion board feet per year is a small amount when prorated across the entire North Pacific. Large driftwood, an important ecological component of Pacific Northwest streams and rivers, interfered with human objectives, however, and was summarily removed. In fact, people throughout North America have systematically cleaned driftwood from streams and rivers for over 150 years.

From the 1800s to around 1915, streams and small rivers were cleaned of driftwood so that logs could be floated from the forests to the mills. Several "splash dams" were built on many streams to temporarily augment the flow of water in order to float logs to mills. The net effect of channel clearance and splash damming was to remove large quantities of driftwood from medium to large streams, which is a significant change from the conditions that formerly existed.

Over the last 100 years, millions of drifted trees and other driftwood have been cleared out of streams and rivers to facilitate navigation and reduce flooding. To this end, streams and rivers have been channeled and dammed and marshes have been drained. In addition, most stream banks have been so altered through logging that they now have dramatically smaller and younger trees of different species than in times past.

Most big western red cedars and Douglas firs have been logged along Cascade Mountain streams and along coastal streams greater than third order. On private land, more than 70 percent of the coniferous trees greater than 14 inches in diameter at breast height have been logged within 100 feet of fish-bearing streams.

Before the great ecological value of driftwood was known, West Coast fishery managers believed that driftwood in streams restricted fish passage, supplied material for driftwood jams, and caused channels to scour down to bedrock during floods. Indeed, during times of flooding such fears might have seemed to be well founded, but we now know that the results of stream cleaning have been ecologically disastrous.

It is now apparent that neither we nor the generations of the future can afford the effects of the loss of driftwood, which connects the forest to the sea and the sea to the forest. The loss of driftwood means the destabilization of streams, rivers, estuaries, complexes of sand dunes, beaches, and sand spits, as well as food chains in the oceans of the world. Sooner or later, it means the loss of such jobs and unique cultural ways of life as commercial fishing, because fish such as tuna and salmon benefit from driftwood during various stages of their life cycles.

Nevertheless, driftwood is being prevented from even beginning its journey to the ocean by the removal of as much wood as possible from the forests as a product for human consumption, lest it remain as an "economic waste." In addition, damming of rivers prevents what little driftwood even begins its journey from completing it. Thus the connection between the forest and the sea is severed.

Even today, county sheriffs, port commissions, and recreational boaters still routinely clear driftwood from rivers for safety and personal convenience. As a result, most Pacific Northwest streams and rivers bear little resemblance to their ancestral conditions, when they flowed freely through pristine forests carrying their gift of driftwood to the sea.

Consequently, the supply of driftwood for food on the bottom of the sea off the coast of North America is both dwindling and becoming more erratic. For the first time in the evolutionary history of deep-sea animals, the availability of food has become unpredictable.

If the mangrove forests, which are composed of evergreen trees with stiltlike roots and stems that grow along coastal shores in the tropics, continue to be destroyed through deforestation, the last direct link of the forest to the sea will be severed. The deep-sea wood-dependent species of the world will then shrink in both number and areas they inhabit, and some or all will become extinct. What does extinction of these species mean in terms of the health of an ocean, especially the deep ocean?

Today, we are substituting for driftwood in the ocean and on beaches such nonwooden human garbage as metal, glass, rubber, plastic, oil, bilge, chemical effluents, medical and household wastes, and raw human sewage—none of which can replace Nature's gift of driftwood. We thus face the certainty of grave, uncomfortable uncertainties through our decisions concerning such renewable resources as driftwood by giving economics and technology higher priority than scientific understanding.

And what has all of this done to the salmon? It has, along with other factors such as loss of habitat due to clear-cut logging, urban development, and unsound farming practices, as well as overfishing and controlling stream flow through placement of dams, caused the extinction of salmon in some rivers and streams of the Pacific Northwest and so reduced many other distinct populations that their survival is severely endangered.

Every stream in which the runs of salmon are either extinct or greatly diminished is impoverished in like measure because it has lost the pulse of nutriments carried from the sea in the salmons' bodies to be released when they die after spawning. Every stream that no longer produces salmon or produces far fewer than during historical times impoverishes the Pacific Ocean in like measure because there are fewer salmon to die at sea and contribute the elements of their bodies to the ocean. Also lost is every indigenous culture whose silent language of spiritual tradition is wrapped around the art and seasonal ritual of fishing for salmon.

Every stream in which the historical component of large woody material is no longer present because of logging is impoverished in like measure. Every stream that no longer produces large woody material or produces far less than during historical times impoverishes the Pacific Ocean in like measure because there is far less driftwood to enter the sea and perform the various functions it once did. And even where streams still produce large driftwood but flow into rivers with dams across them, that driftwood is purposefully stopped and removed at the dams and therefore never reaches the sea. Also lost is that part of every indigenous culture that depended on the mysterious wood delivered to its shores from afar by the ocean.

If healthy streams, rivers, estuaries, oceans, and the salmon they support are important for social benefits, then a renewable supply of driftwood (including whole trees) must be incorporated into land-use planning, especially forests. In addition, society must very soon rethink and change how it uses land to protect not only the remaining salmon and let them regain their biological prominence as part of the ecosystem, which will not be easy or quick, but also the reciprocal relationships between the forest and the sea, as exemplified by driftwood and salmon.

If these reciprocal relationships between the forest and the sea are not restored, all the complex, interconnected, interdependent feedback loops among plants and animals of the streams, rivers, and oceans will gradually simplify, as will all the cultural aspects of humanity that once depended on them. The species of which the feedback loops are composed will be lost forever—and the feedback loops, both biological and cultural, with them. This is how the evolutionary process works. Ecologically, it is neither good nor bad, right nor wrong, but those changes may make the ecosystem less attractive, less usable by species, such as humans, that used to rely on it for their livelihoods and for products. Thus, if we want to think about the sustainability, even the survival, of humans and their communities over the next millennium, we have to think about all interrelationships of animals with plants.

The same types of self-reinforcing feedback loops that take place in streams of the Pacific Northwest of the United States occur in one way or another in all forested streams of the world, and they represent the same four basic elements of diversity: genetic, species, structural, and functional. Genetic diversity is the way species adapt to change; it is the hidden diversity that is so often subjected to the "secret extinctions" mentioned earlier. The most important aspect of genetic diversity is that it can act as a buffer against the variability of environmental conditions, particularly in the long term. Healthy environments can therefore act as "shock absorbers" in the face of catastrophic disturbance.

Here looms a critical concept: the past function of an ecosystem determines its present structure, and its present structure determines its future function. This means that structure is defined by function and function is defined by structure! As we alter the composition of species in an area, as discussed earlier, so we at the same moment alter its function in time. Thus it is that composition, structure, and function go together to create and maintain ecological processes both in time and across space, and it is the health of the processes that in the end creates an ecosystem as we know it, including genetic stepping-stones.

Genetic Stepping-Stones

Species come and go, enriching the world with their presence. Having considered that point, it is time to contemplate the genetics of place, that is, local populations adapted to specific habitats. Their importance lies in understanding that as we fragment the landscape in which we live through such things as urban sprawl, clear-cut logging, or dams in rivers, we are putting our fellow planetary travelers at risk, often without even realizing it.

As we fragment landscapes, both plants and animals become vulnerable to "secret extinctions"—the loss of locally adapted populations, such as people or trees that have evolved over centuries to millennia. Such a loss can be more or less permanent and may inexorably alter the habitat because other populations of the same species might prove unable to reoccupy the habitat or might not even be able to reach it due to major changes in the environment.

Four instances of the genetics of place are presented to help clarify what I mean. The first deals with the Shoshonean peoples of Death Valley, the second with the Temuan culture of Malaysia, the third with sugar maple trees in the eastern United States and Canada, and the fourth with steelhead trout along the Pacific coast of North America.

The People

As continents travel the seas of the world and human knowledge grows and cultures evolve, there comes a once-in-forever instant, flashed on the screen of time, when all the cosmic tumblers click momentarily into place. And it is during this fleeting instant that we humans find the Grace of spiritual harmony with the land, when we are simultaneously transported inward to the center of our deepest being and out of our little selves into Cosmic Unity. Then it is gone.

I suspect that for indigenous peoples those instances of harmony came more frequently than they do for us today, because their lives were in a more holistic balance between the spiritual and the material, intuition and intellect, truth and knowledge. But as intuition gave way to intellect and as knowledge replaced inner truth, harmony between humans and their environment slipped increasingly into the dimensionless past.

Can we in Western civilization recapture that which is lost? I think so, but we will have to acknowledge our inseparability from Nature and live as such. How we participate with Nature in creating our environment is a matter of how we treat Nature and how Nature in turn responds to the treatment received. It is not a matter of management, because we cannot manage Nature; we can only manage ourselves—our motives, thoughts, actions, and the things we introduce into our environment. Once we introduce something, however, such as pesticides, war, or thermonuclear energy, we lose control of its effects and therefore alter the environment, often in negative ways we do not intend.

Nevertheless, in our choice of motives, thoughts, and actions we have free will. Therefore, how we choose will either be the saving grace of human society or its condemnation.

The personal and social dilemma in exercising our free will is that when we assign a price to something and come to know its material cost, we too often lose sight of its spiritual value. In so doing, we are learning the cost of much and the value of little. Something's spiritual value thus becomes its imprisoned splendor.

I, for example, am awed by the use some early indigenous Americans made of the English language and wonder why I cannot speak in my own tongue with such eloquence. The answer seems simple enough. The indigenous Americans were not speaking English. They were speaking their own language—the thoughts of their hearts—through English words, even if they were translations.

They were speaking of their sacred participation with the Earth, while the European Americans were speaking about ownership of land, economic exploitation, and accumulating personal wealth. The indigenous Americans spoke of tangible peace among people and goodwill toward the Earth, whereas the European Americans spoke of an abstract peace on Earth and goodwill toward men.

What makes our union with life and Nature either sacred or profane is how we choose to participate—our attitude, the womb of our thoughts and actions. The sacred is the expression of truth and value enthroned in one's heart, which is straight, simple, open, and spontaneous. The profane is the cost/benefit rationalization of intellectual knowledge, which is convoluted, nebulous, closed, and guarded. Whereas the sacred shines with the crystalline purity of intent and an innocence of execution, the profane is clouded with the murky undercurrents and jagged edges of greed, mistrust, and the overriding will for control and personal gain.

Although we have no choice but to participate with Nature, simply because we exist in and of Nature, we can and must choose how we participate, because participation is the active part of relationship, and we can only exist in relationship.

That we are the products of our motives, thoughts, and actions, those elements of behavior that determine the quality of our participation with life, is illustrated by the Shoshonean people of Death Valley, but they can only be understood in the context of the history of Death Valley and their place in it.[25]

The Shoshonean People

As the last glacial stage of the Pleistocene epoch, which began about 70,000 years ago, reached its maximum development, subarctic plants and animals occurred as far south as what today are the states of Virginia and Texas. During the height of the glacier's development, the Bering–Chukchi platform (also called the trans-Bering land bridge) between the continents of North America and Eurasia was exposed because the sea was approximately 328 feet below its present level. When fully exposed, the Bering–Chukchi platform was a flat isthmus about a thousand miles wide between what is now northeastern Siberia and Alaska. It remained open to migrating plants and animals—including the ancient ones, the ancestors of *some* of today's indigenous Americans—until it was again inundated by rising seas as the climate warmed and the last glaciers melted, between 10,000 and 7,000 years ago. (The origin of indigenous Americans will be discussed in more detail later.)

Between 20,000 and 15,000 years ago, while the ancient ones explored the new land, the valley—today known as "Death Valley," California—was lush and green with streams feeding through interconnected lakes into a huge lake 600 feet deep. In these streams and lakes lived a tiny fish, about three inches long, today called a pupfish.

About 9,000 years ago, approximately a thousand years after the close of the last ice age, the Nevares Spring people moved into the valley. The earliest known inhabitants of today's Death Valley, they camped near springs found on fans of gravel that water washed into the valley as it eroded surrounding mountains. Time has dried some of the springs, and they are now extinct.

These wandering hunters were each armed with spears, usually called darts, and an atlatl, a special stick that forms an extension of the human arm so as to increase the power of a thrown spear. Using spears and atlatls, they ambushed big game, which was plentiful in the well-watered valley, where extensive marshlands surrounded the big lake and where juniper trees covered the lower mountains.

For those who might be unfamiliar with the atlatl, I will explain what it is and how it works,[26] because understanding the atlatl will be important to a discussion on technology later in this book. Atlatl is an Aztec name for a weapon invented in what is now France; the oldest known atlatl in the Americas dates back to about 12,000 years ago. An atlatl is a stick that can be round or flat. Most are three-quarters of an inch to two inches thick, with a half-inch peg projecting from a wooden block at one end and a balancing "bannerweight" lashed underneath near the handle. The spears, called darts in today's vernacular, are 5 to 6 feet long, a quarter- to a half-inch in diameter, and weigh 8 to 12 ounces, compared with about 1 ounce for a modern hunting arrow used with a bow.

The hunter fitted the hollowed rear end of the spear over the peg and laid the spear along the atlatl. Putting thumb and forefinger through two leather loops on the handle near the other end of the atlatl and holding the spear with those fingers, the hunter used the atlatl as a lever to propel the spear with an overhand motion similar to throwing a paper airplane.

Lou Becker, president of the Michigan Atlatl Society, a group dedicated to preserving this Stone Age technology, said, "Tests show that a skilled thrower can generate up to 200 times as much force [with an atlatl] as by throwing a spear by hand. A good thrower can hit a 16-inch circle consistently at 40 to 50 yards." (According to Dr. Rob Bonnichsen, director for the study of First Americans, Department of Anthropology, Oregon State University, Corvallis, who reviewed this book, a skilled thrower can generate up to *five* times as much force throwing a dart with an atlatl as opposed to throwing a spear by hand. And a good thrower, says Bonnichsen, can be *consistent* at 40 to 50 yards, but he questions the figure of consistently hitting a 16-inch circle.) Becker went on to say that a Stone Age hunter who grew up using an atlatl and whose life depended on his skill as a hunter was undoubtedly even more accurate. Such a hunter could throw a flint- or obsidian-tipped spear 200 yards and was sometimes lethal at 150 yards.

Becker used an atlatl to kill a 350-pound wild hog in Georgia. His spear, which hit high on the body behind the hog's head, not only penetrated the length of the hog but also projected about 18 inches from the haunches. "It only ran 20 yards before it dropped," Becker said. "I can guarantee you that an arrow from a compound bow wouldn't have pen-etrated like that. I'm not sure that an arrow would have even reached the vitals from head-on."

Although every picture I have seen of prehistoric men killing the elephant-like mammoth has depicted a group of hunters besieging a single animal, but one hunter in the group skilled with an atlatl could conceivably kill it. Consider the following two examples.

Steve Coleman, who owns the Buckhorn Creek Game Ranch near Vidalia, Georgia, is one of the best atlatlists in the United States. Coleman had an American bison that gave him problems on his game ranch: "He was giving me trouble [by jumping the fences] and I wanted to put one in the freezer anyway, so I decided to try it with an atlatl. It only took one dart [spear] through the lungs. I use a bigger spear than most people do, about 7½ feet and a half-inch thick, and it went right through the bison from 25 yards away. When you consider I'm throwing a 5,000-grain dart at 120 feet per second, compared with a bow throwing a 500-grain arrow at maybe 250 feet per second, you can see why the atlatl hits with so much more force." A grain is a measurement of weight that is commonly used these days for bullets.

Finally, the question of whether a single hunter could kill a mammoth was settled in 1985 in Zimbabwe by Dr. George Frison, an anthropologist at the University of Wyoming. Frison received permission to test Stone Age tools on dead elephants culled by game wardens. As he was preparing to spear one with an atlatl, the presumed-dead elephant suddenly rose to its feet, whereupon Frison threw his spear, which penetrated the elephant's front leg and entered the lung. The elephant dropped to its knees and died.

"I wouldn't have any reservations about hunting elephants with an atlatl," said Frison. "I suspect the way they [Stone Age hunters] did it," he went on to say, "was for one hunter to slip in quietly and put a dart [spear] into its [the mammoth's] rib cage while another hunter held its attention."

Returning to the discussion of Death Valley, somewhere in time, the Nevares Spring people left the valley, probably because the game animals disappeared as the climate became even warmer and drier than it is today, which means summer temperatures ranged anywhere from 110 to over 130 degrees Fahrenheit and the average annual rainfall was about 1.5 inches or less.

Around 5,000 years ago, the Mesquite Flat people came into the valley. They arrived during a wet period and once again lived as wandering bands of hunters who camped low in the valley and on the fans of gravel above the valley's floor. Like the Nevares Spring people before them, they hunted with spears and atlatls.

They augmented their diet of meat by gathering wild plants and by grinding seeds with stone mortars and pestles. The people inhabited the valley for about 2,000 years until 1000 B.C. They lived in the valley before the final lake dried up and formed the flat, salt pan one sees today on the valley's floor.

The Saratoga Springs people came into the valley around 900 A.D. and stayed for about 200 years until 1100 A.D. The climate during this time was much like it is today, although there were brief periods of wetter weather. The Saratoga Springs people camped near the same springs in use today.

Big game was scarce, but the people brought the bow and arrow with them, which was an advantage in hunting. In addition to big game, they also hunted and trapped the abundant small rodents and lizards. The Saratoga Springs people augmented their diet with plants and with seeds ground into flour between smooth rocks.

A few Saratoga Springs people may have been living in the valley when the first Shoshonean people arrived about 1000 A.D. The Shoshonean culture seemed more diverse than those of their predecessors. Although their tools were simple, the people possessed great skill as exemplified by the women's highly developed art of basket making.

The Shoshonean people were the seed gatherers of the desert. Much of the year they lived among the sand dunes in simple shelters of brush where they harvested mesquite beans. But when the seed of the piñon pine ripened, they camped in the nearby Panamint Mountains for the harvest. They also gathered what other seeds they could and, like the people before them, used smooth flat rocks to grind seeds into flour.

In addition to gathering plants, they hunted such small animals as rodents and lizards and even ate adult insects and the grubs of beetles. The ability of these people to find and utilize whatever foods the desert offered was the key to their survival, which brings me to the pupfish.

As the climate began to warm and dry in the time of the Nevares Spring people, the waters connecting the lakes went from perennial streams to intermittent streams to dry beds, and the lakes began to evaporate and shrink, becoming saltier as they did so. Thus, the contiguous population of pupfish inhabiting the originally connected waters of the valley became increasingly fragmented and isolated.

At the time the Shoshonean people arrived in the valley, which by then was the hottest, driest place in North America north of Mexico, the pupfishes had already evolved into nine separate species. And each species was already clinging to existence in completely isolated fragile habitats, some in deep holes, some in salty creeks, and some in warm springs. One of these habitats is Salt Creek (Figure 7).

Salt Creek comes out of deep springs and during the relatively cool months of winter and spring flows on the surface for about two miles before evaporating (Figure 8). In the intense heat of summer, however, the creek shrinks back to the pools of its source (Figure 9).

FIGURE 7   Salt Creek, in Death Valley, California, is home to the Salt Creek pupfish. (Photograph by author.)

Salt Creek is the home of the Salt Creek pupfish, which in the entire Universe is found only there. During winter, when the water is cold, the fish are dormant in the bottom mud and virtually impossible to find. They become active, however, when the water warms in spring, and by March hundreds are visible. As the days get warmer and evaporation increases, the creek and the majority of its pools dry up, and most pupfish die. Only a small percent survive the summer in the deep springs that form the creek's source.

As the land changed over thousands of years, the single species of pupfish became the many species. In addition, various human cultures entered the valley each in its turn and somehow interacted with the pupfish. Although each culture before the days of the Shoshonean people had a relationship with and an effect on the pupfish simply by sharing its habitat, it was during the time of the Shoshonean people that the Salt Creek pupfish became food for humans. In spring, when the fish became

FIGURE 8   Salt Creek flowing into the floor of Death Valley, California, where it both evaporates and sinks into the sand. (Photograph by author.)

numerous, the people collected them in large porous baskets. The fish were then baked in layers between tule reeds and hot ashes and eaten.

The simple society of the Shoshonean people afforded two things that have so far eluded us in modern life—ample leisure time and the peace to enjoy it. Their free time was not, however, devoted to improving their standard of living, as is ours, because that rung on the cultural ladder was unattainable in an environment that permitted no cultural revolution.

Thus, out of the range of available resources, only those that were appropriate to the mode of life of the community, those which in fact were socially necessary and acceptable, were selected. To a community using stone for edge tools and ignorant of the principle of metallurgy, deposits of copper, tin, or iron ore are not only irrelevant but also absent from the society's world picture.[27]

To hunter–gatherers, for example, good farming land is a meaningless concept, which illustrates that a people's technological development limits their ability to exploit their environment. Conversely, however, the tech-

FIGURE 9   One of the deep pools that is the source of survival of the Salt Creek pupfish in summer. (Photograph by author.)

nological capacities of any people depend on their exploitation of raw materials. A community that is relatively static in its technology, however well adjusted, continues to draw on a limited range of products generation after generation. On the other hand, a community with a tradition of practical experimentation and invention will explore, develop, and exploit new potentialities.

The environment in which the Shoshonean people lived also precluded the luxury of war, an activity that requires its own technology. When warlike tribes entered the valley, the residents just slipped quietly away and hid until the intruders left.

In 1849, the first European Americans came into the valley, but they were simply lost. In 1850, prospectors began pouring in. The Shoshone reacted to the influx as they had reacted to all other invaders. However, whereas the previous interlopers had always departed after a time, the prospectors, seeking to exploit the mineral wealth of the valley without interference, both persisted in the valley, claiming it as theirs, and displaced the Shoshonean people.

In 1933, Death Valley National Monument was established, and a different kind of relationship began between the Salt Creek pupfish and humans. Recognizing the pupfish as a distinct species occurring only in this one tiny creek, the people of the National Park Service devised a method of protecting its habitat while at the same time allowing thousands of visitors to experience the marvel of this tiny fish.

Each of these people, in their own unique way, have gained something and have given something through their participation with the Salt Creek pupfish. The Nevares Spring people, the Mesquite Flat people, and the Saratoga Springs people shared the pupfish's habitat in the mutual relationship of life in the valley. The Shoshonean people (some of whom still live around Death Valley) took from the fish its life as food in the great mystic cycle of death feeding life, for which they gave thanks. The employees of Death Valley National Monument, protecting the fish to ensure, so far as possible, its continued existence, are giving it the benefit of human evolution and consciousness and taking with them a sense of moral ascendancy. And the tourists who visit Salt Creek receive from the fish a sense of spiritual enrichment, ecological awareness, and the wonder of Nature while simultaneously affecting the fish by their presence in observing it.

The great irony of this story is that while the Shoshonean people used the pupfish for food, the European Americans stole that source of food by displacing the Shoshonean people from their ancestral home. Having removed the Shoshonean people in whom they saw no value, the European Americans, who were so destructive in their exploitation of the land they stole, ultimately turned around a few generations later and responded to the pupfish through scientific study, protection, and enjoyment (Figure 10). But what about the Shoshonean people of today? They are still displaced, still perceived to be of lesser value than the pupfish. Why? Is their culture of no value to the human tapestry? What are we losing of ourselves as their irreplaceable genetic and cultural uniqueness is lost?

The Temuan People

The second example is the Temuan people, who, living along the fringe of the Malaysian jungle, may be much the same as they were thousands of years ago. This tribal group has stayed remarkably separate through the centuries, with little blending into other nationalities, such as the Chinese, the Eastern Indians, or the British who most recently ruled the area.

The Temuan people display some interesting genetic traits, which they probably maintained by isolating themselves culturally. Among the most

FIGURE 10 Part of the boardwalk constructed by the U.S. Park Service to allow tourists to enjoy the Salt Creek pupfish without damaging its habitat. (Photograph by author.)

significant traits is a special condition of red blood cells, an elliptocytosis (which means elliptical cells), found only in Southeast Asia; it offers some protection against malaria.

Malaria, which has been around for thousands of years, has devastated populations of humans. To the Temuan, resistance to malaria not only has survival value in evolutionary terms but also offers a window into their past. To understand ourselves as a species, therefore, we must learn more about our cultural diversity and about the specifics of our genetic development, because the way we are genetically today reflects our environment of the past.

Although many scientists tend to study only the people of wealthier nations and their characteristics, some other groups of humans around the world represent unique gene pools. In some cases, as history has proven again and again, a disease as simple as the common cold could decimate a particular people who, through isolation, lack immunity to it. And we would rue the day such peoples become extinct, because our global society would lose an irretrievable part of itself. This potential loss reveals the need for a new concept in protecting our environment: the conservation of unique communities of humans. It is an idea worth considering. After all, are not people as unique cultures with their own peculiar genetic makeup at least as important as trees or other species?

The Trees

The third example of the genetics of place deals with sugar maple trees, which in New England range from sea level up to about 2,500 feet in elevation.[28] Populations of sugar maples differ in a number of physiological characteristics depending on the elevation of their habitat. Sugar maples from high elevations, for example, can photosynthesize much faster than those populations at middle elevations. In addition, the structure of their leaves is quite different.

Leaves of sugar maples growing at high elevations are thin. That is, for the same area of a leaf, the weight of the leaf is lowest at the high elevations and highest at the middle elevations, which suggests that sugar maples at high elevations produce cheap, throwaway leaves.

Trees can produce large, thin leaves at far less cost in energy than they can thick leaves. Despite this low investment in leaf tissue, the trees' rates of photosynthesis are very high. It stands to reason, therefore, that such characteristics of low-energy, throwaway leaves coupled with high rates of photosynthesis are best adapted to the short growing seasons of high elevations. Indeed, one would expect leaf-out to occur ten days later at high elevations than at middle elevations and leaf-drop to be ten days earlier—a difference of nearly three weeks in the growing season.

Because sugar maples shed their leaves each autumn and produce new ones each spring, the length of the growing season is critical to the type of leaves they produce. The high-elevation sugar maples are right on the border of conditions to which the maples are suited, and the short growing season must exert a tremendous pressure in selecting for individual trees that can photosynthesize quickly and produce cheap, rapidly deployed, throwaway leaves.

Suppose a population of sugar maples was removed from the top 325 feet of its elevational range. Could it be replaced by sugar maples from middle elevations? You could physically transplant them, but they most likely would not survive, because they lack the local genetics of place. Without the local adaptations necessary to survive at the top of the species' elevational range, sugar maples simply would not be part of the plant community. If the high-elevation population becomes extinct, the high-elevation environment is less diverse by at least one species of tree.

So what if one species of tree is missing from the top of some mountain. Big deal! Let's consider another, more drastic, example. This time, however, the example is hypothetical, because it hasn't happened yet—but it could if global warming is real. Is global warming real? That depends on your view, as eloquently pointed out by Robert L. Park, a physics professor at the University of Maryland.[29]

The great war over global warming, according to Dr. Park, is more about personal values than about science, although it sounds like a scientific debate with numbers and equations thrown back and forth, and the people themselves may even believe they are engaged in a bona fide scientific debate. But are they so engaged? Not necessarily so, says Park, because the average scientist is exposed during his or her formative years to religious and political views at his or her mother's knee, long before he or she is exposed to scientific thought and method.

Such deeply instilled, and perhaps unconsciously held, views have a way of slipping into whatever gaps exist in one's scientific understanding—and there are always gaps, which at times are more like gaping wounds. The debate over climate change is no exception, as Park points out. "There are holes in the data and uncertainties in the computer models, and small changes in the assumptions could result in very different projections." Although both sides of the debate—warming versus no warming, warming as dangerous versus warming as beneficial—acknowledge these limitations, until the numbers are in, says Park, it is easy to be misled. "When uncertainty abounds, scientific judgment has a way of conforming to the religious and political views of the scientist."

Let's assume, therefore, that sugar maples range geographically from Georgia to just north of the Canadian border and that global warming is real. If the climate were to warm up rapidly by an average of three degrees, with correspondingly higher extremes in summer temperatures occurring more frequently, the sugar maples would become stressed throughout their range. In order to survive, the species would have to compensate for the increase in temperature by migrating northward in latitude and higher in altitude.

What happens when the temperature increases and the maples have to migrate northward in latitude? In the past, given Nature's continuous landscape and sufficient time to migrate and to adapt, such a change could have been handled, but now it could not. Why? First, the connectivity of Nature's landscape has been severely fragmented by our cultural tinkerings; this means there are large areas through which sugar maples can no longer migrate because there is simply no suitable habitat for them. Sugar maples cannot, for instance, march through cities or grow in concrete and asphalt. Nor can they grow in many other once suitable habitats, ones that have been so drastically altered that they need time apart from human activity to once again become habitable to sugar maples.

Second, too many of the locally adapted populations of sugar maple within the network of populations no longer exist. They have succumbed to secret extinctions, which means those genetic stepping-stones of place no longer exist as "a corridor of migration."

Forests, like people, migrate. In fact, forests migrate as entire systems—as interactive aboveground–belowground communities of symbiotic plants and animals. Although individual species of trees may migrate singly by means of seeds dispersed by animals or by the wind, this is the migration of trees, not of forests. Even for one species of tree to migrate, however, the habitat requirements of the individual species of tree must be met.

Third, let's assume that global warming due at least in part to our human-induced greenhouse effect is unprecedented in speed and magnitude. Therefore, even if the first two conditions still favored the migration of sugar maples, the speed of climatic change would simply be too fast for the maple to accept. After all, the maples in Georgia would have to migrate at least to New England, and the trees in New England and southern Canada would have to occupy areas that now are boreal forest and tree line in northern Canada.

Even if we set aside this hypothetical case, we must still deal with secret extinctions. When locally adapted, interactive, aboveground–belowground communities of symbiotic plants and animals disappear, they cannot be replaced overnight—if ever. Nor can they be replaced through the myth of "management," a concept through which we give ourselves a false sense of power over Nature.

Until now, the discussion has included relatively stationary beings, people and trees, but what about a fish that spawns in fresh water and migrates to the sea to mature, returning again to fresh water to spawn? How, one might well ask, can that be considered the genetics of place?

The Fish

Steelhead, being a fish that spawns in freshwater river systems and matures at sea, offers a slightly different notion of the genetics of place. In the preceding examples, we dealt with people, who were by most standards relatively sedentary, and with trees, which are, of course, clearly affixed to a given location. With steelhead, however, the genetics of place is not only about a specific location in which to spawn but also about the hidden genetic guidance system that leads them back to their home waters when the time to spawn arrives.

Steelhead, which are in the trout family, range along the entire Pacific coast of North America.[30] Some freshwater populations are already listed as endangered under the Endangered Species Act, including that of the lower Columbia River system. These listings raise two questions: (1) How did we arrive at the necessity of listing the steelhead under the Endangered Species Act in the first place? (2) What makes wild steelhead of the Columbia River system so special, considering that hatcheries raise and release thousands of them each year? Is it just that they are considered a prime game fish?

The answer to the first question, according to Will Stelle, northwest regional director of the National Marine Fisheries Service, is simple. Dams block access to rivers, where steelhead lay their eggs. Logging, road building, and development have stripped from the banks of rivers and streams trees that are needed to keep the water cool enough for young steelhead to survive. Clear-cut logging along the banks of streams has eliminated woody debris-filled places that young steelhead need to hide from predators and has led to erosion of soil, which in turn fills streams with fine sediment and may even clog them. Regulating the flow of water through dams for shipping and large irrigation projects has drastically changed the temperature of dammed rivers and the way they flow. "It took us a generation or maybe two to dig ourselves the hole we are in now," says Stelle. "It will take a generation or more to dig ourselves out."

The answer to the second question lies in something called an *evolutionary significant unit*. Think of an evolutionary significant unit as a discrete "freshwater population" of steelhead that is defined not only by its place of spawning within the river systems of the Pacific Northwest but also by its genetics. This is an important distinction because, like salmon, steelhead appear to a fisher as an aggregate "marine population" when at sea.

Unlike mass-produced hatchery fish, wild steelhead have forged unique adaptations to conditions in their often fickle rivers and streams of origin. These adaptations are encoded in subtle genetic characteristics that have evolved over the last two million years. Although subtle, the genetic codes are distinct enough for biologists to divide steelhead into 15 freshwater populations or evolutionary significant units.

Each distinct freshwater population must be reproductively isolated from other freshwater populations of steelhead to be scientifically valid.

Such isolation allows members of a freshwater population to adapt to the unique conditions of the stream in which they were hatched and lived for a time prior to their migration to sea, where they matured; it also allows them to return as adults to the place of their origin to spawn. By studying units of DNA in wild fish, biologists can determine just how closely knit a freshwater population may be and thereby map its respective geographical distribution.

Each freshwater population is specifically adapted to a number of conditions within its particular river system, the variables of which are secreted in the genetic code within each member of the population. A few of the conditions are as follows: (1) the dynamics of how the water flows, such as periods of low flow and flooding; (2) the amount of time they spend in fresh water after hatching; (3) the length of time they spend in the brackish water of an estuary, where they acclimate to the salt water before entering the sea; (4) where they migrate to once in the ocean; (5) the number of times they spawn, because steelhead, unlike salmon, do not die after spawning but return instead to sea; and (6) the kinds of spawning gravel they prefer. There are additional variables, from a steelhead's eye view, that distinguish freshwater populations from one another.

The upshot is that steelhead in the lower Columbia River have a very different ancestral lineage than steelhead that spawn in the Snake River system or in the coastal streams. Thus, according to Rob Jones of the National Marine Fisheries Service in Portland, Oregon, wild steelhead in the lower Columbia River are designated as a freshwater population or evolutionary significant unit 4.

The adjustments of plant and animal communities over thousands of years make the genetics of place vulnerable to thoughtless human tinkering. Each secret extinction of a locally adapted population weakens and impoverishes the genetic network of diversity, the sum of which constitutes not only the species as it survives today but also what the species must become if it is to survive tomorrow, which raises the specter of changes in habitats.

WHEN HABITATS CHANGE

In addition to the genetics of local populations, there have been and again will be drastic changes in habitats, changes that affect whole groups of plants and animals. On a small scale, for example, changes in the Fort Rock Basin of south central Oregon, east of the High Cascade Mountain

Range, which today is a shrubby, cold-desert steppe, caused species to become extinct in a particular area.

Past Changes in Habitat

During the Wisconsin glacial stage, between 70,000 and 10,000 years ago, the Fort Rock Basin was filled by a large lake (Figures 11 and 12). The basin's habitat was a mixture of grassy plains, riverbank woodlands, and water. Two species of horses and a camel lived on the grassy areas of the lowland glades and upland prairies. The stream valleys, with strips or clumps of woodland, were suited to the large ground sloth, woolly mammoth, and a bear, while the streams themselves held a giant beaver and muskrats.

These animals were hunted by wild dogs called dire wolves and by people, who are thought to have moved into the basin about 11,000 years ago. Three species of carp and two species of suckers as well as trout and Chinook salmon lived in the lake and streams. All these species except the salmon are extinct. Presence of the salmon reveals that there was an overflow through an outlet to the Pacific Ocean, which allowed the salmon to reach Fort Rock Lake. When the overflow ceased, the salmon

FIGURE 11   Fort Rock, rising more than 300 feet, is the remnant of a tuff cone, rock formed from compacted volcanic ash. Much of the erosion was caused by wave action in a lake that covered the floor of the valley during the Pleistocene epoch. (Photograph by author.)

FIGURE 12   Close view of Fort Rock shows erosion at its base caused by centuries of waves in the Pleistocene lake. (Photograph by author.)

became landlocked but persisted in the lake until the end of its existence about 10,000 years ago.

Not all species that became extinct in the Fort Rock Basin, however, died out as a whole. Some species simply migrated with their habitats and live today in other areas. Before 7,000 years ago, for example, white-tailed jackrabbits lived in the lower elevations of the present Fort Rock Basin. The white-tailed jackrabbit is adapted to the colder climates of higher, more northerly regions and tends to occupy grassy habitats. Sage grouse, elk, and bison, each with similar habitat affinities, all lived in the Fort Rock Basin. In addition, the pika or rock rabbit lived in jumbles of broken rock.

Then the climate began to change. As the area warmed and dried, the existing plant community became destabilized and shifted from one made up primarily of northerly grasses and herbs to one made up primarily of southerly shrubs. The shift in plant communities caused the local extinction of the white-tailed jackrabbit, sage grouse, pika, elk, and bison. None of the other species was affected, however.

The pika and the elk moved up in elevation, whereas the white-tailed jackrabbit, sage grouse, and bison followed the migration of their habitat eastward toward what today is the state of Idaho. The mountain cottontail and black-tailed jackrabbit moved northward into the Fort Rock Basin as the habitat changed, because both are adapted to the warmer climates of lower, more southerly regions and tend to occupy shrubby habitats.

As we have seen, habitats change. Sometimes they evolve slowly and gradually and sometimes quickly and drastically, but regardless of the way they do it, all habitats change. When they do, there is a general reshuffling of plants and animals. More adaptable species may for a time survive a change in habitat, even a relatively drastic one, but in the end they too must change, migrate elsewhere, or become extinct.

Occasionally, however, a species like the coelacanth changes but little within its habitat over vast periods of time. This stability of habitat allows such species to exist for millions of years with little or no apparent need to adapt further—that is until now, a time in which they have no place else to go.

Present Changes in Habitat

We humans have changed and are changing the global ecosystem and all of its component habitats at an exponential rate. Today, we have become the major cause of extinctions and evolutionary leaps. Some ecosystems and their habitats may be able to mitigate the alterations to which we subject them. But alas, most alterations are damaging to the ecosystem as we know it and are prone to spread. Others evolve into ecosystems that we humans find less desirable, often because the new species, which quickly replace those lost, cannot live up to our human expectations. Consider, for instance, what human society is doing to the Amazon.

Deforestation in the Amazon, as well as in the Pacific Northwest and across Canada, shows that, as a culture, we have learned but little. Just imagine the forests from the crest of the Cascade Mountains in western Oregon and western Washington to the Pacific Ocean, about a third of each state, all burning up within a year. That is roughly equivalent to the amount of land burned in only one year in the Brazilian Amazon. Each year, an area 80 percent the size of the state of Oregon burns in the Brazilian Amazon alone.

The major cause of deforestation by extensive burning is that people are converting the tropical forests to pastures for cattle. Simple harvesting of timber also causes problems, however, because once the canopy of the forest is opened, the understory environment changes drastically, and the forest can no longer sustain itself.

Never in the history of humanity has so much of the world's tropical forests been disturbed in such a foreign and catastrophic way on such a large scale as during the last 30 years. Today, at least half of the Amazon rain forest is dry as a tinderbox, raising the specter of the world's largest wild area exploding in flames, which would indeed be an ecological disaster of tremendous magnitude. About 12 percent of the two-million-square-mile jungle is already gone, and burning was so intense in 1997 that a lake caught fire, in addition to which people in cities surrounded by the jungle had to be treated for respiratory ailments.

Think for a moment that tropical rain forests—one of the world's oldest ecosystems—occupy only 7 percent of the Earth's surface and are home to more than 50 percent of all the Earth's species. What does this mean in terms of the Amazonian tropical forest?

An intact rain forest creates its own internal and external climate, in which about half of all the rainfall originates from moisture given off by the forest itself. When large areas of a rain forest are destroyed by such things as logging, local and regional weather patterns change.

Once the forest is gone, the result is usually drought, which not only increases the probability of fire in the cutover areas and decreases the probability that the forest will ever return but also increases the likelihood of fires consuming the remaining forest. In 1997, for example, a seven-year study suggested that the burning may get much worse than in the past because the rain forest—including its pristine core—is dangerously dry and flammable as a result of logging activities on a massive scale; deliberate burning around the jungle's edges, which lets the drying wind penetrate it; and the current effects of El Niño.[31]

A test in October 1997, in which American and Brazilian scientists threw a lighted match on kerosene that had been sprinkled on a small piece of undisturbed jungle in the eastern Amazon, showed unnerving results. Whereas the normally moist jungle would be almost impervious to fire, the 300 acres erupted in flames.

"We're on the edge of a catastrophe," said Daniel Nepstad, a research scientist from Woods Hole Research Center in Massachusetts who studied sites across the Brazilian Amazon forest. Researchers in October of 1997 dug 35-foot-deep shafts into the clay soil of unlogged Brazilian jungle at five different sites. Several years earlier, they had struck deposits of water at that depth, but this time they found nothing, which explains why all the fires set by the researchers at the same sites "just took off." That would not have happened, remarked Nepstad, if the pools of water deep in the soil had been available for the trees to tap into.

But the deep-soil pools had dried up across the Amazon during the last two years. The drying of the Amazon was due in part to the logging of precious hardwoods, which created scattered openings in the Amazon's canopy that permitted more sunlight to enter the forest, drying the normally moist air, ground layer of vegetation, and soil. It was also due in part to farmers who are drying out the deep, underground pockets of water in forest adjacent to the openings by burning scrub vegetation within the cleared areas to fertilize the nutrient-poor soil. Finally, such human activity was exacerbated by a drought caused by El Niño, the ocean–atmospheric phenomenon that disrupts global patterns of weather.

"A lot of the Amazon has lost its capacity to protect itself from fire," warned Nepstad. "When the forest is this dry, small fires can turn into giant ones and take off into primary forests," which are the equivalent of virgin old-growth forests in the Pacific Northwest of the United States and southwestern British Columbia, Canada.

The environment in the deforested areas of the Amazon has been altered to such an extent that the ecological processes that once maintained the tropical forest are changing irreversibly. Once the forest has been even partly cleared or logged, environmental conditions change swiftly and dramatically.

Removal of the trees alters the forest's internal microclimate by exposing the heretofore protected, moist, shaded interior of the forest to the sun. It also leaves behind large accumulations of woody material exposed to the sun's drying heat. As a result, daily temperatures soar in the deforested areas by 10 to 15 degrees above temperatures in the forested areas, causing the woody fuels to dry and become extremely easy to burn.

It is therefore not a matter of whether the area will burn but when it will burn. The ultimate result is a quick, dramatic change from a dense closed-canopy forest virtually immune to fire to a weedy, flammable pasture in which fires are common and often occur repeatedly. In those conditions, a new forest cannot grow.

The Amazon and other rain forests were scorched by fire in 1997 as never before. The massive fires that burned for so many months in the Indonesian jungles that year released an amount of carbon that equaled all the emissions from the burning of fossil fuels in Europe during the same year. In fact, said Philip Fearside, an American scientist who works at Brazil's National Institute for Amazon Research in Manaus, burning half of the Amazon would release 35 billion tons of carbon into the atmosphere, which is equivalent to all the emissions from burning fossil fuels in the whole world for a period of six years, and would make extinct many as yet undescribed species.[32]

Marc van Roosmalen, also working in Brazil, spent a year searching the Amazon rain forest for a new species of monkey and found not only the one he was searching for but also three other new species of monkeys, a new species of porcupine, as well as a new tapir and a new jaguar. Even more startling than the number of new species Roosmalen discovered is the fact that they were all found barely 190 miles from Manaus, the largest city in the Amazon, which in turn is 1,800 miles northwest of Rio de Janeiro.

The species for which Roosmalen originally searched occupies a total geographical distribution smaller than Rhode Island within a triangular patch of land between the Madeira and Aripuana rivers.

"I really believe the area has the highest biodiversity in the world in terms of primates and maybe in general. But not a single hectare of the region is protected by law," says Roosmalen. From the point of view of protecting not only the biodiversity known to exist but also those as yet undiscovered species still hidden from science, Roosmalen's concerns are well founded.

New roads and improved navigation along the Madeira River are part of a massive grain project nearby, which almost certainly will open the area to logging. This means that the biological wealth of plants and animals may disappear from the area before science discovers them because, contends Roosmalen, without protection, most of the animals will be gone within 20 years. Could such a wealth of species be reclaimed should the habitat be allowed to heal itself? That depends on what has been lost in the interim. Consider what has happened to Lake Erie.[33]

I remember flying over Lake Erie some years ago and seeing a part of it bright orange from chemicals discharged into its water by unconscious, unthinking human beings. What happened?

Its fisheries gone and the quality of its water worsening, Lake Erie, the 12th largest lake in the world, was used for a century as a cesspool into which everything from raw sewage to solvents was poured. The lake became increasingly eutrophic, which means its mineral and organic nutrients increased, thus reducing the dissolved oxygen and producing an environment that favored plant life over animal life. The eutrophication came about because the growing populations of Detroit, Cleveland, Toledo, Erie, and Canadian towns along the lake's northern shore dumped their personal and industrial wastes into the lake. With the eutrophication came mats of slimy, decaying algae and a shortage of oxygen so acute that by the late 1960s the lake was declared officially dead.

The lake was not "dead," however; it was teeming with organisms— but the "wrong" kind. Those organisms still thriving were "nuisance species," including algae, which gave the water an obnoxious flavor and odor, and "junk fish," species for which human society had found no economic use.

Over the last 30 years or so, the lake has been "cleaned up," but some of the damage caused by pollutants and human activities, such as over-fishing, seems irreparable. Blue pike, for example, a favorite sport fish unique to Lake Erie, is considered to be extinct. Exotic species of fish, such as coho and Chinook salmon, help keep the lake clean but were introduced artificially and thus tend to change the balance of populations of native organisms.

The chemistry of the lake's original water has been altered through increased amounts of potassium, calcium, and sodium from the runoff waters from urban, suburban, and rural lands. Lake Erie's original chemistry is extinct. Today, Lake Erie is a different lake, one whose water has been redesigned with the cultural chemistry of human society. And so it is that once pristine lakes, which evolved to the cyclical, rhythmic beat of Nature's sun-powered baton, may now be in secret completing their death throes in response to artificially high levels of energy dumped in them by a society using fossil and nuclear fuels.

As Habitats Go, So Go Their Species

Species are disappearing into extinction worldwide.[34] The following groups of animals have been documented to be in rapid decline with respect to their diversity of species: mammals, including primates; birds; amphibians; reptiles; and fish. In the number of species racing toward extinction, however, the vertebrates collectively constitute but a fraction of the Earth's diminishing biodiversity. "Not everyone who learns of this collapse is shocked by it," says Ed Ayres of Worldwatch Institute. "Many are indifferent; they don't see why it matters. And some are unapologetically hostile to any form of wildlife that interfere with human hegemony...."

To make his point, Ayres cites the frequent anger of U.S. ranchers toward the coyote, of Zimbabwean farmers toward elephants, or Japanese fruit growers toward the Japanese macaque, a monkey. Ayres goes on to say that while spending time in the Mojave Desert of California, where the desert tortoise is endangered, he learned that "the single largest cause of tortoise death is bullets to the head, delivered by land owners who fear they will be prevented from 'developing' the land by the tortoise's protected status." Ironically, he says, their protected status has made the tortoise even more endangered.

John Tuxill, also of the Worldwatch Institute, in writing about the rapid demise of primates, which he titles "Death in the Family Tree," says, "As the human population continues its unprecedented expansion, the populations of more than half of the world's other primates continue their unprecedented decline."[35] It all began more than two million years ago with little apes that made East Africa home, a home in which they hardly dominated the existing patchwork of forest and savanna. While they spent most of their time getting out of the way of predators, somewhere in time those small, vulnerable creatures embarked on a unique evolutionary journey—"a line of development," as Tuxill puts it, "that would one day confer on their descendants a power without precedent in the entire history of life [on Earth]."

Although the two million or so years between then and now is only a brief moment in evolutionary time, Tuxill says, "the rift that has opened since then between ourselves and our fellow primates—modern apes, monkeys, lemurs, and lorises—is momentous on any scale." Humans share 98.4 percent of their gene pool with chimpanzees, which means that only 1.6 percent of our human genetic constitution is uniquely ours. "But," writes Tuxill, "that seasoning of distinctly human DNA has, in a sense, catalyzed a reversal of our ecological role. We are no longer molded by the ecosystems in which we live—we mold them." He goes on to say that our ecological dominance has a price, as we are learning, and no one "is paying more heavily than our closest relatives."

Embedded in Tuxill's article is a story from Sarawak, which is part of Malaysia on the island that used to be called Borneo. The story was told by Dató Mikaail Kavanagh, executive director of World Wildlife Fund–Malaysia, as quoted in the September 1996 issue of *Daniaku*, a publication of World Wildlife Fund–Malaysia:

> Back in 1981, WWF–Malaysia sent me to Sarawak to help the Forest Department there with its orangutan conservation work. This work took me deep into the forest, near the Kalimantan border [Kalimanta is the current name of the Indonesian portion of what used to be called Borneo], and involved many a night in Iban [people's] longhouses. Once, when I was in the Batang Ai area, long before today's Batang Ai National Park was established, a Tuai Rumah told me the following story.

"In my grandfather's time, a man died and the people laid him out in the bilek for burial the next day. But early on the following morning, when his son entered the bilek, his father's body was gone. Instead, there was a maias [orangutan] standing there, and the maias said to the man, 'I am your father. I am not dead, but because I have turned into a maias, I can no longer live in the longhouse. I must go and live in the forest. But because I am your father and I am joining the other maias, we must have a bond between people and maias.'

"So saying, the maias gave the man a ring and said, 'Keep this ring for eight generations. So long as you and your descendants have the ring, the people of the Batang Ai must regard all maias as their family. Do not harm us and we will know that you are our friends, and good fortune shall be yours.'

"With that, the maias left the longhouse and disappeared into the forest. His son kept the ring carefully and right now it is in the hands of his son's family, although they moved to a new settlement along the Sungai Skrang [which means "River Skrang" in Malay] some years ago.

"Because this happened, we the Iban people of the Batang Ai do not hunt or kill any maias and that is why you can see many of them in our area. They even make their nests where you can see them from our longhouses. We have six more generations to go of this peace between us and our maias neighbours. After that, who knows? I shall not be here."

I have often thought about this tale. And I have often thought about how there are many orangutans in the Batang Ai, yet almost none in similar, nearby areas. I even saw orangutan nests in the tops of rubber trees near the longhouse where the man told me this story. Is it true? I only tell you what I heard. You decide for yourself what you think is true in your world. But I do know that a world with this story is a better place for maias than a world without it.[35]

In addition to the changes in habitat wrought by the physical hand of society, changes in climate and patterns of weather also play a role in changing habitats.

WHEN CLIMATE CHANGES

Although there is no such thing as an independent variable within a dynamic system, especially when part of that system is composed of living entities, the dynamics of climate and weather are leading contenders for stimulating changes from the local scale to the global and across time and landscapes. Although a landscape is usually thought of as a finished product in the sense of a view or vista of scenery or as that aspect of the land characteristic of a particular region, the idea of a landscape as finished because we see it as a snapshot in time is erroneous. I have learned over the years to think of a landscape as a dynamic kaleidoscope of all the elements and all the scales of relationships and events focused for an instant, this instant, in the center of the Universe.

I say "the center of the Universe," because I am here participating in creation as an active observer. I therefore stand at the exact center of the Universe, because as an individual human being, I am the center of all interdependencies; all interdependencies radiate from me and come back to me. As I am the center of the Universe, so are you; so is everything in Creation. The center of the Universe is therefore everywhere and nowhere.

Thinking of a Landscape

In considering a landscape, think first of the dynamic *geological processes*, which evoke every conceivable scale of time, space, and relationship that formed the land and the resultant *macroclimate* (the prevailing climate of the times as it affects a continent). In turn, the geological processes and the climate act together on the *parent materials* (the original rock from which a particular soil is derived in a particular location). The result is the *topography* of the area. These are the long-term ecological variables that control and define a landscape in space through the long reaches of time.

Geological processes constantly alter the surface of the Earth. One such process is the collision of the oceanic plates with the continental plates as the former moves under the latter, thrusting the Earth's crust upward into folds and buckles, sometimes with the punctuated aid of volcanoes, from which ranges of mountains are born. These mountains have a profound impact on the overall climate of an area. They determine the amount and pattern of precipitation that falls in a given time, and they dictate the accompanying temperature. They determine, for example, when, where, and in what way precipitation falls.

The type of parent material or rock of which the mountains are composed determines not only the way in which they will erode but also the type of soil that will be formed as a result of being exposed to a particular climatic regime over time, which is known as weathering. The initial formation of the mountains, their size, shape, and the type of parent materials of which they are composed determine part of the pattern of weathering and erosion. The prevailing climate also determines part of the pattern of weathering and erosion. Taken together, climate and weathering help to form the resulting topography or the physical features of a particular place or region at any given point in time.

In addition to and within the control of the long-term ecological variables, there are such dynamics as *disturbance regimes, hydrological cycles*, and *microclimate*. These are the short-term ecological variables that control and refine the definition of a given landscape in space through the short reaches of time.

Regimes of catastrophic disturbance, such as fire, volcano, flood, landslide, and tornado, to which North American ecosystems are continually subjected, are determined by and influenced by such things as macroclimate in conjunction with topography, the hydrological cycles, and the microclimate of a given area. A hydrological cycle has four apparently discrete parts: (1) the way water falls as rain and/or snow, (2) the way it sinks into the soil and is either stored or flows belowground, (3) the way it runs over the surface of the soil in streams and rivers on their way to the sea, and (4) the way it evaporates into the atmosphere to be cycled again as rain and/or snow. Microclimate, as used here, is the climate of an immediate area as determined by the topography and the vegetation, which exerts a local influence over the macroclimate, the prevailing climate of the times.

Between the nonliving long- and short-term ecological variables of a landscape and the living components of the landscape (its plants and animals) lies the *soil*. The soil, as a combination of both nonliving and living components of the landscape, is an exchange membrane, much like the placenta through which a mother nourishes her child. The soil, which is derived from the parent materials laid down by the geological processes, is built up and enriched by the plants that live and die in it. It is also enriched by the animals that feed on the plants, void their bodily wastes, and eventually die, decay, and return to the soil as organic matter.

And then there are the *individual* living organisms, which collectively form the *species*, which in turn collectively form the *communities* that spread over the land. These organisms, through the exchange medium of the soil, are influenced immediately by the short-term ecological variables even as they themselves influence those same variables through their life cycles. The dynamic interactions of plant and animal communities and soil are controlled and influenced by both long- and short-term ecological variables that collectively help to form the *landscape*. And it is the landscape that we humans arbitrarily delineate into *ecosystems* as we try to understand the dynamic interactions between nonliving and living components of our world.

To gain a sense of the dynamic nature of a landscape through time, we will take a peek at the changes wrought to the central portion of the United States, that which today is the Great Plains. Our view begins as the last glacial stage, the Wisconsin, reached its maximum development and then receded into history.

While the glacier was at its maximum, temperatures lowered on the North American continent, and subarctic plants grew as far south as what is now Virginia, Oklahoma, and Texas. Coniferous trees, like pine and spruce, grew in what is now the Great Plains, along with some deciduous trees.

As the last glacier receded and the climate warmed, the deciduous forest began to take over from the coniferous. The center of the continent continued to warm and dry, and fire began to play an increasingly important role in shaping the vegetation. Although the coniferous forest became confined to the cooler climates of the Rocky Mountains and westward, the grassland in the center of the continent expanded and withdrew as temperatures waxed and waned. During times of warmer temperatures, the deciduous forest retreated eastward and grassland filled the area—and vice versa. Because the climate continued to warm and dry, wind-driven grass fires increased and helped the grassland eventually take over from the trees and shrubs to form the Great Plains of today.

Thus, although climate was a factor in the evolution of the grasslands that greeted the early European explorers in the center of the North American continent, so too were the vastness and the flatness of the Great Plains and the annual fire-carrying dieback of the grasses.

When thinking about landscapes in the Pacific Northwest, I am often reminded of the fires, both large and small, that over the millennia shaped the great forests I knew as a youth. Later in life, as I studied the interactive connections between animals and forests, I found the recurring cycles of the birth, growth, and death of individuals; the waxing and waning of habitats and of plant and animal communities; and the evolution of species that eventually returned again to the distant unknown.

What seems clear to me now is that the universal cycles are not perfect circles, as they so often are depicted in the scientific literature and textbooks and as I was taught they were. Rather, they are a coming together in time and space at a specific point, where one "end" of a cycle approximates—but *only approximates*—its "beginning" in a particular place. Between its beginning and its ending, a cycle can have any configuration of cosmic happenstance.

Further, Nature's cycles seem most "real" and discernible to me as they pertain to and influence living organisms, those beings with which I share the gift of life. Beyond that, in the nonbiological reaches of the cosmos, cycles become more and more abstract as they extend either backward or forward into the continuum of time. Thus, while cycles give dimension, context, and texture to the landscape, they are more real to me in the living here and now than they are when they penetrate into the formation of the short- and long-term ecological variables as they affect any given place on Earth.

In discussing the attributes of a landscape, one must be aware of all of the factors that have come together to create a particular place as one perceives it, not just the events themselves but also the cycles in which the events are embedded. With this notion in mind, one might well ask while viewing a landscape how the seemingly infinite dimensions of scale and process come together as ecological variables to mold and sculpt our planet with composition, structure, and function.

How Ecological Variables Interact with Climate to Form a Landscape

When dealing with scale, scientists have traditionally analyzed large interactive systems in the same way they have studied small orderly systems, mainly because their methods of study have proven so successful. They thought they could predict the behavior of a large, complicated system by studying its elements separately and by analyzing its microscopic mechanisms individually. Such thinking is the traditional linear thinking of Western civilization that views the world and all it contains through a lens of intellectual isolation. During the last few decades, however, it has become increasingly clear that many apparently chaotic and complicated systems do not yield to that kind of traditional analysis.

Instead, large, complicated, interactive systems like components of landscapes and even whole landscapes themselves seem to evolve to a critical state in which even a minor event starts a chain reaction that can lead to an unpredictable, monumental, even catastrophic change.

Although such systems produce more minor events than catastrophic ones, chain reactions of all sizes are an integral part of the systems' dynamics. The mechanism that leads to minor events is the same mechanism that leads to major events. Because such systems are open (which means they can be influenced by such things as the gravitational pull of the moon), they never reach a stable state, but rather evolve from one semistable state to another.

In this sense, ecosystems as portions of landscapes are dissipative structures, as discussed earlier. This is not surprising to me, however, because ecosystems and landscapes are networks of relationships rather than collections of objects. Not understanding this, analysts who try to figure out why catastrophes happen typically blame some rare set of circumstances, some exception to the rule, or some powerful combination of mechanisms. Therefore, when a tremendous earthquake shook San Francisco, geologists traced the cataclysm to an immense instability along the San Andreas fault. When the stock market crashed on "Black Monday" in 1987, economists pointed to the destabilizing effect of trading through the mechanization of computers.

Although these factors may well be causative, systems as large, complicated, and dynamic as the Earth's crust, the stock market, and an ecosystem can break down not only under the force of a mighty blow but also at the drop of a pin. Large interactive systems perpetually organize themselves to a critical state in which a minor event can start a chain reaction that leads to a destabilizing breakdown. After the breakdown, the system will begin organizing toward the next critical state, and so on.

Another way of approaching this is to ask: If change is a universal constant and nothing is static, what is a natural state? In considering this question, one soon begins to realize that the "balance of nature" idea in the classical sense (disturb Nature and Nature will return to its former state when the disturbance is removed) fails to hold. Although one usually perceives the pattern of vegetation on the Earth's surface to be stable, particularly over the short interval of one's lifetime, in reality the landscape and its vegetation are in a perpetual state of dynamic unbalance with the forces that sculpted them. When these forces create novel events that are sufficiently rapid and large in scale, they are perceived as "disturbances."

Perhaps the most outstanding evidence that an ecosystem is subject to constant change and disruption rather than in a static balance comes from studies of naturally occurring external factors that dislocate ecosystems. For a long time, ecologists failed to consider influences outside ecosystems. Their emphasis was on processes internal to an ecosystem even though what was happening inside was driven by what was happening outside.

Climate appears to be foremost among these factors. By studying the record laid down in the sediments of oceans and lakes, scientists know that climate has fluctuated wildly over the last two million years, and the shape of ecosystems with it; witness what is going on today around the world. The fluctuations take place not only from eon to eon but also from year to year and season to season and at every scale in between, which means the configuration of ecosystems is always changing, creating different landscapes in a particular area through geological time.

With this notion of perpetual change in mind, consider that all of us can sense change—the growing light at sunrise, the gathering wind before a thunderstorm, or the changing seasons with spring's new leaves, summer's swaying blossoms, autumn's golden harvest, and winter's stark, naked trees and chilling winds. Some of us can see longer term events and remember that there was more or less snow last winter compared to other winters or that spring seemed to come early this year.

But it is an unusual person who can sense, with any degree of precision, the changes that occur over the decades of his or her life. At this scale of time, we tend to think of the world in some sort of "steady state," and we typically underestimate the degree to which change has occurred. We are unable to directly sense slow changes, and we are even more limited in our abilities to interpret their relationships of cause and effect. This being the case, the subtle processes that act quietly and unobtrusively over decades are hidden and reside in the "invisible present."

The invisible present is the scale of time within which our responsibilities for planet Earth are most evident. Within this scale of time, ecosystems change during our lifetimes and the lifetimes of our children and our grandchildren. To see how interactions of scale in time, space, and proportion work in unison with climate, let's examine some of the geological history of Zion National Park in the state of Utah.[36]

Where today the deep canyons and massive walls of stone enthrall visitors (Figure 13), 245 million years ago a sea in which marine fishes lived covered the area of Zion. Over a period of roughly 35 million years, about 1,800 feet of sediments was deposited on the floor of the sea, along the coastal plain, and along the inland streams.

As the climate warmed, the sea changed into a gigantic swamp. Here, 210 million years ago, crocodile-like plant-eating dinosaurs swam in the sluggish streams whose floods carried drifted trees on their swirling waters from distant forests to form logjams. Here too, small, fragile dinosaurs hunted along the streams' banks. As the climate once again became more moist during the next 40 million years, the swamp became a lake and the

FIGURE 13   Canyon wall at Zion National Park. (Photograph by author.)

sand, silt, and clayey mud of the streams and the swamp gradually hardened into rock.

The lake for a time had fish living in it, but then some of its waters became shallow and eventually disappeared. Existing streams spread silt and sandy mud over the sediments deposited on the lake's bottom. Toward the end of this 40-million-year interval, the climate began to dry, and in a short space of time, geologically speaking, the now intermittent streams deposited more sediments.

Then, about 170 million years ago, the ancient sea, the swamp, the lake, and the intermittent streams became buried beneath a desert of marching sand dunes of the "Navajo Time." This now hostile environment had little life associated with it, and the few hardy plants and animals that did exist often died during the great storms, which blew clouds of hot, dry sand into dunes. As the dunes were built, destroyed, and built again, some of the plants and animals became entombed and are the rare fossils of today in what is now the Navajo Sandstone, which ranges from 1,500 to 2,000 feet thick. Although the source of the sand eroded away 150 million years ago, evidence indicates that the source had been a region of highlands in what is today the state of Nevada.

For a brief period following the creation of the Navajo Desert, flood-waters carrying suspended sediments buried the dunes in deposits of red mud, after which the climate returned to more desertlike conditions.

Again the climate changed, and 145 million years ago a vast, shallow sea once more covered the area, drowning the Navajo Desert. Now the once sterile desert with its cap of red mud became the floor of the sea and the home of sea lilies (crinoids) and shellfish. When the warm, teeming waters retreated, they left behind, buried in limey silt, shells that produced the present fossils.

Over the millions of years, in response to changing environmental conditions, various materials were deposited in the sediments. The Zion area experienced shallow seas, coastal plains, a giant swamp, a lake, intermittent streams, and a desert filled with massive wind-blown dunes of sand. While the shallow seas covered the area, mineral-laden waters slowly filtered down through the layers of sediment. Minerals such as iron and calcium carbonate were deposited in the spaces between the particles of silt, sand, or mud, cementing them together, turning them into stone. The weight of each layer caused the basin to sink and maintained its surface at an elevation near sea level. This process of deposition–sinking–deposition–sinking continued layer upon layer until the accumulation of the successive sediments became 10,000 feet thick!

Geologists believe that Zion was a relatively flat basin with an elevation near sea level from 245 million years ago until the last shallow sea dried about 10 million years ago. At that time, Zion was a featureless plain across which streams meandered lazily as they dropped their loads of sediment in sandbars and floodplains.

Then, in an area extending from Zion to the Rocky Mountains, a massive geologic event began. Forces deep within the Earth's mantle started to push upward on the surface of the Earth. The land in Zion rose from near sea level to as much as 10,000 feet above sea level.

Zion's location on the western edge of the uplift caused the streams to tumble off the Colorado Plateau, flowing rapidly down a steep gradient. The Virgin River, for example, drops more than 4,000 feet from the northeast corner of Zion National Park in Utah to Lake Mead in Arizona, 145 miles away; in comparison, consider that the upper Mississippi River drops only 210 feet from Lake Itasca in Minnesota to Grand Rapids, Minnesota, also a distance of 145 miles.

Because fast-flowing water carries more sediments and larger boulders than does slow-moving water, these swift streams in Zion began eroding down into the layers of rock, cutting deep, narrow canyons. In the ten million years since the uplift began, the North Fork of the Virgin River has not only carved Zion Canyon but also has carried away a layer of rock nearly 5,000 feet thick, a layer that once lay above the highest existing rock in Zion National Park.

The uplift of the land is still occurring, and so the Virgin River is still excavating. The river, with its load of sand, has been likened to an ever-moving strip of sandpaper. Its grating effect, coupled with the steepness of the Colorado Plateau, has allowed the river to cut its way through the Navajo Sandstone in a short time, geologically speaking.

The cutting of Zion Canyon created a gap in the solid layer of resistant sandstone, and the walls of the canyon relaxed and expanded ever so slightly toward this opening. Because rock is not very elastic, this expansion caused cracks, known as pressure-release joints, to form inside the canyon's walls. These cracks run parallel to the canyon about 15 to 30 feet inside the walls and occur throughout the Navajo Sandstone (Figure 14).

The grains of sand that form the Navajo Sandstone itself were once driven bouncing across the desert by the wind, only to be caught within the steep face of a dune, where they became buried. Over time, the cement of lime tied grain to grain, creating the stone of sand.

Today, however, the process is reversed, and a new cycle has begun. The layer of siltstone and sandstone directly beneath the Navajo Sandstone is softer and more easily eroded than is the Navajo Sandstone. Thus, as the walls of Navajo Sandstone are undermined by the erosion of this

FIGURE 14   Note the pressure-release joint inside the canyon's wall (arrows). These joints or cracks run parallel to the canyon about 15 to 30 feet inside the walls and occur throughout the Navajo Sandstone. (Photograph by author.)

softer material, water from rain and snow seeps into the joints, where it freezes in winter, wedging the walls of the joints ever farther apart.

In addition to freezing, the water, one drop of rain at a time, one melting flake of snow at a time, aided by chemical action, dissolves the cement. The structure gradually weakens. A last grain of sand holding the undermined wall in place moves, and the massive piece of rock falls, breaking away along the line of least resistance, leaving the graceful sweep of a huge arch sculpted in the face of the cliff a thousand feet above the floor of the canyon (Figure 15). And so is revealed yet another vertical face previously hidden as a crack or pressure-release joint inside the wall. Below, the rock, shattered by the fall, gradually returns to sand and is once again scattered by the wind or carried toward the sea by the restless Virgin River.

FIGURE 15 A massive piece of rock falls, breaking away along the line of least resistance of a pressure-release joint inside the canyon's wall, leaving the graceful sweep of a huge arch sculpted in the face of the cliff a thousand feet above the floor of the canyon (arrow). (Photograph by author.)

In the end, Zion, cemented together grain by grain over millions of years, is being dissolved over millions of years one grain at a time by the persistence of water from snow and infrequent thunderstorms. But while Zion undergoes its inevitable changes, it is home for 670 species of flowering plants and ferns, 30 species of amphibians and reptiles, 125 species of resident birds, and 95 species of mammals. Gone, however, are the wolf, grizzly bear, and bighorn sheep, all extirpated within the last hundred years by the invading European American settlers. Thus are tipped the scales of change, of creation and extinction, in some of its many dimensions. Having said this, it seems apparent that Zion Canyon is a relatively permanent fixture of the landscape that will surely span many human generations, but what about ecosystems that are not constrained by such massive geological features?

Climate Change and the Migration of Ecosystems

The freezing level in the atmosphere, which is the height above sea level at which the temperature of air reaches 32 degrees Fahrenheit, has been rising in altitude at a rate of nearly 15 feet per year since 1970, which means that both tropical and subtropical glaciers are rapidly melting. Ellen Mosley-Thompson, a member of an Ohio State team of researchers studying glaciers, was asked if she was sure of her results. She replied, "I don't know quite what to say. I've presented the evidence....It just comes back to the compilation of what's happening at high elevations: the Lewis glacier on Mount Kenya has lost forty percent of its mass; in the Ruwenzori Range, all the glaciers are in massive retreat. Everything, virtually, in Patagonia, except for just a few glaciers, is retreating....We've seen...that plants are moving up the mountains....I frankly don't know what additional evidence you need."[37] Ellen Mosley-Thompson's response to the question reminds me of a statement by Henry David Thoreau: "It takes two to speak the truth—one to speak, another to hear." In Mosley-Thompson's case, I wonder who there was or is to hear.

There have been and again will be drastic changes in habitats that affect whole groups of plants and animals due to changes in climate. In fact, there is a theory that the beginning of the last ice age, named the Wisconsin glaciation, may have been rooted in arctic plants.[37] John Kutzbach and Robert Gallimore, climatologists at the University of Wisconsin in Madison, suggest that a shift in arctic vegetation could have helped to cool the Earth enough 115,000 years ago to trigger the ice age.

The temperature of the Earth is affected both by the tilt of the planet's axis and the time of year when the Earth is closest to the sun. About

115,000 years ago, according to the theory put forward by Kutzbach and Gallimore, these two phenomena coincided in such a way to produce a really cold summer, but not cold enough in itself to start an ice age, according to the computer-generated model used by the two researchers. Only when changes in vegetation were added to the formula did temperatures drop far enough to initiate the buildup of ice.

There is evidence that about 115,000 years ago the boreal forest was dying and being replaced by arctic tundra, which is composed of such short plants as mosses and lichens. Since it requires little snow to cover the tundra, expansive snowscapes formed and, according to the model, reflected as much as 70 percent of the sun's heat in that region back into space, which could have cooled the Earth even further and allowed the ice sheets not only to form but also to spread.

Because plants and animals help create a given habitat through their aboveground/belowground symbiotic interactions, in the sense that habitats change, they, too, can be thought of as part of the evolutionary process. After all, plants and animals together help create new habitats as well as the extinction of old ones. To gain a sense of what I mean in a shorter, more dynamic way than the triggering of an ice age, consider conditions in eastern North America at the close of the Wisconsin glaciation, about 10,000 years ago.

The modern northern flora and fauna of eastern North America are composed largely of post-Wisconsin glacial-stage plants and animals that immigrated to ground previously stripped of life by glacial ice. Competition therefore favored species adapted to harsh northern environments, species that could disperse rapidly. Groups of animals composed of species from northern and temperate habitats lived on the southern edge of the glacier. Unadaptable temperate species continued to inhabit local areas of relatively unaltered climate, while those that could adapt to some degree survived where the glaciers had not encroached.

As the climate changed, habitats around the glacier slowly changed. Those covered with ice were created and destroyed more rapidly than those along the edge of the ice. The gradual changes created a continuum of small habitats, which supported a richer collection of plants and animals than the flora and fauna in previously glaciated areas.

As the glaciers receded, most mammals followed habitats northward, migrated to higher latitudes, underwent physiological adjustments, or became extinct. The varied habitats and the adaptability of other mammals allowed them to survive by moving southward ahead of the advancing Wisconsin glaciation and then northward again as the glacier melted. Only the less adaptable larger species were particularly prone to extinction.

Habitats change, especially under the influence of a growing human population. Sometimes habitats evolve slowly and gradually and sometimes quickly and drastically, but regardless of the way they do it, all habitats change. When they do, there is a general reshuffling of plants and animals. More adaptable species may for a time survive a change in habitat, even a relatively drastic one, but in the end they too must change, migrate elsewhere, or become extinct.

We humans have changed and are changing the global ecosystem and all of its component habitats at an exponential rate. Today, we have become the major cause of extinctions and of evolutionary leaps. Some ecosystems and their habitats may be able to mitigate the alterations to which we subject them. But alas, most alterations are damaging to the ecosystem as we know it and are prone to spread. Others evolve into ecosystems that we humans find less desirable, often because the new species, which quickly replace those lost, cannot live up to our human expectations.

Be that as it may, all evidence of changes in the global climate points to the need, once again, for habitats and ecosystems to migrate across the landscape, both in elevation and in latitude, as they have done for millennia. Only this time, they will not be able to extend their geographical distributions fast enough to keep up with the pace of climate change now predicted. A staggering one-third of the world's forests could be forced to migrate as a result of the effective doubling of the concentrations of carbon dioxide projected by the year 2100, according to Steven Humburg, a forest ecologist at Brown University.[38] We humans must therefore help ecosystems, such as forests, by consciously, purposefully keeping corridors of migration free of human-caused obstructions across the landscapes with which we interact as communities, singly and in aggregate.

The long-term sustainability of human communities depends on the long-term sustainability of the habitats and ecosystems of which they are a part. In the face of rapid change in the global climate, sustainability means protecting the ability of habitats and ecosystems, and human society along with them, to adapt to change by wandering at will across landscapes. But what are the effects of short-term patterns in climate, such as El Niño?

Short-Term Patterns in the Climate

What will be called short-term climatic patterns in the following discussion range from the effects of roughly a 60-year cycle, to a 1-year impact of a recurring climatic event—El Niño,[39] to a dust cloud of a few days.[40] Let's begin with the 60-year pattern. According to Peter Lawson, a research biologist with the National Marine Fisheries Service, rainfall, temperature, and other conditions appear to shift in cycles of about 60 years and may have dramatic effects on different species of fish.

Although researchers are learning that climatic conditions vary over cycles of 60 years or more, recorded data describing those cycles exist for less than 150 years. In the absence of recorded human observations, scientists are turning to such things as growth rings in the trees of Arizona dating back 1,500 years. Ensconced in these growth rings are 50- to 60-year cycles that in turn indicated patterns of wet/dry and hot/cold in the climate.

These tree-ring data were then compared with other data by Tim Baumgartner, an oceanographer with the Scripps Institute of Oceanography in La Jolla, California. Baumgartner analyzed sediment cores off the coast of Santa Barbara, California, for the scales of anchovy and sardines. His data, reaching back 1,500 years, showed 50-year cycles in the abundance of anchovy and sardines. The abundance of sardines increases dramatically, for example, when the waters of the Pacific warm off the coast of California, which offers biological evidence of the boom-and-bust nature of some populations of fish in the Pacific.

Because existing data are not refined enough, and may never be, "...it's a lot easier to make general statements about the kinds of things we can expect to happen over the next 60 years than it is to say what's going to happen with a specific stock [of fish] over the next five years," says Lawson, which means that the fishing industry must accept planning for uncertainty.

How does this uncertainty come about? According to George Taylor, the state climatologist at Oregon State University, the answer lies in a convincing theory of how weather intended for one part of the world ends up in another part. This theory is thought to act like a "conveyor belt" that transports water between the Pacific and the Atlantic, which causes two ocean-weather phenomena—El Niño and La Niña. Taylor said that while the concept makes sense physically and explains a lot of what has been seen over the last 100 years, it may take reviewing up to 50 years of data on oceans from satellites before the theory is accepted as fact. Such data are necessary because the oceans of the world are dynamic.

Currents of marine water ring the Pacific Ocean like giant rivers. Cold, wide currents flow southward toward the equator along the eastern edges of oceans (the western edges of continents). These southward-flowing currents, such as the California Current, are tightly interlinked with the upwelling of cold water that creates productive fisheries. The current, warming on its way to the equator, then travels westward along the equator toward Japan, where it turns northward as a deep, warm current along the western edge of the country and becomes known as the Kuroshio Current. The counterpart of the Kuroshio Current of Japan is the deep, warm, northward-flowing current along the east coast of the United States, called the Gulf Stream, which flows with 5,000 times the volume of the Mississippi River.

It is complicated for people of the land to think about directions when dealing with oceans because the west coast of the United States is ca-ressed by the eastern Pacific, just as the east coast of the United States is bordered by the western Atlantic, which is totally backwards from the way people on land think about directions. Let's look, therefore, at the interchange of water between the Pacific and the Atlantic as simply as possible: Water from the typically warm Pacific flows through the Indian Ocean into the Atlantic, where it encounters cold water traveling north-ward. As the warm water cools, it sinks because cold water is heavier than warm water. As it cools and sinks, it eventually reverses direction and sets up a subsurface countercurrent that takes cold water from the Atlantic back through the Indian Ocean into the Pacific. Taylor stresses that it is not so much the volume of water being exchanged that makes the dif-ference, but rather the temperature of the water being exchanged.

The effect of this interchange of water between the Pacific and the Atlantic works something like this: El Niño cools the water of the south-western Pacific Ocean near the equator, which is the point of origin for many storms striking the Pacific Northwest of the United States. At the same time, El Niño warms the ocean off the west coast of South America, which generally produces milder, drier winters in the Pacific Northwest. While El Niño normally produces relatively mild, dry winters in the Pacific Northwest, it simultaneously causes wetter, stormier winters from south-ern California to Texas and along the coast of South America. Then, about 9,000 miles away, La Niña reverses the trend off the coast of Indonesia, where it warms the waters of the southwestern Pacific Ocean, cools the southeastern portion, and sends wet weather to the Pacific Northwest of the United States.

Although the El Niño phenomenon is only now beginning to be understood, its effects are known to date back at least 2,500 years in Peru. Somewhere around 500 B.C. a tremendous El Niño-caused flood brought about the demise of the Mochas, an ancient civilization on Peru's north coast in which the people built an intricate series of canals and water entrapments. Another cataclysmic El Niño-caused flood along the northern coastal desert of Peru took place in 1100 A.D. and has been named the Chimú Flood. The Chimú Flood was so named because it affected a great civilization, the Chimú dynasty, which had nine monarchs and lasted from 1000 A.D. to 1400 A.D. The Chimú capital, Chan Chan, was located near the present-day town of Trujillo, where it covered more than six square miles and was surrounded by a 30-foot-high wall. According to 16th century chroniclers, the last Chimú monarch, Minchançaman, was defeated by the Incas, who conquered the Chimú Empire in about 1470.

El Niño was so named by Peruvian sailors from the port of Paita in northern Peru, who frequently navigated either north or south along the coast in small vessels. They named the current in which they became entrained El Niño because it was most noticeable around Christmas. El Niño is Spanish for "child" or "boy" and when capitalized refers to the Christ child.

As in ancient Peru, the atmosphere plays a central role in regulating the patterns of weather in the Pacific Northwest and the conditions of the Pacific Ocean. Under normal conditions, a large, powerful low-pressure system, known as the Aleutian low, sits in winter off the Aleutian Islands of Alaska and brings cool air from the Arctic into the Pacific Northwest. The Aleutian low is the primary force behind the winds of winter, which generally flow northward, along the coast.

Conditions in the atmosphere change abruptly during the summer as the Aleutian low decreases in intensity and migrates westward. At the same time, a subtropical high-pressure system, usually located along the coast of California, increases in strength, while a smaller low-pressure system forms over North America. The northward-blowing winds of winter switch direction accordingly and blow southward in summer.

The usual conditions of the Pacific Northwest are frequently interrupted, however, by variations in conditions of the atmosphere and the ocean. These fluctuations assume many forms and are usually characterized by the magnitude or scale of their effects. For example, winter storm systems, which bring precipitation and strong winds into the Pacific Northwest, usually last only a few days and affect relatively small areas. In contrast, large-scale variations tend to persist for a longer period of time and affect larger areas. The effects of El Niño, for example, persist for approximately 12 months.

Some of the more pronounced changes in the atmosphere involve variations in the strength and position of the Aleutian low in winter. During certain El Niños, the winter Aleutian low intensifies and migrates southward, westward, or both and thereby alters the course of the jet stream, which increases the force of the northward-blowing winds. These changes generally result in drier conditions, warmer temperatures, and lower precipitation in the Pacific Northwest. Not all El Niños have the same effect, however. Strong El Niños can bring severe winter floods to Oregon and Washington.

A strong El Niño can also have interesting local effects, such as moving sand more than ten feet deep off of a beach in one winter, thus exposing more than 200 stumps of an ancient forest that was growing 2,000 years ago, when evidence suggests that a powerful earthquake offshore dropped the coastline by as much as seven feet and submerged the coastal forest of Sitka spruce and western red cedar trees. Some of these ancient stumps made a brief appearance during another El Niño 15 years ago.

In addition to uncovering a surprise on a single beach, however, El Niño also affects an entire suite of marine organisms, from plankton (the tiny plants and animals that are the basis of the marine food chain) to salmon and seabirds. Salmon will be used here as an example of an immediate local effect that a global shift in climate can generate. Our guide for the discussion of El Niño's effects on salmon will be Bob Hannah, a fisheries biologist with the Oregon Department of Fish and Wildlife who is stationed at Newport on the Oregon Coast.

Hannah says El Niño can affect salmon in three ways:

1. El Niño can cause high mortality of juvenile salmon in the ocean by affecting their source of food. When young salmon reach the ocean, they need the rich source of food (plankton) that is brought up from the deep, cold water by upwelling. Upwelling, which is caused by the east winds during spring, sets the marine dinner table for the newly arrived juvenile salmon. In addition, salmon are not only healthier in cold water but also safer in the murky greenish-brown water that decreases visibility for waiting predators.

   The effect of an El Niño is to stop the east winds of spring, which also stops the upwelling that in turn produces three effects detrimental to the young salmon. The water warms, which is unfavorable to the growth of the juvenile salmon. Without the upwelling, the abundance of food in the form of plankton decreases drastically, and the resulting clear blue of the ocean water allows good visibility for predators, many of which, like mackerel, move up with the warm water from the south.

2. Adult salmon in the ocean can starve because the warm water can deprive them of their usual cold-water-dependent prey. Although starvation cannot be proven, the few salmon that returned to spawn during the strong El Niño in the winter of 1982–83 were skinny and undernourished; this included both coho and Chinook.

3. Depending on timing and severity, El Niño also affects the inland habitat of the salmon by causing either floods or drought in the Pacific Northwest. El Niño typically splits the jet stream, which is a high-altitude wind that generally moves in a westerly direction at speeds often exceeding 250 miles per hour. This split in the jet stream generally brings warmer and drier weather to Oregon than is normal in winter.

Such warm, dry winters would not have a severe effect on salmon if the streams in which they live and reproduce are healthy and remain cold. But nearly 12,000 miles of streams in Oregon are listed in noncompliance with the Endangered Species Act in terms of standards for water quality, such as temperature, which is higher than that in healthy streams—those good for salmon.

Not all winters affected by El Niño are warm and dry, however. When the jet stream does not split over Oregon, as was the case in 1982–83, the extreme weather can cause tremendous coastal storms. These storms do the most damage to the salmon when they cause flooding that occurs before the salmon's eggs hatch. In this case, everything depends on the timing of a given event. In 1982–83, for example, severe flooding took place prior to the hatching of the salmon's eggs, and the distribution of age classes of salmon for that year did not fare well. But if the floods had come after the salmon had hatched and moved out of the gravel, they would have been okay.

In addition, different species of salmon require dramatically different habitats, both inland and at sea. Coho, for example, lay their eggs in the gravel of small streams, where the young fish spend a year before migrating to the sea. Once at sea, they spend two years feeding near the surface. Chinook, on the other hand, primarily spawn in rivers and large tributaries. They spend most of their juvenile lives in the lower rivers before migrating into the deeper regions of the ocean to mature.

Short-term variations in climate, such as El Niño, are one of the reasons so much genetic diversity is necessary in populations of wild fish, like salmon in a particular river system, if they are to survive in the long term. Over the course of several El Niños, which appear to be cyclical in their occurrence, a given life-history strategy seems to work better for one species one time and another some other time. With good diversity in the various populations of wild salmon in their respective rivers, the aggregate population of salmon ought to do well over time. What all this amounts to, says Hannah, is that "salmon have a big backyard" and need not only healthy water catchments, streams, and rivers inland but also a healthy ocean in which to mature if they are to survive over time.

Thousands of miles away, El Niño had its way with the world's largest tribe of Stone Age people, the Yanomami Indians of the Amazon. The Yanomamis are just one example of the plight of people minding their own business and thus simply living within the bounds of their diverse cultures before falling prey to the invasion of ruthless foreign cultures.

On the Yanomami reservation in Brazil, the sun glowed red in 1998 through the ghostly shroud of smoke from the worst forest fires in this remote area's known history. Burning out of control for three months, the fires charred 1.5 million acres, just across the Mucajai River from the reservation. Although fire fighters struggled to protect the 9,000 Yanomamis who live on the reservation, the blaze at one point reached 12 miles inside of it. To the Yanomamis living on the reservation, the fires were a sign of the apocalypse, as they may also be to the 11,000 or so Yanomamis who live just across the border in Venezuela. And they may be right because the dozens of smaller fires burning unchecked within the reservation scared away the game that sustains the Yanomamis.

Some Yanomamis beat on the walls of their houses in an effort to exorcise the evil spirits while others performed the Xabori ritual, drawing on the ground and chanting to bring rain, but modern forecasters did not expect rain for at least another month, until mid-April of 1998. Barely a quarter of an inch of rain fell that year in Roraima, a wedge of land situated between Venezuela and Guyana. The unusual dry spell is the effect of El Niño.

Enough about El Niño. One big storm in Asia on April 15, 1998 produced so much dust that it traveled intact as a cloud across the Pacific Ocean in roughly three or four days and arrived on the west coast of North America. It apparently traveled on low-level currents of air at about 35 to 45 miles per hour. By the time it reached the west coast of North America, it stretched from northern California to the Canadian border, where it became integrated into a coalescing high-pressure system and parked an estimated 20 to 40 million tons of dust over the state of Washington alone. The dust cloud posed a health hazard because it consisted mostly of particles that were 2.5 microns or smaller, which made them small enough to be inhaled deeply into the lungs, where they could cause damage to delicate tissue. Even in British Columbia, officials asked residents to curtail the use of vehicles because the quality of the air was so poor in the lower Fraser Valley and lower mainland.

Could the dust cloud from Asia have been at least partially a result of human activities? Such was the case in the dust storms of the 1930s in the American Great Plains, which were a result of poor farming practices. This raises the question of how we humans are influencing the global climate.

Possible Effects of the Human Influence on Climate

The average temperature of the surface of the globe is determined by a complex of factors, including the amount of energy received from the sun, the properties on the Earth's surface that absorb the sun's heat (such as the size and distribution of oceans, snowfields, forests, and deserts), and the absorptive properties of the atmosphere. A high proportion of the energy that is absorbed by the lower atmosphere and by the Earth's surface is emitted as heat. Some of the heat passes through the atmosphere into space, but the rest is absorbed into the atmosphere and passed back toward Earth.

At the root of the predicted changes in climate is the accumulation of an array of gases in the atmosphere that trap heat as it is radiated outward from the Earth's surface. Carbon dioxide has to date received the most attention, but other gases are involved as well, including water vapor, ozone, nitrous oxide, chlorofluorocarbons, and methane.

Although there is uncertainty as to how the climate will respond, there is no doubt that greenhouse gases are accumulating. Atmospheric carbon dioxide began to rise in the latter part of the 19th century as a result of clearing forests and plowing prairies, both of which released into the atmosphere carbon dioxide that had once been stored in the living tissues of plants and in the soil. Burning of fossil fuels, such as coal, and accelerated deforestation since the 1940s have greatly exacerbated the problem.

Although public attention has focused on the problems caused by deforestation in the tropics, problems also exist in the Northern Hemisphere. On the one hand, burning of tropical forests converts about 50 percent of the badly needed nitrogen contained in the forests' biomass to a gas, which is lost from the forests to the atmosphere. It also causes vast amounts of smoke, which can alter the internal physical structure of clouds so that severe repercussions may be in store for the water cycle in the tropics. On the other hand, clear-cutting old-growth Douglas fir forests in the Pacific Northwest results in a net release of the carbon dioxide stored in the stems of the live trees into the atmosphere. It takes several centuries to recoup this loss, even when the cut forest is replaced with young, fast-growing trees in tree farms.

In many areas of the world, including parts of Canada, the United States, and Central America, logged forests are not being successfully regenerated with young trees. In Central America, for example, deforestation has been rapidly accelerating during the past three decades. If it is not slowed, there will be little but scrub forest left by the end of this century. If important areas of forest, particularly those that serve the major rivers and water catchments of the region, are not protected soon, no amount of social or economic reform will be able to provide for the many basic needs of the increasing population of the region. This also means that the carbon dioxide lost to the atmosphere by cutting the old-growth forests is not being mitigated by the capacity of young trees to use carbon dioxide and thus remove it from the atmosphere.

With a doubling of the preindustrial atmospheric concentration of carbon dioxide (which will be reached sometime during the 21st century), temperatures in the conterminous United States are predicted to increase in winter to the equivalent of a four- to six-degree shift southward in latitude. In summer, the temperature increase would be the equivalent of a 5- to 11-degree shift southward in latitude. This would be like shifting southern California to central Oregon, which is a difference of about ten degrees in latitude.

Note that a greater warming is predicted in summer than in winter. The magnitude of warming is also predicted to vary from east to west across the United States and Canada. The greatest warming will take place in the area of the Great Plains, where North Dakota may have a climate similar to that which presently exists in Texas. And what about the climate in Texas? Will it include heat waves in the future?[41]

Heat waves are given neither the catchy names assigned to hurricanes nor the dramatic media coverage devoted to tornadoes, floods, or earthquakes, but they are the deadliest form of weather. Although the hurricane that killed 6,000 people in Galveston, Texas, in 1900 is often considered to be the nation's worst natural disaster, more than 9,500 people died when a heat wave settled in the Midwest a year later. Nevertheless, heat waves seldom make the headlines because they kill people one or two at a time, which hides the enormity of the danger.

"Prolonged periods of very hot weather...claim more lives nationally than any other natural disaster, including floods, tornadoes and hurricanes," a congressional report noted a few years ago. Even so, many believe the death tolls are understated because only those who succumb directly to heat-related conditions are counted. "No one can know," according to the Weather Service, "how many more deaths are advanced by heat wave weather, how many diseased or aging hearts surrender that under better conditions would have continued functioning."

In addition, a recent study by botanists at Duke University indicates that global warming could produce drier conditions on the northern Great Plains that would probably result in grasslands spreading eastward into areas that now are forested, with a corresponding increase in wildfires.[42] In addition, the models predict a warming in the mountains that will be equivalent to roughly a 2,000- to 3,000-foot decrease in elevation. This means that most, if not all, of the subalpine and alpine areas would probably disappear in the United States south of the Canadian border.

If current trends in the emission of greenhouse gases continue, increases in carbon dioxide and the other gases are predicted to result in "doubled carbon dioxide" temperatures in less than 50 years. It is therefore the consensus of the mainstream scientific community that there is no alternative but to reduce carbon emissions.[43]

Other greenhouse gases, although less abundant in the atmosphere than carbon dioxide, have a much greater warming effect per molecule. For example, one molecule of methane has 3.7 times the potential of one molecule of carbon dioxide to warm the atmosphere. A single molecule of nitrous oxide has 180 times and chlorofluorocarbon-12 has 10,000 times the potential capacity of one molecule of carbon dioxide to warm the atmosphere.

The models of climatic change are less consistent in predicting the greenhouse effect on precipitation, which is a crucial factor in how an ecosystem will respond to changes in climate. However, it is generally agreed that warming will be greater at high latitudes than at lower latitudes. The consequence of such warming will be the narrowing of the global temperature gradient, which in turn seems likely to alter global patterns of precipitation, but what these changes might be remains unclear. Nevertheless, a warming climate, even with no change in precipitation, should increase drought because of the greater evaporative demand brought about by generally higher temperatures.

"We are already feeling the early effects of an altered climate," says Christopher Flavin of the Worldwatch Institute. In northwestern Ontario, Canada, for example, the climatic, hydrologic (refers to the scientific study of the properties, distribution, and effects of water on the Earth's surface), and ecological records for the Experimental Lakes Area show that air and lake temperatures have risen by 3.6 degrees Fahrenheit and that the length of ice-free days has increased by three weeks over the last 20 years.[44]

Further, higher than "normal" evaporation and lower than average precipitation have occurred, resulting in a decrease in the rate of renewal of water in the lakes. In addition to other changes within the lakes themselves, the concentrations of most chemicals have increased in both the lakes and the streams because of the decreased renewal of the water and because of forest fires in the water catchments. These observations may provide a preview of the warming effects of increased greenhouse gases on boreal lakes.[44]

In the Mediterranean Sea, on the other hand, a growing number of species of tropical fish are making the sea their permanent home, a migration attributed to a rise in the temperature of the water during the past 30 years, according to Icram, Italy's leading marine research center. The tropical fish, indigenous to the Atlantic Ocean off Africa and to the Red Sea, are now thriving in part because populations of fish indigenous to the Mediterranean have been weakened by a combination of overfishing and deteriorating environmental conditions.[45]

In addition, there has been a dramatic warming of Antarctica in recent decades, which has caused a chunk of Antarctic glacier the size of the state of Rhode Island to collapse into the South Atlantic. British scientists are now warning that the massive Larsen B ice sheet is breaking up in Antarctica, where temperatures are rising five time faster than the global average and grass is now growing along the edges of the icy continent. According to the British Antarctic Survey, the 8,000-square-mile ice sheet is "critically unstable" and may collapse within the next two years. Should that happen, the event could alter the warm Gulf Stream ocean current and affect the climate as far away as northern Europe.[46]

Siberia is now warmer than at any time since the Middle Ages. In northern Europe, there has been a series of warm winters and severe winter storms. Related to this warming trend is the retreat of alpine glaciers, which is exposing ice and rock for the first time in thousands of

animals whose reproductive cycles are finely tuned to the
s of renewal of these resources.

he way these patterns of flowering and/or fruiting syn-
the animals' cycles of breeding could lead to serious
these cycles. Those disruptions could lead to rates of
ove and beyond those already being experienced. Taken
her, the loss of those species of animals that act as
nd dispersers of seeds would lead ultimately to the loss
dent species of plants—in short, to the total alteration of
tal forests as habitats.

er 30,000 scientifically described species, which, of course,
at those we know nothing about, are threatened with extinc-
g to the *Global Biodiversity Assessment* of the world's fading
H genetic diversity. As a consequence, deadly diseases are
ged all over the world because natural medicines, which
aved lives, have simply vanished before their benefits could
H. In addition to the increasing number of endangered spe-
ort chronicles the loss of genes, habitats, and even entire
e[49]

ity," according to a summary of the report, "represents the
von of human existence. Yet by our heedless actions, we are
biological capital at an alarming rate."[49]

t cites an example of protecting such seemingly unimpor-
t as the day-flying moth (*Urania fulgens*) found in Mexico
america. The moth metamorphoses from a caterpillar that
ively on a particular variety of trees and vines known as
C

y defoliation caused by the feeding of the caterpillars in turn
c ants to produce a protective chemical toxin, which makes
th able to the moths. The plants' toxic compounds have been
e nst the AIDS virus in test tube experiments. There is a caveat,
h toxin is produced only when a plant interacts with a large
p of caterpillars.

g to the report, the loss of genetically distinct populations of
es poses consequences almost as serious as the loss of whole
report then cites several reasons for the decline in both
distinct populations and species themselves: (1) increased
nd economic development deplete biological resources; (2)
re to consider the long-term consequences of actions that
tat, exploit natural resources, and introduce nonindigenous

years. Also, the interior areas of northern India have experienced life-threatening summer heat waves in recent years.[38]

Beyond this, scientists from the British Antarctic Survey have measured a five-mile drop in the Earth's upper atmosphere during the past 40 years, which they say is a litmus test for change in the global climate.[47] These data were obtained from radio-wave-monitoring studies carried out in Antarctica since 1958. The scientists go on to say that they believe the shrinking is caused by cooling aloft, which is linked to heat trapped at the surface that in turn is causing global warming. The altitudinal decrease in the ionosphere, an electricity-conducting layer of the upper atmosphere, was similar to results obtained from separate studies in Europe.

During a meeting in the late summer of 1995, the Intergovernmental Panel on Climate Change concluded that "a pattern of climatic response to human activities is identifiable in the climatological record." The panel's assessment projects an additional rise of 1.4 to 6.3 degrees Fahrenheit in the average global temperature by 2100. Although the projected increase shows a wide range of variation, even at the lower end it is a faster change than any experienced since human civilization began.[38]

Although this may not seem like much of a change, the average global temperature was only 5.4 to 9 degrees Fahrenheit cooler during the last ice age than it is today. If geological history has anything to teach us, one of its most important lessons may well be that the faster the pace of global warming, the harder it will be for humanity, as well as ecological systems, to adapt to the changes.[38]

It is therefore noteworthy that the Intergovernmental Panel on Climate Change concluded in its 1995 report that any rate of change in temperature above roughly 0.18 degrees Fahrenheit per decade, which is about twice the rate of temperature increase experienced over the last century, could cause considerable havoc. Yet the upper end of the panel's projected increase in average temperature (6.3 degrees Fahrenheit) represents a rate of increase that is more than 0.54 degrees Fahrenheit.[38]

It is not so much the relatively modest increase in the projected average global temperature that is of concern to scientists, but rather the possible disruption of atmospheric and oceanic systems that regulate weather. Recent studies indicate that global warming will cause the "extremes" in climate to become more common, which will place unprecedented stress on ecosystems as well as the human economy. According to the 1995 Intergovernmental Panel on Climate Change, "the incidence of floods, droughts, fires, and heat outbreaks is expected to increase in some regions" as global warming occurs.[38]

In a time when many people live in air-conditioned homes, work in air-conditioned buildings, and eat fresh food grown hundreds or thousands of miles away, it is easy to ignore and then forget about our dependence on climate. This is especially true for people who do not travel widely. Nevertheless, people still live in areas where the supply of water is adequate, if not abundant, and their nutritional and material requirements are met. Although societies can and do cope with isolated episodes of drought, heat waves, or floods by obtaining relief supplies such as medicines, water, and food from elsewhere, simultaneous disruptions of even a moderate magnitude in several regions could be unmanageable.[38]

One possible result of disrupting the global climate is more frequent and prolonged droughts. This could exacerbate an already critical shortage of water that currently plagues 80 countries with 40 percent of the world's population, according to the World Bank. Moreover, the availability of water for agriculture is already a major constraint in many areas of the world and is getting worse as rivers and underground aquifers are gradually being depleted. And this says nothing about urban areas, which are competing for the same water.[38]

Because some of the projected scenarios about global warming show increasing drought in various areas, such as the mid-continental "Great Plains," the greenhouse effect may also alter fire regimes and in some areas contribute to an increased frequency of forest fires. There may be some difficulty, however, in determining potential effects of global warming on the fire regimes, because most historical studies, termed chronosequences, are hampered by effects of unknown historical events, which can result in erroneous interpretations.

It is therefore particularly important to study the major ecological processes in an integrated fashion, because mechanisms are interdependent. From an ecological point of view, the variability in fire regimes is more likely to be important to plant communities, especially forests, than are the mean values computed from some arbitrary period of fire history.

For example, unusually long periods without fire may lead to the establishment of species of plants that are intolerant to fire. The simultaneous occurrence of such fire-free periods and wetter climatic conditions may also be extremely important to such species of plants as ponderosa pine that have episodic patterns of regeneration (specific, discrete episodes) as opposed to plants whose patterns of regeneration form a continual, yearly process.

Therefore, while statistical summaries of fire useful in understanding the general comparisons ent forests, the influence of fire on an ecosystem process. Hence, forests of the southwestern United a product of relatively short-term and unusual period frequency than of average or cumulative periods of climate and fire frequency.

How change in the global climate will affect habitat communities living within them is not known exactve facing a change in the global climate that is predictee a speed unprecedented in human history.

In mountainous areas, for example, a predicted rise temperature would mean that subalpine and alpine hmpen sate for the increased temperature, would have to ard in elevation about 1,600 feet. That dramatic a migration w affect the plants and animals of those habitats.

Such migration would lead to a reduction in both nt and the number of areas of subalpine and alpine habitats, those animals that require large home ranges within these spts may become extinct as their habitats shrink. Given this scca two-degree rise in temperature over the next 50 years coulextinction of 10 to 50 percent of the animals now living in ne and alpine "habitat islands" on the tops of isolated moun Great Basin of the American West.

Further, the major impact of such a fast rate of come not from average changes in the weather but rattriking climate events like prolonged drought in the Amerest or increased rainfall in the Indian subcontinent. Such ange could lead to increased flooding in both India and h. though the total amount of rainfall may not be criticaturb habitats, such as forests, changes in the timing of rns rainfall would be catastrophic for many species than current weather patterns for part of their life cycdi increased temperature will cause polar ice caps to mel to rise, with potentially devastating effects on habit coastal areas and the people living there.

What would happen, one might ask, to the biodi forests if no rain falls in the wet season or if rain falls The patterns of flowering and/or fruiting of many spec be disrupted, and that disruption would dramatically species; (3) failure of economic markets to recognize and accept the true value of protecting and maintaining the variety of species; (4) increased human migration, travel, and international trade; and (5) the spread of pollution affecting the quality of air and water.

We human beings, as a young species, as relative newcomers within the world, are redrafting the evolutionary play. We are choosing the characters that will survive to perform again, those that will meet their extinction in which act, and those relative unknowns that will come from backstage to command the spotlight of the future because all habitats must now pass through the hands of time as well as the hands of human society. I say this if for no other reason than we have polluted the atmosphere and, through the air, the quality of the sun's light, the soils, and the waters of the world. And such pollution now reaches from miles above the highest mountain even to the coelacanth in the far, deep recesses of the sea!

Today, in the United States alone, some 592 species of plants and animals are threatened with extinction, and the United States is not the world's richest country when it comes to either biological or genetic diversity. In our arrogance and informed denial of the problems, such as the current political struggle over the survival of salmon in the Pacific Northwest and the international struggle over warming of the global climate, we continue to direct our impromptu play—without any real idea of the long-term consequences of what we are staging.

Be that as it may, opposition to the treaty on global warming drafted in Kyoto, Japan, is so strong in Congress that many lawmakers want to "eliminate funding *for even talking about* [emphasis added] climate change— whether in public forums or administration planning sessions."[50] "I want to keep the treaty from being implemented—front door or back door," said Representative Joe Knollenberg, R-Michigan, who drafted some of the restrictive language.

"There's no question they're [the Clinton administration] trying to make an end run around Congress," insists Robert E. Murray, president of the American Coal Company, who at a congressional hearing in July 1998 characterized global warming as a "hoax." This is also the tenor of lobbyists from industries that deal with fossil energy, who have accused the Clinton administration of trying to squeeze electric utilities and the coal industry in anticipation of a treaty on global warming. But then, much of the carbon dioxide, which is considered to be the number one heat-trapping greenhouse gas targeted by the Kyoto accord, comes from burning fossil fuels, such as coal.

Today as never before, the evolutionary script is in our hands. Through politics, we are writing, editing, and rewriting the next scene of the play, and the next, and the next. Through our motives and our behavior, we set in motion the direction in which the evolutionary tree will grow for better or ill because it is axiomatic that what we do to Nature—to places, plants, and animals—we do to ourselves.

PURPOSELY CREATED EXTINCTION

For millennia, ever since our first conscious human perception of the horizon beyond life, we have been discussing creation and extinction, life and death—at least our own. Over time, the term "extinction" has been used most often in discussing the evolution of plants and animals, including human beings. The concept of extinction seemed fairly simple; it had but one face: a form of life came into being, existed for a time, and then ceased to be. And because people tend to think of time, life, and death as linear—since we seem to have time only once—we view birth, death, and everything in between as discrete points along the linear continuum of time. In this sense, creation is conceived of as but a flicker and extinction as forever.

Extinction is thrusting itself into our consciousness, however, as a much more complicated matter than heretofore assumed. From today forward, the many faces of extinction will become reflected more and more clearly in society's mirror as contemporary Americans are forced to recognize their society's purposely caused extinctions of both species and ecological processes in the name of short-term economic/political expediency. The many faces of extinction will increasingly gain the spotlight in our lives because, as author Paul Shepard said, "we live in a world where that humility and tender sense of human limitation is no longer rewarded."

The ominous reflections of these extinctions signal the creation of a world in which society as we know it is in imminent danger not only of forming the "Museum of Extinctions" but also of becoming its curator. Unless we reverse the growing problem of global pollution, we doom ourselves as a species to the selfsame museum, and we will have made ourselves extinct by our own hand. Even with ourselves the irony is that we find a concrete entity in an individual person, but an abstract thought in humanity as a species.

Extinction: The Individual versus the Species

Humans often rush to the aid of wildlife: a whale trapped in a pocket of open water as the ice begins to freeze the polar sea, deer and elk starving during very cold and/or stormy winters, feral horses dying of thirst during severe drought. Ironically, people will mobilize to rescue animals from imminent death through Nature's impartial evolutionary processes while doing nothing to prevent the extinction of entire species through purposeful exploitation or environmental degradation.

Why will society mobilize to rescue an animal in distress yet turn its back on a whole species facing extinction? What is our "need" to rescue? I think we will find it is not as benevolent an act as we would like to think, but rather a way to reduce our discomfort with participating in the impartial ways of Nature, ways we do not understand and therefore want to control.

Deer and elk, for example, starve periodically in great numbers when they become overpopulated in relation to their food supply. To rescue them under these circumstances may relieve our stress from being out of control but will prolong the overpopulation. Our attempt to rescue is a form of participating only with the symptom, which likely will allow the cause to worsen. If, on the other hand, we do not interfere and allow Nature to treat the symptom in relationship with the cause, often created by our human tinkerings, the entire herd will rebuild toward the next moment of balance, which will last only until the next correction must be made.

We must therefore ask ourselves how we can live in the fullest measure of the moment, to say "YES" unconditionally to life, particularly when that moment is decidedly uncomfortable or even hurts. For it is by living consciously in every moment that we can participate most fully in the mutually beneficial evolution of our home planet by honoring the God-granted integrity of our fellow travelers—the nonhuman animals. Alas, even after all these thousands of years of cultural evolution, we still find it easier and more gratifying economically to drive species to extinction rather than change our thinking and consequently our behavior. Put differently, we find it easier to take rather than to share, which thus far leads inevitably to the trilogy of extinction.

The Trilogy of Extinction

George Horace Latimer wrote: "It's good to have money and the things that money can buy, but it is good [also] to check up once in a while and make sure you haven't lost the things that money can't buy."

Despite Latimer's admonition, we are today moving through an accelerated process of losing many things that "money can't buy," such as our
spirituality, the quality and livability of our environment, and our dignity
as human beings. We are also losing an ever-increasing number of fellow
travelers on our planetary home in space. Such losses come about because we are progressively linear and materialistic in our view of the
world and in our measures of success. We have accomplished all of this
through the introduction into human culture and society of economically
oriented, purposely created extinction.

The motive behind this introduction is something called conversion
potential, which is oriented almost completely toward the control of
Nature and the conversion of natural resources into economic commodities. Conversion potential dignifies with a name the erroneous notion that
Nature has no intrinsic value and must be converted into money before
any value can be assigned to it. All of Nature is thus seen only in terms
of its conversion potential. It is this distorted, fun-house-mirror view of
Nature that gave birth to the trilogy of extinction: intellectually created
extinction, the economics of extinction, and manifested extinction.

Intellectually Created Extinction

The trilogy of extinction begins in the human mind as a tiny worm of
blindness that distorts wholeness into salable parts and relegates the
"leftovers" to the trash bin. Old-growth trees are a case in point.

In Nature's forest, old trees often develop root rot, which so weakens
them that they are easily blown over by strong winds. This is how Nature
reinvests biological capital in the soil, which in turn nurtures and grows
the trees of tomorrow's forest. In the mirror of our linear, materialistic,
human-centered society, such wholesome reinvestment is seen only as
"economic waste."

Neither seeing nor understanding the life and processes of a fallen old-
growth tree as Nature reinvests it in the soil of the forest floor, economists
and people of the timber industry at large continue to seek ways of
eliminating such "wasteful loss of wood fiber." To them, trees blown over
by the wind just lie on the ground rotting and are "good to nobody."

This concept of economic waste drives the corporate/political planning
system to liquidate all possible old-growth trees because the corporate/
political pundits think of them simply as "free profit that will be wasted
if not cut and used." And there is no plan to ever again allow trees to
reach old-growth status; when they are cut, they are gone—not only the

large live tree but also the large snag (a standing dead tree) and the large fallen tree. "Intellectually created extinction" is a person's conscious thought coupled with his or her purposeful plan to eliminate something from a particular area. The effect of an intellectually created extinction too often makes a potentially renewable resource into one that is definitely finite.

In addition, the capitalistic idea of getting the maximum profit out of all resources—be they renewable or nonrenewable, such as fossil fuels—with the minimum investment is used not only to dictate but also to justify the unmitigated corporate/political exploitation of our home planet. In this vein, the purposely planned permanent liquidation of every available old-growth tree, without recompense and without replacement, to feed the corporate/political machine's appetite for free profit constitutes the "intellectually created extinction" of the world's old-growth forests.

The Economics of Extinction

Intellectually created extinction through the process of economic planning is the precursor of the economics of extinction. It leads to the completion of the trilogy in the concept of manifested extinction and is thus the epitome of the materialistic, utilitarian view of the world, a view that totally disregards the sanctity of life and its ecological/spiritual functions.

The motto of the economics of extinction is *profit over all*—even if it means the loss of most of the world's species of plants and animals and the ecological functions they perform. Liquidation pays, even in the purposeful extinction of a species; conservation costs, and cost is unacceptable to profiteers.

In North America, the "profit over all" motto is therefore the guiding force of those in the timber industry who justify the liquidation of as much of Nature's remaining old-growth forests as humanly possible. They then use this same motto to justify the conversion of the liquidated forests into economically designed croplike plantations of young trees to be harvested—theoretically, at least—over and over and over into the distant future, like fields of corn. But trees are only one part of a forest, the only part to which our distorted vision assigns "conversion potential." By converting a forest into a repetitive plantation, the rest of the forest is destroyed, its soil impoverished, and its myriad organisms and processes dismissed as useless junk and impediments to the sanctity of the profit margin.

In 1908 President Theodore Roosevelt, concerned about the "profit over all" attitude in general and the timber industry in particular, convened the first-ever meeting of all the governors of the states to address the topic of the environment. His opening address to the conference is as pertinent today as it was 90 years ago. He began:

> I welcome you to this Conference at the White House. You have come hither at my request, so that we may join together to consider the question of the conservation and use of the great fundamental sources of wealth of this Nation.
>
> So vital is this question, that for the first time in our history the chief executive officers of the States separately, and of the States together forming the Nation, have met to consider it....
>
> This conference on the conservation of natural resources is in effect a meeting of the representatives of all the people of the United States called to consider the weightiest problem now before the Nation; and the occasion for the meeting lies in the fact that the natural resources of our country are in danger of exhaustion if we permit the old wasteful methods of exploiting them longer to continue.[51]

What Roosevelt went on to say is as pertinent today as it was in 1908: "Just let me interject one word as to a particular type of folly of which it ought not to be necessary to speak. We should stop wasteful cutting of timber; that of course makes a slight shortage at the moment. To avoid that slight shortage at the moment, there are certain people so foolish that they will incur absolute shortage in the future, and they are willing to stop all attempts to conserve the forests, because of course by wastefully using them at the moment we can for a year or two provide against any lack of wood."

Roosevelt's argument was that any right-thinking parent strives to leave his or her child reasonably prepared to meet the struggle of life and a family name to be proud of. "So this Nation as a whole," said Roosevelt, "should earnestly desire and strive to leave the next generation the national honor unstained and the national resources unexhausted...."

Even in Roosevelt's time, intellectually created extinction led to the economics of extinction, which claimed the hearts and minds of those individuals who sold their souls to the corporate/political machine. Thus are the thoughts of the human mind translated into action *against* Nature. Now, almost a century later, we see the trilogy of extinction nearing completion with the visible loss of not only species but also whole ecosystems.

Manifested Extinction

How does intellectually created extinction, which leads to the economics of extinction, translate into manifested extinction? When, for example, the old-growth forests in the Pacific Northwest are liquidated, no more old trees will stand as living monarchs (Figure 16), to die and stand as large dead trees (Figure 17) and to topple as large fallen trees and lie for centuries decomposing (Figure 18), providing a kaleidoscope of habitats and performing their myriad functions as they recycle and reinvest their biological capital into the soil from which they and their compatriots grew. As the trilogy of extinction is consummated in the forest, the standing large dead tree and the large fallen tree, which are only altered

FIGURE 16 A live old-growth Douglas fir (right foreground) and a decomposing, fallen Douglas fir, which has been on the ground for well over a century. (USDA Forest Service photograph by James M. Trappe.)

FIGURE 17   A large standing dead old-growth ponderosa pine, which has stood in northeastern Oregon for several years. In the lower foreground note the woodpecker holes in the snag. (Oregon Department of Fish and Wildlife photograph.)

states of the live old-growth tree, will go the way of the oldest living thing on Earth, the old-growth monarch of the forest: down the economic hall of extinction.

And with the old-growth forest will go such species as the northern spotted owl (Figure 19) and the marbled murrelet, which have evolved

FIGURE 18 A large fallen old-growth Douglas fir. The man standing next to the fallen tree is six feet seven inches tall. (Photograph by author.)

in concert with that particular habitat. In fact, the owl and the murrelet have adapted to particular features of that habitat.

The northern spotted owl nests in tall broken-topped old-growth Douglas fir trees. The marbled murrelet, a seabird, nests on carefully selected large, moss-covered branches at least a hundred feet up in old-growth trees, with other branches close overhead to protect the nest site. The murrelet's nest tree is located several miles inland from the coast, where the murrelet feeds. Being so specialized in the selection of its reproductive habitat, neither owl nor murrelet is capable of adapting to the rapid changes wrought by the liquidation of the old-growth forest.

Now comes an interesting twist to the story. It is not only species of plants and animals that will become extinct with the liquidation of the old-growth forests; so will the "grandparent trees" (Figure 20). As young trees replace liquidated old trees in crop after crop, the ecological functions performed by the old trees, such as creation of the "pit-and-mound" topography on the floor of the forest with its mixing of mineral soil and

FIGURE 19 The northern spotted owl is tied closely to some of the habitat characteristics produced only by old-growth forests in the Pacific Northwest. (U.S. Department of the Interior, Fish and Wildlife Service, Oregon Cooperative Wildlife Research Unit photograph by Gary Miller.)

FIGURE 20 When all the grandparent trees are gone, there will be no way for large woody material to reach the floor of the forest, such as this grandparent tree whose roots have been loosened by fungus and wind. (USDA Forest Service photograph by James M. Trappe.)

organic topsoil, become extinct processes. Why? Because there are no more grandparent trees to blow over.

The "pit" in pit-and-mound topography refers to the hole left as a tree's roots are pulled from the soil (Figure 21), and "mound" refers to the soil-laden mass of roots, called a rootwad (Figure 22), suddenly projected into the air above the floor of the forest. The young trees that replace the grandparent trees are much smaller than the old trees and different in structure. They cannot perform the same functions in the same ways.

Of all the factors that affect the soil of the forest, the roughness of the surface caused by falling grandparent trees, particularly the pit-and-mound topography, is the most striking. It creates and maintains the richness of species of plants in the herbaceous understory and affects the success of tree regeneration.

FIGURE 21 Pit-and-mound topography caused when an old tree blew over in a severe wind. (Photograph by author.)

One way uprooted trees enrich the forest's topography is in creating new habitats for vegetation. Falling trees create opportunities for new plants to become established in the bare mineral soil of the root pit and the mound. With time, the fallen tree itself presents habitats that can be readily colonized by tree seedlings and other plants. Falling trees also open the canopy, and the opening allows more light to reach the floor of the forest (Figure 23). In addition, pit-and-mound topography is a major factor in mixing the soil of the forest floor as the forest evolves.

The extinction of the grandparent trees changes the entire complexion of the forest through time, just as the function of a chair is changed when the seat is removed. The "roughness" of the floor of the forest, which over the centuries resulted from the cumulative addition of pits and mounds and of fallen grandparent trees, will become unprecedentedly "smooth"— without pits and mounds, without large fallen trees (Figure 24).

Water moves differently over and through the soil of a smooth forest floor, one that is devoid of large fallen trees acting as reservoirs, storing water throughout the heat of the summer, and holding soil in place on steep slopes (Figure 25). Gone are the huge snags and fallen trees that acted as habitats for creatures wild and free. Gone are the stumps of the

FIGURE 22   Rootwad of an old-growth Sitka spruce along the Oregon Coast. For scale, a six-foot-tall man is standing to the left of center in front of the rootwad. Note the top of another fallen Sitka spruce on top of the rootwad in the upper left-hand corner of the photograph. (Photograph by author.)

grandparent trees with their belowground "plumbing systems," which guided rain and melting snow deep into the soil.

This plumbing system of decomposing tree stumps and roots comes from the frequent formation of hollow, interconnected, surface-to-bedrock channels that drain water rapidly from heavy rains and melting snow (Figure 26). As roots rot completely away, the collapse and plugging of these channels force more water to drain through the soil matrix, reducing

FIGURE 23   Western hemlock growing rapidly out of a large centuries-old buried fallen tree in an opening in the forest caused by the fall of two old-growth giants. (USDA Forest Service photograph by James M. Trappe and the author.)

soil cohesion and increasing hydraulic pressure, which in turn causes mass soil movement. These plumbing systems cannot be replaced by the young trees of plantations.

Suddenly the artistry and the ecological sustainability of Nature's ancient forest have vanished, and with their banishment go the lifestyles of a special breed of logger, log-truck driver, and mill worker, perhaps never to be replaced. Where once stood Nature's mighty forest in the parade of centuries now stands humanity's pitiful, ecologically sterile economic plantations—the epitome of the nonsustainable specialization embodied in the corporate/political motto "profit over all." Now the trilogy of extinction is complete.

A Lesson in a Box

The trilogy of extinction—beginning in secret with the hidden intellectually created extinction, passing through the hidden economics of extinc-

FIGURE 24 Fallen high-elevation old-growth Douglas fir trees. The Douglas fir with the bark on (center) fell as a live tree in a recent windstorm. The whitened Douglas fir was a standing dead tree for many years before it blew over and fell across the live tree, perhaps in the same windstorm. Large fallen trees add the diversity of "roughness" to the floor of the forest. (Photograph by author.)

tion, and completed with the visible manifestation of extinction—is a result of the linear, product-oriented thinking of our Western society. Such thinking is based on the linearity of economic and statistical theory, neither of which accounts for the novelty of Nature's creative processes, because neither economists nor statisticians understand Nature. And Nature in turn cares not a whit about the lack of understanding of economists or statisticians.

Linear economics and statistical theory focus on the wrong end of the biophysical system. They not only omit the novelty of Nature's creative processes but also omit humanity itself. This omission was recognized by Albert Einstein in 1931 when he wrote: "It is not enough that you should understand about applied science in order that your work may increase man's blessings. Concern for man himself and his fate must always form the chief interest of all technical endeavors, concern for the great un-

FIGURE 25 Remains of fallen old-growth Douglas fir lying along the contour of a gentle slope. Note the soil held in place by the presence of the fallen tree (lower right corner of photograph). This old tree is saturated with water and acts as a reservoir throughout the year. Pencil is used to indicate scale. (USDA Forest Service photograph by James M. Trappe and author.)

solved problems of the organization of labor and the distribution of goods—in order that the creations of our mind shall be a blessing and not a curse to mankind. Never forget this in the midst of your diagrams and equations."

The upshot is that we are focusing on the wrong end of the system in our attempt to "manage" it, be it a forest, a grassland, an ocean, or our society. "Management," after all, is only a metaphor through which we justify our impact on a system, whatever the system is. The concept of management allows us to focus on the desired economic product rather than the ecological processes that produced the product in the first place. In "forestry," therefore, we see only the trees, not the forest.

What, one might ask, does focus have to do with management? If you walk to the door of your living room and stop to survey the room, you see everything in your living room in focus and in relationship (the

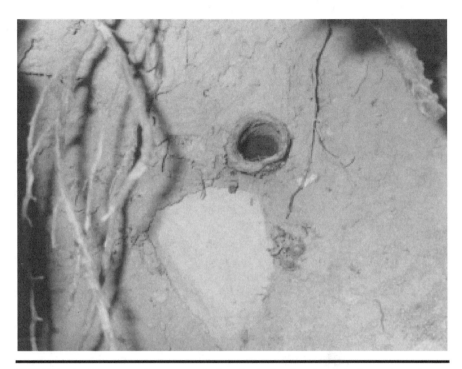

FIGURE 26 The root of a mountain hemlock that has been hollowed out by rot and acts as a conduit for water from the surface of the soil to deep within the soil. (Photograph by author.)

forest). But if you walk to the coffee table in the center of the room, pick up the newspaper, and begin to read a story on the front page (the tree), your focus on the story causes everything else in the room to effectively disappear from view—to go out of focus.

This narrowness of focus brings us to "a lesson in a box"—a box of cake mix, that is. A critical ecological lesson lies inherent in making a cake from scratch. If I were teaching a course in ecology, every student would have to learn how to make a cake from scratch because then she or he would know what ingredients go into a cake, why they are important, and why the cake comes out of the oven as it does.

Today, however, few people know how to make a cake from scratch. Instead, they buy a box of cake mix and erroneously think they have purchased a cake—which, of course, they have not. They have bought a box of some of the ingredients for a cake, but they don't know what those ingredients are, where they came from, what proportions they are in, their quality, who or what put them into the box, and whether or not everything is as it should be inside the box. They are taking all these things on faith.

Suppose you buy a box of cake mix, bring it home, and dump the contents into a bowl. Is there an instant cake in the bowl? No. Why not? Where is the cake? Then what is in the bowl? A dry, powdery mixture of some of the ingredients for a cake.

If you read the instructions on the box, you will find that you must add two eggs, a half cup of oil, one and a half cups of water, and stir. Now do you have a cake in the bowl? No. What do you have? You have the batter, a gooey blob, which consists of all the ingredients now in the bowl. But where is the cake? Why don't you have a cake?

If you continue reading the instructions on the box, you will find out that you must heat the oven to 375 degrees Fahrenheit, transfer the gooey blob to a cake pan, and bake it for 40 minutes.

When the 40 minutes has passed, you open the oven and withdraw the pan. Is there a cake in the pan? Yes. Why? What happened in the oven that did not happen in the bowl when you first emptied the contents of the box into it? First of all, you didn't have all the necessary ingredients in the box, so you had to add some. But even then something was missing: heat. It was the heat of the oven that caused the chemical interactions to take place among the ingredients, interactions that in turn caused the cake to come into being. The heat was the catalyst driving the chemical–physical processes that "created" the form and function of the cake.

The point is that you can understand a cake, including what happens when an ingredient is omitted, only when you make one from scratch, because only then can you see all the ingredients and their interrelationships among one another before and after being heated. A cactus, grass, a shrub, and a tree are much the same as a cake. Each is but the physical manifestation of the chemical–physical interactions among, in their case, a seed, soil, water, air, sunlight, climate, and time.

Thus as a bakery produces cakes, so a forest produces trees. But as a cake does not make a bakery, a tree does not make a forest. A bakery is housed in a building with electricity, water, ventilation, sewage disposal, an owner, a baker, a bookkeeper, a salesperson, delivery trucks that maintain a supply of ingredients, and so on. And part of the profits from the bakery must be reinvested in it to ensure that it functions properly if it is to continue producing cakes to sell. Now consider that if a bakery is the sum total of the chemical–physical constituents that combine to make the cakes, so a forest is the sum total of the chemical–physical constituents that combine to make the trees.

Suppose you enter the bakery as a customer with only one thing on your mind: to buy a cake. At that moment, your thinking is not only linear but also focused only on the product you want to purchase. If, however, the bakery can produce only 75 cakes a day and 76 customers, each intent on buying his or her own cake, show up, self-centered competition rules, tempers flare, and the polarization of duality sets in—mine versus yours, right versus wrong. And if one person buys two or even three cakes, for whatever reason, real trouble ensues.

So it is in a forest. Each timber company enters the forest as a customer intent only on securing as many trees for itself as possible, at the least cost, to maximize its own profits in the shortest possible time. Thus, while timber companies and "environmentalists" fight over who is going to get the last old-growth tree, for whatever reason, society loses sight of the forest and the need to understand the complexities of its processes, because all the focus is on the tree.

What society has forgotten, however, in its linear, competitive drive to harvest trees, is that the quality and the quantity of the ingredients—seeds, soil, water, air, sunlight, climate, and time—and the interactions of the chemical–biological processes among them constitute the forest, which produces the trees. This is the "lesson in a box"—the error of focusing solely on the product while ignoring, even disdaining, the processes that produced the product to begin with. What is the moral of the lesson in a box? The moral is that focusing on the products one would exploit to the exclusion of the processes that produce them is the major cause of extinctions worldwide.

Extinction as a Moral Issue

We have made the extinction of species a moral issue when it really is a biological issue, a condition of creation. And we have ignored the extinction of processes and habitats at our peril. Extinction of any biologically oriented phenomenon is as much a biological issue as is creation, and it is neither good nor bad, right nor wrong, moral nor immoral. The morality of the issue attaches not to extinction as an act but rather to the choice one makes about whether or not to cause an extinction and for what reason.

Consider that humanity purposely caused the eradication (equals extinction) of smallpox as a marvelous feat of modern medicine. Was that choice moral or immoral? Why? By the same token, if a mosquito in the old-growth forests of the Pacific Northwest were on the brink of extinction, would we halt logging? How about the northern spotted owl or the marbled murrelet? How about indigenous peoples, such as the Indians living in the rain forests of the Amazon? Where is the line of morality drawn? Where is the balance in the milieu of social values?

Consider, for example, the sentiments of the "turtle-shell artisans," craftsmen who include handicapped Japanese survivors of the World War II atomic bomb blasts.[52] They complained in 1991 that the U.S. government was "driving them to extinction" by naming the marine hawksbill turtle as an endangered species whose bodily parts it is illegal to sell or own.

The Japanese people, explained Bunki Nakakoga, president of the Nagasaki Tortoise Shell Federation, have a "special feeling" toward turtle-shell products. "America," he said, "has only a 200-year history, yet your country is going to destroy a 400-year-old technique." But critics of the turtle-shell industry saw the conflict as just one more example of Japanese refusal to acknowledge or accept moral, biological limits on resources from parts of the globe not under Japanese jurisdiction. This attitude of allowing a species to be exploited to extinction to save an industry for a little while longer is described as "village morality," in which one thinks only about one's own village.

The morality of the issue lies not in the manifested biological act but in the *intent* residing in one's soul. In turn, the extinction of a species is almost always caused by the destruction of its habitat, the morality of which stems from the *intent* of the destroyers. Although we seldom think of habitats becoming extinct, that is exactly what happens when habitats are so altered that they no longer can function in a way that sustains a particular species—or group of species.

Let's examine an example of a species on the brink of extinction because its habitat has been systematically destroyed in society's myopic pursuit of profits. The California condor once graced the sky of southern California, riding the thermals on its ten-foot wingspan. The sky is now all but empty of this majestic bird.

Personnel of the U.S. Fish and Wildlife Service have captured the last condor to give it a stay of extinction, but at the cost of its dignity. And what about our dignity? Is not our dignity linked with that of every living thing that shares the planet with us? How can our dignity be intact when we unilaterally *choose* to erase even one form of life from the Earth? Extinction is forever, and the species we make extinct have no voice in that decision.

It is difficult for me to write about the condor because I am also writing about myself and society as a whole. Both the condor and I also represent ecological functions without which the world will be impoverished. True, someone else may be able to take over my individual functional role, but what creature can take over that of the last condor? And we are more than simply creatures that perform ecological functions; we represent the health of the ecosystem.

If the condor becomes extinct, its ecological function becomes extinct, and both the condor and its function become extinct because the habitat required to keep the condor alive has become extinct, through its alteration to serve the economic gains of society at the cost of the condor's existence. All this means that the whole portion of the ecosystem of which the condor was once a part must now shift to accommodate the condor's annihilation. Do we know what this means in terms of the ecosystem? No, we do not!

What about the hundreds or thousands of species the industrialized West and Japan are making extinct around the world through the motive of "profit over all," which inevitably leads to the trilogy of extinction through the destruction of habitats? How will the ecosystem respond on a global basis to these cumulative losses? What repercussions will human society face as the ecosystem adjusts to their absence? How much of the world must we humans destroy before we learn that we are not, after all, the masters of Nature but an inseparable part of Nature and thus exist at Nature's forbearance?

Victor Frankl, a psychiatrist who survived the Nazi death camps of Auschwitz and Dachau, understood the feeling of extinction. He could remember the men who walked through the huts comforting others, giving away their last piece of bread. They may have been few in number, said Frankl, but they offered sufficient proof that everything can be taken from a human being but one thing: the last of the human freedoms, the freedom to choose one's attitude in any given set of circumstances, to choose one's own way.[53] Can the California condor choose its own way behind its prison bars, or is that right also usurped through human arrogance?

Frankl quoted a fellow prisoner who said, "There is only one thing that I dread: not to be worthy of my sufferings." The condor, by its nature, is worthy of its suffering. The question is: What have we as a society learned from its suffering?

We have relegated the condor to death row, making it pay for our iniquities and transgressions. Then, to salve our social conscience, we plucked it from the sky and put it behind bars, and we continued to destroy its habitat. Now we spend money on breeding programs and free a few individuals.

Would it not be more honest simply to restore all the remaining condors to the dignity of freedom, to watch them become extinct in the majesty of the sky, and to accept responsibility for our human failings? How else can we grow in consciousness of the effects we cause with our greedy ways than to watch the sky slowly become empty of a child of millennia, a creature that took from the beginning of our planet to perfect, to watch the sky become empty by an act of humans, not of Nature or God?

If we as a society were called before the throne of judgment today, how would we answer the questions of each species' intrinsic value in the universal balance, of the trusteeship we each inherited as custodians of our home planet for those who follow? I do not know, but I think a good place to start is to restore the condors to their birthright, the freedom and dignity of the sky. Then perhaps our consciousness will be raised a little, and their suffering and ours will have value. And should the condors survive, their survival might lead to a time in history when human society and condors can live together. But the question remains: Who makes this decision, and based on what motive?

Questions about morality, human society, and the environment are becoming more urgent in their need to be recognized, asked, and faced, because, when all is said and done, we will find that the morality of an issue lies embodied in the questions we ask. After all, the questions we ask are but the outer reflections of the inner harborings of our souls—our individual notions of morality, which are among the many faces of extinction.

The Choice Is Ours

A human social system is governed by the same Universal Laws that quite literally "grew us" and that govern the survival and evolution of all living things. This is true even though a human society is composed of individually conscious and unique beings, each of whom possesses *free will*. We have, in the short term, compounded this simple statement, however, because we have superimposed our human will onto Nature's cycles and balances in the biosphere.

That the Universal Laws govern human beings and their societies the same as they govern Nature was not understood, or perhaps even considered, when the Europeans invaded the New World. Thus it is little wonder that they spoke grandly over the decades and centuries of "clearing the land" and "busting the sod," of "harnessing the rivers" and "taming the wilds." In keeping with this mentality, they begrudged the predators a right to life—and in the process became what they were against: the most voracious predators the Earth has ever hosted. And yet they only did the best they knew how in their time and their place in history. How could they have done otherwise?

We stand today at a different time and a different place in history. We are present *now*, and we are making history. Yet even today, at the dawning of the 21st century, we fail to understand and accept that the physical and biological principles by which the world is governed function perfectly, that only our *perception* of the way the world functions is imperfect. What distorts our perception is that we focus only on that portion of the world we intend to exploit, the products, and we ignore the ecological processes that produce those products. This warped sense of Nature as a mechanical being gave rise to the platform of "deep ecology."

A group of Norwegian environmentalists, primarily the philosopher Arne Naess, introduced the term "deep ecology" in the early 1970s. The term is meant to characterize a way of thinking that approaches environmental problems at their roots in such a way that the problems can be seen as symptoms of the deepest ills of our present society.

The idea of deep ecology contrasts with "shallow ecology," which I think of as *material ecology*, because it merely addresses the symptoms through technological quick fixes, such as the installation of pollution-control devices and other regulations theoretically imposed on industry. It does nothing, however, to heal the problem. Although "new" technologies and reforms in our current political system are much easier to implement than any fundamental changes in our thinking and our materialistic sense of values, these "material solutions" and the people who propose them are clearly avoiding the heart of the problem. This avoidance of the real issues faced by human society—those seated in spiritual bankruptcy, for which there is no Chapter 11 protection—may ultimately cause the collapse of our social system.

There is a marked difference between the linear thinking of humans and the cyclical diversity of Nature, in which all parts are interactive and unified by the novelty of the creative process—particularly the spark of life—in which everything is always in the process of becoming something else. We industrialized humans have chosen the linear metaphor of a machine not only for ourselves but also for our world. While a machine has many parts, it has neither internal intelligence nor moral sense to guide it. In addition, the parts are unaware of either their purpose or their functions. And while we can usually find or make one or more "spare" parts for a machine, we cannot do so with Nature. Therefore, if the condor becomes extinct, it is extinct. There is no way to reproduce one, no matter how noble the reason.

Thinking like machines is only one step away from *living like machines*. Such a synthetic lifestyle not only alienates us from ourselves and from one another but also alienates us from Nature. In addition, such a mechanistic lifestyle leads to economic problems through the separation of social classes and to philosophical problems of the duality of thought in terms of either/or, right/wrong, and so on. Our synthetic, linear, mechanical thoughts and lifestyles pit us against Nature, which makes our lives increasingly complicated beyond the total complexity of Nature's diversity.

And it is precisely because of our mechanistic thinking that we contend we can have more and more of everything simultaneously if only we can control Nature—manage Nature, as it were. In so doing, we save the pieces we value and discard those we do not. We are thus simultaneously simplifying the biosphere and separating its parts by purposely discarding and accidentally losing pieces of it. We are redesigning our home planet even as we throw away Nature's blueprint in the form of both species and processes. In short, we focus so narrowly on the *products* that we are destroying the *processes* that produce them.

We in Western society have become so linear and mechanical in our thinking and so irrational in our knowledge and the use of it that we have forgotten that everything is defined by its relations to everything else. In the end, we must both understand and accept that everything—*everything*—is a relationship that fits precisely into every other relationship and is changing constantly. The paradox is that the only constant in life is change.

As human beings of Western society, the way we deal with and fit into this pattern of constantly changing relationships is by thinking. We must thus recognize that any human influence on the landscape or in the biosphere—positive or negative—is a product of our own thoughts, because our thoughts, after all, precede and control our actions. We do nothing without first having the thought to do it. This means that the problem of pollution, for example, is in neither the soil, water, or air but in our minds (the cause); the problem only manifests itself (the effect) in the soil, water, and air.

We cannot, therefore, find a solution through science, technology, or the activities of land management without changing our thinking, because all these things, which lie outside of ourselves, are the results of our thoughts. The only possible solutions to our social–environmental problems lie within us. Until we turn the searchlight inward to our own souls and consciously change our thinking, our motives, and our attitudes—and thus our behavior—we will only compound our problems.

CULTURE AND DIVERSITY

PART II

> *[Americans'] one primary and predominant object is to cultivate and settle these prairies, forests, and vast waste lands. The striking and peculiar characteristic of American society is, that it is not so much a democracy as a huge commercial company for the discovery, cultivation, and capitalization of its enormous territory....The United States is primarily a commercial society...and only secondarily a nation....*
>
> Emile Boutmy

For a society to function so that its human components can survive, Nature must maintain its cycles in such a way as to provide enough energy for society to use. If some of the cycles we humans tinker with and alter begin to deviate too much from the evolutionary track that Nature has established, then we tend to introduce "corrections": we seek new sources of energy, we nurture new varieties of plants, and we invent new modes of production.

When, however, enough human-altered cycles break down simultaneously, we must call into question the logic of our social system itself. Such scrutiny is wise, because what society thinks of as "corrections" are really self-reinforcing feedback loops, the outcome of which is not necessarily in keeping with our desires, regardless of what we try to do. Human societies therefore either transform themselves in a truly corrective

173

sense—evolve in a culturally moral sense, realigning themselves with the Universal Laws that sustainably integrate the diversity of life—or they vanish.

Life and society are tenable as long as a particular human population remains within the biological carrying capacity of its habitat, where carrying capacity is the number of individuals that can live in an area without degrading the ecological processes and thus the habitat that supports them. When, however, the limits of carrying capacity are exceeded, the social system must (1) change and correct the way it overtaxes the environment's source of energy; (2) disappear into its smaller, more strongly bound components, such as tribes, families, or even individuals; or (3) become extinct.

To survive, all societies must evolve in response to environmental changes, usually those brought about by their own activities. So far, groups of humans have passed through stages of gathering food, hunting, nomadic herding, agriculturalization, industrialization, and now postindustrialization. Each stage has had a successively greater impact on the environment, and each cultural shift has brought with it the need to transcend the socially created environmental problems it has caused.

Today as never before, the environmental transgressions of a few powerful societies like the United States, Japan, and Europe affect the whole world. Human society as we currently know it, in all its various stages of cultural evolution and technological development, stands at the crossroads of extinction.

If the industrialized nations insist on maintaining their present course of environmental destruction, human societies, including ours, will collapse. If, on the other hand, we humans are wise enough to transcend our destructive ways, we can, through conscious decisions, create the opportunity for our societies to evolve more harmoniously into the future than might otherwise be possible. Such harmony would entail a cooperative, coordinated global undertaking—beginning here, at home, in the United States.

Note that I have used the word "evolve" in connection with human society, despite the fact that I have been resoundingly criticized in the past for using the concept of evolution in such a connection because, I am told, society cannot, by any ecological criteria, be regarded as evolutionary as it in no way adapts us for a better life on our home planet. I contend, however, that evolution is also a process of "weeding out" those species that cannot cope with life as it is presented to them by Nature.

Extinct species, archived in the fossil record, did not survive because they were confronted by a given suite of circumstances and were ill adapted to cope with them. Here an interesting question might be asked: Did they, through conscious choice, cause their own demise? Probably not; they simply could not adequately adapt when adaptation was the requirement of life.

Now consider us, *Homo sapiens*. We are so adaptable that we have changed the world more than any species before us, and we continue to do so. Through our incredible adaptability, we are causing changes in the world that are proving to be deleterious to the health and sustainability of our very life-support system. For us, therefore, the question is: Are we so adaptable that we will, through the decisions we make, be both the authors and the chroniclers of our own demise? Put differently, are we weeding ourselves out of the evolutionary parade because for a time—a very short time geologically speaking—we can exert just enough control over Nature's processes that we think ourselves invincible and are thus so blinded by our own arrogance that we are writing our own evolutionary tragedy? It has happened with whole civilizations in the past. What is there to prevent it from happening to *Homo sapiens*, as a species, in the future—unless we ourselves consciously prevent it?

CULTURE, DIVERSITY, AND EVOLUTION 5

The independence with which cultures evolve creates their uniqueness not only within themselves but also within the reciprocity they experience with their environments. Each culture and each community within that culture affects its environment in its own peculiar way and is accordingly affected by the environment in a particular way. So it is that distinct cultures in their living create in the collective a varied culturalized landscape, which in some measure is reflected in the myths they hold and the languages they speak.

For us and our children and our children's children to continue protecting the historical context of our cultural evolution, we need to protect one aspect of our culture that we normally neglect: language. Perhaps one of the greatest feats of humanity is the evolution of language, especially written language, which not only made culture possible but also archives its history.

Language, which we seem to take for granted, is not something we generally think of as becoming extinct. And yet languages are disappearing all over the world, especially those of indigenous peoples that are spoken languages only. As languages disappear, so too do the cultural variations of the landscape they allowed, even fostered, because a unique culture cannot exist without its own unique language to protect its history and guide its evolution.

LANGUAGE: THE KEY TO CONSCIOUS EVOLUTION AND TECHNOLOGICAL DEVELOPMENT

Of all the gifts of life, language is one of the most incredible. I can, in silence, understand what I think you wish me to know when you write to me. And I can perceive what I think your thoughts are and ask for clarification when you speak to me. You speak and you write, and you allow me to share a small part of you.

Through language, we can create, examine, and test concepts, those intangible figments of human thought and imagination. Concepts can only be qualified, not quantified; only interpreted, not measured. And concepts can be requalified and reinterpreted hundreds, even thousands of years after they were first written. Language thus guides thought, perception, and our sense of reality by archiving knowledge.

Knowledge, in turn, is the storehouse of ideas, and language is the storehouse of knowledge. Language therefore allows each succeeding generation to benefit from the knowledge accrued by generations already passed. It is a tool, a catalyst, a gift from adults to children. By means of language, each generation begins farther up the ladder of knowledge than the preceding one.

One of the greatest values of knowledge is that it allows us to search for truth, while language allows us to share our knowledge as we strive to attain those ideals that we, as a society, perceive to be right and just. In this sense, language has become an imperative for the survival of human society, not only because the tenets of society are founded on language but also because our understanding of the interconnectedness of everything in Nature and our place in the scheme of things is founded on the same language. We simply must understand one another if our respective societies are to survive.

Every human language—the master tool representing its own culture—has its unique construct, which determines both its limitations and its possibilities in expressing myth, emotion, and logic. So long as we have the maximum diversity of languages, we can see ourselves—the collective human creature, the social animal—most clearly and from many points of view in a multitude of social mirrors. And who knows when an idiom of an obscure language, a "primitive" cultural solution, or the serendipitous flash of recognition spurred by some ancient myth or modern metaphor may be the precise view necessary to resolve some crisis in our "modern" global society.

A case in point is the mystery of the way Mayan farmers fed their huge population in the tropical forest of the Yucatán peninsula. Rather than cutting down the forest and practicing the destructive slash-and-burn agriculture of today, they managed the tropical rain forests with ecological acumen and cultural harmony long before the Spanish conquistadors set foot in the New World.

The Mayans practiced sustainable agriculture for centuries by constructing *pet kotoob* (plural of *pet kot*, Mayan for "round wall of stone"). These constructions are rock walls two to three feet high enclosing a small area about the size of a backyard garden. Within these *pet kotoob*, the Mayans grew many kinds of agricultural plants not native to the region.

The *pet kotoob* offers today's farmers in the Yucatán peninsula a form of sustainable tropical agriculture and forest management should they choose to create them, but only because the "tool"—*pet kotoob*—is still alive. What if the word *pet kotoob* had been lost to antiquity, and with the word the idea had become extinct?

How many potential answers, how much ancient wisdom, will be lost, because we are losing languages, especially obscure, "primitive," or indigenous ones, to "progress"? As languages become extinct, we lose their cultural knowledge along with their perceptions and modes of expression. Because language is the fabric of culture, when a language dies, the demise of the culture is imminent.

One such dying language is that of the coastal Tlingit Indians of southeastern Alaska.[54] Richard and Nora Dauenhauer have raced against time to collect the Tlingits' tales before the language dies with the few elders who still speak it. Nora remembers when speaking her native Tlingit tongue brought punishment at school and shame on the streets. Now it is too late for Tlingit to survive as an everyday language. To survive at all, it must be preserved as literature.

Nora began collecting Tlingit stories in the 1960s, and only 3 of the 12 elders whose tales are printed were living when Richard and Nora were interviewed in 1987. "We only know of two young men who can speak Tlingit, two under the age of 40. All of us who can speak it are now grandmothers," Nora said.

With the loss of each language, we also lose the evolution of its logic and its cultural myths and rituals—the metaphors of Creation that give the people a sense of place within the greater context of the Universe. Each time we allow another human language to become extinct we are losing a facet of understanding, a facet of our collective selves. As a global society we are slowly making ourselves blind not only to ourselves and to one another but also to our relationship within the Universe.

Our growing blindness through the extinction of languages is exacerbated by the global spread of such languages as English, German, and French. They are replacing more obscure ones at a tremendous cost of lost cultural history, lost myths, and lost human dignity.

Some people have been pushing English as the "official language" in America.[55] Those who support the "English-only" movement claim that "bilingualism creates cultural divisions and hinders new immigrants' abilities to assimilate," but critics believe the English-only movement is a cover for racism. This may well be so, for as poet Allen Ginsberg said, "Whoever controls the language, the images, controls the race." Regardless of the motive, to lose one's cultural myths, which only one's own language can adequately portray, is to lose one's sense of place and identity in the human family and in the Universe.

If diversity at some point does equate to the stability of a dynamic society, we are simplifying and therefore destabilizing society not only through the loss of languages and their cultures but also through the proliferation of a few chosen languages. Both of these things are destroying the spiritual vitality of humanity's cultural myths and the rituals on which they are founded, which brings us to the notion of "evolution" versus "development" as it pertains to modern societies.

EVOLUTION VERSUS DEVELOPMENT

I know that I am, in some people's minds at least, on thin ice in attempting to make a distinction between evolution and development, but I think it is a necessary risk. In fact, I think the distinction has already been made by General Omar Bradley of World War II fame, who once said: "We have grasped the mystery of the atom and rejected the Sermon on the Mount....The world has achieved brilliance without conscience. Ours is a world of nuclear giants and ethical infants. We know more about war than we do about peace, more about killing than we know about living." This is but saying that our intellectual ingenuity (the basis of our material/technological development) has far outstripped our moral ascendancy (*how we use* that material/technological development, which is the basis of our evolution). I thus see the notion of development, as it is most often used today, being subservient to but part of humanity's evolutionary process.

WHAT IS MEANT BY DEVELOPMENT?

Of the several facets reflected in the term "development," we in the United States have chosen to focus on a very narrow one: development as material growth through centralized industrialization, which we glibly equate with social "progress" and economic health. The narrowness of this view is, I believe, behind the notion of "developed" versus "developing" nations.

"Progress," writes Buddhist monk Bhante Y. Wimala, "is like a race without a finish line, a road without a destination. We are all frantically rushing, but we don't know exactly where we are heading." Wimala goes on to say that the "pursuit of progress is a meaningless mission that wastes a precious life" because we are "trying to run faster than what nature has prepared us for."

I have over the years worked in a number of countries without giving much thought to the notion of "progress" in the sense of "developed" versus "developing" or, as some would put it, "underdeveloped," although I have spent time in both. During a trip to Malaysia, however, I was profoundly struck by the arrogance and narrowness of such thinking.

Malaysia is the only place in which I have ever heard the people refer to their own country as "developing," as though they are somehow behind the "developed" countries and must somehow "catch up" to be equal. Yet the Malaysians have a national unity the likes of which I have never before seen, not even in the United States, where all my life I have been taught about and heard about an equality that is not practiced.

Malaysia is as great a mixture of cultures, national origins, and religions living in as small a space as I have ever seen. Yet when I asked people what their ethnic background was, their answers—to a person—reflected national unity. They referred to themselves as Malaysian Chinese, Malaysian Indians, Malaysian Sri Lankans, and so on. Were I to ask people the same question in the United States, however, the response would be Afro-American, Chinese American, Japanese American, German American, Italian American, and so on. While the difference may be subtle, it is profound. The Malaysians focus on their unity, while we in the United States focus on our divisiveness.

On any given day in Malaysia, I might eat my breakfast the Malay way, using both hands, with a spoon in one and a fork in the other. At lunch, I might eat with chopsticks, and at supper, I might eat as much of the world eats, with my right hand as the only utensil. There were even four one-hour evening news programs on separate channels, one each in Malay, Indian, Chinese, and English. Of course, there are social problems, but I have never before experienced such integration of differences into an amalgamative sense of wholeness.

As a guest and stranger in Malaysia, I felt that sense of wholeness encompass me. I felt welcomed and accepted for what I am—not who I am. In a strange, undefinable way, I felt more at ease and at one with the people of Malaysia as a whole than anywhere I have ever been.

If this is not development, in what I would call the social evolutionary sense, I do not know what is! But then it depends on how one defines development. If development is defined as a certain material standard of living based on the consumerism of centralized industrialization, Malaysia is indeed behind the United States, despite the fact that it was a British colony until the 1960s. But if development is defined as social civility and tolerance, the United States, compared to Malaysia (a nation far younger than the United States), is a developing country.

And what about indigenous peoples who not only have civility and tolerance but also have a long-term sustainable relationship with their environment. Are they not developed?

It is ironic that the very people who consider themselves to be developed and therefore "civilized" are the ones who have so ruthlessly destroyed the cultures of those they unilaterally brand as "undeveloped" and therefore necessarily "uncivilized." Fortunately, despite the continuing onslaught of "civilized" peoples, there are a few remaining indigenous ones who are still relatively uncontaminated by "development," some of whom live in the deserts of Australia and the jungles of South America, as well as other parts of the world.

I say fortunately, albeit they are severely endangered, because there is much about development and sustainability that we in the industrialized world can *relearn* from them. After all, our ancestors were also at one time indigenous tribal people. Our problem of late is that we have forgotten most, if not all, of the wisdom they once knew. And it is precisely this loss of ancient wisdom that is forcing us to focus on a contemporary question: How must we view development if the concept is to be equitable and sustainable?

Make no mistake, "develop," "developed," and "development" must be viewed by all parties as equitable if development is ever to become sustainable because technological development is making society not only ever-more specialized and unjust but also ever-more vulnerable to social collapse. And yet we continue to march from generalization toward ever-narrower specialization without regard to the necessary balance between the two.

THE MARCH OF CULTURES

6

Although the genus *Homo* emerged "only" about 2.5 million years ago and modern humans, *Homo sapiens*, around 120,000 years ago, it has become remarkably adaptable and successful. Unlike most genera, which exist somewhere between five and ten million years before fading into extinction as other genera take over, we modern humans face no such immediate threat of extinction. There is a caveat to this comforting statement, however; one must count as a threat all the cumulative, unintended consequences of our own technological developments, such as pollution of the air, water, and soil and the increasing number of chemical-resistant diseases, through which we are making our home planet unfit for our own existence.

Having to add this caveat calls to mind two telling sentences in the journal *Science*: "Ecologists traditionally have sought to study pristine ecosystems to try to get at the workings of nature without the confounding influences of human activity. But that approach is collapsing in the wake of scientists' realization that there are no places left on Earth that don't fall under humanity's shadow."[56]

Here one might ask what is meant by "the confounding influences of human activity."[57] Overprescribing antibiotics is fast helping bacterial and viral disease organisms to mutate so medicines no longer work when they are really needed. Resistance to antibiotics is a worldwide problem that appears "to be on the verge of desperation," said Nobel laureate Joshua Lederberg, who chaired a panel of top bacterial experts convened by the private Institute of Medicine, at the request of the U.S. government, to monitor the issue.

Although doctors once predicted that antibiotics would vanquish infectious diseases, the "bugs" are rapidly overwhelming today's medicines:

- Over 90 percent of the strains of *Staphylococcus aureus* are resistant to penicillin and other related antibiotics.
- Forty percent of the strains of pneumococcus, a bacterium that causes pneumonia, are partly or completely resistant to multiple antibiotics in some parts of the United States.
- A growing number of disease organisms are developing resistance to vancomycin, the antibiotic of last resort.

Despite several years of repeated warnings, overuse of antibiotics is the main reason disease organisms are becoming immune to drugs—and the culprits are not just doctors and patients. Antibiotics are overused in animals raised for food. The new trend of putting germ-resistant coatings on toys, high chairs, and other items used by children may also be a problem, according to Gail Cassell, vice president of Eli Lily & Company.

In fact, Dr. James Hughes, director of the National Center for Infectious Diseases at the Atlanta Centers for Disease Control and Prevention, looking at one infinitesimal but important aspect of humanity's existence on Earth, says: "Today, we have only one drug to treat some infections. Once they become resistant to this drug, then we will basically be back in the preantibiotic era."[58]

The evolution of chemical-resistant diseases is but one infinitesimal cumulative effect of humanity's domination of the Earth.[59] Jane Lubchenco, a professor of zoology at Oregon State University and one of four contributors to an article in *Science* on the human domination of ecosystems, said recently that "too many people, from the general public to global political leaders, have not yet realized that the problems facing the Earth's environment are mounting rapidly and greatly transcend those of the past." Lubchenco went on the say, "Altogether, these problems threaten Earth's most important role—and perhaps one most taken for granted—as a life support system."

The problem is not singular—not just global warming or depletion of the ozone layer, pollution of the oceans or extinction of species, or the increasing degradation of our forests, farmlands, fisheries, and supplies of potable water. The problem is cumulative—the synergistic effect of all the above elements and many others because we humans dominate the planet as never before, not only by virtue of our numbers but also by virtue of the way we use energy and resources and generate waste.

There are several points of relative scientific certainty that underscore the severity of the above-mentioned problems: (1) between one-third and one-half of the surface of the land has been altered by human activities, which is the overall driving force behind the loss of biological and genetic diversity worldwide; (2) concentration of carbon dioxide in the atmosphere has increased nearly 30 percent since the beginning of the Industrial Revolution; (3) over half of all the accessible fresh water on the surface of the Earth is used by humanity; and (4) roughly one-quarter of all the species of birds on Earth have been driven to extinction by such human activities as alteration of habitats.

Changes such as these are now coming home to haunt us in the guise of global warming, new and drug-resistant diseases, and degradation and collapse of ecosystems that provide food, water, shelter, or fuel for humanity. A compelling example of the interactive linkages among environmental degradation, human health, and economics, said Lubchenco, is illustrated by the provision of drinking water for New York City. Filtration and purification of water used in New York City were once provided free by the water catchment of Catskill Mountain, but now a study shows that it may cost $1 billion just to restore that water catchment, or up to $8 billion in capital costs, as well as an additional $300 million annually, to perform the same function artificially.

"And," according to Lubchenco, "that calculation only considers the cost of replacing a single function of this single watershed. It does not include the flood control, air purification, soil generation, timber, recreation, inspiration, and education also provided by that forest [of Catskill Mountain]."

In addition, humanity's modifications of species and genetically distinct populations of organisms are substantial and growing without bounds. Although extinction and genetic modification are natural, biological processes, the current rate of loss of genetic variability of populations and of species is far above the rate prior to the advent of modern human society. This loss is not only ongoing but also represents a wholly irreversible global change. At the same time, people are transporting species around the world, introducing them into new areas, where they can—and often do—disrupt existing systems, and in the process people are homogenizing the once diverse richness of local indigenous species.

Many introductions of exotic species into local areas are effectively irreversible because once an introduced species becomes reproductively successful in a new area, eradicating it is difficult and expensive at best. Moreover, introductions of some species have undreamed of consequences, such as degrading the health of humans and indigenous species; after all, most infectious disease-causing organisms are introduced as exotics over most of their geographical distributions. Other introduced species cause economic losses amounting to billions of dollars; the zebra mussel is a well-publicized example. Some exotics disrupt biological processes and in so doing alter the structure and thus the function of entire ecosystems. Finally, the introduction of exotic species is a major driving force—after human alteration of habitats—in the loss of indigenous populations of species, as well as whole species themselves.

The upshot is that the rates, scales, kinds, and combinations of changes being wrought by humanity are fundamentally different from those at any other time in history. We are changing the composition, structure, and function of the Earth more rapidly than we are perhaps able to understand—or grasp the consequences. Here a critical lesson in prudence might be usefully gleaned from the notion that we, like a successful parasite, cannot afford to kill our host—planet Earth.

As we the people become increasingly aware of the silent, often hidden, values of a healthy environment and the huge cost of trying to replace any of its functions, which is all but impossible without losing still other hidden functions because there is no such thing as an independent variable, one can hope that we the people will begin to take those values less for granted and become more responsible in our behavior to protect them. In Seattle, Washington, for example, the old adage "waste not, want not" is taken seriously, and garbage is now weighed. The less it weighs, the less you pay to have it removed. The sooner we begin to accept and face these problems, the more options we will have not only for ourselves but also to pass to our children.

Even having said this, I suspect humanity as a species can probably continue living on planet Earth for thousands of years, but human society is sick and in crisis. The culmination of the crisis may well cause the extinction of today's dominant social systems (witness the collapse of the former Soviet Union) and the emergence of new ones. The point is that human beings are generalists, while human societies are specialists. The distinction between the two is both precise and critical.

A generalist, in either a biological species or a biological system, can survive under a wide range of environmental circumstances, can use numerous kinds of energy, and can either fit itself to a wide variety of conditions or fit a wide variety of conditions to itself. A specialist, on the other hand, is fitted to a highly specific set of circumstances within its environment and can derive and use only certain kinds of energy to certain ends.

We as members of the human species are about the most successfully adaptable generalists on Earth. People live in the frozen tundra and along the sea ice above the arctic circle, throughout the temperate forests and plains, in the hot deserts, and in the depths of steaming tropical jungles. We live on every continent and at every latitude between the two polar circles, and we have found cures for enough diseases to vastly increase our numbers and our longevity. In addition, we are generalists in the social sense because we have built and live in societies ranging from nomadic food-gathering tribes to sophisticated postindustrial civilizations and from raw military dictatorships to "grass-roots" democracies.

Although we as individuals and as a species are adaptable generalists, our modern societies are becoming more and more rigidly specialized as we allow ourselves personally to become specialized not only through our professions but also through our technology. I have observed, for instance, that a politician who "creates" jobs and takes credit for his or her accomplishment seldom accepts equal responsibility for the built-in obsolescence of those same jobs. Yet the more specialized the jobs are, the more certain is their built-in obsolescence, which means that many people holding those jobs are destined to become outdated. Ultimately, therefore, those people will again be out of work when the economy changes, when the need for their jobs disappears, or when the resources on which their jobs depend, such as old-growth forests and large stocks of fish, run out.

Because change is inevitable and because there are few "guaranteed" jobs for specialists, other than undertakers, over the long term, one is wise to remain adaptable. Nevertheless, specialists appear to have an advantage in the job market in the short run, while generalists have a corresponding disadvantage. But generalists have a great advantage in the long run because rather than being rigidly set in their ways (as are most specialists), they are versatile and open to learning many things. Such versatility allows generalists to flow with unforeseen changes and makes them rich in the experience of life, while specialists too often become encrusted in their specialities and are increasingly cut off from the experiences of life.

In graduate school, for example, I chose natural history, the broadest and most integrative area of the biological sciences that I could find, because I wanted to study as many aspects of life as I could without being forced into an ever-narrowing mental box. I was, however, told by one professor, who specialized in physiology, that my interests were all "Indian lore" and that we had learned all we needed to know about that a century ago. Then one day, this same professor called and asked me to come to his laboratory, where he explained that he had just worked out how the kidney of a particular animal functioned. Although he was excited by his findings, he asked me what kind of animal it was and what significance for the animal's survival its unique renal function might have.

To the extent that individuals become rigid specialists, communities and society at large become rigidly specialized. This specialization is increasingly apparent through the unfolding impact of the global division of labor and the centralization of global corporate politics, where mergers are placing more and more control in the hands of fewer and fewer people at the tremendous social expense of humanity as a whole. In contrast, a Stone Age village and its neighbors could care for every basic need of its people. Short of such catastrophic disturbances as floods and volcanic eruptions, the Stone Age folk could cope with the vicissitudes of Nature.

Today, however, fewer than perhaps a dozen societies (excluding pockets of pure indigenous cultures) can produce enough food to supply the necessities of their own population, and the same can be said of energy, water, wood products, transportation, and communication, not to mention the myriad consumer goods most people seem to regard as their birthright. When societies are economically specialized and thus inexorably interdependent because of that specialization, they are more or less at the mercy of other societies for the items they lack. Japan, for example, offers high technology in exchange for almost everything else it needs to survive as a modern society. An example of the other side of the coin is Gambia in West Africa, whose economy depends on the export of groundnuts. There, a crop failure spells economic disaster.

The interdependence of societies in the political arena is much more obvious. Almost no country today, including the United States, thinks it can any longer assure its own materialistic defense without military allies, strategic bases, earth-circling spy satellites, and networks of collaborating intelligence agencies—all of which create and maintain what is increasingly apparent to be not peace but a balancing act of trying to contain apparently random and carefully orchestrated global violence and the terror it embeds in people's hearts and souls.

The increasing specialization in almost all dimensions of contemporary societies makes them more and more vulnerable to collapse from economically powerful competition and/or sudden changes in the environment itself. Specialists are unstable and subject to extinction (unemployment) as their usefulness comes and goes, such as the logger when the trees run out, whereas generalists continually improvise, adapt, and adjust to new ways.

Modern human societies are lured into specialization by the linear thinking of quick monetary gains and materialistic security implied by industrialization. Today's societies, each strongly interdependent on one another as they live side by side, have created an inherently precarious global social system. When we add to this already precarious system the introduction of new technologies of production and communication that further isolate us from one another as human beings, the system becomes risky in the extreme, and the imminence of a systemwide social crisis should come as no surprise.

Since World War II, social specialization has been global. Society has become specialized and interdependent in the way it extracts resources from Nature; in the way it cultivates Nature; in the way it uses energy, food, and raw materials; in the way it builds dwellings and cities; and in the way it disposes of its own wastes. This is an unstable social system at risk of extinction; again witness the collapse of the former Soviet Union. Another system could take its place, however, because humanity itself is a generalist and is not condemned to live and die in the superspecialized societies it has created in the postwar era. This may all be well and good, but how did we get to here in the first place? It began with the first purposeful cultural alteration of a landscape.

THE CULTURALIZATION OF LANDSCAPES

As human beings, we are continually changing the landscape in which we live. The ways in which we change the landscape depend on the level of our consciousness of the effects we cause when our thoughts are translated into decisions, which are in turn translated into actions. In the beginning, for example, humanoids (creatures resembling humans) had relatively little impact on the landscapes in which they lived. Their impact increased as they evolved languages, cultures, and societies, because through these devices they could participate with Nature in more intensely organized ways. Today, the human species has essentially altered the landscapes of the entire world through airborne and waterborne pollution and through the unbridled exploitation of Nature's bounty.

Human society changes the dynamics and the design of every land-scape with which it interacts, and it has been doing so for thousands of years. The history of England is an example.[60] About 330,000 years ago, the early humanlike creature *Homo erectus* was already living in what today is England, which was at that time attached to the European continent. As the Pleistocene epoch drew to a close between 12,000 and 10,000 years ago, the ice withdrew, although not in a single smooth recession. During this time, Paleolithic cultures ("Old Stone Age," earlier than 12,000 years ago) of "modern humans" (*Homo sapiens*) occupied the warmer places in the south of what today is England, where they seem to have had an ecological impact with their selective dependence on wild horses and reindeer for food and raw materials.

As the climate ameliorated, the trees that had survived the glaciation in southern Europe and the Caucasus gradually returned to the once glaciated areas until climax-stage mixed deciduous forest was established about 8,000 years ago. The Caucasus is the region between the Black Sea and the Caspian Sea, which covers some 154,250 square miles in extent.

Then about 7,000 years ago, that part of the European continent that today is England separated from the mainland. Mesolithic hunter-gatherers (Middle Stone Age, between 12,000 and 5,000 years ago) still inhabited the newly formed island, and they remained until the coming of agriculture about 5,000 years ago.

The earliest cultural landscapes of the area—those purposely manipulated with fire—were formed in the middle to late Mesolithic period, between 7,000 and 5,000 years ago. As far as we know, that first cultural landscape came from the conversion of a mixed deciduous forest into a mosaic of high forests, open-canopy woodlands, and grassy clearings with fringes of scrub and bracken fern, patches of wet sedge, and bogs of peat. Among these habitats, groups of late Mesolithic peoples without knowledge of crop-based agriculture moved about gathering food.

The coming of agriculture from Asia around 5,000 years ago was one of the great turning points in western Europe, the beginning of the Neolithic or New Stone Age culture, which began with the advent of agriculture. For Neolithic people, the advent of agriculture was not gradual. Instead, the full complement of agricultural tradition and myth probably came as a fully developed package from the East, even if accessory hunting persisted. The model of the earliest agriculture in western Europe is a mosaic of small clearings, which were abandoned as the fertility of the soil became exhausted or the weeds became too bothersome. As new clearings were made, abandoned ones reverted to forest. And so began, in that far distant time, the humble tinkerings with the environment in which humans attempted to gain greater control of their destiny; the cumulative effects of such tinkerings through the millennia have become the human-caused fragility of ecosystems.

FRAGILITY OF ECOSYSTEMS

Ecosystems are designed by the *variability of the variability* of natural phenomena, such as volcanoes, climate, fires, floods, and the cyclical nature of populations of organisms; they are not designed by the predictable averages of anything. Ecosystems are designed by novelty and uncertainty, not by static surety.

In addition, while incremental changes in an ecosystem may seem to us humans to be insignificant and their effects for a time to be invisible, ecosystems operate on thresholds with unknown margins of safety. Once a threshold is crossed, however, it is crossed. There is no going back to the original condition. It is thus necessary to understand something about the relative fragility of simplified ecosystems as opposed to the robustness of complex ones.

Fragile ecosystems can go awry in more ways and can break down more suddenly and with less warning than is likely in robust ecosystems, because fragile systems have a larger number of components with narrow tolerances than do robust ones. As such, the failure of any component can disrupt the system. Therefore, when a pristine ecosystem is altered for human benefit, it is made more fragile, which means that it will require more planning and maintenance to approach the stability of the original system. While sustainability means maintaining the critical functions performed by the primeval system, or some facsimile thereof, it does not mean restoring or maintaining the primeval condition itself.[61]

If one looks at ecosystems along a continuum of naturalness (the most pristine being the most natural end of the continuum and the most humanly altered being the most cultural end of the continuum), the notion of system fragility not only makes sense but also offers humanity a range of choices. And it is, after all, the array of choices that one generation passes to the next that conveys the sustainability of potential outcomes.

For example, the less we humans alter a system to meet our necessities, the more the system's functional requirements are met internally to itself. This in turn makes it easier and less expensive in both time and energy (including money) to maintain that system in a relatively steady state because we have maintained more of the diversity of native flora and fauna than we might otherwise have done.

Conversely, the more altered a system is, the more that system's functional requirements must be met through human-mediated sources external to itself. This in turn makes it more labor intensive and more expensive to keep that system in a given condition because we have maintained less, often far less, of the diversity of native flora and fauna than we would otherwise have done.

But why, I am often asked, do we need such a variety of species? What effect does a variety of species have on an ecosystem anyway? Because this question is such an important one, I will briefly reiterate some points from Part I of this book.

One marvelous effect a variety of species has is increasing the stability of ecosystems through feedback loops, which are the means by which processes reinforce themselves. Strong, self-reinforcing feedback loops characterize many interactions in Nature and have long been thought to account for the stability of complex systems. Ecosystems with strong interactions among components, which are contributed by feedback loops, can be complex, productive, stable, and resilient under the conditions to which they are adapted. When these critical loops are disrupted, such as in the extinction of species and the loss of their biological functions, these same systems become fragile and easily affected by slight changes.

It is the variety of species that creates the feedback loops. That is what makes each individual species so valuable. Each species by its very existence has a shape and therefore a structure, which in turn allows certain functions to take place, functions that interact with those of other species. All of this is governed ultimately by the genetic code, which by replicating species' character traits builds a certain amount of redundancy into each ecosystem.

Redundancy means that more than one species can perform similar functions. It is a type of ecological insurance policy, which strengthens the ability of a system to retain the integrity of its basic relationships. The insurance of redundancy means that the loss of a species or two is not likely to result in such severe functional disruptions of the ecosystem so as to cause its collapse because other species can make up for the functional loss. But there comes a point, a threshold, when the loss of one or two more species may in fact tip the balance and cause the system to begin an irreversible change. That change may signal a decline in quality or productivity.

Although an ecosystem may be stable and able to respond "positively" to the disturbances in its own environment to which it is adapted, this same system may be exceedingly vulnerable to the introduction of foreign disturbances (often those introduced by humans) to which it is not adapted. We can avoid disrupting an ecosystem supported by feedback loops only if we understand and protect the critical interactions that bind the various parts of the ecosystem into a functional whole.

Diversity of plants and animals therefore plays a seminal role in buffering an ecosystem against disturbances from which it cannot recover. As we lose species, we lose not only their diversity of structure and function but also their genetic diversity, which sooner or later results in complex ecosystems becoming so simplified they will be unable to sustain us as a society. Therefore, any societal strategy aimed at protecting diversity and its evolution is a critically important step toward ensuring an ecosystem's ability to adapt to change. Diversity counts. We need to protect it at any cost.

Although ecosystems can tolerate cultural alterations, those functions that have been disrupted or removed in the process (often through a loss of species) must be replaced through human labor if the system is to be sustainable. The more a system is altered and simplified, the more fragile it becomes and the more labor intensive its maintenance becomes. When alterations exceed the point at which human labor can maintain the necessary functions, the system collapses.

Collapse in this case means that it becomes something other than that for which it was originally groomed, and in the process, it becomes nonproductive of that for which it was altered. The degree of human alteration determines which way a system will go, either back toward its original condition or toward something totally different, which brings us back to the Neolithic peoples of England and agriculture, because agriculture places an often misunderstood and frequently ignored primacy on the health of the soil if human society is to survive its march toward specialization with any semblance of well-being and dignity.

SOIL AND AGRICULTURE

"We belong to a mystery that will never belong to us," says poet John Daniel, "yet it is freely given to all who desire it. Though we distance ourselves and fail to see, it is granted everywhere and all the time. It does not fail us [although we may fail it]." Soil is a part of the vast mystery to which we belong. "To forget how to dig the earth and tend the soil is to forget ourselves," wrote Mahatma Gandhi.

Many cultures have emphasized the trusteeship of the soil through religion and philosophy. The biblical Abraham, in his covenant with God, was instructed: "Defile not therefore the land which ye shall inhabit, wherein I dwell."[62] The Chinese philosopher Confucius saw in the Earth's thin mantle the sustenance of all life and the minerals treasured by human society. A century later in Greece, Aristotle thought of soil as the central mixing pot of air, fire, and water that formed all things.

In spite of the durability of such beliefs, most people cannot grasp their profundity not only because they are intangible but also because the march toward specialization isolates us increasingly from Nature and our inseparable place in it. The invisibility of the soil is founded in the notion that it is as common as air and therefore, like air, is a birthright and taken for granted.

Although soil seems "invisible" to many people, it is at the same time thought to be divisible in the sense that one may carve it into personal boundaries of outright ownership. In reality, however, soil is a seamless whole, unknown in its complexity to virtually all people.

Whether most people understand it or not, soil is important for at least five reasons.[63] First, soil is the stage on which human life and its many constructs are physically supported. Second, soil shelters seeds and provides physical support for their roots as they germinate, grow, and mature into adult plants that seed and thus perpetuate the cycle. Third, soil stores elements that, in the proper proportions and availability, can act as nutrients for the plants growing in it. Fourth, soil plays a central role in the decomposition of dead organic matter, and in so doing not only renders harmless many potential pathogens, including those of humans, but also adds to its store of potential nutrients. Fifth, soils of various kinds, acting in concert, are a critical factor in regulating the major elemental cycles of the Earth—those of carbon, nitrogen, and sulfur.

When one thinks about it directly, one realizes that human society is inextricably tied to the soil for reasons beyond measurable riches, for the historical wealth of the Earth is archived in soil, a wealth that nurtures culture even as it sustains life, as illustrated by the following quotes: "The social lesson of soil waste is that no man has the right to destroy soil even if he does own it in fee simple. The soil requires a duty of man, which we have been slow to recognize" (H.A. Wallace, 1938). "In the old Roman Empire, all roads led to Rome. In agriculture all roads lead back to the soil from which farmers make their livelihood" (G. Hambrige, 1938).

Although both of these statements are as true now as the day they were uttered, it is the doom of people that they too soon forget. Having said this, however, I must acknowledge that few people know what soil really is. Soil, the very foundation of life, is a long time in the making, as will be discussed in the following sections. Sacred as soil is, it nevertheless is all too quickly profaned and depleted! Today, for example, nearly 20 percent of the vegetated surface of the land on Earth has been degraded by human activities.[64]

Genesis of Soil

Soil is the result of two opposing geological forces: construction and erosion.[65] The fiery volcanism that builds mountains and the erosive power of wind, water, and ice that works to level them are some of the agents of these opposing forces.

A volcano is a vent or opening in the Earth's crust through which gases and melted rock, called molten lava, are ejected. A volcano that is ejecting gases and molten lava is said to be active; it is in creation. On the other hand, a volcano that has "run its course" of activity is said to be extinct because the "life" has gone out of it.

A volcano is built from within by fire and is eroded from without by wind and water and ice. It defies gravity in its growing and falls to gravity in its dying. A volcano is born and dies and is reborn as something else. This means that volcanoes, which form mountains, are not eternal, but, as with all mountains, come and go, are born and die, in concert with all living things.

Consider that children, flowers, and grasses are living entities, which at given times grow almost fast enough to actually watch them increase in size. Trees grow more slowly. And some rock-dwelling lichens, which are a combination of a fungus and an alga, grow just a fraction of an inch in a century—so slowly that historians use their growth to date events.

And rocks also grow, but more slowly still. At a rock's pace of growth, the history of the Egyptian pyramids is a wink and that of the Rocky Mountains a yawn.

Rocks even have a cycle of birth and death and birth again. Some geologists estimate that since the Earth was born 4.5 billion years ago, its rocks have been through ten generations.

As mountains are born and die, as pieces of continents come and go like ships at dock in a harbor, the rock formed on the floor of the sea is raised to the tops of mountains only to be eroded and returned to the floor of the sea where it once again begins its journey through the Earth. In approximately 450 million years, the rock may reappear on the surface of the continent to begin a new life.

The constructional processes, such as volcanism, sedimentation, metamorphosis, and tectonics or deformation in the Earth's crust, are the physical and chemical methods by which discrete bodies of rock are formed, assembled, and given their physical and chemical characteristics. Igneous processes in which rock is melted, for example, may produce large bodies of homogeneous rock, such as a large flow of basalt or an intrusion of granite, whereas tectonic processes (those causing the deformation of the Earth's crust) would produce in the same area a large mass of heterogeneous rock.

In contrast, through weathering processes (exposure to the effects of weather), landforms are shaped by wind, water, and ice, as rock is broken down physically and chemically into smaller and smaller pieces that eventually become soil. Soil, which is like an exchange membrane between the living and nonliving components of the Earth, is dynamic and ever changing.

Derived from the mechanical and chemical breakdown of rock and organic material, soil is built up by plants that live and die in it. It is also enriched by animals that feed on plants, evacuate their bodily wastes, and eventually die, decay, and return to the soil of their origin as organic material.

Soil, the properties of which vary from place to place within a landscape, is by far the most alive and biologically diverse part of a terrestrial ecosystem. The processes through which soil develops are divided into two categories of weathering, physical and chemical, both of which depend on (1) properties of the "parent" rock, such as its physical and chemical composition; (2) patterns of regional and local climate; and (3) the kinds of plants and animals that are available and capable of becoming established in the newly forming soil.

Physical Weathering

Physical weathering refers to the mechanical fragmentation of rock through the actions of freezing and thawing, wetting and drying, heating and cooling, or transportation by wind, water, or ice. Freezing and thawing is an important means of fragmenting rock in climates that have cycles in which the temperatures are cold enough to freeze rock and warm enough to thaw it. Before freezing and thawing can be effective, however, there must be cracks in the rock for water to enter. Once inside, water expands about 9 percent as it freezes. If water expands in a confined space, it can exert a pressure in excess of 30,000 pounds per square inch, which far exceeds the strength of rock.

I have watched, for example, as some of the rocks that I used to make borders around the flower beds of my garden become saturated in the rain. Then, on occasion, the north wind comes blasting out of the Canadian arctic and freezes the rocks. Although I cannot see them expand, when they thaw, I often find them split into several pieces. Awesome indeed is the hidden power and effect of ice.

Cycles of wetting and drying can also break down rocks, particularly those with fine grains, although the exact mechanism is not understood.

Heating and cooling is an effective process for the gradual conversion of coarse-grained rock into smaller and smaller pieces on its journey to becoming soil. The various minerals of which a rock is composed have different capacities to absorb heat and to expand when heated. So it is that changes in temperature result in stresses that lead to fracturing along the boundaries between the minerals that make up the rock or even within some kinds of minerals themselves.

The results of heating and cooling can be seen as the flakes loosened from exposed boulders following a forest fire or at times from the rocks used to ring a camp fire. I vividly remember one experience many years ago when I camped along a stream with a limestone bed. I collected rocks from the stream's bottom and constructed a ring in which to build my fire.

My fire, burning cheerily in the middle of the circle of rounded rocks, heated the water in the limestone, which expanded as steam. Before I knew what was happening, the limestone began exploding, which sent some fragments whizzing past my head into the night beyond, while others bombarded the flames. Fortunately, none of the flying limestone projectiles found me as their target as I scurried into the night. As with many lessons in my life, this one took but once to learn!

Finally, we come to the transportation of rock. Sand blowing along a seashore or across a desert is an example of rock being transported by wind. Rocks can also be tumbled by the swift waters of streams and rivers or by the pounding surf of the ocean and can be moved by ice in glaciers. This all results in abrasion, which is yet another way rocks are reduced into progressively smaller pieces.

Having dealt with the physical breakdown and transportation of rock by gravity and water, we must now turn our attention to chemical weathering, which is also driven by the environment.

Chemical Weathering

A rock's primary mineral composition reflects the temperature, pressure, and chemical makeup during its formation, often at a high temperature deep within the Earth. At the Earth's surface, where temperatures and pressures are lower, water and various organic and inorganic acids, as well as other chemical compounds, mediate a tenuous state of ever-changing balance. As rocks adjust to the environment at the Earth's surface, the primary minerals may be transformed into secondary minerals through chemical weathering.

Minerals weather at different rates, depending on their chemical composition and crystalline structure. Small pieces of rock and small grains of mineral break down more rapidly than large ones because small ones have a much greater surface area compared to their mass than do large ones. For this reason, a particular rock may be more susceptible to physical decomposition than to chemical decomposition. Nevertheless, initial weathering must precede the formation of soil from hard rocks. Once soil is formed, however, the intensity of chemical breakdown is generally greater than it is in the rock itself, which brings us to the importance of organic material in soil.

The Addition of Organic Material to Mineral Soil

One of the first recognizable manifestations of organic material in soil is the formation of a dark layer near the soil's surface. This organic material comes from lichens and higher plants, such as grasses and herbs, which are capable of becoming established in raw mineral soil. In fact, their presence greatly increases the rate at which soil is formed because they not only add themselves as organic material but also act as catalysts for chemical reactions.

There are distinct differences in the distribution of organic material in soils. These differences depend on climate, slope, and the type of vegetation growing on the site. Soils of grassland and prairie, for example, contrast distinctly with those of a forest in their distribution of and processes associated with organic material.

To better understand what I mean, consider the midwestern United States, where oak forest and prairie coexist, although in distinct patches under a similar regime of climate. Both areas have a similar amount of organic material: live vegetation, vegetative litter on the surface of the soil, and organic material within the soil. But the oak forest has more than half of its total organic material tied up in the trees aboveground, whereas 90 percent of the organic material in the prairie is found within the soil.

The decomposed organic material, which lends soil its dark color, is termed *humus*, the Latin word meaning "the ground, soil" or alternatively the New Latin word *humos*, which means "full of earth." Incorporation of organic material into the surface of the soil, where the dark layer of "topsoil" is formed, is rapid when considered in the scale of geological time but exceedingly slow when considered in the scale of a human lifetime.

The molecules of humus provide many important functions, including absorbing and holding water, acting as weak acids, and forming structure within the soil, such as the pores, which allows biological activity to exist. The porous nature of the soil also provides a mechanism for holding in place both water and chemicals, which are required for chemical interactions. In addition, soil quite literally resembles a discrete entity, which lives and breathes through a complex mix of interacting organisms—from viruses and bacteria, to fungi, to earthworms and insects, to moles, gophers, and ground squirrels.

The activities of all these organisms in concert are responsible for developing the critical properties that underlie the basic fertility, health, and productivity of soil. The complex, biologically driven functions of the soil, in which soil organisms are the regulators of most processes that translate into a soil's productivity, may require decades to a few hundred years to develop, and there are no quick fixes if soil is extensively damaged during such activities as intensive farming.

Infrastructure of Soil

Organisms in the soil, such as bacteria, fungi, one-celled animals called protozoa, and worms, play critical roles in maintaining its health and fertility. These organisms perform various functions in the cycling of chemicals that are required as nutrients for the growth of green plants. Some of these functions are (1) decomposing (recycling) plant material by bacteria and fungi; (2) improving the structure of the soil, which increases such things as the soil's capacity to hold water; (3) mediating the soil's pH, a determinant of which plants and animals can live where and which chemical reactions can take place where; and (4) controlling disease-causing organisms through competition for resources and space. Without the organisms to perform these functions, the plant communities we see on the surface of the Earth would not exist.

As the total productivity of an ecosystem increases, the biological diversity within the soil's food web also seems to increase. The greater the number of interactions among organisms that decompose organic material (decomposers), their predators, and the predators of the predators, the more nutrients that are retained in the soil. It is only through the belowground food web in the soil that plants can obtain the nutrients necessary for their growth; without the belowground food web, the aboveground food web—including us humans—would cease to exist.

One must therefore have the humility to accept that one will never fully understand the soil; only then will one have the necessary patience to protect the organisms that perform those functions through which soil is kept healthy. Soil health *cannot* be maintained solely through applications of commercial fertilizer.

When, for example, commercial fertilizer is applied to agricultural row crops, which disrupts the biological infrastructure of the soil, much may be lost as it leaches downward through the soil into the groundwater, which it then contaminates, because neither the soil nor the organisms in the soil's disrupted food web can retain the added nitrogen. Contamination of the groundwater through the use of fertilizers is a major problem in agriculture throughout the United States and the world.

Agriculture fouls more than 173,000 miles of streams and rivers—a figure that does not include the hundreds of thousands of miles of ditches—with chemicals, erosion, and the runoff of animal wastes in commercial feedlots and poultry farms. It is also the largest overall source of pollution in U.S. waterways.[66] According to the U.S. Environmental Protection Agency, farming is responsible for 70 percent of the pollution in streams and rivers in the United States, outstripping the combined discharges from sewage treatment plants, urban storm drains, and pollutants deposited by air. The problems laid at agriculture's doorstep include those that harm aquatic life and/or restrict human use of streams and rivers, to say nothing of the oceans of the world, where all of this pollution ultimately accumulates and concentrates because oceans cannot flush themselves like flowing waters.

In some cases, adding fertilizer even acts like a biocide, killing the organisms in the soil's food web, which further degrades the soil. It is much wiser, therefore, to work in harmony with the soil and the organisms that govern its infrastructure because they are responsible for the processes that in turn provide those nutrients to the plants.

The development of soil in a forest or a grassland relies on self-reinforcing feedback loops, where organisms in the soil provide the nutrients for plants to grow, and plants in turn provide the carbon—the organic material—that selects for and alters the communities of soil organisms. One influences the other, and both determine the soil's development and health.

The soil food web is thus a prime indicator of the health of any terrestrial ecosystem. But soil processes can be disrupted by such things as decreasing bacterial or fungal activity, decreasing the biomass of bacteria or fungi, altering the ratio of fungal to bacterial biomass in a way that is inappropriate to the desired system, reducing the number and diversity of protozoa, and reducing the number of nematodes (roundworms as opposed to segmented worms like earthworms) and/or altering their community structure.

A model of a soil food web, composed of interactive strands, is enlightening because it shows that there are higher level predators in the system whose function is to prevent the predators of bacteria and fungi from becoming too abundant and thus altering how the system functions. In turn, these higher level predators serve as food for still higher level predators.

In this way, mites, predatory roundworms, and small insects are eaten by organisms that spend much of their time aboveground. Additionally, predators in the third, fourth, and fifth upper strands of the food web are eaten by spiders, centipedes, and beetles, which in turn are eaten by salamanders, birds, shrews, and mice, which in turn are eaten by snakes, still other birds, weasels, foxes, and so on.

If, therefore, part of the biological diversity of the belowground organisms is lost, the soil as a system will function differently and may not produce a chosen crop in a way that meets our economic expectations or may even produce a plant community not to our human liking, such as a hillside of shrubs instead of commercially valuable trees. If the predators in the soil are lost, which disrupts the governance of the soil, the mineral nitrogen in the soil may be lost, and the plants suffer and thus exhibit poor growth and produce fewer seeds. Conversely, too many predators can overuse the bacteria and fungi, which results in slower decomposition of organic material that is needed to fuel the system of nutrient uptake by the plants. A reduction or loss in any part of the food web affects at least two strands of the web at other levels. If we, as individuals and a society, poison the soil directly for whatever reason or otherwise damage its delicate infrastructure indirectly by condoning the pollution of our air and water, we help to destroy the stage on which life depends—including ours!

But, one might ask, can we not learn to live in harmony with the land as the indigenous Americans are reputed to have done? That is a good question. How, exactly, did the indigenous peoples of the Americas live before the Europeans landed?

Although the indigenous peoples of the Americas, prior to the European invasion, did not have European technology with which to alter their environment, they did alter it. In fact, they created a humanized landscape and a human-dominated ecological system throughout most of the Americas over thousands of years of continuous habitation, as the Spanish discovered when they first invaded the shores of the New World.

INDIGENOUS PEOPLES OF THE AMERICAS

I have long heard that the North American continent north of Mexico was all but uninhabited, except for a few "savages," when the Europeans invaded. And even today, people speak of restoring some ecosystems to their "pristine" conditions of presettlement times, meaning pre-European times. If by "pristine" people mean untouched by the hand of humanity, they are in for a rude awakening because the indigenous peoples from north of the Canadian border to the southern portion of South America had long modified the lands they inhabited.[67]

The Landscape

If one were to have traveled over the landscape of the Americas in 1492, the human imprint of the indigenous peoples would have been obvious; it was neither benign nor localized and ephemeral. In fact, the use of resources by indigenous peoples was not always ecologically sound. Sometimes the indigenous peoples lived in harmony with Nature, and sometimes they did not. Nevertheless, they changed their landscape nearly everywhere; they could do nothing else simply because they existed and used Nature in order to live. Consider, for example, the Mayans of the Petén region of northern Guatemala, an area populated sparsely today but an enclave for the Mayans between 1000 B.C. and 1000 A.D.

Over hundreds of years, the population of the area had grown as much as tenfold, and the forest had been cut down for planting, building, and fuel. Because the tropical forest held most of its nutrients in the plants and little in the soil, much of the available nutrients was lost as the trees were cut. As the habitat disappeared, the animals, which provided a major source of protein, also vanished.

Here there is an interesting twist to the story. As the Mayan culture was collapsing, the forest was rejuvenating itself. What is sobering about this scenario is that the Maya were ingenious and knowledgeable conservationists. They knew a great deal about their own ecology, and all their systems of land management were sophisticated, as demonstrated by the Mayan farmers who fed their huge population in the tropical forest of the Yucatán peninsula.

So rather than cutting down the forest to practice the destructive slash-and-burn agriculture of today, they managed the tropical rain forests with ecological acumen and cultural harmony. As mentioned earlier, they practiced sustainable agriculture by constructing *pet kotoob* (plural of *pet kot*, which is Mayan for a "round wall of stone" two to three feet high). Each such enclosure is about the size of a backyard garden. Within these *pet kotoob*, the Mayans grew many kinds of exotic agricultural plants, such as herbs, shrubs, and trees, along with indigenous plants.

The Maya did not move in, raze the land, and move on. Yet it is as if the Mayan civilization choked itself on its own success. As the people caused the land to produce more, their population grew, and as their population grew, they coaxed more from the land. As more and more was demanded from the land, it began to change in subtle ways. These changes took place over a period of 2,000 years and were imperceptible to the people at any given time. Yet the hidden environmental damage caused by centuries of population growth increasingly taxing the land, which we today term "cumulative effects," undoubtedly played a large role in the eventual collapse of the Mayan civilization.

By 1492, therefore, indigenous peoples throughout the Americas had modified the extent and composition of the forests and created and expanded grasslands through the use of fire, much as the Mesolithic peoples did between 7,000 and 5,000 years ago in what is today recognized as England. In addition, indigenous peoples of the Americas rearranged microrelief through countless human-created earthworks. Agricultural fields were common, as were houses, towns, roads, and trails.

Indigenous Americans, for example, changed their environment through a variety of means, some of which were so subtle that European settlers mistook the altered landscapes for ones untouched by human hands. They used such methods as (1) creating raised agricultural fields; (2) creating actual terraced fields in which to raise crops; (3) establishing complex systems of irrigation; (4) using fire to create parklike areas in which it was easy to hunt, collect nuts, and cultivate crops; (5) using fire to create and maintain grasslands for hunting big game animals; and (6) constructing major cities, such as those of the Aztecs, Mayans, Incas, and other peoples.

The size of indigenous populations, associated deforestation, and prolonged intensive agriculture led in some regions to severe degradation of the land's carrying capacity. Such was the case in central Mexico, where by 1519 the pressures to produce food may have brought the Aztec civilization to the verge of collapse even without the Spanish invasion. There is good evidence that severe erosion of the soil was already widespread and not solely the result of plowing the land, grazing it with livestock, and deforestation carried on by the Spanish. So it seems that the degradation of the land, in some areas at least, was as much a matter of long-term intensive use by indigenous peoples as it was intrusion by the Spanish.

All of these human artifacts had local effects on soil, microclimate, hydrology, and wildlife. By 1750, however, the landscape of 1492 had all but vanished, not because the Europeans superimposed their design on it but because the indigenous peoples had declined in numbers so precipitously through the war waged on them by the invaders and through diseases the invaders brought with them to which the indigenous peoples had no immunity. Therefore, the landscape of 1750 appeared to be more "pristine"—less humanized—than that of 1492.

The Indigenous Population

Whoever watched as Columbus came ashore, if any indigenous people did, witnessed the beginning of a conquest destined to cause the greatest destruction of human lives in history. When the Spanish landed in the islands of the Caribbean in 1492, the indigenous population of the Americas was about 53.9 million. Accepting a margin of error of about 20 percent, the population falls between 43 and 65 million.

The 53.9 million figure is thought to be divided as follows: 3.8 million indigenous peoples in North America, 17.2 million in Mexico, 5.6 million in Central America, 3.0 million in the Caribbean, 15.7 million in the Andes, and 8.6 million in the lowlands of South America. As you consider these figures, bear in mind that the landscape of 1492 reflected not only the extant population of the times but also the cumulative effects of a growing population over a period of perhaps 40,000 years or more.

Recent discoveries of ancient skeletons, dwelling sites, histories of language, and genetic evidence suggest that not all of the ancient ones may have migrated across the Bering–Chuckchi Platform connecting Siberia and Alaska and then fanned out into the Americas within the last 12,000 to 20,000 years, as was previously thought. Although a dwelling site in Monte Verde, southern Chile, dates to some 12,500 years ago and radiocarbon dates from another archaeological site in northern Peru indicate that people with stone-tool technology were there about 11,650 years ago, findings from archaeologists, linguists, and geneticists combine to indicate that humans may have traveled extensively in both North and South America as long as 40,000 years ago.

In addition, new evidence suggests that the first Americans did not all come from one area in Siberia in a single migration, as has long been assumed, but rather in three, or perhaps four, distinct migrations. Scientists at Emory University, studying the genes of indigenous Americans from North, South, and Central America, have found that they descended from four primary lineages, some of which originated in geographically distant regions of Asia. "The peopling of the New World is a much more complicated issue than has been thought before," says Dennis Stanford, curator of Paleo-Indian anthropology at the Smithsonian Institution in Washington, D.C. "The old model that we read about in our textbooks is no longer valid."

New evidence suggests that the earliest immigrants to North America came from Asia by skin-covered boats, rather than crossing the Bering–Chuckchi Platform from Siberia about 11,500 years ago. Emerging data from archaeological sites indicate that these Asian seafarers moved along the Pacific coast into Alaska and northwestern Canada and eventually southward to Peru and Chile during the last ice age, about 15,000 to 10,000 years ago. At that time, the level of the sea was 300 feet lower, exposing much of the continental shelf, which at that time would have been inhabitable. "The coastal environment," according to Rob Bonnichsen, director for the study of First Americans, Department of Anthropology, Oregon State University, "would have provided more subsistence than an interior route. Current thinking is there were some refugia [areas free of ice] along the coast, spots that weren't glaciated. Coastal routes provide for easier, faster movement of people." E. James Dixon, curator of archaeology for the Denver Museum of Natural History, adds that the coastal route "would have been more viable" for transporting families and supplies.

According to Dixon, the oldest human remains found in Alaska are the bones of a 23-year-old man found in a small cave on Prince of Wales Island along the coast of southeast Alaska; testing indicates that the remains are from 9,200 to 9,800 years old. The man's diet consisted primarily of such marine mammals as seals and otters. Michael J. Moratto, an archaeologist at California State University at Fresno, says Daisy Cave on an island in the Santa Barbara Channel off the coast of southern California shows evidence of human habitation 12,000 years ago, which implies that watercraft were being used at that time. Ruth Gruhn, professor emeritus in the Anthropology Department at the University of Alberta, Canada, notes in addition that numerous coastal sites in Peru, Ecuador, and Chile are being studied that are from 10,800 to 12,000 years old.

C. Loring Brace, a professor of anthropology at the University of Michigan, thinks three or possibly four migrations took place. Brace, an expert on skull and facial features, said that some of the remains he has studied appear to be related to the ancient Ainu, an aboriginal Caucasian people that inhabit the northernmost islands of Japan. Other immigrants are related to people in northeast Asia, southeast Asia, and China. "It's quite clear," asserts Brace, "that different migration brought different groups of people."

According to Douglas C. Wallace and Theodore G. Schurr, both molecular geneticists as Emory University, the first group came from the Baikal region of Siberia 25,000 to 35,000 years ago and eventually migrated to the interior of North and South America. Dr. Schurr speculated that the second group came from Eurasia, possibly coastal eastern Asia, and made its way to the interior of North America and the northern portions of South America. The third group, originating in coastal eastern Asia, followed the western coast of the Americas to Peru. The fourth group, which crossed the Bering–Chuckchi Platform from Siberia 8,000 to 10,000 years ago and today speak the Eskimo–Aleut and Athapaskan languages, now live in northern Canada and Alaska. The pattern and timing of those migrations, which are inferred by genetic evidence, agree well with the pattern inferred by studies of linguistics.

Johanna Nichols, a professor of linguistics at the University of California at Berkeley, said she calculated through her studies of language that it would have taken about 7,000 years for the ancient peoples to have traveled south by stages, once they entered the North American continent, from the Bering–Chuckchi Platform to Monte Verde, some 8,000 miles to the south. "So," she concluded, "that points to an entry date of 19,500 years ago, minimum." Nichols presented her data as one of six scientists who participated in a session on "The First Americans: A New Perspective" at the annual meeting of the American Association for the Advancement of Science.

Nichols went on to say that she believes the first people may have arrived even before the peak of the last ice age, between 14,000 and 22,000 years ago. She pointed out that indigenous American languages fall into about 140 families, and she estimated that it would have taken 30,000 years for that number of language families to develop had there been a continuous migration into North America. "But there was a break in migration, and I believe that I can confidently say that the population of the New World, based on linguistics, is about 40,000 years old."

Most of the languages share certain traits, contends Nichols, with no evidence of outside influence for many thousands of years. Only along the western coasts of the Americas do languages appear to have come from immigrants who arrived later than 14,000 years ago. In addition, she noted that the pattern in which languages spread suggests that immigrants from Siberia first traveled south and then moved north into the interior of North America, where they diversified, as the Wisconsin glaciation receded.

With respect to the aforementioned dwelling site in Monte Verde, southern Chile, there is some evidence that people may have lived there as early as 33,000 years ago, according to Tom Dillehay of the University of Kentucky, who first began excavating Monte Verde in 1979. Dillehay, also a speaker at the conference, concluded by saying that how the people arrived in and occupied the Americas is a very complex process, "which is borne out in the biological and cultural diversity that we see in the archaeological, linguistic, genetic, and environmental records."

But the European invasion of the Americas abruptly reversed this trend of a growing population. The decline of indigenous peoples was rapid and severe—probably the single greatest demographic disaster in history. With European disease as the primary killer, populations of indigenous peoples fell by 90 percent or more in many regions, particularly the tropical lowlands, during the first century after the initial invasion.

The estimated declines of indigenous populations during this time are as follows: Hispaniola (formerly Haiti, an island in the West Indies) dropped from 1 million in 1492 to a few hundred 50 years later (more than 99 percent). In Peru, the population declined from 9 million in 1520 to 670,000 in 1620 (92 percent), in the Basin of Mexico from 1.6 million in 1519 to 180,000 in 1607 (89 percent), and in North America from 3.8 million in 1492 to 1 million in 1800 (74 percent). Thus, the indigenous population declined from 53.9 million in 1492 to 5.6 million in 1650, which amounts to an 89 percent reduction.

This decline is not surprising, however, because even in what today is the United States the Spanish controlled the land in the mid-1500s from the Carolina coast as far north as La Charrette, the highest settlement on the Missouri River, to at least San Francisco Bay in California. Decimation of the indigenous population affected the human landscape accordingly, although there was not always a direct relationship between the density of a human population and its impact.

Recovery of the Land

A strong case can be made for a significant environmental recovery of the land and a reduction of indigenous cultural features by 1750. For example, on his fourth voyage in 1502–03, Columbus sailed along the north coast of Panama, which his son, Ferdinand, described as well peopled, full of houses, with many fields and open land with few trees. Lionel Wafer, in contrast, found most of the Caribbean coast of Panama covered with forests and unpopulated in 1681. And so it was all over the Americas: forests filled in, soil erosion became stabilized, agricultural fields changed to scrub and forest, and indigenous earthworks became overgrown.

By 1650, indigenous populations had been reduced by about 90 percent in the hemisphere, whereas the numbers of Europeans were not yet substantial by 1750, and European settlement had only just begun to expand. As a result, the fields of indigenous peoples had been abandoned, their settlements vanished, forests recovered, savannas retreated as forests expanded, and the subsequent landscape did indeed appear to be sparsely populated wilderness.

Here it is important to point out that, prior to the invasion of Europeans, human impact on the environment was not simply a process of increasing change in response to the linear growth of the indigenous populations. Instead, the landscape was given time to rest and recover as cultures collapsed, populations declined, wars occurred, and habitations were abandoned. The effects of human activities may be constructive, benign, or destructive, all of which are subjective concepts based on human values, but change is continual, albeit at various rates and in various directions. All changes are nevertheless cumulative, and even mild, slow change can show dramatic effects over the long term.

Although there was, of course, some European impact during this time, it was localized. After 1750, however, and especially after 1850, populations of European Americans expanded greatly, exploiting the resources more intensively and greatly accelerating their modification of the environment, which continues to the present.

Inventing the National Myth

The grand American myth in the United States is imagined pristine Nature across an entire continent of wilderness filled with wild beasts and savages, which was probably not as difficult for settlers to conquer as has been imaginatively conceived.

The ignoble savage, nomadic and barely human, was invented to justify stealing the land from the few remaining indigenous North Americans and to prove that the indigenous peoples had no part in transforming an untamed wilderness into a civilized continent. When the Europeans walked into a forest, which they described as "parklands," and they did not see the indigenous people creating it, they did not see what came before they arrived on the scene and put the best spin on it by assuming it was "natural."

With the indigenous peoples branded as indolent and incapable of the art of civilization, the United States was made, according to official historical texts, by Puritan saint, yeoman, mountain man, frontiersman, pioneer, sodbuster, and cowboy, all of whom are painted as overachieving, self-glorifying Americans. Today, whether denigrated as subhuman savages or idealized as Native Americans living in perfect harmony with their environment, the indigenous peoples of North America are given no credit for having evolved well-developed cultures that molded the North American landscape into open woodlands in the east and stately pine forests in the west, for creating and maintaining much of the continent's grasslands, and for transforming hardwoods into piney woods through the use of fire.

In essence, whether through ignorance or, perhaps and more probably, through deliberate informed denial of the role played by the indigenous peoples in shaping the landscape over a very long period of time, the Europeans, such as the British, downplayed the evidence of cultivation and permanent settlements. To morally and legally justify stealing the land from the indigenous peoples, the British had to do two things: (1) portray the indigenous peoples as nomadic hunting–gathering savages that were forever an incorrigible and uncivilizable part of the wild and untamed continent and (2) demonize the indigenous peoples as indolent, untrustworthy, murdering heathens—and hence the enemy of pious civilized people like the British, who, incidentally, paid bounties for the scalps of indigenous men, women, and children to encourage people to shoot them on sight. In other words, if the indigenous people were not really using the land, they had no title to it, and the British could feel justified in taking it.

In fairness, and paradoxically, it must be stated that the European Americans undoubtedly found much more "forest primeval" in 1850 than had existed in 1650. Nevertheless, writers and historians, both consciously and unconsciously, denied evidence of the indigenous people's having created a culturalized landscape over millennia in order to ennoble the European enterprise of pirating the land. This approach to creating a national myth for the fledgling United States—ironically founded on the premise of human equality—helped European Americans envision themselves as single-handedly taming a vast, wild continent, to which they would ultimately bring civilization—Manifest Destiny.

Despite how the European Americans envisioned themselves, Robert Hine, professor of history at the University of California at Riverside, wrote that "…it takes time to beat the Indian out of the soil, and how could that typical pioneer tame the land if he was always moving on, always settling, never settled! He seemed to love his land so little that he was willing to sell or leave at the drop of a hat. One observer of the West, a man from Scotland, where land was cherished, found Americans without qualms in abandoning their land."[68]

In the Name of History

"History is a pageant and not a philosopher," wrote Augustine Birrell, English author and statesman. To understand this, we must look at history naked.[69] A letter written in 1793 decried capital punishment in the beheading of Louis XVI during the French Revolution. A year's collection of letters in 1897 debated what to do about the homeless people. A Union soldier fresh from battle against General Robert E. Lee's Army of Northern Virginia, having served in "almost every Corps and Division of the Army of the Potomac," wrote, "I have yet to find one man in favor of [President Abraham Lincoln's Emancipation]…Proclamation." These are some of the naked views of history. Author Gerard Stropnicky asks why such issues and dates are surprising when they remain unresolved today. After all, history is not only written by the "winners" but also "is compressed into popular generalizations by an academic process," which begins by setting out to prove a thesis, not to stimulate controversy and contradiction.

Historians love debating the fine points of history among themselves, says Stropnicky, but, he adds, by the time their work is processed ("like Velveeta cheese") into a standard high school curriculum, what contradiction there might have been is "well squeezed out." I have found in science, as Stropnicky has found in history, that we tend to be uncomfortable with messy variables and so we tend toward averages and generalizations not only because they are "true enough" but also because they are easier for us to accept.

The so-called facts of history look clearer in black and white. In contrast to such crystal-clear images of yesteryear, the present seems hopelessly complex and muddled, as did the past to those people who lived it as their present. But when one looks at "naked history," one finds spousal abuse among the mythologized pioneers, animal rights activists in the 18th century, people campaigning against secondhand smoke during the presidency of Rutherford B. Hayes, homelessness in the 1890s, and racists during the American Civil War in uniforms of blue as well as gray.

Yesterday in its nakedness was just as uncertain and perplexing as is today. With this in mind, Stropnicky suggests that the aphorism "those who forget the past are condemned to repeat it" needs to be restated and suggests the following: "Those who generalize their history are condemned to be nostalgic for a past that never was."

Today, through the exploitation begun by the European invaders and the ever-advancing technology of specialization, the landscapes of the North American continent are vastly different from the way they were when the Europeans first invaded the shores of the New World over 500 years ago.

THE SACRED AND THE PROFANE

7

W hen the Spanish invaded the "New World," they not only brought their own culture but also ruthlessly superimposed it on the indigenous peoples, as later did the British. But it was the Canadians and Americans who ultimately forbade the indigenous people to speak their own language or practice their spiritual rites. Forbidding a people to speak their own language is to murder their culture because language makes culture possible in the first place by allowing a group of human beings to evolve a unique ever-increasingly complex social order that eventually becomes a society.

A society is a group of human beings broadly distinguished from other groups by mutual interests, participation in characteristic relationships, a common culture, and shared institutions and agencies. Culture, in turn, is the totality of socially transmitted behavioral patterns, arts, beliefs, institutions, and all other products of human work and thought characteristic of a community or population.

HOW PEOPLE THINK

People think in one of two ways: (1) in a linear pattern that causes one society to focus on producing and accumulating material *products* as the primary purpose of life and (2) in a cyclical pattern that causes another society to focus on being an integral part of the *processes* constituting the spiritual center of life's cycle.

213

Cyclical Thinking

Thinking in cycles ultimately causes us to see our lives as a circular dance in which certain basic and necessary patterns of use and renewal, of life and death, are repeated endlessly. This is the ethical basis of indigenous American spiritual thought, as exemplified by Black Elk:

> Everything the Power of the World does is done in a circle. The sky is round, and...the earth is round like a ball, and so are all the stars. The wind, in its greatest power, whirls. Birds make their nests in circles, for theirs is the same religion as ours. The sun comes forth and goes down again in a circle. The moon does the same, and both are round. Even the seasons form a great circle in their changing, and always come back again to where they were. The life of a man is a circle from childhood to childhood, and so it is in everything where power moves.[70]

Those who think cyclically humbly accept the mysteries of the Universe. They allow Nature to teach them, and Nature's reflective lessons of infinite universal relationship are intrinsically valuable. To use something for its own sake and then to be the source of its renewal is to see it as a re-source. In the original sense of the word, "resource" was a reciprocal relationship between humanity and Earth, a circle of taking and giving and taking again. The very structure of the word—*re* and *source*—means reciprocal relationship, a cycle, to use something from the Earth and then to be the source of its renewal. "It is only in the processes of the natural world, and in analogous and related processes of human culture," says Wendell Berry, "that the new may grow usefully old, and the old be made new...."

People who see life as a great circle see everything as interdependent and nothing as independent. In Nature, there is no such thing as an "independent variable." Everything in the Universe is patterned by its interdependence on everything else, and it is the pattern of interdependence and change that forms the only constant. This constant is the principle of both creation and infinite becoming.

The cyclical vision is at once realistic and generous. Those who accept it recognize that in creation lies the essential principle of return: what is here will leave and will come again; what I have, I must some day give up. They see death as an integral and indispensable part of life, for death is but another becoming, a view beyond a horizon.

Some cycles revolve frequently enough to be well known in a person's lifetime. Some are completed only in the memory of several generations;

hence the notion of the invisible present, that which is ongoing but not seen now, and yet will manifest itself later. Still other cycles are so vast that their motion can only be assumed. Such is our galaxy and the Milky Way, but even they are not aloof from our humble, daily activities, for we are kept in touch with the Universe by just knowing they exist.

Linear Thinking

In contrast to cyclical thinking, which arises from a desire to be in a harmonious relationship with the Universe, our Western linear thinking is oriented almost strictly toward the control of Nature and the conversion of natural resources into economic commodities—into money, the god of Western materialism. We suffer from "affluenza"!

Wendell Berry offers an interesting point with respect to these two patterns of thought. He believes that while natural processes may be cyclical, "there is within nature a human domain the processes of which are linear; the other, much older, holds that human life is subject to the same cyclic patterns as all other life."[71] If the two are contradictory, says Berry, it is not so much because one is wrong and the other is right but because one is only partial and the other is complete.

Berry goes on to say that the concept of linearity is the doctrine of progress, which is supposed to bring us into a human-made material paradise. Within this concept, society discards old experiences as new ones are encountered. Although in our minds we never "repeat" the old ways or the old mistakes, in reality we repeat them constantly. We deny it, however, in our blind drive for material progress. We therefore never learn from history.

The point Berry makes is that there is but one definition of progress: onward and upward forever, an endless cross-country voyage of discovery. To return is merely to come back to the used, because progress means exploiting the new and the innocent.

Characteristic of the linear vision is the notion that anything is justifiable as long as and insofar as it is immediately and obviously good for something else. Linear thinkers require everything to proceed directly, immediately, and obviously to its perceived value. What, we ask, is it good for? And only if it proves to be immediately good for something are we ready to raise the question of its value: How much is it worth? By this we mean how much money it is worth, because if it can only be good for something else, then obviously it can only be worth something else. An excellent example of this type of thinking is portrayed by Clyde Martin, of the Western Pine Association, who wrote in the *Journal of*

Forestry in 1940: "Without more complete and profitable utilization we cannot have intensive forest management....When thinnings can be sold as a profit and every limb and twig of the tree has value, forest management will come as a matter of course."[72]

Martin's notion still predominates. Anything without monetary value has no value, and anything with immediate monetary value is wasted if left unused by humans. Short-term economic profitability of resources seems always to be the bottom line.

Current dictionaries define "resource" in a strictly linear sense as the collective wealth of a country or its means of producing wealth: any property that can be converted into money. Linear thinkers therefore discount intrinsic value in everything touched, including human beings.

It is not surprising, therefore, that in our own culture the intrinsic value of Nature is still largely discounted. The same can be said of the intrinsic value of human beings when our military capacity for the destruction of the "foreign enemy" takes magnitudes of precedence over the domestic welfare and tranquillity of our citizenry. Where does this kind of thinking lead us when we consider ourselves and one another only as "human resources"?

We can begin by looking at the education of our "resource managers." As soon as we demand, in this lifeless, linear sense, that education serve some immediate purpose and that it be worth a predetermined amount, we strip education of its intrinsic value, and it becomes mere "training." Such is the traditional training of foresters, range conservationists, fishery biologists, and game biologists, all of whom are trained in the traditional schools of "resource management" which abound in North America. Once we accept so specific a notion of utility, all life becomes subservient to its use; its value is drained of everything except its "specialized use," and imagination is relegated to the scrap heap. In turn, these patterns of thought determine the core of a society's culture.

Jules Henry, a psychiatrist, says we Americans are a driven people and all our activities are related to our drivenness. I have to agree because the linear pattern of human thought produces a culture like ours, of European heritage, in which *economics of acquisition is the force* that drives the society, determines its mode of institutions, and relegates religion to the bottom rung of the social ladder. On the other hand, the cyclical pattern of human thought produces a culture like that of the indigenous peoples of the Americas prior to the invasion by Europeans, in which *spirituality is the force* that drives the society and determines the mode of its economics and institutions.

Culture is based on and organized by the dominant patterns of human thought. Through the cultural dynamics of human–land interactions, these patterns of thought determine the care a given society takes of its land and the patterns it designs on the landscape. Because a society's culture is the product of its dominant mode of thinking, given two identical pieces of land each culture would, within a century, produce a different design on the landscape as a result of the pattern of its thinking, which is the template of individual values expressed in the collective mirror— the land. Because the land and the people are inseparably one, people unite with the land through their culture.

As the social values determine the culture, so the culture is an expression of those values. The care taken of the land by the people is therefore the mirror image of the hidden forces in their social psyche. These secret thoughts ultimately express themselves and determine whether a particular society survives or becomes a closed chapter in the history books. And history books are replete with such closed chapters as the great empires of Mesopotamia, Babylonia, Egypt, Greece, and Rome, all of which destroyed their forests and the fertility of their topsoil with their linear thinking, insatiable drive for material wealth, and warlike nature. In view of this catalog of extinct civilizations, one might ask where contemporary society in the "New World" of the Americas is headed.

A CLASH OF CULTURES

The Spanish, Portuguese, French, English, and Russian invaders came to the "New World" from afar, from the pastoral scenes of Europe, and they saw not a land to be understood and nurtured but a continent they rationalized to be free for the taking because it was peopled by heathens. Beginning with the secular Spanish, who sought gold and silver, they stole whatever they valued from the indigenous peoples with ruthless cruelty, based on murder and slavery. With them came the great irony of the religious orders who, under the guise of saving the heathens from the everlasting fires of purgatory, began the task of stealing the culture from the very souls of the indigenous peoples in the name of Christian righteousness and piety.

As the Europeans beheld the vast riches of the Americas beyond the gold and silver, they not only began an insidious drive to remove the indigenous peoples from their rightful lands in order to steal them but also were so infected with the green-eyed monster of greed that they fought among themselves to see who could grab the most and hold it. This kind of behavior caused Austrian psychoanalyst Alfred Adler to say, "It is the individual who is not interested in his fellow men [humans] who has the greatest difficulties in life and provides the greatest injury to others. It is from among such individuals that all human failures spring." And it is through this kind of behavior that the Europeans stole the indigenous peoples' ways of life throughout the Americas and purposefully denigrated their cultures, leaving some of the people with tiny pieces of land on which they could not possibly sustain themselves, totally eliminating others through genocide and disease, and confined a few to lands that offered a meager subsistence.

Then the Europeans felt justified in simply taking the products of Nature, the gifts of millennial processes, such as fertile soil for farming, forage for livestock, timber for building, clean water for irrigation, clean air, and abundant wild animals to be commercially hunted and trapped. These products seemed both limitless and free for the taking. That some-day environmental consequences would result from their wholesale destructive exploitation of the land was not part of their thinking. Why? Because they came from "civilized" countries with "civilized" myths and rituals and felt they were being thrust into a "rude" and "uncivilized" continent inhabited by "savages" and wild beasts, the conquest of which was their duty—Manifest Destiny again.

The invaders did not understand that their myths belonged to another place and another time in the evolution of human society and were incompatible with those of the indigenous peoples of the New World— or with the New World itself, for that matter. The myths of the indigenous peoples belonged to the land they inhabited, whereas those of the invaders belonged to a land halfway around the world. In line with a perfectly human tendency, the Europeans' first inclination was to *survive* in the wild, unknown continent, as they perceived it, and then to seek the familiar and comfortable by trying to force their myths from an "old" known world onto a "new" unknown world.

At best, the European myths had already become rigid through long tradition and so were inharmonious with the land, with the indigenous peoples, and with the reality of constant change. At worst, they were on a collision course with the survival of human society on Earth as we know it.

As the indigenous peoples of the Americas, in keeping with their myths, viewed the land as something that could not be owned in fee simple and considered themselves to be an inseparable part of its spiritual harmony, so the Europeans, in keeping with their myths, sought to conquer, harness, subdue, and own the land. And, with a few exceptions, the invaders probably neither understood nor cared about the indigenous peoples' values or points of view, because, according to Genesis, humans were given dominion over the world, and the Europeans viewed "savages" as little more than wild beasts.

This idea, as mythologist Joseph Campbell points out, is "not simply a characteristic of modern Americans but is the biblical condemnation of nature, which...[the Europeans] inherited from their own religion and brought with them, mainly from England. God is separate from nature, and nature is condemned of God." In other words, Nature is here to be exploited. We are here to master Nature and, as masters, to improve Nature's ability to function.[73]

Indigenous people of the Americas, on the other hand, had lived on and with the land for thousands of years. Although they had the common human foibles of war, murder, slavery, greed, and infidelity, their spiritual beliefs tended toward viewing the land and all it contained as a "Thou," something holy and to be revered, whereas the European invaders viewed the same land and all it contained—including the indigenous people—as an "it," simply an object to be exploited. The Europeans therefore invaded the New World and saw the land as a vast unlimited commodity to be openly exploited for their own short-term private gains.

They dominated the New World; slaughtered its indigenous peoples; introduced European diseases; squandered its resources, including its commercially exploitable wild animals; and polluted its soil, water, and air in little more than 500 years, because they lacked a spiritual connection with Nature. Their connection was only with the potential for personal economic gain from the commodities Nature produced.

The Europeans brought their science and technology to the New World and relied on these, as they had in the past, to solve their social problems. What they failed to understand, however, is that science and technology are human tools and as such are only as constructive or destructive, as conservative or exploitive, as their users.

Although many examples of our human insistence on trying to control Nature through science and technology can be cited, I choose instead to share highlights from Professor Robert Bartlett's 1988 article about North Dakota, "Adapt or Get Out: The Garrison Diversion Project and Controversy."[74] This article captures succinctly the unchanging rigidity of the traditional European heritage embedded in the United States by its founders, a tradition that comes almost solely from a linear product mentality. In fact, Bartlett begins his case study by quoting a 1955 suggestion by native North Dakotan Carl Kraenzel that the solution to the difficulty of living with limited water in the Plains is to "adapt or get out." Bartlett says wryly, "The phrase, 'technology can solve many problems,' could become North Dakota's epitaph."

Thirty years after Kraenzel's declaration, says Bartlett, even after the environmental movement, the energy crisis, major changes in the developmental policies for the nation's water, and the economic and agricultural recessions of the 1970s and 1980s, controversy continues over the construction of the Garrison Diversion Unit, a huge, federally financed irrigation project in North Dakota that was begun in 1889 and was only 20 percent completed in 1988.

Accepting the existing conditions of the environment and adapting to them is still not a readily accepted strategy for dealing with Nature's blueprint imposed by life on the Plains. Clearly, European Americans have difficulty adapting to either environmental circumstances or evolving ideas. In fact, the social order established by settlers in North Dakota after 1880 was, from the very beginning, incompatible with the ecological limitations of the land. And little progress has yet to be made in tailoring North Dakotan life to the reality of Nature's blueprint and limited resources.

North Dakotans have hotly debated the issues of forcing the ecosystem, working against Nature, irreversible environmental damage, long-term operating costs, and the irretrievable commitment of resources. Like most Westerners living in arid regions, the people of North Dakota have long assumed, almost unquestioningly, that we can overcome the ecological limitations of scant rainfall through the science-based technology of managing water.

Belief that the magic cure for all environmental–economic ills is somehow locked within the scientific–technological complex, and that all we humans have to do is turn the key, has been held "so strongly, so widely, and for so long," Bartlett declares, "that it is an article of faith in the North Dakotan civic religion." And it persists even in the face of much evidence to the contrary.

The same can be said of logging the old-growth forests and the extinction of the spotted owl in the Pacific Northwest. The same can also be said of deforestation, which is spreading across Canada and throughout the tropics like a cancer as the remaining old-growth forests are cut at an exponential rate. The same can be said as well of water in the American Southwest and of oil in the Alaskan arctic.

An escape from the shackles of our European heritage, a culture that emphasizes a rigid human arrogance toward Nature, does not appear imminent for the landscape of North Dakota or elsewhere in North America. Professor Donald Worster put it well:

> History is always easier to understand than it is to change or escape. In the case of the West, a reversal of past trends must be regarded as a small possibility—and nothing more than that. Long the mythic land of new beginnings, it is now a region heavily encased in its past. What has been done there with the water and land over the past century and a half has had consequences for the people as well. It has handed them a fate, and there will be no quick release from it.[75]

As with most environmental limitations to activities desired by humans, the Garrison Diversion project for North Dakota had its origins in the conscious rejection of the need for humans to adapt to Nature's preexisting circumstances. The untested assumption of human arrogance that people can solve most or even all problems largely through science and technology is ingrained in North Dakota. Historically, the people have been motivated by the belief that they can somehow escape the dictates of Nature, that they can not only overcome them but also create an economy that is not bound by them.

The great irony of our European heritage is that we project the blame for our failures onto everyone and everything outside ourselves, but we seldom turn the searchlight inward, where all too often lies the cause of all our problems: our linear thinking with its unbending, arrogant, materialistic motives. Because the people of North Dakota cannot get what they want environmentally and therefore economically, for example, they feel a sense of disadvantage, exploitation, and betrayal, in which, according to Bartlett, their political culture has come to be characterized as a victim.

By subscribing wholeheartedly to the myth of technological salvation, North Dakotans have for nearly a century avoided the need to change and to adapt institutions and politics to new and different times—a common political failing. Citizens have translated the failure of technology to deliver as expected into a myth of political deception, treachery, and selfishness. The political elites claim that the national politics of interest-group liberalism have betrayed them; the state of North Dakota had in the 1940s pinned its hopes on those politics. And the people have yet to accept and face the problem of intellectual rigidity and the unwillingness to adapt.

As Worster states, a change in thinking from the domination of Nature to the *accommodation* of Nature will be difficult to achieve anywhere in American culture, and nowhere will it be more difficult to achieve than in the parched reaches of the West. Yet just because people must adapt to the physical realities of limited water in the American West does not mean that the West should not have been settled or that water should not be managed. The West, says writer Wallace Stegner, has splendid, inhabitable parts for a limited population that is willing to live within Nature's rules of sparseness and mobility. Stegner believes that the original sin was not only unrestrained engineering of water but also one of scale because anyone who wants to live in the West has to manage water to some degree. When Stegner says the sin was one of scale, he means the scale as measured by the hugeness of human arrogance.[76]

Besides a presumptuous rejection of Nature, our European heritage is encrusted in a rigid adherence to traditions and traditional ways of doing things, not to mention a determined resistance to change at any cost. Such thinking and behavior are a patent refusal to accept our responsibilities to the future in the face of necessary change.

Instead, we pass on the ecological cost of our arrogance to the generations to come. A 1986 statement by engineering educator James C. Fletcher about the space program is an excellent example of the arrogance of the moment: "There simply is no way, in our system of government, to get a long-term national commitment. Neither the President, Congress, nor the Budget Director can commit their successors." Of course they can commit them; ecologically, *we commit the future all the time.* But just because the president, Congress, or the budget director commit their successors to something, regardless of the nobility of the commitment, does not mean that commitment will be honored.

This lack of commitment is an old and traditional tune of our European heritage, one that many of us have heard for years, both in and out of the government. The traditional tune says that whatever you want to have done "can't" be done, that no options exist to do it, so there is no responsibility attached to the actions of the person who refuses to accommodate your request; all the while that person is merely resisting change. But as the Buddha said more than 2,000 years ago, "Doctrine is like a raft that carries you to the opposite bank. But who would be so foolish as to carry the raft on his shoulders and go on dragging it over dry land simply because it was useful on the water?" Thus far in our history, I think we the American people have been so foolish because we have insisted on dragging our out-of-place, out-of-date European heritage over dry, barren land.

Perhaps because we continue to drag with us many of our outmoded doctrines, we tend to see the world as black and white, right or wrong, either/or, which brings us back to science and technology. Science and technology have no sensitivity, no experience, no morals, and no conscience. It is neither scientific endeavors nor technological advances that affect the land, including its people; what ultimately affects the land are the thoughts and values of the people who create and use tools like science and technology and who simultaneously espouse such ideas as the rights of private property and the ownership of land.

THE RIGHTS OF PRIVATE PROPERTY AND THE OWNERSHIP OF LAND

Although the indigenous peoples of the Americas did have a sense of private property and the right thereto, it was confined to their personal possessions, which more often than not they made themselves. That same sense of the rights of private property did not pertain to the land per se. No one could own the land, as they saw it; one could only borrow it from one's children. The European invaders, on the other hand, felt they had the right to take whatever they wanted and the right to kill or enslave the indigenous peoples if they in any way resisted. Why? That depends on one's view of what a "right" consists of and who possesses it.

What Is a Right?

In medieval literature, brave knights came from across the land to be considered for membership at the Round Table. King Arthur designed its circular shape to democratically arrange the knights and give each an equal position. When a knight was granted membership at the Round Table, he was guaranteed equal stature with everyone else at the table and a right to be heard with equal voice.

Today, one understanding of a "right" is a legalistic, human construct based on some sense of moral privilege. Although a right in a democratic system of government is created by people and defined and guaranteed by law, access to a right is seldom, if ever, equally distributed across society. Conversely, a right does not apply to any person outside a select group unless that group purposely confers such a right on a specifically recognized individual, such as the disenfranchised.

In a true democracy, the whole protects all of its parts and the parts give obedience to the will of the whole. Ostensibly, therefore, a right in democracy gives everyone equality by sanctifying and impartially protecting certain socially acceptable behaviors while controlling unsanctioned ones. There is, however, a price exacted for having rights, even in a true democracy.

Rights have responsibilities attached to them. Thus, whenever a law is passed to protect the rights of the majority against the transgressions of the minority, everyone pays the same price—a loss of freedom of choice, of flexibility—because every law so passed is restrictive to everyone. Put succinctly, we give up personal freedoms in order to gain personal rights.

The problem is that rights, as granted by humans to one another in daily life, including in the United States, are based not on equality but rather on access. Access is determined by some notion that one race, color, creed, sex, or age is superior to another, which means that differences and similarities are based on our subjective judgments about whatever those attributes are. In American society, for example, men are judged more capable than women in most kinds of work because society has placed more value on certain kinds of products, i.e., those demanding such masculine attributes as linear thinking and physical strength as opposed to those demanding such feminine attributes as relationship, physical gentleness, and empathy.

With notable exceptions, the stereotype holds that perceived differences in outer (superficial) values become social judgments about the inherent (real) values of individual human beings. Superficial characteristics are thus translated into special rights or privileges simply because the individuals involved are different in some aspects and either perform certain actions differently or perform different actions. The greater the difference I perceive between another person and myself, the more likely I am to make black-and-white judgments about that person's real value as expressed through my notion of that person's rights.

Such judgments are made against the personal standard I use to measure how everything around me fits into my comfort zone. I thus judge people as good or bad depending on how they conform to my standard of acceptability, a standard taught and reinforced by my parents and later by my peers and teachers. Such judgments are erroneous, however, because all I can ever judge is appearances. In addition, my standard is correct only for me; it is not validly imposed on anyone else. Nevertheless, I use socially constructed, hierarchical couplets of extrinsic differences (white male versus white female, white male versus black male, human versus Nature) as a basis for judging the equality of such things as one race versus another, men versus women, secular versus spiritual, right versus wrong, good versus evil, and so on.

The most extreme example of personal judgment is the use of superficial differences to justify a social end. One group of people thus declares itself superior to another group because it wants what the other group has. The "superior" group tells the "inferior" group that it has no rights, and through this denial of rights justifies its abuse of fellow human beings. Indigenous peoples have long been warred upon, condemned as savages, and condescended to as primitive, too uncivilized and brutish to step onto the escalator of consciousness and civility.

When, for instance, the invading Spanish conquered the Pueblo Indians, they could not accept, let alone acknowledge, that they and the Pueblos were equally human. Had they acknowledged that truth, they could never have justified the wholesale murder of the Indians and theft of their land. In turn, when the invading Anglos conquered the Spanish, they could not accept, let alone acknowledge, that they and the Spanish were equally human. Had they acknowledged that truth, they could never have justified the wholesale murder of the Spanish and theft of their land. As modern conquests continue, so does the cycle.

The same principle holds for the indigenous peoples of the South American tropical forests. If the cattle barons ever admitted that the indigenous peoples living in the forests are their equals, they could not clear-cut and burn the forests to gain pasture for their herds of beef cattle at the expense of the indigenous peoples. In creating the pastures, the cattle barons destroy an ecosystem and strip the indigenous peoples not only of their current livelihood but also of their future options and those of their children. If the cattle barons were to admit that the indigenous peoples are in every way their equals, then they would have to treat them as their equals. And that, in turn, means sharing control of their mutual social destiny.

Here one might ask an interesting question. If we deny rights to humans with whom we do not want to share control of our destiny, have we as humans conferred legal rights to animals? The answer is no. Animals do not have rights in the legal sense that humans confer to one another.

We have instead assigned to animals such things as hunting seasons for sport and control of populations, trapping seasons for profit from their pelts, fishing seasons for profit and sport, and bounties to be paid on the death of unwanted individuals and species, but these are not rights; they are economically motivated conditions. I suggest, therefore, that animals do not have rights; they have integrity, which is unimpaired universal wholeness and unity. Rights are granted by humans, an animal that deems itself superior to all others, but integrity lies beyond the power of humans to grant.

What would the world be like if all humans had, in fact, equal rights under both the heart and the letter of the law and were so treated? What would the world be like if we humans then extended those rights to animals?

It is not a question of who is better than whom. Rather, it is a question of who has internalized all the assumed differences and therefore perceives another human being as an unknown entity of lesser value. It is a question of who is so afraid of losing control of their perceived rights that they will do anything to keep control, regardless of social and environmental consequences.

Rights of Use Became Rights of Private Property

"It's my land. I can do with it what I want!" It was not always this way, but the concept of property has changed dramatically over the centuries.[77]

Property, says natural historian George Monbiot in writing about England, used to be a matter of possessing the right to use land and its resources, and most areas had some kind of shared rights. Today, the land itself is considered to be property, and the words for the British rights of old have all but disappeared: "estovers" (the *right* to collect firewood), "pannage" (the *right* to put one's pigs in the woods), "turbary" (the *right* to cut turf), and "pescary" (the commoner's *right* to catch fish) are no longer in the British vocabulary. Now, while the landowner's rights are almost absolute, the common people no longer have the right of access to most lands in England. The people's rights are effectively nonexistent.

There was a similar kind of shared rights among the indigenous Cherokee peoples of North America. In the traditional Cherokee economic system, both the land and its abundance would be shared among clans. One clan could gather, another could camp, and yet a third could hunt on the same land. There was a fluid and common right of usage rather than an individual right to private property. The value was thus placed on sharing and reciprocity, on the widest distribution of wealth, and on limiting the inequalities within the economic system.

The Cherokee notion of the common right of shared usage fits well into Monbiot's commentary, the upshot of which can be stated as follows: The exclusive right to do with a piece of land as one will to the exclusion of other people (present and future) is perhaps the most obvious of class barriers. "We [the common people] are, quite literally, pushed to the margins of society," laments Monbiot. "If we enter the [English] countryside, we must sneak around it like fugitives, outlaws in the nation in which we all once had a stake. It is, in truth, not we who are the trespassers but the landlords. They are trespassing against our right to enjoy the gifts that Nature bequeathed to all of us."

George Monbiot, writing about Southeast Asia, Brazil, East Africa, and his native England, says that rural communities are forced to take seriously the welfare of their land because its resources are all they have to meet their diverse requirements. When the land is privatized, that which had been the people's communal commons passes into the hands of people whose priority is to make money, and the most efficient way to do that is to select the most profitable product and concentrate on producing it.

Without the security of land tenure and autonomy of decision making, writes Monbiot, people have no chance of defending the environment that provides their livelihoods. Brazil needs land reform; Kenya and Indonesia need to recognize and protect the traditional land rights of the indigenous peoples. By themselves, these policies will not guarantee environmental protection, but without them, environmental destruction is guaranteed.

If a land-use decision arises from an informed consensus of the local people, including everyone in a given development whom it might affect, says Monbiot, we are likely to see, reflected in that decision, the people's interests become vested in the quality of their surroundings and hence in the quality of their lives. If, on the other hand, a decision emerges from an impenetrable cabal of landowners, developers, and government officials, accountable to no one but the corporate/political elite, none of whom have to suffer the adverse consequences of their land-use choices, the forthcoming decision is likely to have a far more negative effect on both the environment and its inhabitants.

Concerning England, Monbiot gives the following commentary: The developers have "the most extraordinary legal powers to subvert the democratic process and impose their projects on even the most reluctant population." If ordinary people do not like a local authority's decision to approve a particular development, there is nothing they can do about it. But if a developer does not like the local council's decision to reject his or her proposed development, he or she can appeal to the secretary of state for the environment, in other words, the central government.

The developer knows that such an appeal will cost the local council hundreds of thousands of pounds to contest. Therefore, time and again, developers use the threat of an appeal to blackmail a local council into compliance with their wishes.

If, however, a local council has sufficient funds to fight the appeal, and if the secretary of state for the environment rejects the developer's plans during the appeal, all the developer need do is submit another almost identical planning application, and the whole process begins again. This cycle can go on until both the money and the willpower of the local council and local citizens are exhausted, assuming the developer has the financial wherewithal to outlast them. Thus developers get what they want. Does the dilemma in England ring a familiar note in your own city?

"The results of this democratic deficit are visible all over our cities," writes Monbiot. "Where we need affordable, inclusive housing, we get luxury, exclusive estates; where we need open spaces, we get more and more empty office blocks; where we need local trade, we get superstores...." In addition, traffic becomes increasingly congested, affordable housing is relegated to the countryside, and communities lose the resources that held them together. If this suspension of accountability is onerous in the town, it is worse in the countryside.

This stringent notion of the absolute rights of private property not only was part of the European myth forced on the indigenous peoples of the Americas but also precluded them from being allowed to share the land coveted by the European invaders. So the Europeans, and later the European Americas who were enticed westward by the government's promise of free land, simply took what they wanted by force, coercion, lies, and betrayal. The indigenous peoples had no recourse because they were merely ignorant "savages" with no "legal" documents and thus no claim to land in the European legal sense. To the Europeans and their descendants, the tenure of indigenous peoples on a particular piece of land, even for thousands of years, had—and has—no legal merit to prevent them from taking what they wanted, as the following historical sketches of the Aztecs, the Paiutes, and the Yanomami illustrate.[18,78]

Aztecs

Prior to the European invasion of North America north of Mexico, the Spanish invaded parts of South and Central America and took over Mexico. Prior to 1519, the Spanish had encountered chiefdoms (*cacicazgos*) of the Caribbean islands and along the Isthmus of Panama that had limited social organization or centralized authority. Here the Spaniards focused on the exploitation of gold and slave labor.

But the state organization of the Aztec empire in Mexico, and later that of the Inca empire in Peru, offered much more attractive possibilities, not only in the size of the accumulated wealth but also in the apparently limitless flow of state revenues. Even before the invasion and conquest had been completed, however, the Spanish had garnered considerable wealth, including both the spoils of war and the "gifts" extorted from the indigenous rulers. The sealed treasury of Moctezuma and the rooms filled with gold that belonged to Atahualpa are perhaps the best-known examples. Moctezuma, also known as Montezuma II (1480?–1520), the last Aztec emperor, was overthrown by Hernando Cortés. Atahualpa (1500?–1533), the last Inca emperor, was put to death by Francisco Pizarro.

With the treasures laid open for the taking, ornaments of inestimable artistic and cultural value were melted down and shaped into bars of gold. A fifth of the looted gold was claimed by the king of Spain and another fifth by the leader of the expedition, who also deducted his expenses as generously as possible, which left little for anyone else.

After the conquest of Mexico (1519–21), the Spanish coopted the administrative structures of the indigenous peoples, allowing the king of Spain and the new colonial government to usurp the traditional revenues of the region. At first, the indigenous rulers were allowed to act as nominal heads of state, while the conquistador-in-chief assumed control of the monetary tribute flowing from the economies of the subjugated regions.

The directive from the king of Spain to Cortés in 1523 stated explicitly that the indigenous peoples must pay monetary tribute to Spain, to wit: "They will give and pay us for each year as much revenue and tribute as were given and paid until now to their priests and lords." In order to accomplish this in terms of organization, the lower echelons of the indigenous administration had to be not only maintained but also integrated into the structures of colonial government. Other than the initial high cost of conquest, the Spaniards thought this arrangement would provide both the crown and the privileged conquerors with a seemingly permanent source of revenue.

Because the supposedly permanent source of revenue went to the king and his direct representative and agents, another means of recompense had to be found to satisfy the local petty rulers who had placed their lives and health at risk. The only practicable solution was to award these Spaniards a combination of tribute from and slavery of the indigenous peoples, called *encomienda*. According to the wishes of the king, personal *encomiendas* were to be reserved for the first generation of conquistadors only, yet, following the lead of Cortés, these privileges were repeatedly expanded with the support of the colonial administration.

Although *encomienda* did not legally confer the rights of private property for land, the holders of the privilege received most of the earliest land grants and had the advantage of virtual slave labor during the seasons of planting and harvesting. As the system of *encomienda* was gradually reformed and phased out, farming, which included the raising of livestock, became the major source of income for the increasing number of rural Spanish settlers. By 1525, ownership of public lands was overwhelmingly given to officials, the military, and the colonial elite.

By 1534, agricultural work was relegated to the indigenous peoples and property became the focus of competition between these people and the Spanish, ending in the partial dispossession of indigenous lands by the early 1600s. On the other hand, the indigenous peoples were not simply victims because they themselves participated in the sale of their property at very low prices, which effectively supported the growth and consolidation of Spanish estates.

The process of transferring land from the indigenous peoples to the control of the Spanish in the heartland of Mexico took about a century. Although traditional lands of the indigenous peoples were protected under Spanish law, that protection had the proviso that the land must be under cultivation. This proviso would work well for the Spanish if the indigenous population decreased, which it did.

In addition to the tremendous mortality within the indigenous population as a consequence of actual warfare during the Spanish invasion and subjugation of the people, the primary cause of the crash in the indigenous population was the high mortality associated with the pandemics of European-introduced diseases that swept across Mexico at short intervals after 1520. A mortality of 50 percent can be estimated for the smallpox epidemic of 1520, while the pandemics of 1545 and 1576, with mortalities of 50 to 90 percent locally, led in the cumulative to even greater collapse of the indigenous population. In addition, the many minor epidemics in between the major ones affected each district differently but were important in the collective impact. Between 1560 and 1600, a period that includes only one of the pandemics, the indigenous population of central Mexico declined by two-thirds, which means that a substantial part of the indigenous lands must have been uncultivated by 1600, thus opening them to acquisition by the Spaniards.

The demographic collapse of the indigenous population was reinforced by the resettlement of indigenous peoples in newly created centralized towns, where the people were not only separated by great distances from their traditional lands but also easier for the Spaniards to control through local colonial administration. The transfer of indigenous landholdings to the Spanish began on a large scale after 1580, and by 1620 most of the land in the Basin of Mexico and around Puebla had been given as land grants to Spaniards. Outside of Mexico City, the history of each regional settlement differs in detail, depending on the size of the indigenous population, the quality of the land, and the proximity of larger Spanish towns and major roads.

Leaping forward in history for a moment, modern Mexico City is built over the ancient Aztec city of Tenochtitlan, which in turn was constructed on a network of irrigation canals stemming from the long dried-up Lake Texcoco. Today, however, Mexico City is sinking at a rate of about 18 inches per year and has thus far sunk 33 feet because of the rate at which the groundwater is being pumped out to supply the city's 20 million people.[79] This is just one more legacy of European conquest of the Aztecs.

Bear in mind that the preceding account is a simplistic presentation of a highly complex process that took over a century to complete. In comparison, the Mormons' land grab from the Paiutes happened in the blink of an eye.

Paiutes

Lost in the eons of the past is the moment when the first humans entered the Valley of Fire, in what is now southern Nevada, during the latter part of the great ice age, some 11,000 years ago. Although the great ice sheets did not reach the valley, cool moisture-laden winds from the melting glaciers blew southward into the valley, which was a profusion of vegetation and flowing streams of cool water. Herds of deer, elk, and antelope grazed in the valley along with horses, camels, and a close relative of the present-day mountain goat. There were also ground sloths along the streams' margins and giant beavers within their waters. One of the main predators was a large doglike animal called a dire wolf.

Other humans existed in the valley 4,000 years ago, during a time when the climate was cooler and wetter than today and bighorn sheep were abundant. From 2000 B.C. to 300 B.C., the valley was occupied by people organized into small groups called nuclear families, each consisting of two to four men who, with their wives and children, wandered amongst their favorite hunting areas.

The men, using spears and atlatls, hunted bighorn sheep, the most important source of food. The women and children caught rabbits, hares, tortoises, and other reptiles and collected and prepared plants to supplement their diet of sheep. After the bighorn population declined from overhunting or because they became wary of the hunters, the families abandoned their camps only to return as the sheep once again repopulated the area. During times of good hunting and leisure, these people created elaborate artistic designs (called petroglyphs) on some of the rock faces by carefully pecking into the black desert varnish on the surface of the sandstone.

The climate became warmer and drier over time, gradually forcing the growing culture to adapt to the changing conditions. Between 300 B.C. and 700 A.D., food was too scarce in the valley to permit long periods of occupancy, so the people settled in the valleys of the Virgin and Muddy rivers outside the Valley of Fire. Even here, hunters, formerly dependent mainly on bighorn sheep, had to pursue such small game as rabbits, hares, ground squirrels, lizards, snakes, and birds to augment their kill of desert bighorn sheep and mule deer. The atlatl, still in use during the early part of this period, was eventually replaced with the bow and arrow, which was easier to carry, more accurate, and allowed repeated shots within a short time.

Gathering seeds, tubers, and berries became increasingly important in maintaining subsistence, as did the people's reliance on the streamside areas where the plants grew. With increasing dependence on plant food, risk of survival lessened and the population grew, placing an ever-increasing pressure on the fragile environment and forcing the people to move to less productive areas.

At some point during this period, farming was brought to the area by people migrating northward from Mexico. These migrants were called the Anasazi (Ah-nah-*sah*-zee), a Navajo word meaning "ancient ones." These early Anasazi people, often referred to as the Basket Makers, began to cultivate corn, squash, and beans near their villages along the riparian bottomlands of the Virgin and Muddy rivers and to store food for lean times.

Around 300 A.D., the Anasazi learned how to use clay to make sun-dried cookware, a technique that was gradually refined into the making of pottery. Pottery making became an art that played an important role in transforming the culture of the growing Anasazi population into a more highly organized, ritualized society.

Somewhere around 700 A.D., the Anasazi discovered they were not alone; the Lower Colorado Yuman people migrated into the area from the south, and about 900 A.D. the Paiutes also migrated into the area. As economic competition grew between these diverse people, the climatic conditions became even hotter and drier. The Anasazi abandoned the region around 1150 A.D., which left the area, including the Valley of Fire, to the Southern Paiute culture.

The Paiutes had already adapted to the desert and, unfettered by the ties of extensive farming and village life, lived in close ecological balance with their surroundings. The Paiute population was low, as small family groups lived a nomadic life of hunting and gathering, following the seasonal harvests from one place to another.

The valley, with its wide altitudinal range, was ideally suited for the seasonal use of the Paiutes. The season of greatest use was probably in the spring, when water would gather and remain in depressions in the rocks and edible plants would be in greatest abundance.

The Paiutes believed that the land would supply their needs, and with their simple but effective technology and hard work, the land did indeed grant them an adequate lifestyle. They were conscious of and dependent on Nature's cycles. They did not seek to conquer the desert, for they neither considered that they owned it nor that Nature was their enemy. Their way of life was thus harmonious with their environment and they asked from the land only that which it could supply. In the end, it was the Paiute that the European Americans found living in the valley when they first entered the area.

The first European to reach what is now southern Nevada was Francisco Garces in 1776. Few followed until half a century later when Jedediah Smith, the famous mountain man, led the first party of fur trappers along the Virgin River in 1826. During the 1830s and 1840s, traders and travelers from Santa Fe, New Mexico, followed Smith's route, known as the Spanish Trail, along the Virgin River.

The number of travelers increased greatly in the late 1840s. The old Spanish Trail, which had been used mostly by pack trains, gave way to new immigrants coming via Salt Lake City, Utah, on their way to California. The trail from Salt Lake City became the Mormon Road and was used mostly by wagon trains; it remained the primary route through the region until the San Pedro, Los Angeles, and Salt Lake Railroad replaced it in 1905.

The sudden, intrusive arrival of the European culture was traumatic to the Paiutes. Although there were occasional hostilities between the invaders and the Paiutes, often over the ownership of animals, the most devastating effect on the Paiutes was the European Americans' belief in private property.

Beginning in 1864, the Mormons, coming from what is now the state of Utah, settled along the Muddy and Virgin rivers and simply evicted the

Paiutes from their own land. The Mormons took away from the Paiutes their most productive riparian environments and then diverted water from the rivers and springs for intensive irrigation of agricultural crops, and in so doing destroyed the Paiutes' way of life.

In addition, the Mormons felled for fuel and timbers for mining operations the piñon pine forests on which the Paiutes relied for food. They also introduced vast numbers of grazing livestock and European diseases. The former destroyed the Paiutes' food and medicinal plants, and the latter all but decimated the Paiutes.

Once again, a resident human culture, having evolved a sense of place and mutual reciprocity with the land over many centuries, was immediately condemned and struck as valueless by an invading one, which considered itself superior. Finally, in 1872, their culture destroyed, the Paiutes were forced onto the Moapa Indian Reservation, which consists of about 72,000 acres along the Muddy River. Little of the Paiutes' material culture survives, but they still take pride in their indigenous philosophies and attitudes.

The Valley of Fire was established as Nevada's first state park in 1935, and is still its largest, but the Paiutes are forever gone. Every time we lose a culture, we forfeit an irretrievable part of ourselves, a part that evolved over hundreds, thousands, even millions of years, and it is still happening in South America.

Yanomami

The notion of the exclusive rights of private property coupled with the notion of superiority in the form of "rights" explains why so many species, both nonhuman and "primitive" humans, such as indigenous peoples in the Amazon Basin, are threatened with extinction. We perceive any organism that does not contribute obviously and directly to the workings of the dominant linear economy as having no intrinsic value in and of itself.

The only time one group of human beings makes another group of human beings extinct is when the first group sees itself as superior to the second group and wants—for nothing—what the second group has. In other words, in South America, as in all parts of the world, the "civilized" peoples of a nation see indigenous peoples as subhuman—only a little above the animals with whom they share the wild habitat.

The reason for this attitude is that one cannot forcibly take land from indigenous peoples and justify that theft if the indigenous peoples are seen as equals. The owners must therefore be viewed as subhuman. This view allows the thieves to exploit resources at the expense of the original owners—even to the point of their extermination. Consider the Yanomami Indians.

Bitter disputes over gold and diamonds by miners, soldiers, and priests are endangering the lives of the Yanomami Indians, the largest primitive tribe in existence. The Indians are threatened by a gold rush mentality in the remote northern Brazilian territory of Roraima, a region about the size of Minnesota. Most of the mineral wealth lies buried where 9,000 Yanomamis live spread out in four groups along the savanna clearings of the tropical Amazon rain forest and its border with Venezuela. An equal number inhabit the Venezuelan side of the frontier.

Although it is believed the Yanomamis migrated from the Caribbean region thousands of years ago, evidence of their presence in Roraima can be traced back only 120 years because they burn their dead and drink a solution of the ashes.

Because the Yanomamis have little or no contact with the modern world, they have no immunity against common viruses and can easily die from flu or cold, as did the indigenous North Americans during colonial times. Disease is the main reason the number of Brazilian Indians shrank from five million when the Portuguese reached Brazil 500 years ago to 220,000 today. Although armed violence has become a growing threat, it is bacteria and viruses that will ultimately kill the Indians.

The great irony is that no one has asked the Yanomamis how they feel about being treated as subhumans. But then no one asked the indigenous North Americans or the African slaves how they felt either. The slaves were viewed simply as private property, as are all slaves, which is a phenomenon made possible by linear thinking.

Private Property and Linear Thinking

We humans are quite willing to make a group of people extinct if we covet its resources and can find no alternative way to justify our covetousness! To realize this, all we have to do is witness history from the era of the Old Testament of the Bible to the present.

Threatened and endangered species result from linear vision. When we think in a linear way, we look fixedly straight ahead with the notion that in order for an economic endeavor to be healthy, it must be ever expanding. In linear thinking, we never look back, for our premise is there can be no return. Linearity is above all the doctrine of possession.

This doctrine is not complemented by one of relinquishment, replenishment, and/or sharing.

It comes as no surprise, therefore, that our concept of "use" does not imply wise use, conservative use, or even good use. We simply trade quality in on quantity. Is it any wonder that we find ourselves wallowing in our own waste from our love affair with disposability?

Similarly, linear thinking means that we squander both time and life without respect for death. Through the lens of linear vision, death becomes accidental, the chance interruption of a process that might otherwise go on forever, and so it is an unacceptable surprise and always feared. After all, say the high priests of linearity, it is the length of life, the quantity, that counts; thus medical progress to many people means to prolong life at any cost—regardless of its quality.

Linear vision flourishes in fear, ignorance, and contempt for the processes on which it depends. As linear thinkers, we do not, for example, see the forest for the trees, because in the face of these processes our concepts of linear, mechanical, expansionistic management are so unrealistic, so impractical, they have the nature of science fiction.

Processes are invariably cyclical, rising and falling, giving and taking, living and dying on ever-expanding ripples of time. Yet linear vision places its emphasis only on the rising phase of the cycle—on production, expansion, possession, youth, and life. It fails to provide for returns, idleness, contraction, giving, old age, or death.

Waste is a concept born only from a vision of economic linearity and specialization. According to this notion of life, every human activity produces waste, because every human activity is linear and specialized and in order to be of social value must produce something of economic value. "This," says Wendell Berry, "implies a profound contempt for correct discipline; it proposes, in the giddy faith of prodigals, that there can be [everlasting] production without fertility, abundance without thrift. We take and do not give back, and this causes waste. It is a hideous concept, and it is making the world hideous...." But even worse than this is the ever-growing concept of owning diversity.

Trying to Own Diversity

The most important distinctions to people in the post-Cold-War world are not distinctions of ideology, politics, or economics but rather of culture.[80] People are trying desperately in our current global upheaval to answer the most basic of human questions: Who are we? What value do we have?

They are trying to answer these questions in the only way they know how, the traditional way, by referencing those things that mean the most to them. People define themselves in terms of ancestry, language, values, customs, sense of place, and history in such a way that they highlight their cultural affiliations, such as tribes, ethnic groups, religious communities, and nations. Politics is the tool that people use to advance not only their personal interests but also their identities, which brings us to the Western corporate bid to control the world through what it calls universalism. The rest of the world, however, calls this corporate ploy imperialism. Put simply, the corporate world is trying to own and thus control diversity.

To the corporate mind, with a few exceptions, control is tyranny, whereas being out of control is freedom. An economy that is out of control is a "free" market. But there is no such thing as absolute freedom; freedom is relative and always within constraints. The critical questions thus become: What sort of constraints do corporations accept? Are corporations other-centered in their interests and therefore ethics-centered in their operations, or are corporations self-centered in their interests and therefore self-serving in their operations?

Corporate Power

Corporate freedom relates to corporate power, and absolute power corrupts absolutely. Therefore, while corporations want absolute freedom from the "tyranny" of outside controls, which are in the public favor, they want to impose the tyranny of corporate control in politics in order to secure corporate control of the global market, which is in the corporate favor.

As Professor Noam Chomsky puts it: "Power is increasingly concentrated in unaccountable institutions. The rich and powerful are no more willing to submit themselves to market discipline or popular pressure than they ever have been in the past."

In considering democracy, Chomsky points out that power is continually shifting away from parliamentary institutions into the hands of huge transnational corporations. Power is flowing to corporations and their supporting structures, all of which are completely unaccountable. The corporation itself has a stricter hierarchy than any human institution, which Chomsky says is a form to totalitarianism and unaccountability that is tantamount to "economic fascism." This is the reason corporations are so strongly opposed to classical liberals.

Thomas Jefferson, who lived just long enough to witness the early development of the corporate system, saw the handwriting on the wall. He said in 1799 that "banking establishments [his term for corporations] are more dangerous than standing armies." Jefferson warned in his last years that money and banking establishments (corporations) would destroy liberty and restore absolutism, effectively nullifying the ideals for which the American Revolution was fought.[80]

Preoccupied with consumption for its own sake, economics, since Jefferson's time, has increasingly been confined to the shallowness of appearances. Economists remain mesmerized by the theory that more rational analysis of the material world can and will provide all the necessary answers, despite the acknowledged limitations of "objective" reasoning in the physical sciences, says Frances Hutchinson.[81] "Economics as practised by professionals is, indeed, the 'dismal science' from which life itself is banished." She asserts that economists hide behind a "smokescreen [they] erected...to obscure the fact that they know nothing about the real world."

The marketplace satisfies only temporarily our collective neuroses, while hiding the values that give meaning to human life. Although one's work can offer intense personal satisfaction, the economist has no mechanism to register the joy (utility) derived from work, which leaves the economist incapable of recognizing the fulfillment rendered by labor. Therefore, "environmental economics," which attempts to place monetary value on the nonmarketable aspects of both culture and Nature, dwells in the same murky habitat as marketplace economics.[81]

Gross materialism and gross poverty are equally ugly, and both are the result of an economic system that reduces everything of value to the cash nexus. When, for example, labor becomes a mere commodity, subjected to the laws of supply and demand, statistics substitutes for real human value. "People become things, children born and unborn are material possessions, a beautiful landscape has a price, and all are disposable in the name of economic rationality."[81] And thus, prophetically, Jefferson's foresight comes to pass, exemplified most poignantly by the advent of genetic engineering.

Stealing the Diversity of Life

"Ever since the genetic revolution began," writes author George Monbiot, "biotechnologists have attacked the activists who challenge their work for knowing next to nothing about science, and yet presuming to warn of its consequences." Now that the consequences of genetic engineering reach into every corner of our lives, continues Monbiot, it is surely time for citizens to challenge those biotechnologists who are so cavalier as to dismiss as irrelevant or misguided society's concerns about the potential and unpredictable consequences of genetic engineering.[82] Talking about biotechnology, Alastair McIntosh, a Fellow of Edinburgh's Centre for Human Ecology, feels that "we are witnessing...the emergence of a cult camouflaged as science but without the ethical foundations." McIntosh goes on to say that "the bottom line ethical question in biotechnology is the same as that for all walks of life: does it augment that beauty which is the fruit of love made visible?"[83]

According to Alan Simpson,[84] a Labour member of the British Parliament for Nottingham South, the "'Brave New World' of patents on life is all about imperialism in a new guise. The key issue," he says, "is not about biotechnology research, its ethics and its limitations." The conflict, contends Simpson, is who owns the knowledge and discoveries associated with the genetic makeup of the planet, which previously have always been held in the social commons. The unchartered world that corporate interests now want to colonize is how we humans manipulate plant propagation, livestock breeding, and human health.

The divide between health and wealth under the "new patent and plunder regime" is even more stark in the Southern Hemisphere, where the rules of the industrialized countries allow biopiracy on a scale unseen for centuries. Many big pharmaceutical companies have already taken out what Simpson calls "broad species" patents on a whole range of genetically engineered crops, from soybeans to cotton, and use the patents to restrict all outside research on the crops under patent. This, asserts Simpson, is the pattern disputes will take in the future. Helena Paul, of the Gaia Foundation in London, adds that "through gene technology, corporations are invading plants, animals, and indigenous people to maximize power and profit."[85]

Today, the social benefits of knowledge—at times even stolen knowledge, and hence stolen benefits—are subjected to the greed of material hoarding for monetary gain. And greed is a nationality all its own. Consider that a central part of both the General Agreement on Tariffs and Trade and the North American Free Trade Agreement is protection for the ownership of knowledge and technology, which is rights of intellectual property.[86] The purpose of these agreements, says Chomsky, is to ensure that the technology of the future is held in monopoly by huge private corporations, which are usually subsidized by the government.

Chomsky's point is a good one, because the wealthy industrialized nations, having greatly reduced the biological and genetic diversity within their own borders, are now looking to the nonindustrialized countries for genetic resources and traditional medicinal plants. For example, Canadian varieties of wheat contain disease-resistant genes from 14 poorer nonindustrialized countries, and American cucumbers rely on genes from Korea, Burma, and India.[87]

Tropical forests are perhaps the world's greatest chemical factories, which means that less wealthy, less industrialized countries, such as Brazil, India, and the Congo, still have relatively untapped gene pools for food plants and animals and medicinal plants of potential economic importance, although they do not have the financial resources to commercialize them even if they wanted to. Consider the neem tree. Its bark, oil, and gum have been used for centuries by India's peasant farmers as a source of pesticide to protect their crops. Today, the neem tree, regarded as sacred by many Hindus, is the focus of an international dispute over who should control, and profit from, the tree's biological properties—an industrialized country or India, where the tree grows.[87]

I heard much about the neem tree and the controversy surrounding it at a conference on native medicinal plants while I was in Malaysia a few years ago. The point is that the wealthy industrialized countries have the financial capital to study, identify, purify, and commercialize the biological properties of the neem tree, but they do not want to share any of the profits with the country where the tree grows or with the people who long ago learned how to use it. Such naked greed, lack of consciousness, and arrogance are nothing less than intellectual pirating of traditional indigenous knowledge from people who have no voice with which to speak for themselves and cannot afford legal representation—and should not have to! After all, the people living in the environments with the plants, people who learned over millennia how to use the plants' properties, are, as the original discoverers, being robbed of not only their knowledge but also the plants by foreign corporations.

"If the Western scientists and multinationals really want to help developing countries, such as India, they should share their knowledge and shouldn't patent material derived from the genetic resources which those countries possess," says Ashish Kothari, a professor at the Indian Institute of Public Administration. This prompted Kamal Nath, India's former minister of the environment, to say: "What we protect becomes the raw material for the biotechnology industry of the developed countries without any benefits accruing to India."[87] Kamal Nath has touched on a critical but often ignored point: most localities that harbor either the wild relatives of known crop plants or plants of unknown benefit to society are unprotected and severely endangered.

This lack of protecting habitats has the makings of a monumental human tragedy because different populations of the same species of plant may produce different types and quantities of defensive chemicals that have potential use as pharmaceuticals, pesticides, or disease-resistant crop plants. For example, it took many thousands of varieties of rice from different locations to find one that could resist grassy stunt virus, a disease that posed a serious threat to the world's rice crop.[88] Thus, saving only one population of each important species—but failing to protect habitats with other populations of the same species—could well hide a cost society cannot afford to pay.

Kamal Nath went on to say that India is drafting legislation to regulate the removal of such material and may link that regulation to the issue of stronger safeguards for "intellectual property rights" demanded by the United States.[87]

Another example involves Jamaican peasants who use pink-flowered periwinkle to treat diabetes. When scientists grasped the meaning of an opportunity to use the properties of this plant for medicine, they extracted two drugs from it, the annual sales of which exceed $100 million. In the United States alone, $6 billion is spent annually on medicines derived from tropical plants. The as yet untapped potential is spectacular; for every plant that has been examined by Western science, 200 more await study,[89] which spurs the naked greed of corporations.

There are still more sad chapters to the story of trying to own diversity.[90] In Papua New Guinea, a young tribesman of the Hagahai people may hunt wild pigs or harvest yams somewhere in the wild gorges of the Yuat River. Although his heart belongs to the jungle, his blood "belongs" to the U.S. government—or so says Patent No. 5,397,696.

The Hagahai people have lived as tiny bands of hunter–gatherers in the Shrader Mountains for untold centuries. Their remote region consists of rushing rivers and a jungle rich in wild pigs, birds of paradise, and malaria, a disease that has been killing more and more of the Hagahai's children in recent decades. Hearing from other tribes about the outside world, a few Hagahai went looking for help in 1983.

Medical anthropologist Carol Jenkins of Papua New Guinea's Institute of Medical Research responded to their plea. Flying out by helicopter, the American scientist began a long-term study of the Hagahai people, which won her international attention—and a call from the U.S. National Institutes of Health.

Virologists at the National Institutes of Health, engaged in research on retroviruses (the family that includes the AIDS virus), were surveying human populations from remote areas for genetic variants of retroviruses and asked to check the Hagahai people. Jenkins consequently told the Hagahai people that she wanted to see a "binitang" (an insect) in their blood, which she assured them would not make them sick but might help others.

Subsequent blood tests showed that many Hagahai people carry what appears to be a benign variant of the human T-cell leukemia virus, although the Hagahai themselves are not afflicted with the disease. Because it is possible that this variant might help scientists to better understand its deadlier relatives, the National Institutes of Health established a cell line, which is a self-perpetuating culture of virus-infected white blood cells. In 1991, they quietly applied for a patent, which was issued in March 1995.

U.S. Patent 5,397,696 applies to "a human T-cell line (PNG-1)...and to the infecting virus." The patent lists Carol Jenkins and four U.S. government scientists as "inventors" and the U.S. Department of Health and Human Services as "assignee." The patent means that the U.S. government, or a company that buys the rights to the patent, will have the sole right to use the Hagahai tribesman's virus-infected cells for commercial purposes for 17 years.

And what about the Hagahai tribesman? He is neither named in the patent nor listed as a beneficiary, even though the document indicates that the "invention" may be useful in developing a vaccine or in devising techniques for screening human blood for T-cell leukemia. But how can anyone claim to have invented and therefore own someone else's blood and then patent that invention and benefit from it financially? Is this not simply a new and tragic form of colonialism? How is it any different than my insisting that I have invented the exceedingly fertile soil in the Willamette Valley of western Oregon and being granted a U.S. patent for it and the exclusive 17-year right to use and sell it?

The preceding example is hypothetical, but such is not the case with the U.S. National Park Service, which, according to lawyer Joseph Mendelson, "cut a back-room deal and bent laws to allow the commercial exploitation [bioprospecting and biopiracy] of Yellowstone."[91] Mendelson, of the International Center for Technology Assessment, a public interest group in Washington, D.C., went on to say, "The precedent set by this agreement threatens not only Yellowstone, but all of our parks."

The National Park Service has acknowledged that, under the agreement, Diversa Corporation of San Diego, California, would pay Yellowstone

National Park $100,000 over the next five years and donate $75,000 of in-kind services for allowing bioprospecting and potential biopiracy of the tiny microbes in the rare thermal pools that researchers want to patent. Diversa has, as of March 8, 1998, refused requests filed under the Freedom of Information Act regarding the royalties the government would receive as part of the deal. Despite the fact that such biopiracy not only of Nature but also of public property could be worth millions of dollars to Diversa, the National Park Service stated that such information falls under the category of a proprietary trade secret.

As a result of biopiracy in the 1960s, another company is already profiting from a Yellowstone-derived enzyme now widely used in DNA fingerprinting. Although enzymes (the proteins that operate cells) normally break down at high temperatures, the microbes in the hot springs and geysers of Yellowstone apparently are more durable because they have evolved in water near the boiling point.

Such corporate theft as the patented rights of intellectual property is increasing and is just one more example of corporate coercive power to own diversity, in this case primarily through the often surreptitious control of medicines and foods. But where in this country of supposed equality, one might ask, did intellectual colonialism begin?

The Rights of Intellectual Property

On April, 17, 1492, Queen Isabel and King Ferdinand gave to Christopher Columbus all the rights and privileges of "discovery and conquest."[92] A year later, on May 4, 1493, Pope Alexander VI granted to the Catholic monarchs Isabel of Castille and Ferdinand of Aragon, through his "Bull of Donation," all islands and mainlands "discovered and to be discovered, one hundred leagues to the West and South of the Azores towards India," provided they were not already occupied or held by a Christian king or prince as of Christmas 1492.

Author Walter Ullmann, in writing about medieval papalism, said the pope, as the victor of God, commanded the world as though it was a tool in his hands. The pope, supported by the canonists, thought of the world as his private property to be disposed of in accordance with his will. Acts of blatant piracy were thus converted into acts of divine will through charters and patents.

By this notion, any peoples and nations not already colonized did not belong to the pope per se and were instead "donated" to the European monarchs. This canonical jurisprudence effectively made the Christian monarchs of Europe the sovereign lords of all nations, "wherever they might be found and whatever creed they might embrace," and opened the judicial and moral way to justify colonization and genocide of non-European peoples. The principle of "effective occupation" by Christian monarchs, the alleged "vacancy" of the coveted lands, and the "duty" to transform the "savages" into civilized Christians were critical components of the charter–patents.

Although much has changed in the 500 years since Columbus invaded the New World, some things have not. The "creation" of private property through the piracy of another's belongings is the same as it was 500 years ago. Today, however, the "vacancy" of coveted lands has been replaced by the "vacancy" of coveted life-forms, including species manipulated through the new biotechnologies.

The freedom claimed by today's transnational corporations through the trade-related intellectual property rights of the General Agreement on Trade and Tariffs (GATT) is the same freedom claimed since 1492 by the European colonizers, a precedent set by Columbus as a natural "right" of European men. The titles to and grants of land issued by the pope, through the European kings and queens, were the first patents, giving the holders the freedom to subjugate and enslave the indigenous peoples in order to acquire private property and personal wealth. This violent takeover was rendered a "natural" right by stereotyping all indigenous peoples as savages who were less than human and thus deserved to be enslaved as free labor.

These European notions of the right to commit piracy for personal gain and the right to protect that property once stolen are the bases on which the intellectual property right laws of GATT and the World Trade Organization are framed. The Western industrialized societies are still driven to discover, conquer, own, possess, and control all they see, even if it means the extinction of whole cultures and species. To accomplish this, the assumption of unoccupied or empty lands, "terra nullus," is now extended to "empty life," such as seeds and medicinal plants that are "empty, vacant, unoccupied" as defined by Western science and culture, freeing them for the taking.

Commandeering the resources of indigenous peoples was justified by colonists on the basis that indigenous peoples did not "improve" their lands as dictated by European standards based on private ownership of land. The same logic is used today by stating that any knowledge, especially aboriginal knowledge, is unimproved if it is not encrusted in the science of acceptable Western standards. Taking unacceptable indigenous knowledge and magically transforming it into acceptable scientific knowledge is therefore used as the measure of "improvement" necessary to freely steal from indigenous peoples without permission, just recognition, or just compensation.

New colonies are being carved out through patents and genetic engineering, colonies that not only denigrate but also threaten the sacred evolution of living things. Physicist, philosopher, and author Vandana Shiva writes that resistance to this new colonization through biopiracy is resistance to the ultimate colonization of life itself—to the future of Nature's evolutionary processes. She goes on to say: "It is a struggle to protect the freedom of diverse species to evolve; it is a struggle to protect the freedom of diverse cultures to evolve; it is a struggle to conserve both cultural and biological diversity. It is a struggle against new and old forms of colonization."

There is another way of learning about medicinal plants, a way that is the antithesis of colonization; it is sharing with those who shared. The Belize Ethnobotany Project, which Drs. Michael Balick and Rosita Arvigo began in 1986, is an example.[93] "When we began the project," said Balick and Arvigo, "we really committed to developing a project that would give back as much or more than we would receive in exchange...."

To do this, Balick and Arvigo asked the community of traditional healers, as well as the individual healers and bushmasters, those persons with great knowledge about the rain forest, to help them develop some of the objectives to be accomplished in the project. Then they met with a number of the traditional healers and learned, in the process, that there was a common theme in many of their requests—to create a book that could simultaneously be used by the healers themselves to teach their children and to serve as a reference that would in some way help support and reestablish the validity and importance of traditional healing in the contemporary world. Their commitment to the healers was to produce a simple, inexpensive, and carefully written book that would archive information on the use of plants in the context of local beliefs, while at the same time providing clinical information, when available, on the efficacy of the plants.

To pay for the publication, Balick and Arvigo each took out a loan, using their respective homes as collateral. They did this to give them not only the freedom to determine how the book would be published and priced but also control over how the royalties would be distributed. As a result, a significant percentage of the royalties derived from the sale of the book has gone directly into a fund to support the traditional healers who so graciously shared their knowledge, something the healers did not ask for. But it is only just, say Balick and Arvigo, because it is, after all, *the traditional healers' knowledge.*

Balick and Arvigo structured the payment of royalties as follows: (1) 15 percent of the retail sales in Belize, not the profits, go to the healers' fund, an important distinction because each of the healers has been assigned a certain number of shares depending on how much time, effort, and knowledge they contributed to the project, and (2) 10 percent of the sales from books sold in the United States and from books sold at lectures given by Balick and Arvigo go to the healers' fund. In addition, Lotus Light, the publisher, has pledged to the healers' fund ten cents per book sold. The healers are paid by check every six months, in June and December.

Beyond the royalties, any income that might be derived from a drug discovery program will be shared with the healers. This is possible through the collaboration of Balick and Arvigo with the U.S. National Cancer Institute and other groups, such as Shaman Pharmaceutical, Inc., that have made such reciprocity an important part of the way they conduct business.

Fortunately, people with the integrity of Balick and Arvigo exist in the world that bridges science, medicine, and commerce; they are, however, few and far between. The norm in today's world of megacorporations is vastly different.

Call It Scientific/Corporate Progress, It Is Still "Biopiracy"

"Biopiracy" is the act of modern colonization by which corporations use the ancient wisdom of indigenous peoples to locate and understand the use of their traditional medicinal plants and then exploit them commercially—unbeknownst to and at the expense of the indigenous people and the nation in which they live.[94] Hoping to find cures worth billions of dollars, scientists from the United States and Europe have even taken blood, hair, and saliva from indigenous peoples, which means biopiracy of the human body, for which there is neither moral justification nor recompense.

"The brave new frontier of genetic engineering," says Andrew Kimbrell, president of the International Center for Technology Assessment in Washington, D.C., "is extending humanity's reach over the forces of nature as no other technology has ever done." Scientists can now program species by isolating, snipping, inserting, rearranging, and editing genetic material, making them the first human architects of life itself, the authors of technological evolution.

While this may be true, Jeremy Rifkin, in his 1998 article entitled "God in a Labcoat," points out that many of today's best-known molecular biologists are imprisoned in the hubris of Baconian tradition. Francis Bacon, who lived in the 17th century and is considered to be the father of modern science through the scientific method of inquiry, viewed Nature as a "common harlot" and thus urged future generations to "tame," "squeeze," "mold," and "shape" Nature in order to be in control of the physical world.

Scientists who embrace this traditional Baconian box view the world through a reductionist lens and, according to Rifkin, deem themselves as "grand engineers, continually editing and recombining the genetic components of life into compliant organisms designed for human service." The Baconian method of inquiry favored by most molecular biologists is one of pseudo-objectivity, for no one is or can be truly objective, if for no other reason than all of our questions are subjective. Nevertheless, those scientists who are trapped in the Baconian box of pseudo-objectivity favor isolation over integration, mental detachment over emotional engagement, and the use of force over trusteeship and nurturance.

This world view suites them well for the corporate world on the global stage. I say this because the technological evolution with which they are engaged is designed to create new species of living organisms that are more profitable to the corporate world and research than are the organisms given to us by Nature. The corporate struggle for ever-increasing margins of profit through ever-more centralized control of global markets and politics has resulted in a frenzied corporate search—a gene rush by biopirates—for living materials found primarily in the Southern Hemisphere.

Legalizing Biopiracy

"Bioprospecting," as Kimbrell calls it, has the potential to be a veritable gold mine for industry and science because the untapped genetic materials found in the nonindustrialized countries of the world may well yield cures for some of society's ills as well as a bounty of cash. The prospect of potential material wealth from Nature's genetic materials has already sent biopirates into countries such as India to steal genetic materials and potential drugs under the guise of improving "unoccupied" knowledge because it has neither been certified by the scientific stamp of approval nor economically exploited within the country, which, according to the biopirates, makes it free for the taking.

Today's biopiracy is not solely the product of scientists wed more thoroughly than in the past to corporate greed for their research dollars; it is also the result of a new law based on a 1980s U.S. Supreme Court decision, *Diamond v. Chakrabarty*. The effect of this little-known court decision is to legalize permission to go bioprospecting with the intent to commit biopiracy, which, according to Kimbrell, is "one of the most important judicial decisions of the twentieth century."

The case began in 1971, when microbiologist Ananda Mohan Chakrabarty, an employee of General Electric, genetically engineered a bacterium that could digest oil. That same year, General Electric applied to the U.S. Patent and Trademark Office for a patent on Chakrabarty's oil-eating bacterium. The Patent and Trademark Office deliberated for several years and finally rejected the application under the traditional legal doctrine that life-forms, which are products of Nature, are not legally patentable.

The case was eventually referred to the U.S. Supreme Court, which handed down a surprise five-to-four decision in June 1980, ruling that the patent was to be granted because the "relevant distinction is not between living and inanimate things but whether living products could be seen as 'human-made inventions.'" Allowing life to be seen as "human-made inventions" and thus patentable is a notion on morally thin ice. Nevertheless, the Patent and Trademark Office ruled in 1985 that genetically engineered plants are patentable and in 1987 extended patenting to all genetically altered or engineered animals. Within a few years, microbes, plants, animals, and human cells, cell lines, and genes were being patented.

By a margin of one vote, the U.S. Supreme Court unilaterally handed over to private ownership the genetic commons of planet Earth. The effect of this modern form of colonialism is profound in that a corporation or government entity can now legally expropriate a natural substance found in a poor, nonindustrialized nation, isolate valuable genetic material, and patent it—without permission or recompense—as private property to be held as a monopoly on commercial uses for approximately two decades. The laws that protect outright international biopiracy also protect genetic engineering, which is just another form of biopiracy, an often domestic form within which there are many potential unknown risks.

Biopiracy Is Steeped in Hidden Social–Ecological Risks

Most supporters of "genetic modification" downplay the difference between genetically engineered organisms and the techniques of time-honored selective breeding. They claim, for example, that the only difference between genetically engineered plants and traditional crops is that genetic manipulation is not only more precise but also faster and cheaper. Although this claim would seem to be good news, it is ecologically misleading and genetically irresponsible.

"Experiments have shown," writes Ricarda Steinbrecher, a genetic scientist and member of the British Society for Allergy, Environmental, and Nutritional Medicine, "that a gene is not an independent entity as was originally thought."[95] Genetic engineers increasingly want to "transform plants and animals into designed commodities," while ignoring the many unknown hazards.

Steinbrecher cites the example of a 1990 experiment in Germany, where the gene for the color red was taken from corn and transferred, together with a gene for antibiotic resistance, into the flowers of white petunias. The only expectation was a field of 20,000 red-flowering petunias. The genetically engineered petunias not only turned red but also had more leaves and shoots, a higher resistance to fungi, and lower fertility. These unexpected results were completely unrelated to the genes for color and antibiotic resistance. Such unrelated, unexpected results have been termed pleiotropic effects, which by their very nature are totally unpredictable.

In this case, says Steinbrecher, the pleiotropic effects were both clearly visible and easily identified without molecular analysis. But what happens, asks Steinbrecher, if pleiotropic effects are not so obvious, if they in secret affect the composition of proteins, the expression of hormones, or the concentration of nutrients, toxins, or allergens? Who is going to monitor all the possible pleiotropic effects before a genetically engineered plant is introduced into the environment or placed on our dinner plates? And there are neither regulations nor voluntary guidelines and practices with which to check for pleiotropic effects.

In addition to pleiotropic effects, there are simple biological and ecological limitations to what is and is not possible. Consider, for instance, that a 1997 report by the World Bank indicated that a 1.5 to 1.7 percent per year increase in grain yields could be expected. With such a rosy outlook, says Lester R. Brown, president of the Worldwatch Institute, the World Bank projects a surplus in the capacity of agriculture throughout the world as a whole, accompanied by declining food prices, but the Worldwatch Institute came up with a very different outcome from the World Bank's analysis.

The difference is that the economists of the World Bank based their predictions on simple extrapolation in which they argued that "historically, yields have grown along a *linear path* [emphasis added] from 1960 to 1990, and they are projected to continue along the path of past growth." Note two things here: (1) the linear nature of the economists' view of ecological systems and (2) the creation of the grain yield as an independent variable, which, of course, cannot exist in an interdependent living system.

Thus, while extrapolating past trends in the grain yield worked well in previous decades, it will not work as it once did because the ecological limiting factors to the ever-increasing production of grain, which always loomed invisibly on the horizon, are becoming undeniably manifest. In contrast, the robust 2.1 percent increase in grain yields between 1950 and 1990 has been replaced with a 1.0 percent increase between 1990 and 1995.

Although one can argue that a five-year increment is too short a time to establish a clear trend, it may nevertheless be a strong portent of the future because it is clear ecologically that when a country's farming practices in growing wheat, or other crops, fall short of their potential, the yield can for a time be rapidly improved until the ecological limits are reached. Beyond that, no amount of money, ingenuity, water, or fertilizer can force more out of the crop.

The projections of the World Bank are hence irresponsible in that they permit governments to become complacent about treating agricultural lands as a commodity of which there is a perceived surplus that is then available through the rights of private property to be subdivided for houses, paved over as shopping malls, or otherwise frittered away with self-centered impunity. A result of this kind of thinking is visible in the Central Valley of California, where housing projects march unimpeded up the valley, consuming some of the world's finest farming land. In China, the government is paving over millions of acres of agricultural lands so automobiles can replace bicycles. And the fertile riceland of Indonesia is being converted to golf courses.

Losing farmland to other uses is not the only irreversible problem; losing water is another. In Texas, where farming has historically relied on irrigation, 14 percent of the irrigated area has been lost since 1980 as a result of depleting the aquifer. Water for irrigation is also being lost in

California, Kansas, and Oklahoma. Water is being diverted from irrigation to cities in the Hebei Province of China to satisfy the soaring urban and industrial demands for the precious liquid. In the agricultural areas surrounding Beijing, farmers have been prohibited since 1994 from using water stored in reservoirs because all the region's water is now preempted by the capital city's growing thirst.

"So what," one might think, "there still is the opportunity for genetic engineering. We will simply design organisms to meet our changing needs despite the supposed ecological limiting factors." Yes, we can work on this, but it is a gigantic gamble with all of the future just to avoid acting with personal responsibility. And that gamble is the outcome of the effects we cause when we introduce an unknown product of any kind into the environment.

To examine this gamble, let's begin with a new buzzword, "transgenic technology," which is taking one part of an organism's genes and placing it into the genes of another organism. Transgenic technology is, after all, far from a precise practice because genes are not machines that can simply be snipped from their host and placed somewhere else without opening the possibility of totally unpredictable, unwanted, and potentially uncontrollable results. Consider that a trait which is not evident in one organism and is said to be suppressed may come out of hiding, as it were, and become visibly expressed when working in concert with the full set of chromosomes present in a normal reproductive or germ cell of another organism.

Roughly two-thirds of the transgenic research in agricultural crops is aimed at creating plants that can resist stronger than normal dosages of pesticides and herbicides. The reason is that most crops developed through selective breeding during the "Green Revolution" can compete only weakly with weeds. Corporate reasoning might go something like this: If the crop plants of the Green Revolution are easily outcompeted by weeds and our chemical herbicides are detrimental to both the weeds and crop plants, then we must create genetically engineered crop plants that can withstand more of our chemical herbicides. In this way, the crops will be protected; we sell more herbicides, kill the weeds, and the world is better fed. But this line of reasoning did not work, as demonstrated by the "parrot beak" fiasco, which took place during 1997 in the southern United States.

Monsanto, in 1997, made its first commercial planting of "Roundup Ready" cotton, which was created by Monsanto to withstand high dosages of the powerful herbicide Roundup. By October, over 30,000 acres planted to Roundup Ready cotton were in serious trouble because the cotton bolls were falling off the plants throughout the South. In fact, the cotton bolls were deformed in such a characteristic way that the farmers named the syndrome "parrot beak."

Although the farmers lost millions of dollars, Roundup Ready cotton had been deregulated, which meant that the U.S. Department of Agriculture did not require Monsanto to report the incident. According to Kelly Wiseman, co-op general manager of the Community Food Co-op of Bozeman, Montana, the company tried to claim that unfavorable weather conditions were at fault, despite the fact that only Roundup Ready cotton exhibited parrot beak. Wiseman went on to say that the ensuing investigation is being conducted by Monsanto, which means the results will most likely remain a closely guarded secret under U.S. patent laws.

What if all the genetic engineering of the world's crop plants were to lead to "superweeds," as there already are "superinsects" and "superbacteria"—all genetically resistant to the chemicals that are supposed to kill them? Then what? After all, many so-called weeds are close relatives of crop plants, especially in the mustard family. And there is good evidence that cross-species mutations can occur within a few generations, which can lead to herbicide-resistant weeds. Farfetched? Not so. In 1996, researchers in Denmark reported that a genetically engineered, herbicide-resistant rapeseed plant transmitted its transgene to a weedy relative, *Brassica campestris*, in the mustard family within just two generations of its having been planted. This was not a predicted result of the genetic engineering.

It is unintended results like this that deeply concern organic farmers. Why such concern? Because organic farmers have for decades relied on a naturally occurring bacterium, *Bacillus thuringiensis*, commonly referred to as Bt, as Nature's own insecticide. Bt was deemed safe because, in addition to being totally "natural," it decomposed within days into harmless components, which precluded any insects that survived from evolving resistance to it. Once again, enter Monsanto.

By taking genes from Bt and incorporating them into cotton plants, Monsanto has created Bollgard, more commonly known as Bt cotton. By incorporating genes from Bt into the germ cells of cotton plants, there is a much greater probability that insects can, through mutation, evolve resistance to Bt and thereby render it useless as a natural insecticide for organic farmers.

In 1996, according to Wiseman, nearly two million acres in the United States were planted with Monsanto's Bollgard cotton. Wiseman goes on to say that "Monsanto made over $50 million from registration fees on the crop alone, despite the fact that the planted Bt cotton suffered major bollworm infestation." The farmers who paid Monsanto had to spray heavily anyway. The upshot is that Monsanto made money, the farmers lost money, and the organic agriculture business waits to see if bollworms develop genetic resistance to Bt.

There are no requirements, as far as I know, that genetically engineered or transgenic species in our food supply be labeled as such, much as I and many others would like to know. About 60 percent of the packaged foods one buys at the grocery store, says Wiseman, contain soybeans in one form or another, but we have no way of knowing whether the products we purchase contain Roundup Ready soybeans. Wiseman contends that large corporations in agribusiness, which control commodities, have been quick to mix transgenic seeds with traditional seeds, thus preventing consumers, in the United States at least, from having any real control over what is in the food they purchase.

The reason for this lack of control on the part of consumers, says Wiseman, is that food labeled "genetically enhanced" or with some other such label has been rejected by consumers. Therefore, Wiseman says, the corporations have lobbied Congress and the Clinton administration to omit the requirement of such labeling, which has so far been granted, keeping consumers in the dark about the quality of their food.

Another hidden risk to our food supply is hybrids. The term "hybrid," as it is technically used, refers to the first-generation progeny of crosses between two different varieties of parent plants, each of which breeds true in its own right when pollinated freely by insects. A hybrid is usually produced artificially to accomplish a particular agricultural objective, such as increased yields. Although hybrids do occur in Nature occasionally, like artificially produced hybrids, they rarely breed true when pollinated freely by insects and thus effectively lose their first-generation hybrid integrity.

In the first half of the 20th century, some of the characteristics of these introduced, genetically identical hybrid plants were extremely beneficial because they induced greater yields in crops with increased vigor. Companies that developed these new plants kept their parentage secret, which meant that seed companies benefited financially because farmers and gardeners had to purchase new seeds every year because hybrid plants do not breed true when pollinated freely by local insects. The increased cost of seed was at first offset by increased yields; farmers could grow 50 percent more corn on 25 percent less land, as well as four times more potatoes and almost three times more tomatoes per acre. But then the downside of such specialization began to show up, as it always does.

Using genetically identical hybrids in large-scale agriculture carries with it the risk of major losses in yields due to disease. Because all the plants are exactly the same genetically, in addition to which they are planted in homogeneous monocultures, there is neither genetic diversity nor structural diversity within a given crop. If, therefore, a crop is susceptible to a disease, it can spread widely in short order and destroy the entire crop, as happened in the Irish Potato Famine of 1845 to 1847 and the corn blight in the 1960s that cost farmers in the United States 15 percent of their crops.

Nevertheless, both the average consumer in the United States and the average farmer appreciate and prefer the uniformity of the hybrid crops, which are both easier to harvest with machinery on a large scale and more attractive in the grocery store. The Plant Variety Protection Act of 1970 was passed to protect the large monetary profits to be made in the production of hybrid seed-propagated plants and the economic investments of plant breeders who develop and patent these new varieties of seed-propagated plants. This law, although less restrictive than such laws in other countries, is nonetheless restrictive.

You can, for example, grow seeds from patented varieties of crop plants as a home gardener, but you can neither sell the seeds nor reproduce the plants vegetatively, which means by cuttings. You may use the patented plants to cross-breed your own varieties, but you cannot sell the new varieties commercially.

To protect the patents of European plant breeders, the European Community has established an official list of legal varieties of plants, and anyone who sells unlisted varieties can be prosecuted, which in effect prevents amateurs from getting their new varieties recognized and sold on the market. But the list supposedly does not prevent them from exchanging seeds.

As mentioned earlier, however, the downside of such specialization is showing up, as it always does—only this time it is hidden in the grocery store. I say this because many of the "improvements" made today by plant breeders who produce new hybrid varieties are either minor alterations or are made with the large corporate-style farmers in mind. These latter "improvements" include such things as tougher skins to better handle shipping from the field to the market and longer usable life of the crop in storage and on grocers' shelves. These "improvements" have little or nothing to do with higher nutrition or better flavor. In fact, based on my experience in many grocery stores over the past 40 years or so, I find that flavor is too often sacrificed on the altar of cost efficiency in the marketplace.

The problem with growing these commercially standard hybrids is twofold: (1) as a home gardener, one gives up one's independence by forfeiting the ability to produce one's own seeds and (2) there is a growing loss of genetic—and thus biological—diversity as artificially produced, patented hybrids increasingly replace local populations that are pollinated freely by insects. The latter is particularly troublesome because it poses greater risk over time of epidemics in populations of local plants.

There is yet another type of biopiracy, perhaps the ultimate form—cloning.

Cloning

Although genetic engineering has biological thievery within its precepts, nothing in life that I can think of has the human arrogance of cloning, in which one attempts to control as completely as possible the diversity and novelty of life. A clone is a group of genetically identical cells descended from a single common ancestor. Cloning, in turn, is the creation of a genetic duplicate of an individual organism. It occurs to some extent in Nature, such as a grove of quaking aspen trees, which are often natural clones. But cloning by humans is another thing altogether. Artificial cloning is inevitably wed to economics, such as a tree with economically desirable characteristics that is cloned through artificial asexual reproduction to capitalize on those characteristics.

Like all things in life, cloning will have its tripartite debate among those who see a new frontier for science, those who see commercial profit, and those who see ethical–practical problems. The ethical side of cloning is being targeted for debate by Stuart A. Newman, a cellular biologist at the New York Medical College in Valhalla, who quietly applied for a patent on a method of producing creatures that are part human and part animal.

Newman's move is expressly designed to reignite debate over the morality of patenting life-forms and genetically engineering humans, which he says he has not done and never intends to. His goal is to prevent the technology from being used and to force both the U.S. Patent and Trademark Office and the courts to reexamine the United States' 18-year history of allowing patents on living creatures.

Although patents are not currently allowed on human beings, there is nothing in the U.S. patent code, according to patent law experts, that would preclude someone from obtaining a patent on a partially human creature. In fact, the U.S. Patent and Trademark Office has already awarded several patents on animals with minor human components, including laboratory mice engineered with human cancer genes. "It is a classic slippery slope," contends Thomas Murray, director of the Center for Biomedical Ethics at Case Western Reserve University. "If we put one human gene in an animal, or two or three, some people may get nervous but you're clearly not making a person yet. But when you talk about a hefty percentage of cells being human...this really is problematic. Then you have to ask...very hard questions about what it means to be human."

The debate, should it arise, is likely to center around the commercialization of life and the meaning of being human. At the very least, the National Bioethics Advisory Commission plans to study patenting genetic materials in the hope of improving public policy. Apart from that, my tack in discussing cloning will be from the vantage of biopiracy and ecology.

Artificial cloning is nothing new. It has been a common practice, for example, in forestry for some time, but, to me at least, it has grave ecological problems waiting in the wings. To see these problems, however, one must get past the short-term linear thinking that makes the notion of cloning attractive in the first place.

Genetic manipulation of forest trees was born out of the concept of short-term economic expediency. By necessity, this process ignores long-term ecological ramifications to and within the forest as a whole, because tenable management practices for short-term profits must be based on *predictable* and *uniform* results. *Predictable* and *uniform* are the operative words in cloning.

Some people consider "genetic improvements," usually based on cloning in some facet of the operation, to be the panacea of forestry. In the short term, this is seen as maximizing return on investments and as creating a predictable and uniform base of raw materials for the benefit of the timber industry. Beyond the short-term economic benefit to timber companies, however, it is imperative to address the immense importance of long-term biotic, genetic, and functional diversity in relation to the adaptability of ecosystems at the scale of the landscape. Current criteria for the economic evaluation of tree farms (even-aged plantations of trees as a crop) do not adequately account for these and other crucial issues that accrue from the manipulation of whole forests for short-term profit.

In reality, the only "panacea" in forestry, from an industrial point of view, is an unlimited supply of virgin timber (such as old-growth Douglas fir) to feed the insatiable appetite of the linearly programmed, expansionistic timber industry. That is not possible, however, because native old-growth forests are an inheritance that we are given only once on each acre of ground. We have spent our own inheritance and are spending that of future generations.

Genetic manipulation, mainly cloning, is therefore the perceived industrial panacea, but it contains hidden costs. Four hidden costs can be shown for tree farms consisting of cloned trees, particularly tree farms of commercial scale, also thought of as industrial forests.

The first hidden cost is lack of predictability; we cannot predict any results, because no one has yet grown a "genetically improved" tree farm for even one full rotation. We are consequently playing genetic roulette with future forests, which is a dangerous game called "untested new products."

The second hidden cost is that by manipulating the genetics of the trees, the function of ecological processes in the entire tree farm is being altered by changing how the individual trees function. For example, if they grow faster, they will have larger cells and more sapwood and less heartwood, which changes the way they recycle in the soil. In turn, all other connected biological functions are altered. And we do not even know what these functions are, let alone what difference they will make in the long-term health of the forest ecosystem over time. We can, however, make some educated guesses.

For example, a central thrust of modern agricultural technology (including forestry under this umbrella) has been to (1) isolate such individual organisms, such as a particular species of tree, which possess desirable economic characteristics; (2) enhance their desired characteristics through breeding; and (3) replicate them on a massive scale. This type of plant is termed an "ideotype" for such an ideal plant model, which literally means a form denoting an idea.

Any management, but particularly that which focuses on individual ideotypes, unavoidably changes other properties of the ecosystem in addition to productivity, which is the target of the change. Genetic diversity and fundamental structural relationships, the architectural aspects of indigenous plant communities, are altered as well. Although numerous ecologists and foresters have raised concerns about this for some time, these concerns have too often been viewed as grounded in unproven criticism, which has little or nothing to do with perceived economic need.

Quite to the contrary, system-level properties are likely to play a seminal role in the health of the ecosystem, and healthy, sustainable forests provide values that are no less real because they cannot be traded in the marketplace. Society will continue to demand wood, and forests will provide it, but forests both produce wood and play a central role in the dynamics of global climate, in addition to which they harbor immense biotic diversity.

The third hidden cost is like a numbered Swiss bank account, which has a complete denomination of its own particular currency. The currency in the forest (called stored genetic variability) is unseen, as is the currency in the bank account. One does not have to see the currency in order to get the correct change, however. If there is an unlimited amount of money in the bank account, as there is genetic variability in the unmanaged forest, then the exact change can be received for any denomination chosen, even from an automatic, mechanical teller.

This means that a forest can, within limits, adapt genetically to changes in climate from a human-caused greenhouse effect, natural climatic changes, increasing air pollution, and so on. When genetic variability (currency) is withdrawn from the forest's genetic account, the ability of the forest to adapt to changing conditions—something it must be able to do in order to survive—becomes artificially limited. Without the ten-cent coin, for example, exact change can no longer be received from the bank account; it becomes limited and loses flexibility in terms of the transactions that can be made.

Let's take this one step further. A forest is cut down across the landscape from northern Washington to southern Oregon and from the Pacific coast to the crest of the western Cascade Mountains. Genetically engineered Douglas fir seedlings, based on cloning in some part of the engineering process, are then planted to grow quickly. In addition, seedlings planted in northern Washington are selected to withstand cold, those in the south to withstand heat, those in the west to withstand wet weather, and those in the east to withstand dry weather and a short growing season. In order to gain genetic selectivity, we have artificially adapted the trees to our set of values. In doing so, we give up flexibility or genetic plasticity—the tree's inherent ability to adapt to changing conditions.

As an analogy, suppose you are traveling in Switzerland and the central bank with your numbered account is in Geneva. Only the central bank has all denominations of currency. As you travel in northern Switzerland, you find satellite mechanical bank tellers from which you can make change, but they only have a denomination of one. In the east you find a teller that only has a denomination of 5, in the south only 10, and in the west only 25.

The selected currency of the satellite tellers restricts your ability to adapt to unexpected necessities, and this loss of flexibility can cause considerable unforeseen hardship. It is the same with a forest. Nature allows for changes in climate and equips trees with the genetic ability to adapt and survive. What happens when a forest is converted to a tree farm selected for warm and dry conditions and robbed of its "excess genes" when a long-term change in the climate results in wet and cold conditions?

Through such genetic engineering as cloning, genetic diversity—and therefore adaptability—is increasingly limited over time as genetically handicapped, identical trees are planted in an environment that changes freely in the invisible present. The more the environment changes, the more the cloned trees, which have been robbed of some portion of their adaptability, appear to remain the same, like a historic relict out of the past. Such relicts are holdovers that cannot adapt fast enough to keep pace with the changing conditions of their environment. Extinction, therefore, is always just around the corner.

The fourth hidden cost is the "secret extinctions" discussed earlier. Secret extinctions are an unnoticed loss of locally adapted populations of species, such as trees, that have evolved over millennia, a loss that can be more or less permanent. Accordingly, if locally adapted populations of a species are extirpated, they might never be replaced because other populations of the species might lack the characteristics necessary to become established in the now vacant habitat. They also might not be able to reach suitable habitat because of major environmental shifts due to the unprecedented speed of the changes brought about in the global climate.

In the case of forestry, liquidation of the indigenous forest and its replacement with genetically engineered tree farms constitutes an economically motivated secret extinction. I say this because the genetic variability of the trees adapted to the site has been purposefully replaced with trees that have been genetically altered and simplified through artificial means, thus robbing them of their full complement of stored genetic variability.

In addition to cloning in forestry as an increasingly standardized method of manipulating crop trees, we have now graduated to domestic animals, such as Dolly the sheep. Here one might ask what the purpose of cloning animals is.

According to Ian Wilmut, one of the scientists who cloned Dolly, the purpose is, in the end, economic.[96] Someday, says Wilmut, a dairy farmer, as an example, might clone a few cows that are especially good at producing milk, resisting disease, and having calves, but a farmer would not want an entire herd of cloned cows because populations require genetic diversity to prevent a lethal disease from eliminating the whole herd. He goes on to say that what scientists are learning about cloning will allow a much more efficient way to insert genes into livestock, which in turn can be used to make animals secrete such things as valuable drugs in their milk.

Where in all this can one find any respect for the life of the animals that are being violated through such biopiracy? And what about humans? Are we next? The answer is yes, according to physicist Richard Seed, who says he will clone a human despite ethical considerations.[97]

Chicago scientist Richard Seed vowed to clone a human being—himself—with his wife carrying the embryo that is to be created by combining the nucleus of one of his own cells with a donor egg. The 50 anticloning bills that emerged from state legislatures across the country, however, ended the celebration of the pharmaceutical companies over the decision by leaders of the U.S. Senate to put an anticloning bill on hold.[98,99] The patchwork of state laws would be "an absolute disaster for medical research," said Jeff Trewhitt, a spokesman for Pharmaceutical Research & Manufacturers of America. Despite these bills, it would be folly to doubt that cloning of a human being will be tried somewhere, by someone—and much sooner than later.

Scientists already use cloning as a technique to test how identical cells react to different substances. They hope cloning can be used to grow new skin for burn victims and to overcome the need for organ donors by creating whole new organs, such as livers and kidneys. Cloning has already led to drugs used for cystic fibrosis and strokes.

Although President Clinton has called for a federal ban on the cloning of human beings, drug researchers point out that the Food and Drug Administration already requires anyone who wants to perform research that uses the technique of cloning to file for permission. Members of the drug industry would prefer a federal ban that forbids only the cloning of a whole human being—if people feel there must be a law based on social morality.

For this reason, two trade groups have launched a state-by-state campaign to fight 50 anticloning bills being considered in legislatures from California to Connecticut. But they were too late to block the first state law against cloning. Pete Wilson, governor of California, signed a bill on October 4, 1997 that makes it a crime to clone a human or to purchase fetal cells to do so. Fines for violating this law can be as much as $1 million.

Although the use of cloning as a scientific technique is clearly a moral issue for society to resolve, there is also a practical aspect to the debate, about which little is heard. The practicality is the fact that genetically engineered parts, individuals, and species are, in the commercial sense, and perhaps even more in the ecological sense, untested genetic products, which are likely to have hidden flaws because the people who create them are working, at best, with a great deal of uncertainty. As Edward Tenner, a visiting professor at Princeton University, says, "It is part of the nature of radically new ideas that they are not the kinds of ideas we thought they would be."[100]

The Untested Product

Genetically "improved" individuals and/or species represent a new, untested product (the first hidden cost), and American business has had much experience with new products. Consider the risk of new product failure.

Industry, its customers, the American public, and society at large, especially future generations, have an important stake in the effective management of innovation and new product processes. Direct expenditure by industry on research and development is large and must be judged by its ability to yield superior new products and processes. During development, the market success of a new product is always in doubt. In fact, a large proportion of all programs are terminated before achieving success in the market.

A number of industries have indicated that less than 15 percent of all development projects result in commercially successful products and that a full 37 percent of all products that reach the market prove to be commercial failures. The seven most convincing studies place the failure rate of products introduced in the market at about 40 percent. It should be emphasized, however, that the types of products examined, the period of time covered, and the definitions used can all have a pronounced effect on the reported rate of failure or success.

Even though the products discussed in the preceding paragraph were all conceived, studied, designed, studied, manufactured, studied, and marketed by people for people, there is no guarantee of success. When we "redesign" trees, we also redesign the entire functional forest, even though we know little about the consequences. A similar caution is given by geneticists David Suzuki and P. Knudtson in their book *Genethics, The Ethics of Engineering Life*,[101] in which they discuss human genetics, which is better understood than the genetics of the life-forms with which people are now tinkering.

A new product on the consumer market succeeds or fails in months. The success or failure of a redesigned industrial forest based on genetically engineered trees will not become apparent for perhaps a century or more. If we fail, who will pay the price? The price will be passed to the generations of the future, as usual. Consider the following scenario.[102]

A plant thought of as a "weed" has been genetically engineered by scientists to resist an herbicide and simultaneously developed a far greater ability to pollinate other plants and pass on its genetic traits. The weed's enhanced ability to pollinate other plants was an unintended result of experiments with *Arabidopsis thaliana*, a species of plant commonly used in genetic research.

Such an unintended result shows that genetic engineering can substantially increase the spread of certain traits from one plant to another, or "transgene escape," as it is technically called. This development raises the possibility of the emergence of "superweeds" that are impervious to weedkillers, which, according to Joy Bergelson, a professor of ecology and evolution at the University of Chicago, are able to fertilize other plants at a rate 20 times greater than the rate of plants that developed their resistance to herbicides through nonengineered mutation.

In our burgeoning, product-oriented society, however, one of the most insidious dangers to genetic diversity is the sadly mistaken perception that indigenous species (1) have no intrinsic value, (2) are a "weed" species if they lack obvious economic value, or (3) must be "improved" before they are of sufficient economic value to count. As far as industry is concerned, the foregoing all too often means that large areas of habitat are not worth protecting in their "wild" state for their long-term hidden potential at the apparent cost of immediate short-term profits. Potential in this case refers to genetic diversity—one of the cornerstones of sustainable life.

The economic shortsightedness with which our Western industrialized society is today imbued is understandable considering that (1) most people view the land and all it contains simply as an object without intrinsic value, which must be converted into something else before value—economic value—can be assigned; (2) Western society focuses predominantly on utilizable products from the ecosystem rather than on the processes that produce the products; (3) renewable "natural" products are largely manifested aboveground, whereas many of the processes that produce the products are invisible belowground; (4) we therefore think about and manipulate what is visible aboveground and tend to ignore the crucial biological processes below the surface of the soil; and (5) short-term economic gain is the driving force behind manipulation of renewable natural resources and our society.

When these points are taken together, they form the foundation of Western economic culture. Reared with this historical background, most people find it difficult to understand the risks to society's future that accompany the genetic violation of individuals and species either in principle or in fact.

There is, however, yet another form of trying to own diversity within our Western industrialized society. It is called centralization. Centralization is the process through which the small, diversified family farms in the United States are being gobbled up by huge corporations, which in turn control the production, preparation, distribution, and therefore the pricing of food.

Controlling Diversity Through Centralization

Since 1930, the number of farms has declined steadily from six million full-time farms to less than one million in 1994. Compared to other businesses, farm debt has risen, and farming is now a more hazardous occupation than mining, according to John Kinsman, a dairy farmer in LaValle, Wisconsin.[103]

"Why protect family farms?" asks Kinsman. Because historically, and probably before, the family farm has been society's primary endeavor both socially and economically, and it has nurtured us physically, emotionally, spiritually, and economically. Communities and villages became possible through the enduring stability of the family farm. Democratic government grew directly out of such agrarian necessities and values as patience, cooperation, coordination, and shared responsibilities.

Compared to corporate factory-style farming, the traditional family farm is far more environmentally friendly and benign. "Family farmers," says Kinsman, "have a vested interest in food, land, water and air quality because they actually live on the land they own, breathe the air, eat the food, drink the water and depend on continued soil productivity for future generations." It is a tragic mistake, present and future, to turn the responsibilities of trusteeship for family farms over to absentee owners who amalgamate them into huge corporate farms, which they see merely as a business, and at times simply as a tax write-off, instead of a way of life in which they have a vested interest. I know this from firsthand experience. I watched it happen to the cattle ranch I used to work on.

Three companies in the United States process more than 80 percent of our beef, four companies control 50 percent of the hog production, and four companies oversee 95 percent of the chicken production. In addition, four corporations control 90 percent of the trade in grain on the world market.

Although economists claim that the efficiencies of large-scale agribusiness are good for consumers, low farm prices do not translate directly into lower retail prices. For example, people who eat beef are probably unaware that the people who raise the beef have not received more than 75 cents per pound since December 1993 and have gotten less than 66 cents per pound since May 1995. But the meat packers have not passed this price on to consumers and have made unprecedented profits.

The price paid to farmers for raw milk has fallen 15 percent since 1980 while retail prices have risen 15 percent. The extra profits are used by the corporate dairy industry to intensify its market presence through mergers and leveraged buyouts. Meanwhile, depressed prices for raw dairy products have in the last 15 years (1980 to 1995) forced more than half of the dairy farmers out of business. While family farmers have virtually no history of consumer blackmail by withholding production to exact higher prices, can the same be said for corporate agribusiness?

In addition to the consolidation of family farms, the efficiency of the worldwide system of food production and marketing that gives the consumer more choices at lower prices comes with a troubling cost—a rise in food poisoning. For example, cases of salmonella, which used to originate mostly in restaurants or at events like church suppers, now originate at times in huge factories through which food is widely distributed before anyone gets sick. In this way, cases of salmonella alone have doubled over the last 20 years. "Industry consolidation and mass distribution of foods," warns the Centers for Disease Control and Prevention, "may lead to large outbreaks of foodborne disease."[104]

In my own backyard, the corporate timber industry, as another case in point, dominates the Coast Range mountains of western Oregon. Tax records for 11 "timber" counties in western Oregon show that 59 percent of the private timberland is controlled by 10 corporate owners, according to a 1995 study by the Coast Range Association of Newport, Oregon. In Benton County, for example, 595 owners control 1,906 acres (1.5 percent) of timber as opposed to 120,137 acres (98.5 percent) controlled by 10 corporate owners. In neighboring Lincoln County, 865 owners control 1,763 acres (almost 2 percent) as opposed to 105,931 acres (98 percent) controlled by 10 corporate owners.[105]

Thus, in those two counties alone, 1,460 small owners control 3,669 acres (less than 1 percent) compared to 400,152 acres (more than 99 percent) controlled by 15 corporate owners. Out of these 15, 4 national and/or international corporations own 221,002 acres (more than 50 percent) of the timberland. In addition, corporate timber owners have a history of shipping unprocessed logs to Japan, where they get larger profits than they would in domestic markets, which bypasses domestic mills and domestic workers.

At the same time, more than half of the large streams, which are critical habitat for endangered stocks of steelhead trout and commercially important salmon, run through private lands. "The fate of coastal salmon lies in the hands of corporate landowners," says Chuck Willer, director of the Coast Range Association. "Many industrial owners...are not at the table and are avoiding hard questions about their land's condition."

"Communists and capitalists are alike in their contempt for country people, country life, and country places," observes author Wendell Berry. "They have exploited the countryside with equal greed and disregard. They are alike even in their plea that it is right to damage the present in order to 'make a better future.'"[106]

"This," says Noam Chomsky, "is the model for the free-market future. The profits are privatized and that's what counts—it's socialism for the rich: the public pays the costs and the rich get the profits. That's what the free market is in practice," and it will surely continue to destroy the communities and cultures of the world until governments, including that of the United States, become accountable to their people. But as Frederick Douglass pointed out so long ago: "Power concedes nothing without a struggle." Mahatma Gandhi, on the other hand, noted that "even the most powerful cannot rule without the cooperation of the ruled."

To conclude this section, 18th century British philosopher and statesman Edmund Burke succinctly addressed the problem of trying to own the diversity of Nature at the expense of one's fellow travelers on this tiny planet spinning in infinite space:

> Men are qualified for civil liberty in exact proportion to their disposition to put moral chains upon their own appetites....Society cannot exist unless a controlling power upon will and appetite be placed somewhere, and the less of it there is within, the more there must be without. It is ordained in the eternal constitution of things that men of intemperate minds cannot be free. Their passions forge their fetters.[107]

On this note, we will proceed to the third and final part of this book. In Part III, we will examine some aspects of diversity as they pertain to our current everyday efforts to come to grips with the notion of sustainable community development.

PART III

DIVERSITY AS THE FOUNDATION OF SUSTAINABLE COMMUNITY

*We used to do things for posterity,
now we do things for ourselves and leave the bill to posterity.*

Anonymous

*In the time of your life, live—so that in that wondrous time
you shall not add to the misery and sorrow of the world,
but shall smile to the infinite variety and mystery of it.*

William Saroyan

As cultures have been and are being destroyed through war and disease, as their languages—and thus their history, myths, idioms, and the construct of their particular sense of logic—disappear from the living library of humanity and pass into the fading halls of extinction, we are not only losing irretrievable parts of ourselves as a species but also homogenizing the landscape in which we all must live. As I watch humanity lose parts of itself to genocide—through both open war and the secret war of technological depersonalization—and the continual productive decline of the planet on which all life as we know it depends for sustenance, I see the peoples of the world increasingly losing their sense of identity and self-worth within the greater context of the extended human family and Nature as a whole.

I also see the cancerous, amoeboid body of fear penetrating ever deeper into the human psyche as economic/political power is continually centralized in the hands of fewer and fewer people and technological machines are increasingly used to put people out of work, denying them, under our capitalistic economic system, the right, power, and dignity of purchasing the basic necessities of life. At the very time we are exponentially losing species, habitats, ecological functions, human cultures, and myriad other components that equate in the collective to the quality of human life, the linear-thinking corporate/political elite is striving for evermore centralized specialization and control over the destiny of humanity without an apparent understanding of or regard for the well-being of today's and tomorrow's children.

Having said this, I am reminded of something Lee Schroeder, a courageous and forthright engineer, wrote in the foreword to one of my recent books: "I tend to be a linear thinker, as do many engineers. When I have been involved with systems behavior, and the parts of the system interact as they always do, the conclusions reached are often too vague to implement. Since I'm always trying to solve problems and I am driven to find a solution, I tend to revert to the linear approach. Show me a mountain, and I'll move it, but don't make me worry too much about anything more than that."

In Lee Schroeder's statement, I hear not only engineers speaking but also economists, politicians, government officials and their staffers, the military, and even university professors. The result of such linear thinking is the continual loss of diversity, wherein lies the greatest long-term threat to the survival of society as we know it. In trying to rectify the dangers of such linear thinking, well-intentioned people coined the adage "think globally, act locally." While this notion may be an unfathomable abstraction to most people as it is stated, it could become a concrete reality if it were turned around: "Act locally and affect the whole world."

LOCAL TECHNOLOGY AND GLOBAL CONSEQUENCES

8

In the consciousness and choices of individual people living and acting collectively in a local community lies a great power to heal *or* to sicken the Earth that supports us all. Before we introduce such things as pesticides into our local environment, therefore, we must learn to ask broad questions about the possible effects of our actions beyond our local borders. With this in mind, there are many examples on which I could draw to demonstrate the concrete nature of the adage "act locally and affect the whole world," but I will restrict myself to two: a ditch and a dam. As you read this chapter, be aware that none of our actions are or can be carried out in isolation from the rest of the world. We cannot divorce ourselves from the systemic way in which the world functions, much as we might like to. Everything we do has an effect, which is beneficial to some things and detrimental to others. Moreover, each effect is the cause of another effect—albeit one we may not intend to have happen, as the following examples illustrate.

A DITCH

Did you ever think about a ditch, say a humble roadside ditch, and wonder how the practice of ditching got started? Most people probably don't even notice ditches, much less think about them. Nevertheless, there was actually a time before ditches, a time when water itself decided where humanity would dwell. Then the ditch was invented as a way to purpose-fully channel water to a given place for a particular reason, and that changed everything.

The First Ditch

The first ditch was likely an idle scratch in the surface of the ground made by some child playing in a puddle after a rain storm or perhaps along a stream in the land of far memory. That first child's play—of leading water from one place to another—on that faraway afternoon has continued through the millennia. I, who just crossed the threshold of 60, still cannot resist leading little trickles of water from here to there by scratching the surface of the ground with a stick or for want of a stick with my finger or the toe of my shoe.

A ditch in the beginning is just a naked furrow in the skin of the Earth until Nature takes over, molding and sculpting the furrow with erosion, using wind and water and snow and ice as implements. Slowly the gaping furrow begins to round and crinkle as flowing water moves jousting grain and shifting pebble here and there. Little by little the ditch bottom loses all sign of human tool, and the once raw wound becomes a labyrinth of nooks and crannies, each with a pair of eyes silently watching the world.

As the ditch's bottom transforms, Nature plants seeds of grasses and herbs along its banks. Each seed, be it as large as a giant lima bean or as small as a gnat's eye, has locked within it the secret code of shape and color for leaf and flower, height of stem and depth of root, season of bloom and season of fruit. Each seed, millions of years in the making, is a crowning achievement in an unbroken chain of genetic experiments that began when life was born.

A dandelion seed drifts ditchward, suspended from its gossamer para-chute. Where will it land? Will it germinate? If it germinates and grows, will it be eaten by a grasshopper or a mouse, or will it mature and add its encoded link to the genetic chain? Of the thousands of seeds that fall on the fertile soil of the ditch's banks, each is an open question.

Relatively few will survive to maturity. The rest will disappear from whence they came, into the Eternal Mystery. Nature thus creates a back-drop of swaying grasses and brightly colored flowers, of protecting shrubs and stately trees. On this stage unfolds her play enacted with the animals that live along the ditch, burrow in its banks, and visit with the seasons.

Somewhere in the recesses of memory that first ditch became a con-scious thought that translated into a conscious act. As the one ditch became many ditches, humanity and plants and animals moved into areas previously uninhabitable by those who needed water in close proximity, and thus was expanded the human arena of choice.

The first ditch irrevocably altered humanity's sense of itself, its sense of society, and its ability to manipulate Nature. Today, a ditch is also a classroom.

Lessons from a Ditch

To me, the concept of humility means to be teachable, even by something as lowly as a ditch. Do not be deceived by humble status, for the humble are mighty in simple, unobtrusive ways. Consider, for example, that to drain a swamp, one needs only to dig a ditch, and to regain the swamp, one has only to fill in the ditch.

Over the years, much has been learned through studies of ditches and through studies of human-made canals (large ditches) that were designed to carry large quantities of water, to let ships pass from one ocean into another, or specifically for research. For instance, studies have focused on how various kinds of vegetation react to floodwaters, such as slowing the water's force, combing out suspended sediments from sediment-laden waters, creating and maintaining the stability of banks, and abating erosion in the banks of streams and rivers. Much also has been learned about the water–land interface and how stream channels, including bed-load materials, react to different velocities of water at different gradients of steepness. Studies also have been made of the geometry of various channel configurations and their effect on the flow of water, the stability of their banks, and other instream processes.

These studies not only have helped us to better understand some of the water-related geological processes but also have helped us to better decipher physical and biological processes that interact in creating the fluid dynamics we call streams and rivers. To go on at length would not serve the purpose of this book. Suffice it to say that the humble ditch, for better or for worse, has forever changed how humanity sees itself and how humanity and the land interact. If we are willing, there is much we can still learn from a ditch about the interdependence of ourselves as a species, about the geological processes of planet Earth and even the Universe, and about the new, truly reciprocal partnership that must be formed between humanity and the land if either is to survive in any semblance of environmental order as we know it. Although the ditch itself is a simple invention, it nonetheless is an integral but unrecognized and ignored part of the stream-order continuum, and as such connects society's culturalized landscapes to all the connected oceans of the world.

The Stream/Ditch-Order Continuum

Although the stream-order continuum was discussed in Chapter 4, it is repeated here both to refresh your memory and to incorporate the ditch into the continuum. The stream-order continuum is a concept devised for streams, but I find many of the same processes in ditches and therefore think of it as the "stream/ditch-order continuum." The stream/ditch-order continuum operates on a simple premise: Just as the heart, arteries, and veins are the arterial system of the human body, streams are Nature's arterial system of the land, and ditches create society's arterial system. As such, they form a continuum or spectrum of physical environments, with associated aquatic and terrestrial plant and animal communities, as a longitudinally connected part of the ecosystem in which downstream processes are linked to upstream processes.

The idea of the stream/ditch continuum begins with the smallest stream or ditch and ends at the ocean. The concept centers around the resources of available food for the animals inhabiting the continuum, which range from invertebrates to fish, amphibians, reptiles, birds, and mammals.

As organic material floats downhill from its source to the sea, it becomes smaller, while the volume of water carrying it becomes larger. Thus small streams feed larger streams and larger streams feed rivers with partially processed organic matter, the amount of which becomes progressively smaller the farther down the continuum of the river system it goes. The same is true for ditches.

A first-order stream is the smallest undivided waterway or headwaters, a description that fits most ditches. Where two first-order streams join, they enlarge as a second-order stream, again a description that fits ditches. Where two second-order streams come together, they enlarge as a third-order stream and so on.

The concept of stream order is based on the size of a stream in terms of the cumulative volume of water, not just on which stream of what order joins with another stream of a given order. For example, a first-order stream (or ditch) can join either with another first-order stream (or ditch) to form a second-order stream (or ditch) or it can enter directly into a second-, third-, fourth-, fifth-, or even larger order stream. The same is true of a second-order stream, a third-order stream, and so on.

In addition, the stream/ditch order influences the role played by streamside and ditchside vegetation in controlling water temperature, stabilizing banks, and producing food. Streamside vegetation is also the primary source of coarse woody debris, such as tree branches or the trunks of large trees with their rootwads attached. Ditches, on the other hand, are usually stripped of their trees long before the trees mature.

Forest trees adjacent to streams supply wood from their branches, trunks, and rootwads, while ditchside vegetation supplies grasses, herbs, and occasionally branches from shrubs but rarely from trees. Erosion also contributes organic material to the stream or ditch.

Wood in streams increases the diversity of habitats by forming dams and their attendant pools and by protecting backwater areas. Wood also provides nutrients and a variety of foundations for biological activity, and it both dissipates the energy of the water and traps its sediments. These functions in ditches are usually performed by nonwoody vegetation.

Processing the organic debris entering the aquatic system includes digestion by bacteria, fungi, and insects and physical abrasion against such things as the stream bottom and its boulders or the ditch bottom and its pebbles. In all cases, debris is continually broken into smaller pieces, which makes the particles increasingly susceptible to microbial consumption.

The amount of different kinds of organic matter processed in a reach of stream or ditch (the stretch of water visible between two bends in a channel, be it a ditch, stream, or river) depends on the quality and the quantity of nutrients in the material and on the capacity of the stream or ditch to hold fine particles long enough to complete their processing. The debris may be fully utilized by the biotic community within a reach of stream or ditch or it may be exported downstream.

Debris moves fastest through the system during high water and is not thoroughly processed at any one spot. The same is true in streams and ditches that do not have a sufficient number of instream or inditch obstacles to slow the water and act as areas of deposition, sieving the incompletely processed organic material out of the current so its organic breakdown can be completed. Accordingly, small streams feed larger streams and larger streams feed rivers, just as small ditches feed larger ditches, which eventually feed streams and rivers.

As a stream gets larger, its source of food energy is derived more from aquatic algae and less from organic material of terrestrial origin, which is comparable for ditches. The greatest influence of terrestrial vegetation is in first-order streams and ditches, but the greatest diversity of incoming organic matter and habitats is found in third- to fifth-order streams and large rivers with floodplains.

Small, first-order, headwater streams (and, where applicable, ditches) largely determine the type and quality of the downstream habitat. They and second-order streams and ditches are influenced not only by the configuration of surrounding landforms but also by the live and dead vegetation along their channels. This vegetation is called riparian vegetation and interacts in many ways with the stream or ditch.

The canopy of vegetation, when undisturbed, shades the streamside or ditchside. The physical energy of the flowing water is dissipated by wood in stream channels and by grasses, sedges, rushes, and cattails in ditch channels, slowing erosion and fostering the deposition of inorganic and organic debris.

Because these small streams and ditches arise in tiny drainages with a limited capacity to store water, their flow may be scanty or intermittent during late summer and autumn, but during periods of high flows in winter and spring, they can move prodigious amounts of sediment and organic material.

The preceding discussion describes the beneficial aspect of the stream/ditch continuum. There is, however, a sinister side to the ditch portion of this story as well, a tragically human side.

Ditches of Death

Ditches form a continuum or spectrum of physical environments (the same as streams) along a longitudinally connected part of the ecosystem in which downstream processes are linked to and influenced by upstream processes. The stream/ditch continuum begins with the smallest stream or ditch and ends at the ocean. Little ditches thus feed bigger ditches and bigger ditches eventually feed streams and rivers, which ultimately feed the ocean. As organic material (food energy) floats downhill from its source to the sea, it gets smaller (more dilute), while the volume of water carrying it gets larger.

But what happens to the continuum concept when a ditch is polluted? To pollute a ditch means to contaminate it actively by dumping human garbage or discharging noxious substances into it (perhaps through the soil of a garden where herbicides have been applied) or passively by motor oil that accumulates from automobiles on roads or by animal waste that seeps from feedlots with large populations of cattle and hogs or from large poultry farms—all of which washes into ditches and in one way or another disrupts biological processes, often by corrupting the integrity of their chemical interactions.

While Nature's organic matter or food energy is continually *diluted* the farther down the continuum it goes, pollution, especially chemical pollution, is continually *concentrated* the farther down the continuum it goes because it gathers its potency from the discharge of every other contaminated ditch that adds its waters to the passing flow. In this way, with every ditch we pollute, the purity of stream and river is to that extent compromised, and the amount of pollution that humanity is dumping into the estuaries and oceans of the world through the stream/ditch continuum is staggering.

Today, for example, Dutch scientists say that human-caused pollution, such as polybrominate chemical compounds, is being found in the bodies of minke and sperm whales that wash up dead on Dutch beaches. These whales feed at depths of 3,000 feet below the surface of the ocean and, according to Jan Boon of the Netherlands Institute for Marine Research, show just how far toxic pollution has spread into the ocean's food chain—much farther than previously thought.[108]

I voice my concern not only because I have seen ditches in North America, Europe, Asia, and North Africa discharging their foul contents into streams, rivers, estuaries, and oceans but also because in 1969 I found a population of montane voles (meadow mice) living along a ditch that drained an agricultural field.[109] The fur of the voles was an abnormally deep yellow when I caught them, but they lost the yellow with their first molt in the laboratory when fed normal lab chow, whereas those along the ditch retained their yellow pelage.

Although I tried, I could find no one in the Department of Agricultural Chemistry at the local university to acknowledge this color deviant, let alone examine it in a effort to find the cause, which was undoubtedly some agricultural chemical compound. They all turned their backs, even when I presented them with the evidence—yellow voles. I thus learned that chemical pollution in the flowing waters of ditches is often not visible to the human eye, but it may become visible in the sickening of the environment if people have the vision and the courage to see such effects and correctly, honestly relate them to the cause.

In 1984, as part of a committee called to Washington, D.C., to help the U.S. Congress frame the ecological components of the 1985 Farm Bill, I learned in far greater depth of the incredible nonpoint source chemical pollution of our nation's surface waters (ditches) and groundwaters (aquifers) from today's chemical-intensive agriculture.

In 1998, based on a study by the Environmental Working Group, which used data from federal records, including those of the Environmental Protection Agency, I learned that 606 corporations in 44 states sent more than 270 million pounds of toxic wastes to farms and fertilizer companies in the first five years of this decade, of which firms in Oregon contributed almost 10 percent or 26 million pounds.[110] Although the practice of turning toxic wastes into fertilizer was first reported in *The Seattle Times* in July 1997, the Environmental Working Group's report was the first account of just how widespread the practice has become.

"We found a bustling toxic commerce between factories and fertilizer makers," noted Ken Cook, president of the Environmental Working Group and a soil scientist. There are currently three legal loopholes that allow toxic industrial wastes to flow into fertilizer. One allows steel companies to sell the ash from their smokestacks without having it tested for toxic chemicals. The second loophole permits material that is considered to be safe for landfills to be used in fertilizers, and the third allows companies to transfer industrial waste directly to farms if it can be safely rendered harmless on the land.

"It does not make sense to spread toxic materials, at whatever level [of toxicity], on the land that is producing our food and fiber," says Bill Leibhardt of the University of California at Davis. Leibhardt, who worked for fertilizer companies before joining the University of California, went on to say: "The preponderance of evidence would say if you're adding heavy metals and dioxins into fertilizer and mixing them up around the countryside, you're playing Russian roulette with the food supply," which says nothing of what these chemicals do to the water passing through the soils to which they were applied.

For example, researchers found that between 1990 and 1995 industry sent the following to farms and fertilizer companies: 90 million pounds of zinc, 49 million pounds of copper, 6.2 million pounds of lead compounds, 1.3 million pounds of chromium compounds, 233,000 pounds of cadmium compounds, 212,000 pounds of nickel compounds, 16,000 pounds of mercury compounds, 223 pounds of arsenic compounds, and 34 million pounds of sulfuric acid. This list does not include methanol, dioxin, acetone, chloroform, chlorine, ammonia, phenol, and methyl ethyl ketone.

Clearly, the loopholes must be closed and all raw materials from which fertilizers are made must be tested for their toxic content. In addition, all toxic chemicals must be monitored and the data must be readily available in an easy-to-read format because people have a right to know what toxic materials, if any, are in the fertilizer they purchase and in what amounts. This knowledge is critical because fertilizers, wherever applied, are a major source of nonpoint pollution with which humanity is poisoning its supply of potable water and making deadly thousands of miles of humble ditches. But fertilizers are not the only culprit; owners of livestock feedlots and poultry farms also pollute the water of ditches with animal wastes.

The time may finally have arrived, however, for the Environmental Protection Agency to develop regulations that will require owners of livestock feedlots and poultry farms to obtain permits not only to pollute but also to control the animal wastes from their operations.[111] The regulations would apply to some 6,000 commercial livestock and poultry operations throughout the United States. This will be the first attempt by the federal government to regulate these facilities under the Clean Water Act.

Although roughly a fourth of the livestock feedlots are currently regulated by states, poultry farms are not subject to either state or federal regulation. Runoff of water following rain or melting snow carries the animal waste into bodies of water that become saturated with nutrients, including nitrogen and phosphorus, which cause oxygen-choking blooms of algae, even massive "dead zones," where fish and other aquatic organisms can no longer survive.

The Environmental Protection Agency's proposal would require permits for feedlot owners with more than 1,000 cattle or 2,500 swine, as well as owners of poultry farms with 100,000 laying hens. In addition, permits could be required for smaller operations that are found to pose an environmental hazard to specific environmentally sensitive waterways. "We are taking a major step to make good on…[their broad plan to protect the nation's waterways] by controlling runoff from animal feeding operations, a major source of water pollution," said Carol Browner, director of the Environmental Protection Agency.

For me, the obvious question is which waterway is not environmentally sensitive, including ditches, since all water sooner or later ends up in the ocean. I still wonder, therefore, if we can learn to care for rivers and oceans if we continually defile the ditches that feed them. The answer is, of course, that we cannot! Consider, for example, just one small local creek, Dixon Creek, flowing through my hometown.[112] The creek drains 4.8 square miles or 3,041 acres, which includes upstream use that is 18 percent agriculture, 20 percent forest, and 62 percent residential.

Dixon Creek, flowing through the heart of north Corvallis, carries traces of nine pesticides in its waters, as well as fecal coliform and *E. coli* bacteria, according to a recent study of water quality in the Willamette River basin of western Oregon conducted by the U.S. Geological Survey. The creek, only a few miles long and almost entirely within the city limits, flows past churches, parks, homes, and even through the campus of Corvallis High School before emptying into the Willamette River, which in turn empties into the Columbia River, which empties into the Pacific Ocean.

The following pesticides found in Dixon Creek are listed in descending order of concentration:

Dichlobenil	An herbicide
Tebuthurion	An herbicide not known to be hazardous to aquatic organisms
Diazinon	An insecticide toxic to fish
Carbaryl	An insecticide moderately toxic to aquatic organisms
Prometon	An herbicide
Metolachlor	An herbicide moderately toxic to both cold- and warm-water fish
Atrazine	An herbicide slightly toxic to fish and other pond life
Desethylatrazine	An herbicide slightly toxic to fish and other pond life, which breaks down in the environment
Simazine	An herbicide of low toxicity to aquatic species

In addition, 20 percent of the water samples from Dixon Creek were hotter than 68 degrees Fahrenheit during summer's low water flow, which is warm enough to cause increased stress on fish. And this is just a small example from my hometown, which can be generalized to streams and rivers throughout the United States and much of the world.

Now consider that these poisons add to the diversity of the environment not only through their different chemical makeups but also in the way they kill, what they kill, in what concentrations they can kill, how they move through the food chain killing as they go, and the deadly synergism of their chemical interactions when they come in contact with one another. Consider also how they alter the ecosystem in which their respective effects become manifest.

Then they collect in the ditches, including street-side gutters, and polluted creeks in and around the myriad small towns and large cities, all of which add their array of poisons to the stream/ditch continuum. To this, one must add the nonpoint chemical pollution from rural areas, from intensive agriculture and intensive forestry, that is leached from the soil through which the water flows.

Now the arsenal of destructive toxins is mighty indeed as it enters the ditches, streams, rivers, and oceans of the world, where all pollution concentrates over time because oceans have no outlets. Oceans lose their water through evaporation, which concentrates the remaining chemicals because there is no way to dilute them without an outlet of some kind to flush the system.

The oceans' inability to flush themselves as do ditches, streams, and rivers causes me to wonder how many of the chemicals we introduce into our environment are toxic and to what degree. It causes me to wonder how many of the chemicals are in fact biodegradable, breaking down into harmless components over what period of time. When I ask such questions, I get very, very few satisfactory answers.

Consequently, I think we must learn to care first and foremost for how we affect the health of humble things in our environment, such as the soil of our own gardens, yards, or agricultural fields through which water passes and the ditches that carry the water to the streams. Only then can we learn how to care for the mighty things in our environment, such as a river or an ocean.

Protect the soil and we protect the ditch; protect the ditch and we protect the stream, river, estuary, and ocean. Defile the soil and we defile the ditch; defile the ditch and we defile the stream, river, estuary, and ocean.

Because our Western industrialized thinking is so linear, so out of touch with Nature, I wonder how long it will take for society to kill the mighty oceans of the world by poisoning the humble local ditches of the land. But we need not poison or kill these things. It is, after all, by choice that we either protect or defile our environment. This being so, we can always choose to choose again, to honor the humble and thereby protect the mighty, for it is ordained in the nature of things that water always knows where it is going—back to the sea. Whether it takes days or years makes no difference.

If, therefore, every person made it his or her personal duty to protect the health of the soil of his or her garden, yard, or field, the world, through the discharge of the humble local ditch, would be cleaned in like measure—as would the oceans of the world. Ditches in many unforeseen ways connect people with one another in both time and space, but how does a rigid fixture like a local dam affect people?

A DAM

Although dams can afford considerable economic and social benefits, their placement and construction must be grounded in sufficient knowledge of the river and its catchment basin to account for long-term ecological consequences. Dams are highly individualistic, and the same physical circumstance may elicit dramatically different responses. The effects of a dam in time and space can be considerable and may become apparent only after a long time. For purposes of illustration, I shall discuss only one dam, the Aswan High Dam in Egypt.

A Warning About the Aswan High Dam

While I was working as a vertebrate zoologist with a scientific expedition in Egypt in 1963 and 1964, a representative of the Egyptian Ministry of Agriculture spent time with us as we worked just north of the Sudanese border along the Nile. One day, three of us from the expedition tried to help this man understand that building the Aswan High Dam across the Nile River would be an ecological nightmare. He could not, however, see beyond the generation of electricity and irrigation, which was the official position of the government for constructing the dam.

We explained to the government representative that building the dam would increase the geographical distribution of the snails that carry the tiny blood fluke that causes the debilitating disease schistosomiasis from below the Aswan Dam (built by the British in the early 1930s) south to at least Khartoum in the Sudan, several hundred miles above the new, yet to be completed dam. At that time, it was still safe to swim above the Aswan Dam, where the water was too swift and too cold for the snails to live, but it was not safe to swim, or even catch frogs, in the water below the dam, where the snails already lived.

We told him that the Nile above the high dam would fill with silt, which would starve the Nile Delta of its annual supply of nutrient-rich sediment and affect farming in a deleterious way. We also told him that the dam could easily become a military target for the Israelis, as German dams were targets for the British during World War II.

The Dam Is Built

The engineers building the Aswan High Dam had intended only to store more water and to produce electricity, which they did. However, deprived of the nutrient-rich silt of the Nile's annual floodwaters, the population of sardines off the coast of the Nile Delta in the Mediterranean diminished by 97 percent within two years. In addition, the rich delta, which had been growing in size for thousands of years, is now being rapidly eroded by the Mediterranean, because the Nile is no longer depositing silt at its mouth.[113]

Until the Aswan High Dam was built, the annual sediment-laden waters of the Nile added a millimeter (a little less than a 16th of an inch) of nutrient-rich silt to the farms along the river each year. Now that the floods have been stopped by the new dam, the silt not only is collecting upriver from the dam, thus diminishing its water-holding capacity, but also is no longer being deposited on the riverside farms, thus decreasing their fertility. Soon the farmers will have to buy commercial fertilizer, something most of them probably cannot afford. In addition, because irrigation without flooding causes the soil to become saline, the Nile Valley, which has been farmed continuously for 5,000 years, will within a few centuries have to be abandoned. Also, schistosomiasis has indeed spread southward to the Sudan. What right does one nation have to knowingly cause the spread of a highly infectious disease into another nation in the name of economic self-interest, or any other reason for that matter?

What About the Nubian People?

In addition, a people, the Nubians, were displaced and their culture thereby destroyed. The Nubians whom I got to know were tall, straight, slender, very black with fine features, and lived many miles south of Aswan on small farms sandwiched between the east bank of the Nile and the Eastern Desert. Their village was neat and clean, and each house was decorated by embedding plates, with designs around their borders, into the outer mud coating of the doorways. The people had a wonderful sense of humor, were quick to laugh, and seemed genuinely pleased that I delighted in playing with their children and vice versa. For their part, the children seemed to have a good sense of self and of each day as an adventure to be lived to the fullest.

But the Aswan High Dam changed all that. The Nubians were moved inland from the bank of the Nile, whose quiet flowing waters and silent guardian desert had been a part of their lives seemingly forever. In place of their freely spaced, cool, airy, self-designed, and self-constructed homes, they were put into government-built, look-alike, minimum-quality housing. Gone was the peaceful silence of the desert. Gone were the songs of the birds in the shrubs along the Nile's banks. Gone was the clean air. Gone was their experience of the quiet, black nights, ablaze with crisply visible stars, including the magnificent Southern Cross. Gone was the Nubians' freedom of choice. Many of them could not adjust to the loss of their place, of their culture, their gentle way of life, and simply died.

How, I wonder, does one tell a whole people, a whole culture that they have no value? How does one tell children that the fate of all their tomorrows is sealed in the concrete of a dam?

An Explosion of Rats

There is another consequence of the Aswan High Dam, one I would never have thought of, even though I had studied the mammals along the Nile. The Nile annually flooded the many nooks, crannies, and caves along its edge, killing the rats whose fleas carry bubonic plague. Because the floods no longer occur, the rat population has soared, and bubonic plague is once again a potential threat.

I learned about this unexpected consequence of the Aswan High Dam from Dr. Wulf Killmann of the Deutsche Gesellschaft für Technische Zusammerarbeit, whom I met in Malaysia. As we visited about the effects of dams on rivers and oceans, I told him about my experience in Egypt. Dr. Killmann then told me that he had been part of a project to figure out how to control the ever-growing population of rats, which had become a serious health problem.

But that is not all; the saga of the Aswan High Dam continues, according to R.G. Johnson of the Department of Geology and Geophysics at the University of Minnesota.[114] "If the Mediterranean Sea continues to increase in salinity," says Johnson, "shifting climatic patterns throughout the world may cause high-latitude areas in Canada to glaciate within the next century."

The Aswan High Dam and Global Climate

The Mediterranean is starving for fresh water because of human activities, such as the Aswan High Dam that cut off most of the annual flow of the Nile River, which is now used for irrigation and no longer enters the sea. In addition, evaporation from the surface of the Mediterranean is increasing due to global warming. Consequently, a larger amount of fresh water is being lost to human activities and evaporation than is being replaced by rainfall and the inflowing of freshwater rivers. All this means that the Mediterranean is becoming more saline and that salinity is being modified at the Strait of Gibraltar, where the waters of the Atlantic and Mediterranean mix. Barring a significant change in the regional circulation of the atmosphere, Johnson contends that the two human-caused losses of fresh water from the Mediterranean (the Aswan High Dam and global warming) will cause the salinity to increase for some time because of the influence burning of fossil fuels has on global warming.

The higher salinity in the Mediterranean will lead to more of the Mediterranean flowing into the Atlantic through the Strait of Gibraltar, which will modify the high-latitude oceanic–atmospheric circulation and, in effect, initiate new glaciation. This hypothesis, says Johnson, arises from his 1997 study of the climatic conditions and inferred changes in the oceanic–atmospheric circulation that probably triggered the last glaciation.[115]

The hypothesis, which is presented here in a simplistic form, works something like this: Leaving Gibraltar, the more saline, and thus heavier, water of the Mediterranean sinks and mixes with the very cold, deep water of the Atlantic, moving northward until it enters the northern gyre, a great circular vortex. As the fast-flowing water of the Mediterranean approaches the shallow banks north and west of Ireland, it comes to the surface by upwelling. The upwelling apparently acts like a fluidic switch that deflects the relatively warmer surface water of the Atlantic past Greenland into the colder Labrador Sea off the eastern coast of Canada, which in turn becomes warmer and, in connection with cloudy, cooler summers, causes more precipitation around Baffin Island and other regions in northern Canada, which in turn causes sheets of ice to grow while cooling the Nordic seas and northern Europe.

Johnson says that "today's climate may be close to the threshold for new glaciation," because the large plateau areas of Baffin Island are already covered with semipermanent snowfields that expanded during the historic Little Ice Age 150 to 350 years ago, a time during which summers were cool and extremely severe winters frequented northern Europe. Initiation of new growth in the ice sheet is of grave concern, says Johnson, because of the strong positive feedback from the enhanced electromagnetic radiation reflected by a growing ice sheet (termed *albedo*, which is Late Latin for whiteness, from the Latin *albus*, white), and denser cloud cover could ostensibly "lock in" the beginnings of an ice age despite global warming. ("Albedo" already exists today over the Greenland Ice Sheet.) The ultimate consequence, warns Johnson, might be a combination of two extremes in which strong global warming in the lower latitudes would nourish the rapid expansion of ice sheets in Canada and Eurasia.

Although there are many unknown variables, Johnson says that if his conceptual model is "approximately correct, a new ice age can be avoided if a partial dam is constructed on the sill across the strait 40 km (25 miles) west of Gibraltar." The idea, which again is presented in simplistic form, is to limit the outflow of the Mediterranean to something like 20 percent of today's rate of flow, which would remove the faster flowing water of the Mediterranean from traveling northward to the shallow banks off Ireland and thus diminish the upwellings. With the upwelling diminished, the warm surface water, now diverted into the Labrador Sea, would once again enter the Nordic seas. Canada would remain dry, and Europe's climate would remain mild and stable.

I find in this scenario an interesting problem, one I see arising again and again. We humans introduce something, such as the Aswan High Dam, into the environment, where it provides some benefits to humanity (electricity and more irrigation) while simultaneously causing untold, unknown, even unimaginable problems. But when the problems begin to manifest themselves, rather than removing the cause—the dam—we want to remedy the problems by introducing more of the same—another dam—into the environment. I have never seen a second dam fix the ecological problems created by the first dam.

On the other hand, what would happen if the Aswan High Dam were removed? While the floods would once again begin fulfilling their many ecological roles, negating the perceived need for a new dam across the Strait of Gibraltar, there would be an immediate problem of how to deal with all the silt trapped behind the dam. Then there is the question of what to do with all the steel, concrete, and other materials of which the dam is built. What would happen to all the economic investments and technological developments that have over the years sprung into existence because of the dam? How would the Egyptian people replace the social benefits engendered by the dam?

Even if all conceivable questions could be answered and most of the effects could be to some extent reversed, there is at least one effect of the dam that is final. The Nubian culture, in which I found such beauty and joy, would still be extinct. Therefore the question is: How reversible in reality are the effects of the Aswan High Dam? Here an observation by the Russian-born, Nobel-Prize-winning chemist and physicist Ilya Prigogine is opportune. Prigogine points out that all large processes in the real world, particularly all chemical processes, are irreversible.

Reversibility of processes, Prigogine contends, always corresponds to idealization.

Having examined a smattering of the possible global outcomes that can result from introducing technology into a local area, it is now time to ponder whether we can control the consequences of that which we introduce into the environment.

CAN WE CONTROL THE EFFECTS OF THAT WHICH WE INTRODUCE INTO THE ENVIRONMENT?

We introduce thoughts, practices, substances, and technologies into the environment, and we usually think of those introductions in terms of development. Whatever we introduce into the environment in the name of development will consequently determine how the environment will respond to our presence and to our cultural necessities. It is therefore to our social benefit to pay close attention to what we introduce.

Introduction of a foreign substance, process, or technology has a much greater impact on an ecosystem's ability to function as we want it to than does taking something away. The things we introduce into the environment represent both our sense of values and our behavior. After all, values—often competing values to which we give no conscious thought—shape the contours of our lives, which raises the question of how one goes about calculating the risk of something that has never before happened and, by our reckoning, is unlikely to occur in the future.[116]

As society develops new technology, draws on the resources of the Earth, and generates unprecedented quantities of unintended industrial products, such as toxic wastes, the above question is being asked more and more frequently because we must understand as best we can what the effects of our activities will be on the sustainability of our environment as a whole. Some people would throw their hands up and say that such predictions are impossible, but that is not entirely true. Over the past few decades, says retired physicist and engineer B. John Garrick, an entire discipline, known as risk assessment or risk analysis, has been formulated around the proposition of "what if."

As such, assessment of risk focuses on three issues, according to Garrick: "What can go wrong? How likely is it? And what are the consequences?" The answers are given as probabilities, which is the language of uncertainties, and learning how to quantify the uncertainties is a critical part of assessing risk.

Many people do not find the probabilities reassuring, however, despite how low they may be. I am one of those people because no matter how low they may be, I know how ignorant we are collectively when it comes to the synergistic effects of interdependent living systems. My doubts are not based on fear, however, but rather concern for the expressed surety of our human knowledge. Nevertheless, every decision has a risk attached to it, and the more we can understand the risks of our proposed actions, the better off we will be.

Making people more comfortable with the probabilities, says Garrick, is a matter of changing the terms of the debate. He goes on to say: "During my 40-plus years in the risk [assessment] business, the questions that have come to annoy me most are 'How safe is safe?' or 'How much risk is acceptable?' These are illogical questions. The only answer that makes sense is 'It depends—on the alternatives available and on the benefits to be gained by making a certain decision.'"

The questions are not illogical to me, as they are to Garrick, because the questions as asked simply point out that the people who ask them are frightened and do not know how to frame the questions in a way that addresses their fears. In addition, they are questions of value, including things likely to be lost, such as some long-cherished, often intangible component of one's lifestyle, which is far more complicated to deal with than the simple, traditional, linear questions asked and favored by scientists and engineers, who can at best measure only tangible effects.

Be that as it may, the best possible assessment of potential risk, as Garrick states, requires participation by the public, either directly or through elected representatives. "Governments and the private sector," admonishes Garrick, "need to develop mechanisms to ensure this input [by the public] without letting the process get bogged down by a few people whose entire agendas may never be expressed and whose actions lead to gross mismanagement of society's resources. Those who spread false information [on all sides] need to be held accountable—especially since the consequences of their actions can cost billions of dollars," to say nothing of destroyed ecosystems and the loss of the services they provide, which add to the misery of countless people.

"If decisions involving risk are not approached rationally, they will be made on political and emotional bases, which usually is not optimal for society," counsels Garrick. But then, all truly *rational* decisions involve—but are not ruled by—emotions, which after all are the foundation of our values as human beings. Politics, on the other hand, is often a case of hidden agendas that determine who wins and who loses. Having said this,

I will be the first to acknowledge that assessing risk in a formal manner provides us with a way to better understand the possible consequences of the choices we face. We thus would be well advised, I think, to make the best possible use of what we know about assessing risks, provided we do not become enamored with the outcome as a sure bet. And a bet on the outcome of adding something to or subtracting something from an ecosystem is all risk assessment is!

Adding Something to the Environment

A simple act by the very people who moved to Phoenix, Arizona, to find relief from their allergies has placed Arizona among the top 10 percent of states in pollen count during the six-week allergy season.[117] Before urban sprawl began consuming the desert, the area around Phoenix was a haven for people who suffered from allergies. Doctors in the 1940s and 1950s sent patients there because the dry air was virtually pollen-free. But many of those people also brought with them their nondesert plants, which subsequently matured and now fill the air with pollen during the spring of each year.

In addition, the dry climate causes pollen grains from nonindigenous plants to stay aloft and ride the air currents, wafting in every zephyr. They are not washed from dry desert air as they are in nondesert areas that experience spring rains. The allergy sufferers themselves inadvertently turned their own haven into their worst nightmare by not identifying and protecting the very environmental value that brought them to Phoenix, Arizona, in the first place—air virtually free of pollen.

Getting rid of all the pollen-producing plants is probably no longer an option for the residents of Phoenix. If this is true, then clearly the introduction of pollen is out of their hands and here to stay.

Now consider that it is not the industrial smokestacks belching plumes of airborne pollutants that pollute most of the air in Oregon; it is cars, trucks, lawn mowers, leaf blowers, and aerosol cans.[118] "Two tons of smog-producing chemicals are put into the air in the Portland [Oregon] area every day just from hairspray," said Marcia Danab, a spokeswoman for the Oregon Department of Environmental Quality.

"Industry contributes just 15 percent [of the pollution]," Danab said. "That's surprising to most people." On the other hand, studies by the Oregon Department of Environmental Quality show that trucks account for 41 percent of the pollution inhaled within the city limits of Portland. An additional 21 percent comes from household items such as paint, solvent, dry-cleaning residues, and chemical air fresheners. Lawn mowers, leaf blowers, boats, and construction equipment account for 23 percent. The French government is, however, dealing with a different kind of culprit.

The French government has launched an investigation into a malady that has killed an estimated 60 percent of the famed honeybees in western France since June 1997.[119] Beekeepers say the insects are becoming increasingly disoriented and thus fail to return to their hives after feeding on sunflowers. The culprit is suspected to be the pesticide Gaucho, introduced in 1994, the use of which was subsequently suspended by French agricultural authorities in the affected areas.

Then there is a very real danger that importing raw logs into the United States and Canada, to offset the industrial depletion of North American forests, would bring unwanted diseases and insects that damage trees.[120] For example, Dutch elm disease, a fungal disease, "is coming to our shores in unprocessed logs," according to William Denison, retired professor of botany and plant pathology at Oregon State University. Transmitted by bark beetles, Dutch elm disease chokes the trees' vascular tissues. There is no cure; diseased trees must be cut down and removed to prevent the fungus from spreading. In addition, a variety of disease-carrying insects, such as the Asian long-horned beetle, penetrate raw logs and can thus be shipped alive around the world in unprocessed wood.

Finally, there is controversy concerning the ski area at Timberline Lodge on Mount Hood, Oregon, where eight million pounds of salt have been strewn across 320 acres of the Palmer Snowfield since 1988 to harden the snow that would otherwise melt.[121] Salt has been spread on the snowfield to keep it from melting since the 1950s. Without salt or a viable substitute, Timberline Lodge, which is the only ski area in the United States where chair lifts operate all year, would lose its profitable niche because people could neither ski nor snowboard in July, now the most profitable month for the owners of the lodge.

Although questions remain as to where the salt goes and what its effects on the environment might be, even 20 months after the state of Oregon began more stringent monitoring of the practice of salting the snowfield, Jeff Kohnstamm, an area operator and president of RLK & Company, the privately held owner of Timberline Lodge, seems to have no doubts. Kohnstamm is reported to have said that the practice of salting the snowfield is sound and that he supports it because it works and because salt occurs naturally on the mountain. One cannot, in this case, argue that RLK & Company has the right to do on its lands as it pleases because Timberline Lodge is situated on public lands administered by the U.S. Forest Service.

Despite Kohnstamm's apparent certainty about the appropriateness of the practice of salting, one estimate projects that between 32 and 91 percent of the salt ends up in the Salmon River. Surely, this must have an ecological impact. The questions remain, however, about the nature and magnitude of the impact. But what about subtracting something from the environment?

Subtracting Something from the Environment

There is today a crisis building in Vietnam.[122] Rats have begun widespread destruction of rice and cereal crops across the country. Nearly 200,000 acres were destroyed in 1998 because farmers and villagers were eating cats, owls, and other predators that normally control the rats.

In an effort to control the rats, the government in Hanoi has closed restaurants that serve cat meat to stop the wave of "catnapping" that has left the rat population free to grow and increasingly devour the crops. Domestic cats have been disappearing at an alarming rate in recent years as new specialty establishments feature "little tiger" dishes on their menus. As a result of the loss of the rats' normal predators, the government is urging residents to catch and kill rats by hand because it is safer for the environment than the use of rat poison. Of course, it would also help if domestic cats, owls, and other predators were allowed to rebuild their former populations and reclaim their useful role in controlling the rats, which is possible.

In the arid western United States, on the other hand, it is time that is being taken away and plants and soil that are being lost. We in Western industrialized society seem to find little or no intrinsic value in Nature unless it is demonstrably "good for something" or can be converted into something for which we can find a material value. In this sense, it seems to have become a largely accepted norm that a piece of land must be producing something we desire almost all of the time or we deem it unproductive. We therefore use land continually, disallowing it time to itself. What might some of the consequences be of taking away from the land its time to rest and heal?

The "skin" of lichens, fungi, and algae that once formed a protective layer over the surface of the soil of grasslands and shrub steppe in the western United States has been frayed to dust by the hooves of livestock, boots of backpackers, and wheels of dirt bikes and all-terrain vehicles.[123]

Today, less than 5 percent of the skin exists in pristine condition. When in excellent condition, the skin can cover as much as 80 percent of the soil and is interspersed here and there only by indigenous grasses and shrubs.

Although the soil can begin to form a "scab" of "living skin," which to me looks more like a "living crust," within a few years of protection, it takes a half-century or more for the complex living skin to develop. A fully developed skin, which can be thought of as a tiny ecosystem, may have more than 100 species of minute to small plants and thousands of bacteria and other microorganisms within it.

This fibrous skin of little plants and microorganisms is imbued with the remarkable ability to build fertility in the soil even while it resists erosion of the soil and lessens the frequency and intensity of summer fires. In addition, the skin helps prevent foreign grasses, the most pervasive of which is cheatgrass, and herbs from gaining a secure toehold where they are not wanted.

Finally, consider Owens Lake near Lone Pine, California.[124] Where waterfowl and steamships once flourished, a barren expanse of white rock-hard ground covered in a fine, ever-shifting layer of sand and dust now exists. When the wind blows, it stirs up the dust and thereby causes the adjacent towns to be shrouded by a chalky fog because 85 years ago an aqueduct was opened, which drained the Owens Valley of its water to satisfy the ever-growing thirst of the people living in Los Angeles.

Years of bitter conflict raged between the city of Los Angeles and the residents around Owens Lake as the water-guzzling people of Los Angeles turned the lake into one of the nation's largest sources of lung-damaging particle pollution. Today, in a single 24-hour period, as much as 11 tons of particles laced with arsenic and other toxic metals blows off the dry lake bed. Such pollution can cause respiratory infections, attacks of asthma, and sometimes even deadly complications from respiratory and heart ailments.

Should the 15-member Los Angeles City Council and the California Air Resources Board agree with the currently proposed plan, the city will rectify the problem by focusing on flooding the shallow parts of the 110-square-mile dry lake bed, planting vegetation, and depositing gravel. Although the lake will not be refilled, the first ten square miles will likely be permanently soaked with a few inches of water. Treatment of those 10 square miles by the Los Angeles Department of Water and Power will be completed by the end of 2001, to be followed by another 3.5 square miles in 2002 and 3 more in 2003. Thereafter, at least two square miles must be treated annually. The progress and plan will be evaluated in 2003 to ensure that federal clean air standards are met by 2006.

The project is expected to cost the city of Los Angeles $120 million, in addition to which the city might permanently lose around 40,000 acre-feet of water. That is enough water to serve 80,000 households.

Both adding to and subtracting from the environment have consequences, albeit adding something is likely to perpetuate consequences that are more out of human control than is subtracting something from the environment. Be that as it may, whatever we add to or remove from the environment depends on the immediate value we perceive the act will net us.

How We Think Determines Our Actions

Vandals on four-wheelers cut through a gate on a road at the edge of the Three Sisters Wilderness of the Deschutes National Forest in central Oregon and gutted a high mountain meadow. They churned about 1,600 square feet of the sensitive wet meadow into a mud pit with ruts as much as a foot deep. "It's entirely ruined," said Rico Burgess, law enforcement officer for the Bend-Fort Rock Ranger District. "It's not one of those crimes [where] you can say, 'I didn't know the rules.' You know you're damaging a resource. This is about the worst I've seen." Restoring the meadow will cost about $2,000 and take about five years.[125]

Our initial introduction into the environment is our pattern of thought, which determines the way we perceive the Earth and the way we act toward it—either as something sacred to be nurtured or only as a commodity to be converted into money. Because our pattern of thought determines the value we place on various components of an ecosystem, it is our sense of values that determines the way we treat those components and through them the ecosystem as a whole, which has caused professor of zoology Jane Lubchenco to call for a new social contract for science.[126] If the 21st century, the "century of the environment," as Lubchenco calls it, is to become one of hope and human dignity, then we also need new, more responsible contracts for technology and economics, contracts that place primacy on long-term social–environmental sustainability as opposed to solely short-term profit margins.

In our linear, product-oriented thinking, an old-growth forest is an economic waste if its "conversion potential" is not realized; that is, the only value old-growth trees have is their potential for being converted into money. Such notions stimulated Professor Garrett Hardin to observe that "economics, the handmaiden of business, is daily concerned with 'discounting the future,' a mathematical operation that, under high rates of interest, has the effect of making the future beyond a very few years essentially disappear from rational calculation."[127] Unfortunately, Hardin is correct. Conversion potential of resources counts so heavily because the economically effective horizon in most economic planning is only five years. In our traditional linear economic thinking, any merchantable old tree that falls over and reinvests its nutrient capital into the soil is an "economic waste" because its potential was not converted into money.

New equipment is therefore constantly being devised to make harvesting resources like trees ever-more efficient. The chain saw, for example, greatly accelerated the liquidation of old-growth forests worldwide. Possessed by this new tool, the timber industry and the forestry profession lost all sense of restraint and began cutting forests far faster than they could regrow. Further, no forested ecosystem has yet evolved to cope ecologically with the massive systematic and continuous clear-cutting made possible by the chain saw and the purely economic thinking behind it.

Nuclear energy is another example. In our search for "national security" and cheap energy, we are introducing concentrated nuclear waste into many ecosystems, the impact of which is both global in scale and complex in the extreme. And there is no safe way to introduce the concentrations we are creating. The meltdown of the nuclear reactor at Chernobyl was not potentially as dangerous as the buried nuclear dump that blew up near Chelyabinsk, in the southern Ural Mountains, in late 1957 or early 1958.[128] "The land was dead—no villages, no towns, only chimneys of destroyed homes, no cultivated fields or pastures, no herds, no people—nothing," said Leo Tumerman. "It was like the moon for many hundreds of square kilometers, useless and unproductive for a very long time, many hundreds of years."

We have not the slightest idea how to deal safely with the concentrations of nuclear wastes we are introducing into the world. Yet instead of committing our efforts to producing safe, clean solar and wind energy, we cling steadfastly to unsafe, deadly dirty nuclear energy and create thousands of tons of nuclear waste annually through the military–industrial complex and peacetime technology.

If we continue this course, the biosphere will eventually adapt to high, generalized concentrations of radioactivity, but most life as we know it will not be here to see that adaptation take place. With this in mind, there are concerns not only here at home but also abroad. Consider the following two examples.

Nuclear Waste at Home

Attorneys in the state of Utah bombarded the Nuclear Regulatory Commission with dozens of arguments against putting nuclear waste in Utah's Skull Valley.[129] The nuclear waste dump would store spent fuel from nuclear reactors on the Skull Valley Goshute Indian Reservation in the west desert 50 miles southwest of Salt Lake City.

The state attorneys told the Nuclear Regulatory Commission that, despite safeguards, high-risk facilities are already located in the west desert, including the Deseret Chemical Depot and the Dugway Proving Ground, which "create a potentially volatile community of institutions," according to state attorney Connie Nakahara. She went on to say that "a number of dangerous scenarios are possible, given the existence of these facilities in the same general area."

These scenarios include the proximity of Hill Air Force Base, where two F-16 jet aircraft crashed in the west desert just two weeks prior to the hearing conducted by the Nuclear Regulatory Commission. In addition, the state cited a recent incident in which a cruise missile was accidentally deployed during a training mission.

On the other hand, attorneys for both Private Fuel Storage, the consortium that wants to build the private storage facility, and the Skull Valley Band of Goshute Indians said the scenarios proposed by the state attorneys are farfetched. "I think we need to have intellectual honesty in these proceedings," said Danny Quintana, attorney for the Goshute Indians. "We can't have the state just reaching into outer space for any excuse at all. We don't require PFS [Private Fuel Storage] to plan for a meteorite falling out of the sky. We don't require them to build a surface-to-air missile battery...these [scenarios by the state] are truly, truly incredible."

If you think the fears the Utah state attorneys expressed over locating a nuclear waste dump 50 miles from Salt Lake City are as unfounded as Danny Quintana indicates, consider the reasoning in the next story concerning nuclear waste from Asia.

Nuclear Waste Abroad

The United States has agreed to take the highly radioactive nuclear waste from Asia to protect it from groups of terrorists and "rogue" nations, either of which could use it to build nuclear weapons.[130] The five shipments, planned over a period of 13 years, will enter San Francisco Bay by ship. They will begin their travel by rail at Concord Naval Weapons Station and proceed through northern California, Nevada, and Utah on their way to the Idaho National Engineering and Environmental Laboratory.

The Department of Energy reiterated its plans to station armed security guards and nuclear emergency response teams on board each train. Other security measures include:

- The governor and appropriate local officials of each state will be notified seven days before a shipment is to reach their state, in addition to which emergency notification systems will be tested in advance.
- State police and local health personnel will shadow the trains as they move through each state.
- Safety inspections will be conducted by the Federal Railway Administration and the California Public Utilities Commission prior to the departure of each train from the Concord Naval Weapons Station.
- Crews running the trains will receive special training, and inspectors will assist dispatchers during each shipment.
- Only "dedicated" trains (those carrying only nuclear fuel) will be used, and they will be given priority status.
- All railroad crossings will be inspected to ensure that gates and lights are functioning properly.
- Cranes will be available to retrieve the casks containing nuclear fuel in the event of an accident.

The mere fact that the United States is willing to bring within its borders nuclear waste from Asia for "safekeeping" indicates that nuclear waste is exceedingly dangerous. I would not want it in my backyard because it would mean that someone else is risking my future above and beyond the vagaries of Nature and life itself. If nuclear waste is so dangerous, I suggest that the only way to "manage" it is to shift our thinking and not produce it in the first place.

Shifting Our Thinking

Thus far, our management of the world's resources has been to maximize the output of material products, putting into operation the notion that conversion potential is the only value, while minimizing the monetary costs of protecting the environment. In so doing, we not only deplete the resource base but also produce unmanaged and unmanageable "by-products," often in the form of hazardous "wastes." In unforeseen ways, these by-products, which in reality are unintended, undesirable products, are altering the way in which our biosphere functions.

Because of unforeseen and usually undesirable effects from many of our introductions, we must shift our thinking from managing for particular short-term products to managing for a desired long-term condition on the landscape, an overall desired outcome of our decisions and actions. To help you understand what I mean, reread the section on "Adding Something to the Environment."

With the above discussion in mind, I suggest that we must become innovative and daring and must focus on controlling the type and amount of processes, substances, and technologies that we introduce into an ecosystem to effect a particular outcome. With prudence in our decisions about what to introduce into an ecosystem and how to do it, we can have an environment of desirable quality to support a chosen lifestyle and an environment that can still produce a good mix of products and amenities, but on an ecologically sustainable basis.

If, for instance, we ensure that all possible material introductions we make into the environment would be biodegradable as food for organisms like bacteria, fungi, and insects, then our "waste" would be their nutriment. In addition, if we use solar- and wind-based energy instead of fossil fuels, and if we recycle all nonrenewable resources in perpetuity, we will shift our pattern of thought from one that is ecologically exploitive to one that is ecologically friendly and sustainable.

Waste that threatens the environment and human life rather than sustaining it must be relegated to the strictly linear materialistic economics of the 20th century. The 21st century must begin the era of balances in which we employ cyclical thinking to maintain ecological harmony while we employ linear thinking to produce the goods and services society requires. This means that an ecologically sound environment must become the measure of economic health in which the welfare of our home planet—in the present for the future—takes precedence over our puny, selfish, materialistic wants. We must understand and accept that it is the cumulative effects of the collective thoughts, practices, substances, and technologies that we introduce into the environment that determine the way in which the environment will respond to our presence and our social necessities over time.

HOW ONE INTRODUCTION LEADS TO ANOTHER

Development of any kind is the collective introduction of thoughts, which inevitably lead to further introductions in terms of practices, substances, and technologies in a strategy to use or extract a given resource or to defend those one already has. Another facet of technology is the sense that it gives us ever-greater control over our environment, which today in Western society is all too often seen as a war against the uncertainties of Nature—against the creative novelty of the Universe itself. To understand this statement, let's look at two simplistic scenarios: weapons and the domestication of animals.

Weapons

Weapons probably initially came about as a means of protecting oneself against predators and for obtaining food. In this simplistic scenario, let's assume that the first weapon was most likely a hurled rock or a piece of wood used as a club. Then, somewhere in the far reaches of past memory, a humanlike creature began to see the advantage of using a long piece of wood to hold some vicious predator at bay. With time, it was discovered that a stick could be fashioned into a more potent weapon by rubbing one end against rough rocks until a sharpened point was effected—a point that caused pain.

Next, it was discovered that such a pointed stick could be hurled at a foe or potential meal, and thus was born the rudimentary art of making and using a spear. Then, perhaps by accident, it was learned that the sharpened point could be hardened by subjecting it to heat from a fire. This may have been followed by attaching a piece of sharp bone as a more lethal tip and finally a piece of stone that was carefully shaped into a sharp, cutting point. Again time passed, and it was figured out that by making and using a throwing stick or atlatl, a spear could be hurled with greater force and penetrating power than simply using one's extended arm.

Next came the bow and arrow, which could be shot faster than a spear could be thrown. In addition, one could carry far more arrows than spears, and arrows were probably more economical to make and thus less of a setback when broken or lost. Over time, experimentation led to attaching parts of birds' feathers to the end of an arrow opposite the point. Gradually it became common knowledge that if the feathers were attached at a slight angle, the arrow would not only spin its way accurately through the air but also travel faster and farther, becoming a still more lethal weapon. This in turn meant that one could shoot at one's opponent or at game from a greater and thus safer distance. Arrows also progressed from stone-tipped to iron-tipped projectiles, and bows became stronger, finally leading to the invention of the crossbow, a weapon much more deadly than the traditional longbow of the time.

The next advance in the lethal capacity of weaponry had to wait for the invention of gunpowder, which made possible the smoothbore musket-type weapon. Smoothbore weapons were eventually followed by rifles with grooved barrels, which greatly increased the accuracy of the bullet because the grooves caused the bullet to spin its way through the air, as opposed to the smoothbore's inaccurate wobble. After more time and experimentation came the invention of smokeless gunpowder and a repeating, high-powered rifle with a telescopic sight. Today's automatic rifles can fire several bullets per minute.

Each technological advance in weaponry not only allowed the weapon to be used from a safer, more distant position but also increased the accuracy and power of the projectiles. Each technological advance also did something else, however. It made both enemy and game an increasingly abstract entity as one could kill at ever greater distances, divorcing oneself from the intimate relationship with either foe or wild animal that the old weapons demanded. This poses an interesting question: Would the indigenous peoples of the Americas, or anywhere else for that matter, have had the same land ethic had they possessed high-powered, repeating rifles prior to the invasion of the Europeans?

Domestication of Animals

We know that early humans domesticated animals, beginning perhaps with a child purposefully taming a mouse or rat sharing the family cave, and so the first pet came into being. At some later time, large animals, such as sheep and goats, were domesticated in the Near East. Still later came the domestication of the ox, a human–animal relationship out of which was born the ability to use animals for work. But an ox by itself could not do much. Something was missing.

Let's suppose that someone, seeing the strength of an ox, began toying with the notion of attaching a hide rope around the neck of his ox and attaching the opposite end to an object, say a large piece of wood, to see if the ox could pull it. New technology was suddenly available.

Then someone began to question whether a better way could be found to use an ox to pull heavy objects. After much experimentation, a crude ox yoke was invented, which revolutionized the possibilities of putting oxen to work. For a time, the focus was on perfecting the design and craftsmanship of the yoke.

With time, someone began to wonder if a better way could be found to move heavy objects with an ox or even a team of oxen, and the idea of the wheel was born. Again, after much experimentation, the first crude wheel was engineered, which meant that a mechanism had to be invented to hook wheels together so they would work in unison. Then someone had to figure out how to hitch the ox yoke to the wheels so that something could be pulled. If two wheels worked well, would four wheels not work better? It was only a matter of time before the first cart was invented.

But oxen are slow compared to a horse. If a yoke could be invented to harness the energy of oxen, could not a similar device be invented to harness the energy of a horse, giving the owner of both oxen and horses a greater array of options for work and thus more potential wealth and power? With this in mind, and after much experimentation, the first crude horse collar was produced, tested, improved, tested, improved, tested, improved, and so on.

Each of these inventions became the means by which the owner of the technology was relieved of manual labor. In other words, technology, by its very conception, was continually designed to make life easier by making as much manual labor unnecessary as possible, while making life as predictable as possible. I say this because it is much easier to ensure a continual supply of wood for the fire if, rather than having to carry it from afar in small bundles by hand, one can, with a team of oxen or horses, haul home a whole tree or log. With a team of oxen or horses, one person not only could haul a greater load but also could vastly increase the distance from which one could glean such a load, thus increasing the effectiveness and efficiency with which one could use one's environment. This in turn allowed one to become more sedentary in lifestyle, but with an increasingly greater impact on the environment in both space and time.

If we leap forward in time by the thousands of years it took to advance from the domestication of animals to the Industrial Revolution, we find that technology was still idealized both as labor saving and as a means of increasing predictability in maintaining material lifestyles. But then something shifted in the human drive for power.

Those who could afford to own the machines, which did more work than one person could, kept more of the profits. Thus, if it originally took ten men to produce a certain amount of goods for sale, each man was paid a certain amount. With the advent of a machine that could now replace nine of those men and still produce the same amount of commodity, the reasoning became something like this: I have invested my capital in the purchase of this machine; therefore, I am entitled to keep nine-tenths of the profits because my machine represents nine-tenths of the productive capacity. And so the first people were put out of work by a "labor-saving" invention.

At some point in history, those who lusted after wealth and power discovered that if they could own the technology, they could use that technology to produce more of a given product with fewer people and thus keep more of the profits for themselves. At that point, labor-saving technology shifted social tyranny because the unspoken purpose of such technology began to move from labor saving in terms of creating a better life for everyone to people being replaced in order to garner more wealth and power for the few who could afford to own the technology. After all, machines do not ask for wages, are not late to work, do not call in sick, make no human mistakes, do not want child care or maternity leave, do not expect health benefits and paid vacations, and so on.

But beware of illusions, such as idealized technology, which many see as the way to wealth and the panacea to all the world's problems. Illusions, in their very idealized perfection, are dangerous entities whose dark sides are far more unpredictable in cumulative effects than anyone could ever imagine.

I say this because the machines of the Industrial Revolution in England forced large numbers of people to abandon their varied handicrafts and village communities and herd together in slums near the mills and factories. This forced migration caused new problems of organization and government, problems for which there are still no solutions, problems of technology inappropriate to sustainability that are increasingly replacing with robotic sameness the diversity of life vital to human beings and Nature. Thus, while fewer and fewer people can afford to live the "good life," where diversity of choice and things from which to choose abound, more and more people are reduced to the homogeneity and sense of hopelessness that are the hallmark of poverty.

Based on a one-night check of shelters and the streets, the Census Bureau reported in 1990 that 228,372 people in the United States were homeless, including 3,818 people in Oregon.[131] One should not read too much into these numbers, cautioned an employee of the Center for Population Research and Census at Portland State University, because "the assumption is, they're under-counted," said Sharon Ordaz, office coordinator for the center. And the numbers have grown, according to Dee

Southard, who herself was homeless for almost six years but is now teaching a class on homelessness at Southern Oregon University.

The census, according to Southard, does not include more than 6,800 homeless children who were enrolled in school in 1990, which means, according to the Oregon Department of Education, that 11,000 children were homeless, including those enrolled in school. That number rose to 20,000 in 1997. Thus, said Southard, between one-quarter and one-third of the homeless are children. Extrapolating from the other figures, indications are that about 50,000 Oregonians were homeless in 1997.

There is an unfortunate twist to this story. Where technology is not yet available to replace people, corporations still find ways of divesting themselves from those people they feel cost more than they want to pay. Many of the homeless who had jobs lost them, Southard said, because corporations moved their plants to countries with cheaper labor. She went on to say that "we have a lot of skilled blue-collar workers who have no work."

As corporations downsize, and as technology increasingly replaces people, lower paying jobs, such as clerks in retail stores and positions in fast-food establishments, fill the gap, but most pay minimum wage or slightly higher, which is not enough to pay for housing, according to Southard—and she knows from personal experience. As a result, says Southard, many people *with* jobs are homeless. That is different than in the past, when a full-time job almost guaranteed a person the dignity of being able to afford housing.

Although I could go on at length, the point about the cumulative impact of technology has been sufficiently made on the one hand. On the other hand, now that we humans in fact have the technological capability to destroy the entire world as we know it, more and more people are beginning to question how we as human beings will cope with many of our so-called technological advances. In this questioning I find hope, because somehow most technology has progressively allowed us to dupe ourselves into thinking that we are in control of and therefore somehow separated from Nature, rather than being an integral and inseparable part thereof. With this in mind, it is time to discuss our human manipulation of diversity as it pertains to the environmental context in which we place ourselves.

DEALING WITH SCALES OF DIVERSITY

9

R ecall from Chapter 6 that the indigenous peoples of the Americas, prior to the invasion of the Europeans, had already greatly changed the landscapes in which they lived not only through their growing populations but also through their development of technology. The systematic demise of the indigenous peoples of the Americas began the day Columbus landed in the New World in 1492. The indigenous peoples were not only progressively slaughtered and enslaved but also subjected to diseases for which they had no immunity and thus succumbed in the millions.

Between the time the Spanish landed and the British began to invade North America, the land, left increasingly uninhabited and untended by the dying indigenous peoples, reverted to a wilder state than had existed for many centuries. Consequently, the British did in fact encounter a less culturalized continent than did the Spanish when they arrived. And it is this experience, as well as the fabrication of the grand American myth of imagined pristine Nature across an entire continent of wilderness filled with wild beasts and a few savages, that became the backdrop of pre-European settlement against which naturalness is today measured when discussing the ideal state of biological diversity of a given landscape. With this in mind, let's consider diversity within the context of time and space.

DIVERSITY WITHIN THE CONTEXT OF TIME AND SPACE ACROSS A LANDSCAPE

An issue I frequently deal with as a consultant is the notion of biological diversity in time and space across landscapes. Biological diversity in its array of interrelating scales across the time and space of a given landscape is little understood by the general public and is thus a subject of much mistrust when agencies, such as the U.S. Forest Service, attempt to deal with landscape-scale diversity. To help clarify what I mean, two scales of diversity will be discussed, one at the scale of a landscape on public lands and one on small-scale forest holdings on private lands.

Large-Scale Diversity on Public Lands

Some years ago, I was asked to conduct a workshop for the people of the Ouachita National Forest, headquartered in Hot Springs, Arkansas. The problem was the public's concept of an acceptable scale of diversity across the landscape, a concept founded on ignorance of scale and distrust, both of which I found understandable.

For many years, the people had watched, often with a feeling of enraged helplessness, as large timber corporations clear-cut one section of forest after another, converting diverse forests into monocultural plantations of row-cropped trees for the pulp market. Where the people had once seen an acre of forest with a diversity of hardwood trees and shrubs, occasionally with a few conifers mixed in, they were suddenly confronted with row after row of pines. As more and more acres were clear-cut and converted to tree farms for the pulp industry, the people developed a bias against what they perceived as economic simplification of their beloved forest solely for some corporation's short-term monetary gains, which came at the expense of the aesthetic quality of the landscape they felt belonged to all of them.

Although the conversion from forest to single-species tree farm came in two scales, the people were consciously aware of only one, that which encompassed an acre. They saw a diverse forest being converted into a simplified, economic tree farm. What they did not see was the larger picture, which would have been even more disturbing had they recognized it. As industry clear-cut first a few acres and then another few acres, often leaving a few acres of standing forest in between because it did not own the land, industry progressively created a homogeneous landscape as well as homogeneous tree farms, something the U.S. Forest Service had done earlier in the Pacific Northwest.

In the Pacific Northwest, vast areas of unbroken forest that were at one time in our National Forest System have been fragmented by clear-cutting and have been rendered homogeneous by cutting small patches of old-growth timber, by converting these patches into plantations of genetically selected nursery stock, and by leaving small, uncut patches between the clear-cuts. This "staggered-setting system," as it was called, required an extensive network of roads, which meant that before half the land area was cut, almost every water catchment had been penetrated by logging roads. The whole of the National Forest System thus became an all-of-a-piece patchwork quilt with few, if any, forested areas large enough to support those species of birds and mammals that required the interior of the forest as their habitat.

The public who used the Ouachita National Forest, on the other hand, was unknowingly advocating a hidden homogeneity in insisting on all possible diversity on all acres all of the time, thus theoretically eliminating any disturbance regimes that might create diversity on a larger scale. The public's insistence on small-scale diversity was based, as noted previously, on both a lack of understanding of how the various scales of diversity nest one inside the other and a distrust of the industrial model of "pulp forestry."

When, therefore, the folks of the Ouachita National Forest began to restore a single-species pine forest and its simple ground cover of grass along the face of a range of mountains, the public erupted with indignation because the people saw it simply as a maneuver to grow an even-aged monoculture of pine trees for the pulp industry. And they had always known they could not trust the Forest Service. That is when I was summoned.

My task was to help all people concerned to understand (1) how exclusively small-scale diversity on all acres all of the time becomes homogeneity of habitat across a landscape; (2) how different scales of diversity not only nest one inside another but also create a collective landscape-scale habitat that is different than the individual habitats created by a single scale of diversity; (3) that the pine/grass community the Forest Service was attempting to restore had indeed existed where the Forest Service was attempting to restore it, according to the journals of early settlers, as a fire-induced and -maintained ecosystem in times of pre-European settlement; and (4) the necessity of landscape-scale patterns of diversity if landscapes are to be adaptable to changing conditions and thus suitable for human habitation over time.

It was critically important for the people to both understand and accept multiple scales of diversity across an array of ecological conditions if the heterogeneity of habitats—and of species—was to be maintained. They needed to understand that diversity is mediated by such events as a falling leaf, a blown-over tree, a fire, a hurricane, a volcano, or an El

Niño weather pattern. Each scale of disturbance alters—both destroys and creates—a habitat, or collective of habitats, by renegotiating the composition, structure, and function of plant communities, which in turn allows and creates a time–space array of still different scales, dynamics, and dimensions of diversity that can be used by animals, which in turn can alter plant communities, which in turn become still different habitats, and so on.

Although the workshop took a few days, the people began to change their thinking about the importance and dynamics of large-scale diversity on public lands. Now let's turn our attention to small-scale diversity on private holdings.

Small-Scale Diversity on Private Lands

There are endless possible scenarios of diversity on private lands, but four will suffice in helping to understand the importance of considering multiple scales and dynamics of diversity in relationship to sustainable community. To keep these examples as comparable as possible, the size of each parcel will be limited to 1,000 acres, and they will be discussed as though you, the reader, owned them.

Example 1

Your forest has a mix of three species of coniferous trees—Douglas fir, western hemlock, and western red cedar—with a few interspersed bigleaf maple and red alder. The forest is relatively uniform in the way it covers the land but is surrounded by a veritable patchwork of industrial clear-cuts, right up to the boundary of your property.

Your thinking, however, stays within the boundary of your property. Thinking your forest lacks diversity, you begin cutting small, dispersed patches of trees throughout the forest to create diversity, but you do so without a clear vision of what you want your forest to look like or why and without any consideration of the conditions of the land surrounding your property, which is all but a sea of clear-cuts. What will your forest look like? Is it what you really want? Will you in fact have created more diversity or so fragmented your forest that you have made it even more homogeneous than it was before? How will the pattern you create fit into the surrounding landscape?

In this case, you are creating diversity within the forest canopy for the sake of diversity without taking into account the various scales of diversity. If, for example, small openings are cut in an opportunistic fashion throughout your forest without accounting for diversity at both the scale of your forest and the larger landscape outside of your forest, there will soon be so many little openings and patches of diverse elements within your forest that it will become like alphabet soup out of which no ecological sense can be made. Diversity, to be ecologically viable, must be created in terms of some pattern.

Consider that as the land around your forest is progressively clear-cut, your forest will become a habitat island that will be ever-more isolated from other similar habitats. The basic consideration, therefore, must be to make your forest as viable and resilient in its ecological integrity as possible for as long as possible, and that means having a vision within which to create the kind of diversity that is more self-sustaining rather than less self-sustaining, which means understanding the relationship among composition, structure, and function.

To maintain ecological functions means that you must maintain the characteristics of the ecosystem in such a way that its processes are sustainable. The characteristics you must be concerned with are (1) species composition, (2) structure, and (3) function.

You can, for example, change the species composition of your forest, which means the composition is negotiable. In this case, composition is the determiner of the forest's structure and function, in that composition is the cause, rather than the effect, of the structure and function.

Composition determines the structure, and structure determines the function. Thus, by negotiating the composition, you simultaneously negotiate both the structure and function. Once the composition is in place, however, the structure and function are set—unless, of course, the composition is altered, at which time both the structure and function are altered accordingly.

The composition or kinds of plants and their age classes (the size of plants, usually trees, at certain chronological ages) within your forest creates a certain structure that is characteristic of the plant community at any given age. It is the structure of the plant community that in turn creates and maintains certain functions. In addition, it is the composition, structure, and function of a plant community that determine what kinds of animals can live there, how many, and for how long.

If you change the composition of your forest, you change the structure, and hence the function, and you affect the animals. The animals in general are thus ultimately constrained by the composition of the plant species and the age classes of the overstory trees.

If, therefore, you want (as part of your vision) a particular animal or group of animals in your forest, you have to work backward by determining what kind of function to create, which means you must know what kind of structure to create, which means you must know what type of species composition of plants (and age classes) is necessary to produce the required habitat(s) for the animal(s) you want. Once the composition is ensconced, the structure and its attendant functions operate as a unit in terms of the habitats required for the animal(s).

People and Nature are continually changing a plant community's structure and function, as well as its attendant animal community, by altering the species composition of the plant community, which in turn affects how it functions. For example, you change the structure of your forest (albeit much of it is invisible to you belowground or unknown to you in the animal community both above- and belowground) by how and when you cut the trees, which in turn will change the forest's species composition of plants and their age classes, which in turn will change how the forest functions, which in turn will change the kinds and numbers of animals that can live there. These are the key elements with which you must be concerned, because an effect on one area can—and usually does—simultaneously affect not only your forest but also the entire landscape. Composition, structure, and function work together to create and maintain ecological processes both in time and across space, and it is the health of the processes that in the end creates the health of your forest.

Scale is an often forgotten component of healthy forests and landscapes, however. The treatment of every stand of timber (a designated group of trees) is thus critically important to the health of your forest and the forest landscape as a whole, which can be thought of as a collection of the interrelated stands.

When you focus your whole attention on one stand of trees, you are ignoring the relationship of that particular stand of trees to other stands, to the rest of your forest, and to the surrounding landscape. It is like a jigsaw puzzle where each piece is a stand of trees. The relationship of certain stands of trees in the collective makes a picture of your forest. The relationship of your forest—and all surrounding clear-cuts—makes a picture of the landscape as a whole.

If one piece is left out of the puzzle, such as the various scales of diversity, the picture on the face of the puzzle is not complete, and you lack the ecological understanding necessary to make your forest as productively sustainable as possible. Thus your understanding of each stand of trees that you in some way manipulate is critically important in its relationship to the health of your forest as a whole. Therefore, the way each stand is defined and treated is critically important to how your forest, within the surrounding clear-cut landscape, both looks and functions over time.

Example 2

In this example, you own a piece of forestland that, due to past human activities both within and outside of your boundaries, is a fairly homogeneous and predominantly coniferous forest, such as Douglas fir, ponderosa pine, and incense cedar, with a mixture of hardwood trees, such as tan oak and madrone. Being interested in the conditions of your forest prior to European settlement, you check the historical records and find that prior to intensive logging and following World War II, when the planting of conifers replaced the groves of hardwoods, your forest had been predominantly a mixed conifer–hardwood forest with numerous patches of pure hardwoods.

Armed with this knowledge, you decide to see if you can return your forest to its pre-European settlement condition as you envision it from the literature. How accurate is the literature? Is your parcel of land large enough to sustain itself as a viable ecosystem once you have altered it? How will the structure of your redesigned forest fit as a patch of habitat into the surrounding landscape? Will it be a large enough patch for pre-European settlement animals to live there if they can get to it in the first place? What will happen to the species of animals that live there now? Will you add, lose, or maintain the diversity of species?

It is important for you to understand the island effect that you are creating because restoration of your forest to an earlier condition is going to severely disrupt the current habitats and existing habitat corridors and replace them with habitats increasingly at odds with the surrounding landscape. Such activity can actually initiate a decline in the viability of an existing local species and/or disrupt existing corridors for uncommon species, thus fragmenting the existing habitat and creating isolated subpopulations that are more prone to local extinctions.

Consider that the spatial patterns you see on the landscape, including those of your own forest, resulted from complex interactions among physical, biological, and social forces. The landscape has been influenced by the cultural patterns of centuries of human use, and the resulting landscape is therefore an ever-changing mosaic of patches of habitat, which vary in size, shape, and arrangement. The European-created disruptions of the existing landscape pattern, which included the extensive use of fire by indigenous peoples, began to cause unforeseen changes in the landscape, changes we are now having difficulty dealing with.

A disturbance, in this sense, is any relatively discrete event that disrupts the structure of a population and/or community of plants and animals or disrupts the ecosystem as a whole and thereby changes the availability of resources and/or restructures the physical environment. Cycles of ecological disturbances, including the indigenous use of fire, ranging from small grass fires to major hurricanes can be characterized by their distribution in space and the size of disturbance they create, as well as their frequency, duration, intensity, severity, synergism, and predictability.

Human-introduced disturbances, especially fragmentation of habitat, impose stresses with which an ecosystem is ill adapted to cope. By restoring the forest on such a small acreage as your land to an earlier condition of habitat, you would be further fragmenting an already fragmented landscape. It is critical to understand this because "connectivity" of habitats with the landscape is of prime importance to the persistence of plants and animals in viable numbers in their respective habitats—again, a matter of both biological and genetic diversity. In this sense, the landscape must be considered a mosaic of interconnected patches of habitats, which act as corridors or routes of travel between patches of other suitable habitats.

Whether populations of plants and animals survive in a particular landscape depends on the rate of local extinctions from a patch of habitat and the rate with which an organism can move among patches of habitat. Those species living in habitats isolated as a result of fragmentation are less likely to persist. Therefore, modifying the connectivity among patches of habitat strongly influences the abundance of species and their patterns of movement. The size, shape, and diversity of patches also influence the patterns of species abundance, and the shape of a patch may determine the species that can use it as habitat.

In this sense, your property is too small a parcel to restore the "original" condition in such a way that any restored habitat area will be large enough to contain a viable population of most species. In addition, restoration of habitats on such a small acreage really means creating new habitats in terms of what now exists and would further fragment the habitat of those species already established in the immediate area because restoration would likely fragment the existing habitat still further in relation to the surrounding habitat.

It is not, after all, the relationship of numbers of pieces or spatial extent that confers stability on ecosystems; it is the relationship of pattern. Stability flows from the patterns of relationship that have evolved among the various species. A stable, culturally oriented system, even a very diverse one, that fails to support these coevolved relationships has little chance of being sustainable. To create a viable culturally oriented forest within your 1,000-acre property, you must not only recognize but also accept that ecological sustainability and adaptability depend on the connectivity of your forest with the surrounding landscape.

Example 3

In this case, you own a 500-acre tree-farm forest that is primarily Douglas fir with a few scattered western hemlock. The oldest trees are 80 years. Your management strategy is to cut and remove a number of trees every few years, selecting the biggest and best trees as well as any diseased and dying trees, regardless of age. The number of trees you remove is determined, to some extent at least, by your perceived monetary requirements for the year. Although the trees are felled and removed carefully, so as not to destroy the naturally seeded young trees, you are having a definite effect on the diversity of your forest. What effect are you having on the composition, structure, and function of your tree farm? Are you making it more or less like a forest? What effect are you having on its potential as habitat for wildlife? What effect are you having on the health of the soil?

True, your tree farm superficially looks more like a forest in some respects than do most tree farms in the sense that there is clearly a mixture of age classes among the trees, but you are nonetheless continually simplifying it in terms of species composition, structure, and function through the severity, frequency, and evenness of your manipulations. The multiple entries are constantly altering—and eliminating—habitat for both plants and animals in time and space, such as large dead standing trees and large dead fallen trees. The resulting uniformity excludes some species of organisms that are critical to the long-term ecological health and sustainability of your property as a viable tree farm.

In short, your tree farm is becoming not only an increasingly simplified and homogeneous habitat but also progressively nonsustainable biologically, with less and less resemblance to an ecologically healthy forest. I say this because the simplification of its biological structure through your practice of selective logging amounts to biological "high-grading" in which the dominant features of the forest structure and function, as well as the organic material available to the soil, are continually and systematically removed to satisfy immediate profitability at the expense of long-term sustainability.

Here it is important to understand that the less we humans alter an ecosystem, such as your tree farm, to meet our desires, the more the system's functional requirements are met within itself. This in turn makes it easier and less expensive in terms of both time and energy to maintain that system in a relatively steady state because we have maintained more of the diversity of indigenous plants and animals—and therefore biological processes—than we might otherwise have done.

Conversely, the more altered a system is by our human attempt to control it, as in the sense of tree farming, the more that system's functional requirements must be met through human-mediated sources external to itself. This in turn makes it more labor intensive and more expensive to keep that system in a given condition because we have maintained less, often far less, of the diversity of indigenous plants and animals than we would otherwise have done.

Although ecosystems can tolerate cultural alterations, like those you carry out on your tree farm, the ecological functions that are disrupted or removed in the process, often through a loss of species, even locally, must be replaced through human labor if the system is to be sustainable. The more a system, such as your tree farm, is altered and simplified, the more fragile it becomes and the more labor intensive becomes its maintenance. When alterations exceed the point at which human labor can maintain the necessary functions, the system collapses. Collapse in this sense means that it becomes something other than that for which it was originally groomed, and in the process it becomes nonproductive of that for which it was altered.

What you must keep in mind, therefore, is that you are continually manipulating the structure and function of your tree farm, as well as its attendant animal community, by altering the species composition of the plant community, which in turn affects how it functions. For example, by how and when you cut the trees, you affect the structure of your tree farm, albeit much of the effect is invisible to you belowground or unknown to you in the animal community both above- and belowground. As your manipulations affect the plant community's composition, they in turn change how the community functions, which in turn will change the kinds and numbers of animals that can live there. These are the key elements with which you must be concerned, because an effect on one affects the others and thus the health and productivity of your entire tree farm. To have a biologically healthy tree farm, therefore, you must learn to see it as a living organism instead of just a collection of trees.

"Well," you might say, "I can't afford to waste merchantable wood. Such waste will affect my livelihood." Yours is an economic concept of waste, which says in effect that anything not used directly by you for your economic benefit is wasted. In a biological sense, however, there is no such thing as waste.

Consider that a tree rotting in your tree farm, composting as it were, is a *re*investment of Nature's biological capital in the long-term maintenance of soil productivity and hence the tree farm itself. Biological capital includes such things as organic material and biological and genetic diversity. To *re*invest means to invest again.

In a business sense, you make money (economic capital) and then take a percentage of those earnings and reinvest them, put them back as a cost into such things as the maintenance of your logging equipment and the road system in your tree farm. You do this to continue making a profit by protecting the integrity of your initial investment over time. In your business, you reinvest economic capital *after* the fact, after you have earned the profits. It is different, however, with biological capital, which is the capital of your tree farm.

Biological capital, on the other hand, must be reinvested *before* the fact, before the profits are earned, which means leaving some proportion of the merchantable trees, both alive and dead, in the forest to decompose and recycle themselves into the fabric of the living system and thereby replenish it. This is crucial because your tree farm *cannot* process economic capital; *biological capital* is required.

Such biological reinvestment is *necessary* to maintain the health of the soil, which in large measure equates to the health of your tree farm. The health of your tree farm, in turn, equates to your long-term economic health as a tree-farm owner.

Your tree farm has awesome complexity both aboveground and below. Adding to the apparent complexity aboveground is the internal hidden diversity that comes about when a live old tree eventually becomes injured and/or sickened with disease and begins to die. How a tree dies determines how it decomposes and reinvests its biological capital, organic material, chemical elements, and functional processes into the soil and thus the health of your tree farm.

A tree may die standing, only to crumble and fall piecemeal over decades to the floor of your tree farm, or it may fall directly to the floor of your tree farm as a whole, potentially merchantable tree. Regardless of how it dies, the standing dead tree and fallen tree are only altered states of the live tree, which means that the large live old tree must exist before there can be a large standing dead tree or a large fallen tree.

How a tree dies is important to the health of your tree farm because its manner of death determines the structural dynamics of the habitat its body provides. Structural dynamics, in turn, determine the biological/chemical diversity hidden within the tree's decomposing body as ecological processes incorporate the old tree into the soil from which young trees must grow.

What goes on inside the decomposing body of a dying or dead tree is the hidden biological and functional diversity that is totally ignored by economic valuation. That trees become injured and diseased and die is therefore critical to the long-term structural and functional health of your tree farm, but such injured and diseased trees are seen by an industrial forester only as economic waste if not cut and converted into money.

Your tree farm is an interconnected, interactive, organic whole defined not by the pieces of its body but rather by the interdependent functional relationships of those pieces in creating the whole—the intrinsic value of each piece and its complementary function. These processes are all part of Nature's rollover accounting system, which includes such assets as large dead trees, genetic diversity, biological diversity, and functional diversity—all of which count as *re*investments of biological capital in the health of your tree farm.

Your intensive, short-term, tree-farming methods disallow the reinvestment of biological capital in the soil, but then you were erroneously taught to see such reinvestment as economic waste. Yet even today, with our vastly greater scientific knowledge, the health of the soil is not only ignored but also discounted because those who analyze soil by means of traditional linear economic analyses weigh the net worth of protecting soil only in terms of the expected short-term revenues from future harvests. They ignore the fact that it is the health of the soil that produces the yields. In short, they see the protection of the soil as a cost with no benefit because the standard method for computing soil expectation values commonly assumes that the productivity of the soil will either remain constant or increase—but never decline.

Given that reasoning, which is both shortsighted and flawed, it is not surprising that those who attempt to manage the land seldom see protection of the soil's productivity as cost effective. If, however, we could predict the real effects of this economic reasoning on long-term yields, we might have a different view of the invisible costs associated with ignoring the health of the soil.

Nevertheless, soil is a bank of elements and water that provides the matrix for the biological processes involved in the cycling of nutrients, which are elements under the right conditions of concentration and availability to plants. In fact, of the 16 chemical elements required for life, plants obtain all but 3 (carbon, hydrogen, and oxygen) from the soil. The soil stores these essential nutrients in undecomposed litter and in living tissues and recycles them from one reservoir to another at rates determined by a complex of biological processes.

With the above in mind, it would behoove you to reconsider how you "manage" your tree farm if you want it to be ecologically healthy and biologically sustainable over time. Remember, your tree farm must be biologically sustainable *before* it can be economically sustainable, which means that you must take the scales of diversity into account, even the microscopic scale.

Example 4

In this final example, you are the manager of a recreational forest owned by the city in which you live. You have had the job for 15 years and have watched as urban sprawl has all but surrounded the forest. Now you are faced with not only increasing use of and damage to the forest by people but also an incursion of domestic and feral cats in the forest and holly trees.

Domestic Cats

Domestic cats, both tame and feral (domestic cats gone wild), have invaded the forest; while adding diversity with their presence, they are decimating the small indigenous animals, largely negating the positive effects of sound habitat management. What are your options?

One option, of course, is to do nothing. But that is not viable because the people who spend time in the forest watching birds are beginning to notice an increasingly sharp decline in species, particularly year-round residents, and they demand that something be done about it. Now what are your options?

You could begin by setting up an education program, with the help of the bird-watchers, to inform the townspeople about the effects their cats are having on the local populations of small birds and mammals in the forest. In addition, the bird-watchers and other interested people could gather support and pass a city ordinance that would make it mandatory to have all pet cats neutered. That would substantially control the population. In addition, you could begin a live-trapping and removal program to eliminate as many feral cats as possible roaming the forest.

If that still does not work, the city could pass an ordinance that would make it mandatory to obtain a license for all cats. Anyone's cat caught beyond some distance in the forest would be taken to the local animal shelter and the owner would be notified. An owner would be given two chances to control his or her cat. The third time a cat is caught in the forest, it would be euthanized.

Although this may sound harsh, if the townspeople really value their forest in its entirety, the cats must be controlled as much as possible. The real problem is not the cats but the owners who are irresponsible and allow their cats to stray. Unfortunately, it is usually the cats who pay the price for their owners' thoughtless negligence.

Holly

In addition to cats, holly trees are beginning to show up in the forest and are taking over the understory at the expense of indigenous plants; in so doing, they are altering the habitat for wildlife. Again, what are your options?

Doing nothing is certainly one of them. But this time, people of the native plant society will not accept that as an option. Now what? You might find out how holly seeds are dispersed, if you don't already know. You will find that they are dispersed by birds, particularly robins. What options does this information give you? It might stimulate further questions, such as where the robins are getting the holly and how far they fly after eating holly. What ideas would such information give you?

In this case, the solution is fairly simple. Since birds disperse the holly seed during winter, people from the native plant society, with the support of other interested parties, can educate the city council and seek an ordinance to limit and/or remove holly trees within some distance of the forest. This is important because if the source of holly seed is not removed, holly trees in the forest will never be controlled.

Having thus far examined some of the possible relationships of diversity on various culturally oriented landscapes, how might one consider diversity with the context of a community?

DIVERSITY WITHIN THE CONTEXT OF TIME AND SPACE OF A COMMUNITY

Nothing in the material world of the human being lasts forever. Couple the certainty of change as a constant with the short, often frightened tenure and uncertainty of a human life and the stage is set for the fear of perceived future loss in whatever form it might take. The sense of impending loss of that which one desires, that which seems to offer material security, often breeds a shortsightedness of view and an irrational impatience with Nature's timetable, which in turn causes potentially renewable natural resources to be overexploited for all the reasons given in Chapter 1.

On the other hand, single resources, such as a vast forest, a mother lode of mineral, or a breed of domestic animals, have lives built around them in the hope they will last at least for the person's lifetime—and they may. But time inevitably takes its toll.

Diversity in the Long View of Time—Relatively Speaking

Although saving capital is one pillar of sustainable economics, the world is rushing with ever-increasing speed into large-scale, capital-intensive production. This is leading society into a crisis of survival, first by making people "machine minders," which does nothing to develop their humanity and robs them of their creative powers, and then by eliminating their jobs. Highly capitalized technology has proven monstrously inefficient and ineffective in solving the human/environmental problems of the world.

In addition, highly capitalized technology stimulates the ratchet effect in resource exploitation. As mentioned earlier, ratchet effect economics generally includes corporate welfare through subsidies, which translates into corporate profits through an immediate monetary expense to taxpayers and a long-range ecological/monetary expense to future generations.

Highly capitalized technology can also be subtle in its destructive power. Consider, for example, extinction of domestic animals, such as the Taihu pig, gembrong goat, and choi chicken.[132] These domestic Asian animals, along with as many as 1,500 other farm breeds worldwide, are as endangered as their wild relatives. The demise of biological diversity on the farm could prove equally damaging to the loss of biological diversity in the wild.

Causes for the decline in farm breeds, according to the U.N. Food and Agriculture Organization, include loss of habitat due to growth in the human population and wars. But the greatest threat comes when farmers in poor nations discard native breeds and switch to Western commercial livestock, which is highly productive.

Western breeds like Holstein cows, Rhode Island red chickens, and Yorkshire pigs are alluring to Asian farmers because of the great quantity of milk, eggs, and meat they produce. For a poor farmer barely able to feed his family, they seem heaven-sent. The problem is that Asian farmers invariably cannot afford the high cost of maintaining and feeding such specialized Western breeds.

Livestock that are bioengineered in Western laboratories for the technology- and money-intensive agriculture of Western industrialized countries may not be suited to other environments, cultures, or methods of farming. Local breeds may well prove better and more profitable in the long run than those marketed by the West.

Local breeds are the result of successful adaptations to particular environments that began when people started domesticating animals more than 10,000 years ago for food, fiber, the power to work, and for their droppings as fertilizer. The following are examples of such adaptations: China's min pig tolerates extreme temperatures, the pygmy hog of northern India is ideal for small villages, and the zebu cattle of Java are disease resistant and prolific. But now 105 such domestic animals are endangered in Asia—and Asia is not alone.

The U.N. Food and Agriculture Organization estimates that 30 percent of the 4,000 to 5,000 breeds of domestic animals thought to exist in the world are threatened with extinction and that 3 breeds become extinct every two weeks. Half of all the domestic breeds that existed in Europe at the beginning of the 1900s, for instance, have vanished, and more than one-third of all breeds of poultry and livestock in North America are rare, which may well have a tremendous impact on rural economies in the future.

The loss of diversity among well-adapted livestock and poultry, particularly in foreign countries, raises some disturbing questions with which I have struggled over the years as I have traveled abroad. When someone or some agency from a Western industrialized country introduces specialized breeds of livestock and poultry into an Asian village, for example, the *assumption* on the part of the person or agency introducing the animals is that the people both want and need our Western-style help. But who said such communities either want or need our help? Who said we should impose our values on them? If the people of a particular village have not, in fact, specifically asked for our help, are we not simply stealing their way of life, which may be perfectly adequate for them, by stealing the adapted diversity of their indigenous animals? Who or what gives us that right? Who really benefits from such noncompatible introductions—the villagers who must live with the often devastating results or those who sell the animals and the technology that goes with them? In my experience, it is almost inevitably the latter.

Before moving on to the next section, I will share with you what I consider one of the more blatantly ill-considered ideas that I have come across with respect to biological diversity and all its ramifications:[133]

> The remote nation of Nepal has a serious deforestation problem [created by the U.S. AID mission in the first place; I know because I was there in 1966–1967 and I watched it]. In Oregon there lives a citizen who raises fast-growing hybrid poplar trees. Sen. Mark O. Hatfield, R-Ore., chairs the Appropriations Committee. The committee earmarked $2.28 million in its fiscal 1986 foreign operations bill to send 2.5 million Oregon poplar tree cuttings to Nepal.
>
> Nothing new there, you say? Happens all the time? Ah, but in this case, Nepal resisted: These poplars might not grow well there. The Agency for International Development also resisted, listening to one of its foresters who argued that the project would be "completely unrealistic, a waste of money" and "an act of extreme folly" because of transport, land availability, and refrigeration problems.
>
> Hatfield was determined. "He really believes that this is an important and valid development project," said aide Rick Rolf....
>
> ...A feasibility study that AID ordered in January—but which committee aides said was a stalling tactic—reported that Nepal does indeed need "a tree such as a poplar" that can be used as fuel, animal feed, brushwood, and a soil holder and wind break. The study, headed by Argonne National Laboratories, said that other varieties of trees should be explored.

Remember that there is no such thing as an independent variable in an interdependent system, yet nothing was said in the article quoted above about using native trees already adapted to the interdependence of the Nepalese forest. How would a monoculture of hybrid poplars from Oregon improve a Western industrialized clear-cut in the forest of Nepal? What impact would such an introduction, based solely on economics and politics in the United States, have on the diversity of indigenous species in the forests of Nepal? What would the long-term ecological ramifications of such an introduction be for the Nepalese people? What unwanted consequences would they have to live with? Such questions are endless. Were they asked by the senator's staff? What were the answers?

If the foregoing discussion is about diversity in the long view of time, what might diversity look like in the medium view?

Diversity in the Medium View of Time

"Town built on nickel sees its mine close for good."[134] Glenbrook Nickel, the nation's only nickel mine and smelter, is closing permanently after more than a century in operation. The closure will put 300 people out of work, which, if one figures four people per family, affects 1,200 people in the small southwestern Oregon town of Riddle. The town was named for J.B. Riddle, who started mining nickel there in the 1880s.

The history of mining nickel in Riddle is as follows:

1865   Shepherds discover mineral deposits on the slopes of 3,500-foot Old Piney, later renamed Nickel Mountain.

1880s   The mineral deposits are determined to be nickel, not copper or tin as had been first believed. William Q. Brown and J.B. Riddle begin mining the nickel.

1892   Riddle Nickel Mining Company, which employs 100 people, is purchased by Chicago-based International Nickel Mining Company, which files for bankruptcy before its smelter is built; the mine is closed.

1936   William Q. Brown dies, having spent much of his life attempting to make the mine fully operational.

1941   World War II demands that Freeport Sulphur Company begin prompt exploration of the mine, but Freeport Sulphur relinquishes its lease after two years.

1947   M.A. Hanna Company of Cleveland, Ohio, obtains the lease and begins to explore the mine and test the quality of the ore.

1953   Hanna begins construction of a tramway to haul ore and a smelter to process it.

1954   The first ferronickel, a combination of iron and nickel, is poured in July. The mine, which employs between 500 and 700 people, operates continually for the next three decades.

1973   A nationwide power crisis threatens to close the mine, which now employs about 500 people and annually produces about $30 million in nickel.

1982   Hanna closes the mine, but reopens it 18 months later after winning concessions for cheaper electricity and negotiating reduced wages and benefits for members of the United Steelworkers of America.

1986   Hanna permanently closes the mine.

1989   Glenbrook Nickel Company reopens the mine.

1993   The low price for nickel ($2.50 per pound) forces Glenbrook to shut down mining operations in July; the closure puts 250 people out of work.

1995   Glenbrook reopens the mine as nickel brings $4.45 per pound and hires back all 250 people.

1998   Able to break even with the price of nickel at $3.00 per pound in September of 1997, Glenbrook announces on January 29 that it will shut down permanently, effective March 30, because the price has fallen below $2.40 per pound and shows no signs of improving in the near future. Closure of the mine in Riddle also forces closure of Glenbrook's port facility in the town of Coos Bay on the Pacific Ocean, a combination that will cost more than 300 jobs.

Bill Duckett, the mayor of Riddle, said the workers from the Glenbrook mine will have a tough time finding jobs that pay a living wage in Douglas County. With the shrinking of the timber industry over the past eight years, he said there is little industry in the county to absorb the workers. Now what?

Another recent example is Charleston, a town along the southern coast of Oregon whose economy is based on fishing.[135] Although waves lap lazily at the pilings of South Coast Seafoods, the fish-processing plant is closed and silent, except for the mewing of a sea gull or the splash of a sea lion.

New federal cuts in the allowable number of fish caught have been devastating to commercial fishers along Oregon's southern coast, sending ripples of despair through communities that are so specialized that they, like Charleston, depend largely on the day's catch to make economic ends meet. At least one dockside restaurant which catered to the commercial fishers has closed. Sales of diesel fuel at the commercial dock are down two-thirds. Crews who work on fishing boats for a percentage of the catch are taking home a pittance.

Fishers grumble that reducing the allowable number of fish caught for such popular bottom fish as black cod, lingcod, rockfish, and Dover sole is based on federal data that are flimsy or worse. The people who regulate fishing (the Pacific Fisheries Management Council and the National Marine Fisheries Service) admit their data are imperfect—and I submit always will be, even as a best-case scenario. Nevertheless, their best information indicates that populations of some species of fish along the Pacific Coast are dangerously low.

All the fishers know for sure, from their point of view, is that for the past decade regulations have been whittling away at the limits of various species of fish that commercial fishers can catch off the coasts of Washington, Oregon, and California. Fishers say the data used by the Pacific Fisheries Management Council and the National Marine Fisheries Service are based on insufficient samples and go against what they see in the ocean. What the fishers see is the catch, however, not the long-term trend in the health of the populations of the various species of fishes.

The decline in populations of marine fishes in not just local or even confined to the coasts off Washington, Oregon, or California; it is global. In fact, data indicate that the catch of marine fishes worldwide is approaching its upper limit.[136] The number of overfished populations indicates that management by the United States has failed to achieve sustainability in fishing, including the indirect effects of fisheries on marine ecosystems. "This failure [of management]," according to Botsford, Castilla, and Peterson, the three scientists who reported in *Science* on the management of fisheries and marine ecosystems, "is primarily due to continually increasing harvest rates in response to incessant sociopolitical pressure for greater harvests [the ratchet effect of linear economics, discussed in Chapter 1] and the intrinsic uncertainty in predicting the [particular] harvest that will cause population collapse." The greatest promise in achieving sustainable harvests of marine fishes is to transform the process of managing marine fisheries to reduce, or preferably eliminate, the pressure for ever-greater harvests.

The cut in the number of fish that are allowed to be commercially caught follows the collapse of the local timber and lumber industries that for decades were the mainstay of the economy in the Coos Bay–North Bend–Charleston area along the southern Oregon coast. The collapse of the commercial fishing, timber, and lumber businesses is a classic example of depletion of a potentially sustainable, renewable resource because of the local people's insistence on overexploitation based on the ratchet effect of linear economics.

I lived just south of Coos Bay in the early 1970s, and I heard the heated rhetoric about how much harvestable timber was going to waste simply because it was not being cut fast enough. I also heard how healthy the stocks of fish were and that more could be harvested; more could always be harvested, regardless of what the best data showed. Anyone who spoke to the contrary was branded a heretic and summarily dismissed. Finally, however, informed denial has come home to roost. Now what?

I have seen dozens of towns attempt to find another specialized economic mainstay, such as ecotourism, to replace the one they lost rather than diversify—really diversify. But ecotourism, should it be viable in the first place, will also fade away unless the people heal the surrounding landscape stripped of its resources in a nonrenewable manner over the past decades to maintain, as much as possible, an economic stability within a community based on a narrowly specialized industry. After all, who would come to look at massive clear-cuts or mine tailings or want to fish in a depleted ocean?

Either people of economically collapsed towns learn to deal with diversity and diversify the social and economic underpinnings of their respective communities or they will relive their self-imposed history. But diversification within a community for its long-term sustainability takes another kind of diversity, a shorter term diversity, which few people seem to recognize when they have it.

Diversity in the Short View of Time

Many a community in trouble makes the mistake of calling in outside "experts" for advice on what it "should" or "should not" do before it has even considered the social capital (collective talents, skills, experiences, and willingness to work = energy) of the people who are the community. Although President Theodore Roosevelt was probably speaking about an individual when he said, "Do what you can with what you have, where you are," the same admonishment applies to a community. And so does Ralph Waldo Emerson's: "This time, like all times, is a very good one, if we but know what to do with it." Thus, before a community calls for an outside expert, it would be wise to see what it can do for itself with its own resident experts whose talents, skills, experiences, and energy are directly relevant to the needs of the community.

Existing Human Talents, Skills, and Experience

Every community has within it many people with known talents, skills, and experiences, but each community also has among its members many hidden, even latent, talents and many unknown skills and experiences. It is unwise, therefore, on the part of community leaders to draw conclusions about the potentialities of the community's membership based solely on past experience. That would be like saying that a dog cannot learn to roll over simply because it has not done so.

While it is of value to recognize what talents, skills, and experiences are already available within a community, it is equally important to realize that people are continually growing and hence so is the pool of talents, skills, and experiences from which a community can draw in the future. Failure to recognize people's potential for continual growth calls to mind a comment by poet William Blake: "The hours of folly are measured by the clock; but of wisdom, no clock can measure."

Talent

"Every man," thought Ralph Waldo Emerson "has his own vocation, talent is the call." Talents and skills differ in that talent is innate to one's being whereas skills are acquired through study, imitation, training, and practice.[137] It is one's talents, not one's skills, that open the door to discovery and innovation, which is not to say that skills are unimportant.

Talents are meant to be shared while abnegating ownership, a lesson Michelangelo learned—and we must too. On the one hand, Michelangelo honored his skill by saying: "If people knew how hard I worked to get my mastery, it wouldn't seem so wonderful after all." On the other hand, he learned that his talent was a sacred gift to be held in trust.

After he completed his first pietà, he heard rumors that another artist was being credited with his work. He thus stole into the cathedral one night and carved his name on the back of his pietà. This act bothered him so much that he later called it an abomination and a desecration. This pietà was the only piece of work he ever signed because he recognized that his talent was a sacred gift and could not be possessed.[138]

Although vision and its purpose marshal talent, more talent is squandered (both personally and as a community) due to a lack of vision and purpose (the kind Michelangelo had) than from any other cause. Recognizing and developing talent is the road to creativity in both the individual and the community, for a community's creative consciousness is raised each time one of its members experiences inner growth.

If a community is dedicated to a vision and its purpose, members of the community will find a way to express their talents through it. In fact, they might even discover new talents. But remember that each person's talent is equally important to the whole. No one's talent is greater or lesser than anyone else's; they are only different and therefore complementary.

Raw talent is that which is undeveloped. Talent is incomplete, however well developed, when it is not aligned with a vision, purpose, and values. When talent is integrated with a vision, purpose, and supporting values, however, there is no telling how far an individual or a community can go, provided the necessary skills are also available.

Skills

While talent is unique to each individual, skill seldom is. Although talent is innate to a person's inner world, skill must be earned in the outer world. More often than not, skill is at least a partial gift from some other person or other people. Nevertheless, we often spend so much time, effort, and money developing our skills that we are loath to admit we may lack talent in the area of endeavor. This is not to say that our skills are wasted, but only that they may be out of harmony with our talents. Nevertheless, each person's skill, whatever it is, is important to sustainable community development.

While some people take their skills for granted or see little value in them outside the immediate necessities of earning a living, others have such low self-esteem that they imagine their skills to be either poorly developed compared to someone else's or of small value to anyone. Yet each person in a community (and her or his respective skill) is a part of the whole and therefore of value to the whole.

Sustainable community development requires the greatest possible participation of community members, and this means all of their assorted skills at some time or another, be they those of a cook, carpenter, electrician, community organizer, facilitator, or custodian. For one's skill to be used to the best advantage, however, one must draw on one's personal experiences.

Experience

Experience is the active participation in events that lead to an accumulation of knowledge or skill, the totality of which in the past of an individual or group of people, such as a community, is archived in language. Every human being holds within the language his or her experiences in and with life, be it a mode of expression carried forward from one's family of origin or the jargon of one's craft or trade. Every human language—the master tool representing the experiences of its own culture—has its unique construct, which determines how one's experiences in life are stored, expressed, and understood, as the indigenous Americans knew well.

DIVERSITY IS THE WEALTH OF SUSTAINABLE COMMUNITY

10

No community today is untouched by the interplay between its traditional self and the greater, more expedient industrial–commercial society. It is not surprising, therefore, that conflicts over the value of place are arising with increasing frequency between those members of a community who hold traditional values and those who hold more modern transient values. In this sense, many communities are in transition between sets of values, which must be carefully assessed, in terms of both human attitudes and the ways in which land is used.

Community can be lost when citizens become reticent to think in terms of maintenance. We Americans seem eager to build but then begrudge providing the local or state tax dollars necessary to maintain our highways and schools, let alone our downtowns, which we effectively abandon. This loss of community is neatly summed up by Scottish author Muriel Spark, who wrote: "Art and religion first; then philosophy; lastly science. That is the order of the great subjects of life, that's their order of importance."

One of the reasons a number of townspeople may be reluctant to spend money on maintenance is their lack of long-term commitment to the town. Where they reside while earning a living does not hold sufficient value for them to retire there. Thus, while they are committed to working in and living as a part of the town, they plan to move somewhere else to spend the rest of their lives. With such thinking, why would they be committed to spending their hard-earned money on maintaining a place they are eagerly planning to leave?

Be that as it may, what we neglect, we lose, be it a house, a street, or a downtown. Communities are not made to be disposable; they are not designed in terms of planned obsolescence. This could be partially remedied if each member of a community would tithe 10 percent of his or her time to do something that would improve the quality of the community.

Tithing a portion of one's time is the beginning of recognizing the difference between real wealth—which lies in natural diversity, including that of human relationships—and money.

WEALTH VERSUS MONEY

Conventional money knows no loyalty to a sense of place, a local community, or even a nation, and so it flows toward a global economy in which traditional social bonds give way to a rootless quest for the highest monetary return. The real price we pay for money, the real cost, is the hold it has on our sense of what is possible—the prison it builds around our imaginations, which American journalist Sydney J. Harris captured in a few words: "Men make counterfeit money; [but] in many more cases, money makes counterfeit men."

According to Bernard Lietaer, of the Center for Sustainable Resources at the University of California at Berkeley, "Money is like an iron ring we've put through our noses. We've forgotten that we designed it, and it's now leading us around. I think it's time to figure out where *we* want to go—in my opinion toward sustainability—and then design a money system to get us there."[139]

Lietaer goes on to say that while textbooks on economics claim that people and corporations are competing for resources and markets, which means diversity, they are in reality competing for money, and in so doing are using resources and markets. "A more fascinating aspect of money," notes author Caroline Myss, "is the fact that it can weave itself into the human psyche as a substitute for the life-force." Through the way in which we spend money, according to Myss, we make our private beliefs into public declarations.

"Modern money," explains David Korten, author of *When Corporations Rule the World*, "is only a number on a piece of paper or an electronic trace in a computer that by social convention gives its holder a *claim* on real wealth," which Korten goes on to say has concrete value in meeting the necessities of and fulfilling our desires for a quality life.[140]

But in our confusion over where real wealth lies, we chase the "Almighty Dollar" and neglect those things that actually sustain a life of quality—both spiritual and material. Money has no intrinsic value, but rather only the potential to be converted into something else that may have real value.

It is striking, notes Korten, that our language makes it so difficult to express the critical difference between money and real wealth. He suggests that if you picture yourself alone on a desert island with nothing to sustain you but a large trunk filled with hundred-dollar bills, the difference between money and real wealth becomes clear.

Korten suggests thinking of the modern money economy as a system comprised of two subsystems: one creates wealth and the other creates and distributes money as a convenient means of allocating that wealth. Wealth means healthy and diverse ecosystems, social–environmental sustainability, human equality and dignity, meaningful work, having a home and food, and so on. In a healthy economy, money serves the people in helping to create and protect the real wealth. Money, in a healthy economy, is neither the dominant value nor the sole or dominant medium of exchange.

One of the most important indicators of economic health is social–environmental sustainability, which means not only quality interpersonal relationships but also quality relationships between people and their environment. A healthy economy is based on love and reciprocity, where people do kind and useful things for one another with no expectation of financial gain. Such mutual caring is the soft social capital that both creates and maintains the fabric of trust, which in turn is the glue of functional families, communities, and societies.

Pathology enters the economic system, writes Korten, when money, once a convenient means of exchange, becomes the factor that defines the purpose of life for individuals and their communities. Then the human, social, and biological capital on which the well-being of any community depends is sacrificed on the altar of making money, at which time those who already have money prosper at the expense of those who do not.

The growing dominance of money as master is also revealed in the increasing "monetization" of human relationships. Not long ago, even in such rich, industrialized countries as the United States, half of the adult population worked without salary to create and maintain home and community, which are among the most fundamental functional values of a healthy, sustainable economy.

Today, financially supporting a household usually requires two adults holding two, and sometimes three or four, paying jobs between them, but at the expense of quality human relationships because, of necessity, they rarely see each other and the care of children and the home is either neglected or hired out. In addition, the once shared mutual caring becomes "community service," which is the work of hired public employees, to the extent the public is willing to pay for it.

As the soft social capital of mutual caring dwindles and the resulting quality of family life withers, a community becomes fragmented and its members increasingly apathetic or competitive. As human relationships become more and more dysfunctional, a community's infrastructure crumbles into ever-greater disarray at an ever-increasing social cost.

MYTHOLOGY, DIVERSITY, AND LIFESTYLE

The underpinnings of social values and therefore chosen lifestyles are rooted in people's thoughts and values, which are based on their cultural myths, translated into their lifestyles, and it is the cultural underpinnings of their chosen lifestyles that ultimately affect the land they inhabit. Lifestyle is commonly defined as an internally consistent way of life or style of living that reflects the values and attitudes of an individual or a culture.

We in Western civilization have made lifestyle synonymous with "standard of living," which we practice as a search for ever-increasing material prosperity. If, however, we are to have a viable, sustainable environment as we know it and value it, we must reach beyond the strictly material and see lifestyle as a sense of inner wholeness and harmony derived by living in such a way that the spiritual, environmental, and material aspects of our lives are in balance with the capacity of the land to produce the necessities for that lifestyle.

Whether a given lifestyle is even possible depends on "cultural capacity," a term that is analogous to "carrying capacity," which is the number of animals that can live in and use a particular landscape without impairing its ability to function in an ecologically specific way. If we want human society to survive the 21st century in any sort of dignified manner, we must have the humility to view our own population in terms of local, regional, national, and global carrying capacities, because the quality of life declines in direct proportion to the degree to which a habitat is overpopulated. Is there a higher moral purpose that will be served by cramming eight billion people into a world where space and the other necessities of life are finite—and shrinking with each new person brought forth who needs, and ideally is given, an equal share of life's necessities?

Take water, for example.[141] According to a report given at the United Nations International Conference on Water and Sustainable Development, at least five million people die annually as a result of filthy drinking water, and the suffering will only increase unless steps are taken to increase the purity of water used for human consumption. "Clean water is indispensable for life," said Dominique Voynet, the French minister for environment, in her keynote address to delegates from 80 countries at the conference, which was held at the Paris headquarters of the United Nations Educational, Scientific, and Cultural Organization. She went on to say that the consumption of water has increased seven times since the beginning of the 20th century and doubled within the last two decades. For its part, the World Bank has noted that only 40 percent of the human population has sufficient water to meet its requirements.

"Fresh water...for human needs is rapidly getting scarce....It is rare to find pristine water anywhere," says Abu Zeid, head of the World Water Council. He goes on to say that about 1.2 billion people already lack access to clean water, and 5 to 10 million, mostly poor women and children, die each year from water-borne diseases. Already today, up to 300 million people in 26 countries face severe shortages of water, he says, and by 2050 two-thirds of the world's population could face such shortages because the situation is aggravated by the massive amounts of pollutants, including sewage, industrial wastes, and hazardous fertilizers, that are being dumped into the world's lakes and rivers, both directly and indirectly.

Water covers 71 percent of the surface of the globe, but 98 percent of it is too salty for human use without expensive, time-consuming purification; it is also unevenly distributed. Sixty percent of the world's drinking water is located in just ten countries, including Russia, the United States, China, Indonesia, and Brazil. In addition, industrialized countries use far more water than rural ones, and rich countries use more than poor ones. The United States, one of the most prodigious consumers of water, uses an average of 150 gallons per day per person compared to 50 gallons a day for Europeans and just 7.5 gallons per day for Africans.

Because the quality of human life and the maximum numerical carrying capacity of people on Earth *cannot be maximized simultaneously*, we must consider an alternative. If we substitute for "carrying capacity" the idea of "cultural capacity," we have a workable proposition for society. Cultural capacity is a chosen quality of life, the quality that can be sustained without endangering the environment's productive capacity. The more materially oriented the desired lifestyle of an individual or a society, for example, the more resources are needed to sustain it and the smaller the human population must be per unit area of landscape. Cultural capacity, then, is a balance between the way we want to live, the real quality of our lifestyle and of our society, and the number of people an area can support in that lifestyle on a sustainable basis. The cultural capacity of any area will be less than its carrying capacity in the biological sense.

Cultural capacity is a workable idea. We can predetermine local and regional cultural capacity and adjust our population growth accordingly. If we choose not to balance our desires with the land's capabilities, the depletion of the land will determine the quality of our cultural/social experience and our lifestyle. So far, we have chosen not to balance our desires with the capabilities of the land, because we have equated "desire, need, and demand" as synonyms for every itch of "want." We have lost sight of ecological reality.

If we desire to maintain a predetermined lifestyle, we must ask new questions: (1) How much of any given resource is necessary for us to use if we are to live in the lifestyle of our choice? (2) How much of any given resource is it necessary to leave intact as a biological reinvestment in the health and continued productivity of the ecosystem? (3) Do sufficient resources remain, after biological reinvestment, to support our lifestyle of choice, or must we modify our lifestyle to meet what the land is capable of sustaining?

"Necessity" is a proposition very different from the collective "desire, want, need, demand" syndrome, and therefore arguments about the proper cultural capacity revolve not only around what we think we want in a materialistic/spiritual sense but also around what the land can produce in an environmentally sustainable sense. Cultural capacity is a conservative concept, given finite resources and well-defined values. By first determining what we want in terms of lifestyle, we may be able to determine not only if the Earth can support our desired lifestyle but also how we must behave with respect to the environment if we are to maintain our desired lifestyle.

To see how this works, let's examine a few examples of cultural capacity. On September 21, 1989, Hurricane Hugo flattened most of South Carolina's beachfront. Since then, houses have been rebuilt and stand once more "eave to eave" as testimony of American's determination to live by the sea.[142] The result is that so many people are trying to buy so little remaining land that a standard city lot may sell for as much as $500,000.

Today, nearly half the American population lives within an hour's drive of a coast. By the year 2010, predicts the National Oceanographic and Atmospheric Administration, nearly 60 percent, or 127 million people, will live in the coastal zone, including the shores of the Great Lakes, Puget Sound in the state of Washington, and the shores of such rivers as the Columbia.

Pollution and destruction of habitats, problems faced in every coastal region of our nation, are fueled both by unchecked growth of the population and by an increasing desire on the part of many Americans to live by the sea or some other shore. The Pacific Northwest is increasingly feeling the pressures of a growing coastal population, which began on the eastern seaboard at the end of World War II, and hopes to avoid both the overcrowding and the building in hazardous areas that have plagued such states as South Carolina.

In Oregon, the demographics of the coastal population are changing with the influx of retired persons, many of whom have some environmental awareness. Nevertheless, as people build their dream homes by the sea and along other shores, they fill in wetlands, cut down forests, and cause the erosion of beaches, thus making changes that threaten the very environment that drew them to the coastal areas in the first place.

A clear example of grossly exceeding the cultural capacity of a chosen area is building on unstable ground (Figures 27 to 30). Consider the fiasco at The Capes, along the northern Oregon coast. It is a perfect example of a predictable natural event spurred by a disaster that was not of Nature's making—poor planning.[143]

An enclave of luxury townhouses teeters on the edge of a crumbling cliff, and officials must decide whether it is feasible or ethical to bend the rules to save them, even if it means endangering other homes. Here one might ask: If a luxury home falls into the ocean because it is built where it is almost certain to fall, will it make a sound? The answer is yes; the homeowners will make a sound. But should anyone listen?

Many local people had warned the developers in the 1980s that the exclusive gated community they proposed to build would be constructed on an old garbage dump and a sand dune, with an ocean-side face that rose over 150 vertical feet from the beach and was known for shifting. But when the luxury housing development, The Capes, was approved by Tillamook County planners in 1991, the doubts raised were few compared to the assurances of the developers.

FIGURE 27   A resort built on an unstable dune, where no one should be allowed to build; note how close to the beach the buildings are. (Photograph by author.)

FIGURE 28   There is more sand next to the dune because of El Niño. (Photograph by author.)

FIGURE 29 In "normal" years, the dune has a sharp edge that is being eaten away by the waves right in front of the resort. Note whole drifted trees embedded in the dune's base. (Photograph by author.)

When Sallie Jacobsen of the Oregon Parks and Recreation Department warned in May 1991, before construction at The Capes began, that "placement of the structures might cause problems for the beach in the future," she was given less credence than engineers paid by the developer. When John J. Marra of the Department of Land Conservation and Development warned in 1993, after construction had begun, that setbacks from the face of the dune did not "provide an adequate safeguard from known or suspected natural hazards," the county said his comments had come too late. The knowledgeable warnings about the instability of the dune were overpowered by the credentials of the geologists and engineers brought in by the developer. Simply put, local knowledge based on personal observation and a history of place were summarily ignored.

Records show that even engineer Charles R. Lane, hired by the developer, noted in 1982 that the dune was prone to slide, or more correctly worded to slump, on its steep face. Lane recommended constructing a rock wall at the base of the slide-prone face and that homes should be

FIGURE 30   The whole drifted trees, which normally hold the sand dune together, are eroding out of the dune and being washed away without replacement because large driftwood has become so scarce in the ocean. (Photograph by author.)

constructed at least 60 feet back from the nearest steep slope. But because the beaches in Oregon are public property, state laws promulgated in 1977 and county rules forbid landowners from walling off the shoreline to protect their homes, which meant no wall on the beach at the base of the dune. There is another reason for the state laws against seawalls; they can cause the currents and flow from stormy seas to shift elsewhere and erode areas that would otherwise be unaffected.

By 1991, however, the county and the developer agreed to a "softer" approach: stabilizing the dune by planting European beach grass, which has long been used to prevent sand dunes from encroaching on the main coastal highway. Having looked at historical photographs, Lane said that the dune had been stable at least as far back as 1939, and thus he thought the soft approach was reasonable. I know from personal experience, having studied the coastal ecosystem along the entire state, that European beach grass is not an adequate contestant when confronted with a raging winter storm along the Pacific Coast, especially a storm fueled by El Niño.

Thus it is not surprising, especially in a winter when El Niño is in full force, as it was in 1997–98, that by December 1997 residents at The Capes had begun to notice the dune was shifting in front of their homes. By late January 1998, county officials began to consider evacuating the $400,000 homes nearest the cliff.

In a two-hour meeting on February 10, residents of The Capes were pitted against their neighbors because people living on the sand dune wanted to have a seawall built to protect their homes, a wall their neighbors argued would shift the tidal erosion to their property. One woman summed it up for those who live outside The Capes when she said that her home had been standing for 65 years, and she now reasoned that her home would be put at risk from erosion to save the homes of people who were where they should not have been.

Both the county officials and the governor of Oregon, John Kitzhaber, to their credit in my opinion, upheld the state laws protecting the diversity and open access to the public beach by refusing to let the homeowners build a seawall below The Capes. Kitzhaber said that he could sympathize with the owners facing loss of their homes, but added, "That is not a reason to erode the integrity of Oregon's beaches." He went on to say that if he did allow a seawall to be constructed for the benefit of The Capes, "I would have to do that for people up and down the coast and put a blemish on our public beaches," which would have undermined Oregon's beach protection law.

Tom Steward, who owns a home at The Capes, helped frame the debate in terms of the homeowners' perspective. "The other day I looked down and saw my dream disappearing below my feet. Don't push us or hold us hostage for mistakes the developer made." Tom Hendrickson, president of The Capes Homeowner's Association, added: "A lot of people said, 'I told you so,' but no one told the homeowners. We're innocent people. We bought these home in good faith."

The next volley came from Brian Chapin, a new homeowner at The Capes, who attempted, in my opinion at least, to extort an exception to the state laws protecting Oregon's public beaches. "The problem we at The Capes have is a problem with the entire country. If we don't stop those houses [32 in danger of falling] from coming down over the cliff, it will be a catastrophic event for Oregon's beaches." He went on to warn that nails, shingles, glass, pipes, and insulation would tumble onto the beach if the houses were undermined and that the debris would be carried "as far north as the currents allow."

By March 13, a team of state geologists and engineers found that prevailing winds had shifted, and accompanying waves were carrying sand back to the beach below the cliff. Thus, erosion at The Capes appeared to have slowed, causing the county officials to lift the evacuation order on 28 of the 32 endangered homes.

The team said the homeowners' new plan to install "tiebacks" to anchor the upper part of the dune to a more stable part of the hill appeared to be a reasonable engineering approach in temporarily mitigating erosion of the slope's surface. The tieback system will not be a permanent solution, according to the team, which warned that the work must be carried out with a minimum of disturbance to the existing slope or further landslides could occur.

And so the saga continues, not just at The Capes but across the entire United States because people are moving in droves to the south, west, and suburbs in search of the sun,[144] and they often want to dictate the conditions of Nature to suit themselves. Consider, for example, the beach "reclamation" projects along the eastern seaboard, which many think are a waste of taxpayers' money.

"Your tax dollars at work," begins one article.[145] "A huge vacuum cleaner [operated by the U.S. Army Corps of Engineers] floats off the coast of Monmouth County, N.J., sucking sand from the seabed, shooting it through a pipeline and onto beaches emaciated by storms and tides. Wet and dark, carrying the scent of underwater life, the sand lands with a splash rather than a thud." With an initial cost of $200 million, the project could well cost $1.5 billion over 50 years, including the price of periodic follow-up work along the 33-mile stretch of coastline.

Now extend the idea of such projects to the hundreds of miles of shoreline stretching from New York to Florida, which some people think could benefit from similar projects. In fact, beach-building projects are either under way or pending in such vacation spots as Sarasota, Florida; Fire Island, New York; Virginia Beach, Virginia; and Myrtle Beach, South Carolina.

"We're going to put a billion dollars worth of sand on a beach, when we know it won't stay put," says environmentalist Beth Millemann. "You stop and think about it, and it's kind of astonishing. Look," continues Millemann, "if the residents of the New Jersey shore...[want] a wide beach, then let them pay for it, because the taxpayer in Topeka, Kansas, is getting no benefit," from the 65 percent of the cost absorbed by the taxpayers because the U.S. Army Corps of Engineers does much of the work.

Although proponents of the corps' involvement in the project say healthy beaches pay for themselves in tourism and through protection of property against damage from storms, David Conrad, a water resource specialist with the National Wildlife Foundation, points out the obvious: "They don't last very long, and they cost a fortune," which brings me to the final example of exceeding the cultural capacity of a chosen area— the decline of the Hawaiian paradise in which many unanticipated, unwanted changes will last forever.[146]

Until people found the Hawaiian Islands, perhaps one new species evolved every 10,000 years. This number is significant because the Hawaiian Islands surpass even the Galapagos Islands, off the coast of South America, in the number of species that evolved from a single ancestor. In Hawaii, at least 50 species have evolved from a common ancestor.

Beginning in the 1700s, the islands became a crossroads for Pacific travel, and early seafarers introduced domestic pigs, goats, horses, and cattle onto the islands as sources of fresh meat. Even within the last 15 years the introduction of foreign species of plants and animals has increased dramatically.

In addition to the obvious introductions of domestic animals, less expected imports affected the islands. Bird malaria and pox, both of which are carried by mosquitoes, have had a severe impact on native Hawaiian birds. Brown tree snakes, which have devastated the native species of birds on Guam, have been intercepted on flights to Hawaii six times.

The banana poka, a passionflower vine, which is kept in check in its native South America by the feeding of insects, has no such controlling mechanisms in the islands. Consequently, since arriving in Hawaii it has smothered 70,000 acres of forests on two islands and is threatening larger tracts.

To date, nearly two-thirds of Hawaii's original forest cover has been lost, including half the vital rain forests. Ninety percent of the lowland plains, once forested, has been destroyed. Of 140 species of native birds, only 70 remain, and 33 of those are in danger of extinction. Eleven more species are beyond recovery. As of November 1991, 37 species of plants native to Hawaii were listed as federally endangered; within two years, 152 more species will be proposed for federal listing. Among the state's rarest species of plants are 93, including trees, shrubs, vines, herbs, and ferns, each of which has only about a hundred known surviving individuals. At least five species have been reduced to just one individual.

The cause of the decline is twofold: (1) the cumulative effect of people's careless, unplanned, unbalanced conversion of the land from

Nature's design to society's cultural design in the form of agriculture, ranching, and residential use and (2) our introduction of nonnative species of plants, insects, and mammals.

The results include the loss of the forests, which once intercepted and generated rainfall and protected the coral reefs and beaches from siltation caused by the erosion of soil. Forest loss, coupled with the extinction of native plants and animals, affects every level of the islands' economy and cultural heritage, such as the generation of unique materials for clothing, textiles, ornaments, canoes, and scientific study. Because its cultural capacity has been grievously exceeded, Hawaii has become largely a paradise lost.

The Hawaiian experience illustrates clearly, dramatically that it is vitally important for humanity, especially in Western industrialized societies, to understand and accept that both biological and genetic diversity are the underpinnings of a sustainable quality of life. The more we strip the world of its diversity in the pursuit of money, the more we degrade our potential lifestyles. It would behoove us, therefore, to get serious about saving diversity.

IF WE ARE SERIOUS ABOUT WANTING A QUALITY LIFESTYLE

We are today at a crossroads in the potential quality of life in the world. I make this a generic statement because it is not only Western industrialized countries that are today selling off their diversity or otherwise destroying it in pursuit of money but also the nonindustrialized countries, because the West is holding some nonindustrialized countries in an economic stranglehold, which leaves them little apparent choice. Nevertheless, if society as we know it, be it Western or Eastern, Northern or Southern, rich or poor, is ever to have a chance of becoming truly sustainable with respect to a quality of life that is commensurate with basic human dignity, it must begin now by openly, purposefully, consciously working together to save all possible biological and genetic diversity. Where and how do we begin? We begin by rectifying some obvious, human-created problems with honest intentions and honest decisions. In this case, wild salmon in the Columbia River system will be used as an example of political/economic willingness to let the run become extinct under the guise of a real effort to save it.

Honest Intentions and Honest Decisions

The question is how to save the dangerously weak runs of wild salmon in the Columbia River system, which includes the Snake River as a major tributary.[147] Three freshwater populations of wild Snake River salmon are already listed as endangered species, as are wild steelhead in the Snake and upper Columbia rivers. In addition, five other freshwater populations of salmon and steelhead in the Columbia River Basin are weak in numbers—and thus in genetic diversity—and were recently proposed for protection.

The people who built the four dams in the lower Snake River promised that human-made hatcheries would keep the salmon swimming back to Idaho despite the 150 miles of lakes that were created behind them, replacing the fast-flowing Snake River, and thereby balance the harm the fish would suffer because of the dams. But 22 years after the last dam was built in the state of Washington, it is clearly evident that the balancing act has failed. Now the U.S. Fish and Wildlife Service is working desperately to keep salmon, an endangered species in the Snake River, from becoming extinct.

This possibility of extinction is clearly echoed by Lorraine Bodi, the Northwest director of American Rivers. "Unless immediate steps are taken to help fish survive the many dams that block the Columbia and Snake rivers as they migrate up and down the waterways, they will be gone in the 21st century."

To help deal with this issue, an 11-member scientific panel was authorized by Congress in 1996 to review the salmon recovery programs in the Columbia River Basin, which have already cost $3 billion during the past 15 years and have failed to stop the decline in numbers of fish within wild runs. The panel was ostensibly formed to separate scientific fact from economic and political fiction in the debate over how to save the runs of wild salmon within the basin. I say ostensibly because, as we will see, the answers, derived from scientific data by an independent panel, are as unwelcome as is the obvious truth, which has unflinchingly stared everyone in the face for years.

The upshot of the panel's report, which strikes at the heart of the long, contentious debate, is to restore the Columbia and Snake rivers—now virtually a series of reservoirs behind huge hydroelectric dams—to their more natural state. This, however, is not a conclusion that industry or the politicians who must deal with industrial constituents want to hear, and therein lies the *real* problem of honest intentions and honest decisions.

It boils down to industry and politicians focusing on trying to avoid an unwanted economic impact rather than focusing on saving the salmon. The real contest is between short-term profits that directly benefit a relatively few people within a given generation and long-term biological and genetic diversity, which is the intergenerational wealth that makes the sustainability of dignified lifestyles possible through time. Brian Gorman, the spokesperson for the National Marine Fisheries Service, put it succinctly: "There will have to be a change in the way we live, because it's the way we've been living for the past 15 to 20 years that's causing these problems [the declines of salmon and steelhead]."

However, according to ecology professor Jack Stanford, who resigned from the panel because the federal agencies refused to grapple with the real causes for the decline in wild salmon, the scientists were being asked to perform "assignments that amount to fiddling while Rome burns." He went on to say that the assignments in which he participated were "fundamentally irrelevant to recovery [of the wild salmon] and a gigantic waste of money and effort." Having been employed as a government scientist for more than a decade, I not only know well the mental gyrations government agencies, industry, and weak politicians with vested interests go through to rationalize and justify their avoidance of the truth but also believe Stanford has put his finger on the real problem.

Although rivers in the United States are owned by the public, developers can apply for a license from the Federal Energy Regulatory Commission to dam a navigable river to create hydroelectric power. The owners of dams and utility companies, which may include you and me if we consciously or unconsciously hold their respective stocks, have historically fared well in the regulatory process of getting operating licenses for dams, each of which lasts for 30 to 50 years, and have had little trouble getting their licenses reissued. Consequently, around 68,000 large and 2 million small dams are holding virtually every stretch of American waterways captive. The result is that most rivers in the United States are devoid of much of their indigenous wildlife, and countless runs of indigenous fish, such as salmon, steelhead, and sea-run cutthroat trout, are prevented from reaching their spawning grounds, which means stocked trout and carp have too often taken their place.

However, one day in the near future, a few sticks of dynamite will be strategically placed into the 917-foot-long Edwards Dam across the Kennebec River in Augusta, Maine, and the river, which has been obstructed for 161 years, will be free. In addition to the Kennebec River, there is reason to believe that other rivers can be restored to something that more closely resembles their original free state, which may well happen because, under a 1986 amendment to the Federal Power Act, the regulatory commission must now take into account a variety of mitigating factors, such as habitat for fish and wildlife, recreational use, and aesthetics, when the owner of a dam applies for relicensing. Now, for the first time since they were built, many dams will face scrutiny because a long list of them is coming due for relicensing.

As one might expect, there is strong opposition from the owners of the dams to do anything that would interrupt commerce, especially something as drastic as removing the dams. Thus it is not surprising that the scientific panel has strongly stated that the proposal made by the U.S. Army Corps of Engineers (which operates most of the big dams on the Columbia and lower Snake rivers of Oregon, Washington, and Idaho) and the Bonneville Power Administration (which markets the electricity the dams produce) to transport even more young fish downriver in barges will not work. The scientists were especially critical of placing young salmon into trucks and driving them past the dams to be released downriver, a tactic based on economics as opposed to the biological requirements of the fish, and were emphatic that this practice must stop immediately.

Chris Zimmer of Save Our Wild Salmon, a coalition of 47 environmental and fishermen's groups, said of the government's proposal to increase barging young fish: "It will just delay the eventual extinction of these fish. What the science says is we have to restore more natural river conditions. Taking fish out of the river and putting them in a steel barge is about as far from natural conditions as you can get." In addition to the panel of scientists and Save Our Wild Salmon, the Inter-Tribal Fish Commission, which represents the four tribes that hold treaty rights to fish for salmon in the Columbia and Snake rivers, has long been critical of barging as a way to save the runs of wild salmon.

The panel of scientists did not rule barging out entirely, but stated that the risk to young salmon must be spread out, which means putting some in barges to protect them from the deadly dams and leaving others in the river while increasing the flow of water through the dams to simulate more closely the river's natural state. Stanford dismissed a recent study that indicated fish are more likely to survive to adulthood if they are transported past the dams rather than left in the river.

"Increased survival associated with barging," wrote Stanford in his letter of resignation, "...is trivial when weighed against the increased survival that is needed to reverse the steep, inexorable decline in salmon and steelhead returns to the Columbia River. Recovery...cannot be accomplished by transportation, more and fancier hatcheries, better screens [to protect fish from the turbines], and continued mixed-stock commercial fisheries." The answers, he said, lie in improving the conditions of habitat within the river, which means if dams cannot be breached or removed, as they will be in some rivers, the flow of water passing through the dams must at least be increased.

Four dams on the Snake River and one on the Columbia River can be breached, according to a panel studying the proposal to help salmon survive by returning the rivers to more natural conditions. Although it will be expensive, the panel indicated that it will not bankrupt the Bonneville Power Administration, at least not in the next ten years. The problem, as is often the case in government at all levels, is that no one wants to make a decision. "The region isn't ready to decide what should be done, and it's not ready to decide who should decide," said Bob Lohn, the Bonneville Power Administration's director of fish and wildlife. What goes unspoken is the finality of extinction.

Beyond the question of what to do about the dams is the growing problem of ecologically sick rivers. Take the Willamette River of western Oregon, for example. The Willamette, a major tributary of the Columbia River, has suffered from years of farming and urban growth that have chewed away at its banks and those of its tributaries, leaving its basin among the least healthy for fish. This finding of a $4 million study by the U.S. Geological Survey released on May 29, 1998 caused Dennis A. Wentz, the hydrologist with the U.S. Geological Survey in charge of the five-year study, to say, "We were surprised to see that stream habitat and fish conditions in the agricultural and urban streams of the Willamette Basin to be among the most degraded."

The report compares the Willamette River Basin to 19 other major river basins, including the Hudson, Potomac, and Connecticut in the East and the Trinity, Yakima, and San Joaquin in the West. "We have a river that has a tremendously altered physical habitat," said Bill Bakke of the Native Fish Council, an environmental group that works on issues concerning the management of fish. "The environmental debt is coming due."

The current report corroborates earlier studies, which found 50 kinds of pesticides in the Willamette River and its tributaries, 10 of which are at levels above those considered to be healthy for aquatic life. Be that as it may, it is the physical contour of the waterways within the Willamette Basin that is so damaging by comparison to some of the other rivers discussed in the study. Years of straightening the main channel of the Willamette, which eliminated most or all of the lesser channels; cutting down the riparian forests that shaded and cooled the water and supplied the ecologically important coarse woody debris to the river, estuary, and ocean; and building berms and riprap on the river's banks have greatly reduced the quality and amount of habitat necessary for many of the indigenous fish to thrive, including salmon and steelhead.

The foregoing discussion deals with declines within indigenous species for which obvious, if unwanted, solutions are readily available. But what about the mass movements of unwanted species from one place to another?

Losing Diversity to Diversity

As stated in the beginning of this book, diversity is mediated by adding something to the environment and/or taking something away. One must be more careful, however, when adding something to the environment, as previously discussed, than when taking something away because what has been removed can, for the most part, be reintroduced; once something, such as an exotic species, is introduced, however, the results of the introduction are out of our hands and usually out of our control. With respect to the introduction of an exotic species, which in a sense is adding diversity, the results may actually be a drastic loss of indigenous diversity, especially if the exotic species is invasive by nature and thus takes over the habitat by displacing indigenous species.

"Imagine you are looking at a beautiful and richly detailed painting when suddenly all of the colors begin running together into blotchy grays," says ecologist Daniel Simberloff from the University of Tennessee in Knoxville.[148] "Something similar is happening to the world's plants and animals. The flow of exotic organisms is increasing rapidly as the world becomes more interconnected. Without action, a growing army of invasive species will continue to overrun the United States, causing immense economic and ecological damage."

Simberloff is speaking about the movement of exotic species into new areas, where they are causing damage to grasslands, wetlands, forests, and other ecosystems. "The world's habitats are rapidly being homogenized," admonishes Simberloff.

The cost to the American public amounts to billions of dollars annually because around one-quarter of the value of agriculture is forfeited to foreign plants and the expense of controlling them. In addition, public lands and waterways are being greatly impaired for recreational use by aggressively invasive aquatic plants, not to mention the nonindigenous species that pose major risks to human health, such as the Asian tiger mosquito from Japan, which is spreading in the United States and is carrying with it encephalitis, yellow fever, and dengue fever.

Although plants and animals have been piggybacking on human travelers for millennia, the rapid growth of current travel and trade, as well as the wholesale displacement of entire human populations due to wars, has created an entirely new problem. In the past, when an organism stowed away in the cargo hold of a ship, it not only had to survive on board ship for months at a time but also had to be transported from a ship into an entirely new environment in which it also had to survive. Today, however, millions of tons of cargo and hundreds of millions of people travel annually on commercial airliners, which greatly increases the chances that a foreign organism will survive.

The brown tree snake, for example, has already devastated populations of forest birds on the island of Guam and has traveled to Honolulu in the wheel wells and cargo bays of airplanes. A giant African snail, which has ravaged agricultural crops on many Pacific islands, was carried from Hawaii to Florida by a boy as a gift to his grandmother. The Asian chestnut blight fungus arrived in New York City in the late 19th century and killed almost all American chestnut trees along the east coast of the United States; the tree was the most common species in many forests prior to the introduction of the fungus. The list goes on and on.

Eradication of these exotic species is not only impossible most of the time but also expensive because chemical, mechanical, and/or biological controls, which can sometimes minimize economic and ecological damage, are frequently harmful to beneficial species.

Unfortunately, the laws that restrict entry into the United States or individual states are generally designed to use what Simberloff refers to as "blacklisting," which means that an organism must first be proven to be detrimental before anything is done about prohibiting its spread. More effective would be what Simberloff calls "whitelisting," which means that all potential introductions of foreign species would be subjected to scrutiny, which in turn would stimulate the scientific research necessary to determine ahead of time if and when a given species has the potential to be destructive if introduced into the United States.

Another obvious requirement to help control the spread of unwanted exotic species is an early warning system with the capability of responding rapidly *before* the species reaches a stage in which it is beyond control. Even if we had such a system, which we do not, the greatest barrier to an effective response concerning invasive exotics, according to Simberloff, is public nonchalance.

In addition, a number of special interest groups, such as importers of exotic plants and animals and owners of pet shops, work to minimize barriers to the importation of exotic species, despite the harm escapees could cause. Such self-centered myopic behavior is, in my opinion, totally irresponsible because an escaped exotic species often becomes not only a severe, ongoing ecological problem but also an ongoing astronomical expense to the public in trying to control it. But without an educated public and educated legislatures, says Simberloff, the special interest groups can and do undermine the ability of government agencies to either place harmful species on a blacklist or keep them off a whitelist.

There is another side to this issue, the supply side.[149] Lawmakers in Hawaii have recently taken the first step toward protecting their colorful indigenous marine fish by limiting the number that can be captured and sold to supply pet shops and home aquariums throughout the United States. Although the committee in the House of Representatives rejected an outright ban on capturing the fishes along the west coast of the island of Hawaii, it adopted a plan to set aside about a third of that area as a sanctuary for the protection of tropical fish. In October of 1999, part of the same area will become a no-capture sanctuary for all fish; the sanctuary will extend to a depth of 650 feet.

The issue pitted some people in the state's $50 million diving tourism industry, which needs the fish to entertain snorkelers and scuba divers, against those in the $10 million industry that captures the tropical fish to supply pet shops and collectors throughout the United States. But in the long term, said Jack Randall, a retired ichthyologist who worked at the Bishop Museum in Hawaii, the sanctuary would benefit both industries, even if it causes economic pain in the short term. Randall went on to explain that the protected area will give fish more of an opportunity to grow larger than they have time to now, which is important because the larger the fish get, the more young they produce.

In fact, some people, such as James Bohnsack, a research fisheries biologist with the National Marine Fisheries Service in Miami, Florida, contend that no-capture marine sanctuaries should not be viewed as an experiment but rather as "the controls, and everything else is the experiment." Bohnsack goes on to say that by allowing fishing throughout the ocean, "we've been conducting a giant, uncontrolled experiment over the entire ocean for years."[150]

To the extent the special interest groups undermine the protection of either indigenous species from being overexploited or the ecosystems into which they may be introduced as an exotic should a species escape and cause damage, they are stealing diversity and thus a greater potential quality of life from future generations. I say this because the continual escape of invasive exotic species, as well as the depletion of indigenous populations to supply the pet trade, will increasingly impoverish the ecosystems our children, their children, and their children's children must inherit.

THOU SHALT NOT STEAL DIVERSITY

How one treats one's land as private property determines not only whether one gives a gift of diversity—biological, genetic, and functional—to the next owner, which is simultaneously a gift of choices that can be made, but also whether one steals such choices from the next owner by degrading the land under one's care. How is it that we in the United States cannot legally steal from our adult neighbors in space (= in the present) but can legally steal from our child neighbors in both space and time (= in both the present and the future) through the degradation and loss of diversity for whatever short-term economic/political rationalization sounds best? Keep in mind throughout the ensuing discussion that private ownership of land is a very recent concept.

Consider, for example, that the pygmies of central Africa, the most ancient of all forest dwellers, hold no enforceable claims to the forests they have inhabited for at least 40,000 years.[151] Moreover, indigenous peoples on every continent find the notion of private ownership of land to be both ludicrous and impossible.

How can an individual human being own something that he or she has not created and therefore cannot control? How can an individual own something that has been around for millennia before he or she was born and will continue for millennia after he or she is dead? How can an individual own something that is so obviously part of the global commons in both time and space that it belongs to every living creature in its turn and so to no one individual in particular at any given time?

Society is divided on this issue. Society must therefore decide. Either this notion of land ownership and the rights of private property, which seems most peculiar to Western industrialized society, will continue or people must accept an alternative, such as custodial trusteeship of the piece of Earth one inhabits or otherwise has deed and title to as a living trust for the beneficiaries of the future. It is a question of self-centeredness versus other-centeredness, which means that the morality of the idea of land ownership and unlimited rights of private property must be opened to rigorous debate. And make no mistake, the question of land ownership and the rights of private property is, at its very root, a moral one.

In such a debate, the questions must be: Does the holder of a deed to land of any kind "own" the land in an absolute sense, or is he or she only a custodial trustee thereof? Does such a holder of a deed have the moral right to degrade the productive capacity of the land, stealing diversity in all its forms, before passing it on to the next person who *must* use it? Put a little differently: Does any person have the moral right to steal options from the future by stealing the diversity on which they are based for immediate personal gain, thereby irreparably degrading the productive capacity of the land? If not, how can one be granted the legal right to do so?

"Where scarcity rules," says Ivan Illich, "ethics is reduced to numbers and utility. Further, the person engaged in the manipulation of mathematical formulas loses his or her ear for ethical nuance; one becomes morally deaf." Consider the following example.[152]

Someone with a backhoe decided to resolve a debate over the rights of private property by demolishing a 12-foot-high dam that created a wetland, known as Heinz Marsh, just south of Leadbetter State Park on the Long Beach Peninsula in the state of Washington. Whoever destroyed the dam also bulldozed open three beaver dams. As a consequence of these illegal acts, hundreds of thousands of gallons of fresh water and dead leaves flooded eastward from the wetland into a drainage ditch from which it spilled into the oyster beds of Willapa Bay.

The marsh, on the mostly undeveloped northern end of the peninsula, was three miles long and a half-mile wide, but now is half that size and still diminishing. "If people wanted to focus attention on that little corner of the world, they couldn't have done any better..." said Martha Jordan of Everett, Washington, a board member of the Minnesota-based Trumpeter Swan Society, which owns the dam.

The 500-member society recreated the wetlands in 1984 by constructing the dam to make up for the marsh destroyed earlier by a developer. Some landowners and developers in the area objected to the dam that belongs to the Trumpeter Swan Society, as well as those built by the beavers, and argued that the level of water in the restored wetland, which was raised 14 years ago, was higher than that of the original marsh and thus covered more land, which may have been true according to aerial photographs.

Sabotaging the dams thus came to represent one side in the debate between conservation of habitat for wildlife and future generations and the landowner/developer perception of the sacredness of private property and the unfettered pursuit of immediate profit on the peninsula's northern rim. The irony is that if a developer had not destroyed the wetland in the first place, there might not be a problem now.

Be that as it may, beyond the immediate area of the dams, the people who harvest oysters in Willapa Bay are concerned that the surge of fresh water, which is still draining the marsh, is still destroying habitat and may also be damaging some of the region's most productive beds of oysters by diluting the saltwater habitat and carrying bacteria potentially dangerous to the oysters themselves. In addition, the dead leaves carried into the beds with the fresh water could stain the oysters brownish and hurt sales.

If the outcome of public debate over the rights of private property and the ownership of land is in favor of the status quo, then biological sustainability is at best an academic question—and so is every other kind of sustainability based on the underpinnings of diversity. Before sustainability can be tenable, the ownership of land and the unlimited rights of private property must be modified. Such modification must be in the tenor of a person's privilege to enjoy being the custodial trustee of the piece of Earth he or she inhabits or otherwise has deed and title to as a living trust for the beneficiaries of the future. Only then is the biological sustainability of the Earth possible.

Should the status quo prevail, it will do so because of what Professor David Orr calls "conservatives against conservation."[107] The following discussion is taken from his insightful article.

"The philosophy of conservatism has swept the political field virtually everywhere," says Orr, and virtually everywhere conservatives have forgotten what conservatism really means. Orr goes on to say that conservative philosopher Russell Kirk proposes six "first principles" of conservatism, based on his "love of order," for which true conservatives are accountable:

1. Believe in a transcendent moral order.
2. Prefer social continuity (i.e., the "the devil they know to the devil they don't know").
3. Believe in "the wisdom of our ancestors."
4. Be guided by prudence.
5. "Feel affection for the proliferating intricacy of long-established social institutions."
6. Believe that "human nature suffers irremediably from certain faults."

Nevertheless, it is 18th-century British philosopher and statesman Edmund Burke who is considered to be the founding father of modern conservatism and, according to Orr, is "as much admired as he is unread."

To Burke, the goal of order is to harmonize the distant past with the distant future through the present, which is the nexus.

Like the Republicans of the U.S. Congress, Burke thought in terms of a contract. But unlike the prevailing Republican contract, which is self-centered for a minority in the present, Burke's contract is between "those who are living, those who are dead, and those who are to be born." Those "possessing any portion of power," says Burke, "ought to be strongly and awfully impressed with an idea that they are in trust." In Burke's contract, freedom is "that state of things in which liberty is secured by the equality of restraint," and not a state in which "every man was to regulate the whole of his conduct by his own will."

As the ecological shadow of the present stretches increasingly over the generations of the future, the wisdom of Burke's concern for the justice and welfare of the generations yet unborn becomes more evident. If conservatism means anything at all, says Orr, it means the conservation of what Burke called "an entailed inheritance derived to us from our forefathers, and to be transmitted to our posterity; as an estate belonging to the people." It does not mean preserving those rules whereby one class or one generation enriches itself at the expense of another, as the mayor of a town in Idaho may be trying to do.[153]

The U.S. Environmental Protection Agency recently announced plans to study the extent of contamination in the Coeur d'Alene River Basin, including Lake Coeur d'Alene, caused by a century of mining in the mountains near the town of Coeur d'Alene, Idaho. The information will be used to develop a plan to clean up the contamination, although the actual cleanup will not necessarily encompass the whole river basin.

"We can't afford it, especially when there's not a proven health risk," said the mayor in his address before the Coeur d'Alene Chamber of Commerce. The mayor went on to say that he is especially concerned about the possibility the study will force posting of signs warning swimmers not to drink water from the lake and the threat to landowners of being tapped to pay for the cleanup.

The mayor is assuming that dangerous levels of contamination will be found in the lake and on its shores, which is not necessarily the case. Nevertheless, the mayor seems willing to risk contaminating tourists by not wanting to know how safe the lake really is.

"How do you overcome that perception in the national mind [that the lake is unsafe]?" asked the mayor during his address to the chamber of commerce. "It will be staggering to tourism and to the image we portray to the rest of the world—that Coeur d'Alene is beautiful."

But what if the lake is contaminated and unsafe? As an elected representative of the people, does the mayor not owe them and the rest of the world the truth? Or are people so quick to become morally deaf to ethical nuances where the perceived scarcity or loss of money is concerned by reducing ethics to numbers and utility, as Ivan Illich said?

Would the mayor of Coeur d'Alene be considered a "conservative" in today's vernacular? Perhaps. His behavior is certainly in keeping with the image many of today's conservative thinkers portray, which brings us back to Orr's discussion of the current notion of conservatism.

"What is conservative," asks Orr, "about squandering for all time our biological heritage [in the form of diversity] under the pretext of protecting temporary property rights?" Present-day conservatives scorn efforts by the public to protect such things as endangered habitats (like old-growth forests), endangered species (like spotted owls, coho salmon, and red wolves), clean air, and clean water. Almost any restriction placed on the rights of an individual to use land as private property in any way one sees fit is viewed increasingly as an unlawful "taking," even when such use would irreparably damage the land and its surrounding environment. How, one might ask, is it any more of a lawful "taking" when one degrades land in the present that must be used in an impoverished condition by someone in the next generation and beyond?

Even John Locke, from whom we have derived much of our land-use law and philosophy, said that "nothing was made by God for Man to spoil or destroy." "The point," says Orr, "is that John Locke did not regard property rights as absolute even in a world with a total population of less than one billion, and neither should we in a world of 5.7 billion."

"What," asks Orr, "is conservative about conservatives' denial of the mounting scientific evidence of impending climatic change?" Climate change will have rapid, self-reinforcing feedback loops that could change the nature of the Earth's hospitality to human life for all time. What right do we have to run such a risk, when the consequences belong to the generations of the future and they are not here to participate in the choice?

What, asks Orr, is conservative about perpetual economic expansion when it not only has changed the Earth more radically than any other force in modern times but also is rapidly destroying communities, traditions, cultural diversity, and whole ecosystems throughout the world? What is conservative about passing forward a despoiled legacy to the future?

Social–environmental sustainability requires no less than the first of Russell Kirk's "first principles": that humanity must be grounded in the belief in a transcendent moral order in which we humans, as trustees for future generations, are accountable to a Higher Authority. Anything less is not sustainable!

Edmund Burke put the capstone on land ownership and the unlimited rights of private property as a sustainable proposition when he wrote:

> Men are qualified for civil liberty in exact proportion to their disposition to put moral chains upon their own appetites....Society cannot exist unless a controlling power upon will and appetite be placed somewhere, and the less of it there is within, the more there must be without. It is ordained in the eternal constitution of things that men of intemperate minds cannot be free. Their passions forge their fetters.

Considering the current notion of land ownership and the rights of private property, can diversity be protected from theft in the present for the future? Put differently, do we even know when we lose diversity?

DIVERSITY—GOING, GOING, GONE

There are many ways to lose diversity without realizing it because the loss of diversity is incremental within the invisible present and because the invisible present is caught up in the cultural trance of the times, be it a war that either unites or divides a country, a struggle for civil rights, or some other event that mesmerizes the focus of society. Whatever the issue, it steals the spotlight from the conscious protection of Nature's diversity.

A prime example is a community's or a society's preoccupation with its own economic growth, where individuals try to position themselves to reap the greatest possible monetary gains despite the environmental consequences passed forward to the next generation. In this self-centered individualism, I find that the most aggressive people tend to determine the direction in which a community will grow unless they are countered and balanced or sometimes just outmaneuvered by someone with a more altruistic bent, which seems to be the eternal struggle for conscious, moral evolution within human society. Regardless of the outcome, the diversity in Nature is usually lost because its intrinsic value, which belongs to everyone and thus no one, is invisible to those who focus solely on the conversion of their private property into cash value. This narrow, self-centered focus is perhaps the major cause for the inadvertent loss of diversity.

Inadvertent Loss of Diversity

The landscape around my hometown was friendly when I was a little boy in the early 1940s. The town was surrounded by fields and forest, which were connected by swift forest streams that fed meandering valley rivers. And I was free to wander over hill and dale without running into a no-trespassing sign on every gate and seemingly every other fence post.

The code of the day was to leave open any gate that was open and to close after passing through any gate that was closed. It was also understood that one was free to cross a farmer's property as long as one respected the property by walking around planted fields rather than through them. If I asked permission, I could wander, hunt, fish, and trap almost anywhere I wished.

Much of the Coast Range and most of the Cascade Range of Oregon that I knew as a boy were covered with unbroken ancient forest and clear, cold streams from which it was safe to drink. Although the streams were still filled with trout and salmon, the forests and mountain meadows were already devoid of wolf and grizzly bear.

In the valley that embraced my hometown, the farmers' fields were small and friendly, surrounded by fencerows sporting shrubs and trees, including apples and pears that proffered delicious fruit, each in its season. In spring, summer, and autumn, the fencerows were alive with the colors of flowers and butterflies and the songs of birds. They harbored woodrats and rabbits, pheasants and deer, squirrels and red valley foxes. The air was clean, the sunshine bright and safe, and the drinking water among the sweetest and purest in the world.

When World War II came along, the seeds of change were sown with respect to community. The war effort pushed mass production to new levels and brought the impersonalization of humans killing humans to the fore with such labeling of cartons containing weapons as "mine, one, anti-personnel," which indicated that the person the weapon was meant to kill was simply a military abstraction.

Although World War II eventually drew to a close, the impersonalization of mass production carried over into the postwar boom years. Gone was the simple wisdom of building communities and neighborhoods within communities for people within landscapes of natural beauty. The simple wisdom that had worked so well in the past was replaced by the strategies of massive wartime production developed in defense factories.

Towns, including mine, started to sprawl rapidly in largely unplanned ways. Cookie-cutter houses were concentrated in developments that were isolated from everything else dealing with community.

Speed rather than care began creeping into the building trade, and I watched as houses sprang up in blocks and lines and circles, built for speculation. As speculation crept into the housing market, speed, sameness, and clustering became marks of efficiency and greater profit, setting the tone for the future—a tone reflected in the night sky as the once brilliant stars of the Milky Way disappeared into a seemingly eternal mask of light pollution.

With the stage set by the postwar housing industry, things began to change noticeably as corporate depersonalization commenced its insidious growth into the heart of community. Shopping malls were connected by roads that became bigger, straighter, and faster and increasingly went through prime agricultural land. Then came larger and larger subdivisions with cheaper and cheaper ticky-tacky tract housing, some of which was constructed in floodplains or on unstable soils.

Centralization had arrived on the landscape as it had earlier in corporations. Driving on superhighways became a necessity, and with it came pollution of air and water, which increased with every extra mile that had to be driven and every additional automobile on the road. The gentle motion and relaxed pace of the traditional street gave way to ever-increasing speed. As author Jean Chesneaux observed: "The street as an art of life is disappearing in favour of traffic arteries. People drive through them on the way to somewhere else." There is no word in English with a positive connotation for going slowly or lingering on streets as a way to participate in a sense of community.

People started losing their sense of connection as centralization within urban sprawl increasingly specialized the human landscape, and communities began falling apart. A sense of place—of a familiar, friendly community, where everyone left their homes unlocked—gave way to a sense of location as more and more people became transients, who arrived to chase the dollar and who disappeared when a bigger dollar loomed somewhere on the horizon.

By the time I was a teenager, it had become necessary to lock the doors to our house, and no-trespassing signs proliferated across the landscape. A sense of distrust had begun its insidious invasion throughout the once closely knit human bonds of mutual caring that in days gone by had characterized a community.

Outside of town, the forests were being cut at an exponential rate, including the town's water catchment, endangering such species as the northern spotted owl and marbled murrelet. The forested streams, where as a lad I drank of their sweet water and caught native cutthroat trout, now have waters unsafe to drink. Clear-cut hillsides began eroding as forests were converted to economic tree farms. Gone are most of the great native trout and the wild salmon that graced the streams from which I drank. Gone are the great flocks of bandtailed pigeons that once greeted me in forest and fen. Gone are the elk and bear that I used to see within ten miles of my house. Gone is the forest of centuries. In its place are acres of comparatively lifeless economic tree farms, some of which may live but a little longer than I.

At the same time, I watched helplessly as the small protected fields of the personable family farms increasingly gave way to larger and larger naked, homogeneous fields of corporate-style farms as fencerows were cleared to maximize the amount of tillable soil, to squeeze the last penny from every field. With the loss of habitat along each fencerow, the bird song of the valley was diminished in like measure, as was the habitat for other creatures wild and free.

Gone are the fencerows with their rich, fallow strips of grasses and herbs, of shrubs and trees, which interlaced the valley in such beautiful patterns of flower and leaf with the changing seasons. Gone are the burrowing owls from the quiet secluded fields that I once knew. Gone is the liquid melody of the meadowlark that I so often heard as a boy. Gone is the fencerow trill of the towhee. Gone are the song sparrows, Bewick's wrens, yellow warblers, and MacGillivary's warblers. Gone are the woodrat nests, the squirrels, and the rabbits. Although these species may still occur along the edge of the valley and in isolated patches of habitat, they are gone with the fencerows from the agricultural fields of the valley floor.

As I now pass 60 years of age, the valley's floor offers little in the way of habitat, other than a great depersonalized open expanse of silent, naked fields in winter and a monotonous sameness under the sun of summer (Figure 31). What happened?

The Corporate Revolution in Agriculture

According to C.J. De Loach, "…the objective of agriculture is to encourage the growth of a foreign organism, a crop, at a high density and to suppress…organisms that might compete with it…."[154] Yet it was not always so cut and dried, as noted by David Pimentel: "When man dug holes here and there and planted a few seeds for his food, ample diversity of species remained, but this resulted in small crop yields both because of competition from other plants (weeds) and because insects, birds, and mammals all took their share of the crop."[155]

FIGURE 31 Today's irony—giving lip service to protecting habitat while simultaneously destroying it. Note the words "Think Habitat. Pheasants Forever" and then contrast them with the huge field, which is mowed every year to harvest a monoculture of grass seed. (Photograph by author.)

"In my opinion," says author Jane Smiley, "the form of agriculture that a society chooses is basic and dictates the whole culture."[156] Smiley's statement is apt in two ways: the first is the destruction of the social structure of agrarian communities and the second is the drastic simplification of the landscape.

First, let's consider the social structure of agrarian communities. Although the following example may appear simplistic, it is illustrative of the larger dynamic. I worked on cattle ranches in northwestern Colorado as a young man. It was not uncommon in those days for a group of four or six ranchers to get together during haying season and move from ranch to ranch helping one another put up their hay. We put up two 20-ton stacks of loose hay each day; I say we because I was usually one of the hands on top of the hay doing the stacking. The rancher whose hay was being stacked on any given day was responsible for feeding the crew. Out of fairness, the order in which a rancher's hay was stacked revolved each year, so that every rancher took his turn being first and last. In those days, almost all of the work was done with teams of horses. Then came the baling machine.

With the advent of the hay baler, the cooperative spirit among the ranchers began to break down as each rancher purchased a tractor and a hay baler and began to put up his own hay with his own crew of hired hands. Although the ranchers still helped one another out as necessary, a crack had begun to form within the community, a crack that in a few years led to the end of the real cowboy way of life I cherished so much, as large absentee corporate owners began to purchase ranches that just a few years earlier had not been for sale. Sadly, I watched not only a way of life passing as the community fell apart but also watched the beginning of the landscape's natural diversity fade into the past as corporate-style agriculture took hold.

Now let's turn to modern agricultural practice in the United States, where large fields are often planted with a single-species monoculture. This specialization has resulted from an ever-expanding centralized corporate power base, aided by technology in an increasingly mechanized society.

In the process of centralizing corporate power, a greatly simplified and therefore increasingly fragile and labor/energy-intensive environment has been created through the following changes in the land:

1. Increased specialization of farms (growing fewer crops in larger fields) caused amalgamation of small, individual fields
2. Increased size of individual farms due to specialized corporate farms replacing small, diversified family farms
3. Increased use of modern machinery that is more easily and more economically operated in large single-species fields
4. Increased clearing of fencerows to gain more land for agriculture, where one mile of fencerow may occupy one-half acre[157]
5. Increased use of large sprinkler irrigation systems that eliminate uncultivated irrigation ditches and their banks
6. Replacement of many uncultivated earthen banks of irrigation ditches with concrete
7. Constant human control of crops with fungicides, herbicides, insecticides, and rodenticides if the desired production is to be forthcoming
8. Federal aid to farmers through the Agricultural Stabilization and Conservation Service for various types of land "reclamation"

Looking at agriculture worldwide, scientists have concluded that the expansion and intensification of cultivation are among the predominant changes to the globe in the 20th century. Intensification of agriculture through use of high-yielding varieties of crops, coupled with fertilization, irrigation, and pesticides, has contributed substantially to the tremendous increases in the production of food over the past half century. A predominant feature of agricultural intensification, however, has been the increasing specialization of production, which has resulted in a decrease in the variety of species grown, leading to more and more monocultures. The net result is that the conversion of land to and the intensification of agriculture have altered the biotic interactions and patterns of available resources in ecosystems, which can, and in some cases already are, having serious local, regional, and global environmental consequences.[158]

As these factors reduced the habitat for many species of wild plants and animals, they also increased the tendency for these same plants and animals, which now surrounded the croplands, to be perceived as exerting a constant negative influence on production. When wild species, especially animals, use agricultural crops as habitat, they are normally termed "pests." However, whether or not a species is a pest is a matter of perception based on some level of competitive tolerance, which wanes rapidly when money is concerned.

Small, diversified family farms were excellent habitat for wildlife. They provided increased structural diversity and therefore increased habitat diversity through a good mix of food, cover, water, and mini open spaces within surrounding, otherwise rather homogeneous, croplands.

The many small, irregular fields with a variety of crops created an abundance of structurally diverse edges, and tillage offered a variety of soil textures for burrowing animals. Uncultivated fencerows and ditch banks provided strips that not only acted as primary habitat for species, such as insectivorous songbirds, but also provided travel lanes between fields for other species.

Replacement of small family farms by large ones, dependent on mechanization and specialized monocultural crops, caused a drastic decline in wildlife habitats within and adjacent to croplands. Because of the decreased crop stability—increased crop vulnerability—resulting from the greatly simplified "agricultural ecosystem," farmers are more and more inclined to view wild or nonagricultural plants and animals as actual or potential "pests" to their crops.

Jane Smiley goes on to say: "If a society chooses mechanized, exploitive, giant-scale agriculture, an agriculture based on the ideal of genetic and economic uniformity, then its relationship to nature is systematically lost. If the relationship to nature is lost, then its relationship to delicacy and complexity of what's around them and who they are is also lost."[156] Smiley's observation is prophetic because in addition to stripping habitats from fencerows surrounding fields to maximize tillable soil and to get rid of unwanted plants and animals, modern agriculture is both killing the soil and poisoning the water with chemicals, which clearly is neither biologically nor culturally sustainable. But there is yet another consequence of modern corporate-style agriculture—local extinctions.

Consider Fender's blue butterfly.[159] The habitat for Fender's blue butterfly and its host plant, Kindaid's lupine, once spread across more than a million acres in the Willamette Valley before settlement began in the 1840s. Today, more than 99 percent of the native prairie in the valley has been lost to agriculture. Fortunately, in this case, the butterfly, once thought extinct, has been found in two small areas, both protected. The U.S. Fish and Wildlife Service is now considering listing the butterfly as endangered and its host plant as threatened. Although such protection is part and parcel of achieving social sustainability, which is, after all, hinged to the diversity of Nature, where is the protection for the diversity of crops?

Loss of Crop Diversity to Economics

"No one would deny that food is essential to life," writes organic gardener and author Amy Knutson.[160] Yet the Seed Savers Exchange estimates that 90 percent of the crops grown for food at the end of the 19th century are no longer available commercially and that two-thirds of the 5,000 freely pollinated varieties of crop plants available in 1984 were gone by 1994. The Food and Agriculture Organization, a branch of the United Nations, estimates that 75 percent of the genetic diversity of agricultural crops has been lost in the United States in this century.

In traditional agriculture, the diversity of crops was maintained by populations of species of plants grown over and over again by local farmers. Such plants were genetically varied, pollinated freely by local insects, and grown repeatedly in the same locale by seed saved from each successive crop, which over time adapted the plants to the particular climate and environment in which they grew.

Although not productive by the same scale of measure as modern agricultural crops, traditional corps survived over time to feed the people who grew them, regardless of conditions. Many of these locally adapted crops are being lost around the world, however, as farmers replace them with new varieties developed by plant breeders. Unfortunately, but as would be expected ecologically, these new varieties are often not only ill-adapted to a particular local environment but also prone to disease. Awareness of this vulnerability and concern over the loss of traditional, well-adapted, disease-resistant germ plasm have led some people to collect and maintain traditional plants at such places as the International Rice Institute in the Philippines.

Another concern is the loss of species of wild plants. Although plants are estimated to be disappearing in this century at the same rate as species of animals, plants are the foundation of the food chain, and it is thus estimated that with the extinction of each species of wild plant, 10 to 30 species of animals that depended on the plant for survival disappear also. Many plants thought of as "weeds," which are plants that either grow where one does not want them to or plants for which society has found no useful purpose, end up being important in medicines, for making new products, and for genetic material that builds useful characteristics into cultivated plants.

Of the 80,000 plants in the world known to be edible, it is estimated that prehistoric peoples ate about 1,500 wild plants, whereas ancient societies cultivated at least 500 major vegetables. Today, however, we in the United States depend on such a narrow range of crops, roughly 30 kinds of plants, for 95 percent of our nutrition that it may be crucial at some point, which I suggest is now, to consciously protect and maintain wild and semidomesticated edible plants.

But herein lies a problem. Most large companies that market seeds are not interested in keeping small supplies of older varieties of plants and therefore they replace them with the currently more profitable new and exclusive varieties. About 100 years ago, for example, Burpee's catalog offered twice as many varieties of plants as it does today. Today, seed companies typically prefer to stock a few "all-purpose" varieties that can be grown just about anywhere, rather than carry those varieties adapted to a specific region. Many large seed companies carry seeds for the Midwest or eastern United States, and nowhere in their catalogs is it mentioned that these seeds often fail to grow well in other parts of the United States.

There is a twist to the economic modernization of agriculture. Many of the well-adapted older varieties of crop plants are maintained in people's home gardens but not necessarily represented in the U.S. National Plant Germplasm System because its goal is to identify, collect, store, and distribute seeds and plant materials that can be used to *improve* crops grown for food and forage in the United States. What most people do not realize, contends Amy Knutson, is that the U.S. Department of Agriculture "is not making any great effort to preserve native American varieties because our 30 main food crops are foreign," which means the U.S. National Plant Germplasm System is biased in its preference toward foreign crop plants.

This notion raises the question of what we and the future are losing by not focusing on species of crop plants that came from indigenous North American parentage, some of which may grow in the open spaces, fencerows, riparian zones, or floodplains within proximity of our own communities. But to save the social wealth of Nature's diversity, we must plan wisely how we use land.

PROTECTING DIVERSITY
THROUGH LAND-USE PLANNING

It is not within the scope of this book to deal at length with the myriad ways a community or society can protect the diversity of Nature—the wealth of society—for the benefit of all generations. Nevertheless, I shall do my best to point out a few of the options that I think will bear fruit of sufficient quality to make their cultivation worthwhile.

Habitat will be used as the example because quality habitat is the basis of biological, genetic, and functional diversity, the sum of which is the basis of natural wealth and thus economic viability, which in turn equates to long-term community well-being. Habitat is composed of food, water, shelter, and space. Further, the environment dictates the composition of the species of plants, which creates a particular structure that in turn allows processes and functions to occur within time and space to create the living portion of habitats for wildlife and people. Understanding and maintaining the viability of these components are therefore key to the sustainability of quality habitat.

If we are really serious about achieving sustainability within our communities, we must learn to understand, accept, and act upon the notion that whether populations of indigenous plants and animals survive in a particular landscape depends on the rate of local extinctions from a patch of habitat and the rate with which an organism can move among existing patches. Those species living in habitats isolated as a result of fragmentation, from such things as urban sprawl, are therefore less likely to persist. Fragmentation of habitat, the most serious threat to biological, genetic, and functional diversity, is the primary cause of not only the often discussed global crisis in the rate of biological extinctions but also the less discussed crisis in the rate of local extinctions.

The Effect of Modifying Habitat

Modifying the connectivity among patches of habitat strongly influences the abundance of species and their patterns of movement. The size, shape, and diversity of patches of habitat also influence the patterns of species abundance, and the shape of a patch may determine what species can use it as habitat. The interaction among the processes of a species' dispersal and the pattern of a landscape determines the temporal dynamics of the species' populations. Local populations of organisms that can disperse great distances may not be as strongly affected by the spatial arrangement of patches of habitat as are more sedentary species.

Our responsibility as adults is not only to make decisions about patterns across the landscape while considering the consequences of our decisions on the potential quality of life for the generations of the future but also to teach these concepts to children in school who are that future. We are, after all, planning the environmental and social conditions of the future to which all children to come must respond; in that they have no choice. Although the decisions are up to us, one thing is clear: the current trend toward homogenizing the landscape, which may help maximize short-term monetary profits for one generation, progressively degrades the long-term biological adaptability of the land and thus the long-term sustainability of society as we know it.

Sustainability flows from the patterns of relationships that have evolved among the various species. A culturally oriented landscape, even a very diverse one, that fails to support these coevolved relationships has little chance of being sustainable. To create viable culturally oriented landscapes, we must shift our focus from fragmentation to *connectivity*. Because ecological sustainability and adaptability depend on connectivity of the habitats, we must ground our culturally designed landscapes within Nature's evolved patterns and take advantage of them if we are to have a chance of creating a quality environment that is both ecologically adaptable and pleasing to our cultural senses—and thus sustainable.

We must move purposefully, consciously toward the connectivity of habitats in the form of well-planned and protected systems of open spaces if we are to have adaptable landscapes with a desirable quality of living, including our indigenous wild neighbors, to pass to our heirs. Such a move will require that we shift our focus to six primary things:

1. Consciously, purposefully integrate cyclical thinking and linear thinking in such a way that we can produce the goods and services necessary to society while simultaneously understanding and protecting the cycles of Nature as a dimension of diversity that makes adaptability to the future as painless as possible for humanity.

2. Consciously, purposefully accord women absolute equality with men because women are, after all, half of the diversity that comprises the whole of humanity. Women are also more oriented toward the cyclical nature of relationship than are men, and men are more oriented toward the linear nature of production than are women, which helps to balance the two basic ways humans seem to think and thus brings humanity toward greater wholeness. Further, women who are afforded their birthright of equality tend to have fewer children and to have them later in life, which is the only way the world's human population will ever be voluntarily controlled.

3. Consciously, purposefully connect, or reconnect, people with a variety of habitats through a well-integrated system of open spaces that includes educational features about the critical importance of quality habitat.

4. Consciously, purposefully protect existing biological, genetic, and functional diversity, which is the irreplaceable wealth forming the foundation of human dignity as it equates to the quality of one's life within any given environment.

5. Consciously account for the sustainable connectivity of habitats, in the form of open spaces and biological richness, which is the price we must pay for the long-term sustainability and ecological wholeness of the patterns we create across the landscape.

6. Consciously choose cultural capacity (the quality of life) as opposed to carrying capacity (the maximum number of humans the world can support) because we cannot maximize both quality (life with dignity) and quantity (mere existence) simultaneously—*we must choose.*

Why are these six focal points important? Their importance can be summed up in one word, "connexity," which according to Geoff Mulgan, a policy adviser to British Prime Minister Tony Blair, is an old English word that better describes the quality of human relationships to one another and their environment than either interdependence (which captures the effect, but not the cause) or globalization (which drains the moral content from relationships).[161]

It is, writes Mulgan, sometimes easy to forget that in the recent past of a few generations, people seldom came across strangers because human relationships were close, intimate, demanding, and generally face to face. There was little one could do that would materially change other people's lives, except for those close at hand. As far as people from neighboring towns or countries were concerned, they might as well have been on separate continents.

Today, however, we affect one another through the global commons of air and water because everything we do that affects either of these affects all people in one way or another. People are also increasingly interconnected through the global economy and computer technology. Coming after centuries and millennia of oppressive hierarchies, says Mulgan, it is not surprising that freedom is valued so highly. But, he asks, is the achievement of new freedoms really compatible with growing interdependence, or is a world that devotes its energy to the pursuit of individual desires necessarily condemned to neglect or destroy the shared environment on which its well-being depends? He answers, "if we cannot cultivate people who are able to bear responsibilities, to recognize their impact on the world, then freedom soon becomes a pathology."

Constraints: The Building Blocks of Protecting Diversity

To design and protect diversity, one must first understand and create a vision of the desired outcome. (For a discussion on how to create a vision, see *Vision and Leadership in Sustainable Development*.[162]) The purpose of a vision is to determine not only what you want but also its feasibility because a vision is based on a series of behavioral constraints.

Constraints are limitations on freedom, which many people in our society view as unnecessarily restrictive to human "rights," however they are defined. What must be understood, however, is that complete freedom does not and cannot exist because everything is defined by its relationship to everything else, and that very relationship, within itself, is a constraint on one's absolute freedom. In addition, all relationships are constantly changing, which means one is and must be constantly responding to changes that are induced outside of oneself and therefore out of one's control; these are nonnegotiable constraints. Nevertheless, by understanding constraints and constructively using those that are negotiable, such as one's behavior in response to circumstances, one can acquire a measure of desired freedom.

The constraints imposed by Nature, such as climate, are for all practical purposes nonnegotiable. Nature's constraints are the ecological circumstances we are given to work with, such as the effects of a volcanic eruption like Mount St. Helens in the state of Washington, over which we have little or no control.

The constraints imposed by society on itself, either consciously or unconsciously, are all negotiable, however, and include trading freedoms, accountability for outcomes, and accountability for the rate of change.

1. Any time a community creates a vision for its future, it is trading freedoms, which means, for example, that to have more open space, one must limit growth in the human population because one cannot simultaneously have unlimited growth and a viable system of open spaces. One must choose, and in so doing, one gains more freedom in a particular area by giving up some freedom in another area. Here it is important to understand that not making a choice is still making a choice, but most likely not a wise one.

2. By imposing voluntary constraints on some freedoms and relaxing constraints on others, a vision becomes both a determiner of the outcome of planning and a mechanism by which the people who created the vision and those who implement it are accountable for that outcome.

3. Because local people, through the crafting of a vision, empower themselves to guide the destiny of their future, they simultaneously become accountable for the rate of change in their own population and thus the rate of change they exert on their community and its immediate landscape.

The farther into the future a community plans, the more diversity it can save, protect, and pass forward to the next generation. There is, however, an important fundamental consideration that one must address at this juncture: the notion of cultural capacity (the quality of lifestyle) versus carrying capacity (the absolute number of individuals a habitat can support). Cultural capacity was naturally built into the indigenous people's nomadic way of life; when conditions of livability became unfavorable, the people moved to an area with favorable conditions or split up into daughter groups. When their life became sedentary, however, with the advent of agriculture, cultural capacity had to become a conscious choice, if for no other reason than the rising problem of what to do with the accumulation of human offal, garbage, and diseases that are part and parcel of a sedentary culture. But cultural capacity as a conscious choice did not materialize immediately.

Cumulative Effects, Thresholds, Lag Periods, and the Continuum

Cultural capacity did not become a conscious choice overnight when the nomadic way of life shifted to a sedentary one because the hidden cumulative effects of humans concentrating their activities in one area did not become immediately apparent. The cumulative effects of human activities had to compound in secret to a point that something in the environment shifted dramatically enough for people to see it. That shift was defined by a threshold of tolerance in the ecosystem beyond which the system as people knew it suddenly, visibly became something else, something undesirable. Once the ecosystem shifted, however, the effect of that shift was, more often than not, irreversible.

The approaching danger went undetected until it was too late because ecosystems operate on the basis of lag periods, which simply means there is a lag in time between when the cause of a fundamental change in an ecosystem is introduced and its visible outcome is apparent. This is somewhat analogous to the incubation period in the human body between contracting a disease and manifesting the symptoms.

We, in society today, spend much time arguing whether an ecosystem is natural or unnatural ecologically, right or wrong morally, good or bad economically. I do not think of ecosystems or habitats as natural or unnatural in the sense of either/or, but rather as a continuum of naturalness. Consider, for example, that a mountaintop untouched by human alterations constitutes the most natural end of the continuum, while a shopping mall constitutes the most cultural end. Such a continuum can easily be symbolized as follows: N—C, where N represents the most natural end of the continuum and C the most cultural end. Everything in between, depending on where along the continuum it falls, represents a degree of naturalness and/or a degree of culturalness.

The question for us today is where along this continuum we must of necessity maintain a piece of land if the whole of the landscape, in the collective of our individual choices, is to be sustainable, both environmentally and socially. To examine this notion, we will discuss three scenarios: open space, transportation, and human population. Each scenario in its turn will be considered as the socially derived, nonnegotiable constraint at the core of a community vision. The order of presentation is important because it will lead us from a vision based on cultural capacity to one based on carrying capacity.

OPEN SPACE

Open space, like water, is available in a fixed amount. Unlike water, however, open space is visibly disappearing at an exponential rate. Once gone, it is gone, unless, of course, rural communities, and perhaps even cities, are torn down to reclaim it—an unlikely event.

Space was once sacred to indigenous peoples, but today it all seems to have a price and to be coveted for that price. Whether it is "outer space, inner space, sacred space, forbidden space, your space, or my space, the more removed we are from original participation with space [which included the sanctity of all space], the more *all* space will continue to be desecrated," writes poet Geoffrey Hill.[163]

Consider, for example, the forested areas around Puget Sound in western Washington State, where the forests have been thinned so dramatically in recent years that "this land of towering evergreens is now relatively treeless."[164] Using satellite imagery, researchers from American Forests, one of the nation's oldest conservation organizations, based in Washington, D.C., found that nearly one-third of the most heavily forested land around Puget Sound has disappeared since the early 1970s.

Satellite photographs from 1972, 1986, and 1996 and computer-mapping software were used to study a 700-square-mile area that stretched across King, Pierce, Snohomish, Thurston, and Kitsap counties. Overall, the heavily forested areas, those where trees covered more than half of the land, fell from 49 percent of the region to 31 percent, a loss of about 600,000 acres. According to the study, places where trees covered 20 percent of the landscape or less grew simultaneously from 25 percent of the study area to 57 percent, an increase of more than one million acres. Why? Because subdivisions, driven by growth in the human population around Seattle and other suburban cities, have gobbled up the available open-space land.

"If people want to know why we are having so many more landslides, if people want to know why it seems to be getting hotter and why rainstorms are more intense, well, this [deforestation] is part of the answer," according to Clement Hamilton, director of the Center for Urban Horticulture at the University of Washington in Seattle. But how do fewer trees make it rain harder?

Trees provide shade, which lowers the temperature of the air. As areas are deforested, they create a phenomenon called "heat islands," where temperatures can increase five to ten degrees or more. Then, because warm air holds more moisture, heavier rains are triggered when the warm, moisture-laden air rises and cools in the atmosphere, which increases precipitation in the form of storm water.

Forested areas typically slow and absorb water from storms, allowing it to infiltrate deep into the soil instead of flowing overland or gushing into gutters, storm drains, and water treatment plants. According to the study, it would cost about $2.4 billion to build a storm-water system that would be equivalent to the one provided free by the trees lost since 1972. In addition, those trees would have annually absorbed 35 million pounds of pollutants, such as carbon monoxide, ozone, and sulfur dioxide. With loss of the trees, however, those pollutants, circulating freely in the air, translated into approximately $95 million in health-care costs and other social impacts.

Thus, while there are multiple reasons why a community might want to save open space, its irreplaceability and value added to community life are critical ones because in the plurality of options saved and passed forward lies the kernel of diversity and choice. Open space, as the non-negotiable constraint around which a community chooses to develop, places the primacy of development on quality of human relationships to both people and Nature. The ability and commitment to maintain a matrix of open spaces within and surrounding a community are critical to the sustainability of its quality of life (its cultural capacity, which is based on protecting its natural wealth) and ultimately the economic viability of the community, especially a small community in a nonurban setting. A well-designed open-space system determines where both urban development and the transportation system will be located.

Communal Open Space

Open space for communal use is not only central to the notion of community but also is increasingly becoming a premium of a community's continued livability and the stability of the value of its real estate. It can also become a focal point around which to organize communities, such as the ecological restoration project in Iowa that became a community project.[165] Of course, continual economic growth, at the expense of open space, will line the pockets of a few people in the present, but it will ultimately pick the pockets of everyone in the future. Can an ordinary citizen do something about saving open space? Yes. Bill McDonald did.[166]

Bill McDonald, a fifth-generation rancher in southeastern Arizona, has used his skills of forging consensus among fellow ranchers, some conservationists, and others, known as the Malpai Borderlands Group, to help save 800,000 acres of open space and with it a way of life. McDonald's aim is to help ranchers become progressive trustees of an area larger than Grand Canyon National Park by keeping the connectivity of its open space intact. The parcel of land is a combination of land owned by 32 ranchers, who collectively own about half the area, and public lands the ranchers lease from the U.S. Forest Service and Bureau of Land Management, plus state trust lands belonging to Arizona and New Mexico. The ranchers' common ground—their vision, if you will—is their love of open space, the way of life it affords, and a deep desire to protect both, which means they must accept personal accountability for their own behavior.

Their achievements to date are as follows:

- Incorporating as a nonprofit organization focused on reducing polarization between the interests of ranchers and conservationists, in particular by limiting the effect of grazing livestock on public lands and in riparian zones.
- Creating a "grassbank" and "conservation easements" intended to help ensure that the ranchers can keep their lands open and that they and their children can continue ranching without having to sell or subdivide parts of their acreages.
- Emphasizing sound scientific study to discern the best approach to restoring ecologically fragile areas that will help endangered and threatened species through a "rancher's endangered species program." A working example of the program is one area ranching family trucking a thousand gallons of water to stock ponds during a prolonged drought to keep alive one of the last populations of Chiricahua leopard frogs.
- Getting federal bureaucrats and officials from two states to agree to reintroduce fir into the ecosystem through prescribed burns to help restore the area's native grasslands.
- Improving the upland areas, including the forage on hillsides, which not only will increase the infiltration of water and thereby reduce soil erosion but also will improve the condition of riparian zones.

For his part, Bill McDonald knows that the extremists, who just want to fight, are still there. But he says, "My hope is that what we're doing will encourage other people to step toward the middle and find solutions and that the extreme positions will be marginalized over time."

For such communal open space to have maximum value over time, a community, like the ranchers, must have a clear and compelling vision of what it wants so that the following questions can be answered in a responsible and accountable way: (1) What parcels of land are wanted for the communal system of open space? (2) Why are they wanted? What is their functional value: capture and storage of water, habitat for native plants and animals, local educational opportunities, recreation, aesthetics? (3) How much land is necessary to fulfill the first two questions? (4) Can one project the value added to the quality of life and/or the consequential value of real estate in the future?[162]

Although it is not possible in this book to discuss all the possibilities of an open-space system, we shall consider some of the more critical and perhaps commonly overlooked components, such as the source and storage of water.

Water

Seventy-five percent of the surface of the Earth is covered with water, but more than 97 percent of it is salt water that makes up the oceans. Another 2 percent is frozen in glaciers and the polar ice caps, which means that only 1 percent of the water is available in usable form for life outside of the oceans. In fact, without fresh water from precipitation, even the oceans would become so salty that life in them as we know it would either have to change or become extinct.

More than 70 percent of the human body consists of water.[167] A 1 percent deficiency of water in your body will make you thirsty, a 5 percent deficit will cause a slight fever, and an 8 percent shortage will cause your glands to stop producing saliva and your skin to turn blue; you cannot walk with a 10 percent deficiency, and you die with a 12 percent deficiency. Today, according to United Nations authorities, 9,500 children die every day from lack of water or, more frequently, from diseases that are carried in polluted water.

Water is a nonsubstitutable requirement of life, and its source and storage capacity are finite in any given landscape. The availability of water throughout the year will thus determine both the quality of life in a community and consequently the value of real estate. It behooves a community, therefore, to take any measure possible to maximize and stabilize both the quality and quantity of its local supply of water.

Local supply refers to water catchments in the local area under local control, as opposed to water catchments in the local area under the control of an absentee owner with no vested interest in the community's supply of water. Such absentee ownership could be a person, corporation, government body, or agency beyond local jurisdiction.

Fresh, usable water, once thought to be inexhaustible in supply, is now becoming scarce in many parts of the world, in addition to which worldwide use of water doubled between 1940 and 1980. The per-capita consumption of water is currently rising twice as fast as the human population of the world is growing. Today, 70 percent of all water used is devoted to agriculture, which uses water inefficiently at best, and forecasters predict that an additional 25 to 30 percent will be needed by the year 2000 to keep pace with increases in irrigated agricultural land.

In the western United States, for example, water pumped from deep underground aquifers is today such a valuable commodity that it is often referred to as "sandstone champagne." Much of North Africa is suffering from droughts that have forced hundreds of thousands of people to flee rural areas for low-paying jobs in cities. In Cherrapunji, a town in northern India that receives 1,000 inches of rain annually—the most precipitation in the world, the people walk long distances to get drinking water, limit bathing to once a week, and have trouble irrigating their crops.

Water, not oil, will be the next resource over which nations and factions within nations will go to war. Twenty-two countries are already dependent on the flow of water that is supplied from sources in other nations. India, Pakistan, Bangladesh, the Middle East, Egypt, and Ethiopia are among the areas with the potential for armed conflict over water. There are even serious disagreements over issues concerning the sharing of water between nations on the best of terms, like Canada and the United States. In addition, China and the western United States may well have factions that are willing to compete for water in armed conflict. Wally N'Dow of Gambia, whom the *Los Angeles Times* describes as "the world's foremost specialist on cities," says bluntly: "The crisis point [over the battle for water] is going to be 15 to 20 years from now."

"It is no exaggeration to say," according to Paul Simon, former senator from Illinois, "that the conflict between humanity's growing thirst and the projected supply of usable, potable water could result in the most devastating natural disaster since history has been recorded accurately, unless something happens to stop it." That something would have to be far wiser leadership at home and abroad than I have thus far seen in my lifetime.

With this in mind, it is wise to use the storage of water for present and future generations as one of the cornerstones in any open-space system. If outright purchase of a water catchment is not possible, a community could conceivably enter into a long-term lease or contract to rent a catchment, with control over what is done on it. Then it might be possible to accrue monthly or annual payments toward the price of purchasing the land at a later date. Such an arrangement could benefit the owner in terms of a steady income at reasonable tax rates while allowing some acceptable use of the land.

Another alternative might be a tax credit payable to the landowner if the community could work in conjunction with the owner to protect the water catchment's inherent value to the community itself. There are probably other options, but the important consideration is to secure the purchase of local water catchments in community ownership as part of the open-space program to maintain and protect the quality of life and the local value of real estate. An added value may be that such water catchments in an open-space system can act as islands of quiet amidst the daily bustle of town life.

Quiet

The past quiet of my hometown is but a memory. Today, there is an increasingly noticeable din from autos, buses, and trucks that seem in perpetual motion at all hours, as well as the rumblings of trains that whistle at the numerous road crossings. If a community designs its system of open spaces to dampen the constant stimulation of urban background noise, people could, for many years to come, find a peaceful quiet in which to relax and hear the songs of birds and the stories of faraway places whispered by the wind.

The relaxation experienced in a quiet place can be consciously enhanced in an open-space system by including farm- and forestlands, riparian areas, and floodplains as buffers against city noise. I know this is possible because I have experienced it in the beautiful Shinto shrine in downtown Tokyo, Japan, an exceedingly busy city.

Surrounding Landscape

The land surrounding a community's municipal limits gives the community its contextual setting, its ambiance, if you will. The wise acquisition of open spaces in the various components of the surrounding landscape, whether Nature's ecosystem or culture's, protects, to some extent at least, the uniqueness of a community's setting and hence the uniqueness of the community itself. And the value added, both spiritual and economic, will accrue as the years pass.

Agricultural Cropland

A community could purchase open space in the form of fencerows along which to allow fencerow habitat to recreate itself. Then, in addition to mini habitats in and of themselves, the few uncultivated yards along each fence could once again act as longitudinal corridors for the passage of wildlife from one area to another. Living fencerows would also make the landscape more interesting, more appealing to the human eye, and add once again the songs of birds and the colors of flowers and leaves to the passing seasons.

The point is to find out what worked sustainably in the past, such as organic farming, and begin recreating it in the present, and where problems arise, as they will, to work together to resolve them. The only way to create, maintain, and pass forward the sense of community is by working together, because the friendliness of a community is founded on the quality of its interpersonal relationships, of which small family farmers are an integral part.

Forestland

If a community is in a forest setting, the forest more likely than not is a major contributor to the community's image of itself, in addition to which it may comprise an important water catchment. Furthermore, if the community is, or has been, a "timber town," then most of the forest may well have been converted into economic tree farms; therefore, maintaining an area of native forest may be of even greater value. If some old-growth trees are included in the area, its spiritual value may well be heightened and its value as habitat for some plants and animals greatly enhanced.

On the other hand, if what surrounds a community is no longer forest but rather an economic tree farm, a purchased area could be allowed to evolve once again toward a forest. As such, its aesthetic and spiritual values will increase, as will its potential value as habitat and for educational purposes. Much can be learned by comparing a relatively sterile tree farm with a real forest.[168,169] One will find, for instance, that a forest harbors a far greater diversity of species of both plants and animals than does a tree farm, even one near the age of cutting.

I have used the forest as an example only because I grew up in one, but the same concepts can be applied anywhere. Outside of Denver, Colorado, for example, is a wonderful open space, which represents a vestige of native shortgrass prairie that once covered the eastern part of the state. It is beautiful! And it is inspirational, creating, as it does, a tangible tie to a now intangible past and an unknowable future.

Riparian Areas and Floodplains

Riparian areas and floodplains are coming under increasing pressures of urban development because of the misguided notion that we humans can unilaterally entrain streams and rivers with impunity, despite much and growing evidence to the contrary. When a levee fails, the response seems always to be more levees and, if need be, more dams. We have yet to understand that a problem caused on one level of human consciousness cannot be fixed on the same level of consciousness.

If we are willing to risk moving to a higher level of consciousness, we can either prevent or repair much of the damage our shortsighted human activities cause. Take, for example, the Snake River near Jackson, Wyoming, where engineers, the Jackson Hole Conservation Alliance, the Wyoming Department of Fish and Game, and local officials are planning to restore part of the Snake River to a more natural condition.[170]

For nearly 40 years, levees that line about 23 miles of the Snake River near Jackson have entrained high water from the melting snows of spring in the Teton Mountains and allowed lavish homes to invade the cottonwood forest of the river's floodplain. Although researchers have known for some time the ecological havoc wreaked by dams, only recently have they begun to recognize the ecologically destructive nature of levees and their "free-form cousin" riprap, which is piles of rock and earth dumped by landowners along streams and rivers to guard against erosion.

It is not surprising, therefore, that the 15-foot-high serpentine piles of rock created by the U.S. Army Corps of Engineers to protect farmers' fields and hay meadows from flooding and erosion have caused serious and unexpected problems along one of the world's most scenic stretches of river. The river had for centuries been true to its rhythm of flooding and receding in a fluid motion that constantly redesigned its five or six channels or braids as it dissipated the energy of its floodwaters each spring. But now, squeezed into one or two rigid channels, the upper Snake River has lost its ability to flood during the spring runoff. This lost ability has increased the velocity of the water from spring runoffs within the levee straitjacket, which in turn has caused the destruction by raging spring torrents of many of the large islands in the remaining channels that were at one time occupied by willows and cottonwood trees. The luxuriant forests of cottonwood that once lined the river's banks are fading into a past era for lack of young trees to replace the dying of the old because cottonwoods need periodic flooding to reproduce successfully. And Snake River cutthroat trout, which need clean gravel in which to spawn, have suffered from the channelization because floodwaters no longer flush and rejuvenate their spawning gravels.

In the autumn of 1998, the Teton County Natural Resource District and the U.S. Army Corps of Engineers began testing methods of breathing old life back into the river by restoring its rhythms of flooding. They hope to begin the full restoration project in the year 2000, which will take a different level of consciousness, as Rik Gay, manager of the restoration project for Teton County, pointed out when he said, "Rivers don't just go downstream. We need to think in three dimensions. Rivers also move laterally and below the ground."

There is a sober reminder in all of this, however. The levees along the upper Snake River not only have narrowed and denuded the river over the last four decades but also have allowed million-dollar housing developments to flourish, which caused Bill MacDonald, manager of the Snake River project for the U.S. Army Corps of Engineers, to observe that restoring the natural flow of the river was "not feasible" because "behind those levees are millions, if not billions, of dollars in real estate." What might an alternative for the future be?

According to Scott Faber, a floodplain expert with the conservation group American Rivers, what really needs to be done to protect the ecological integrity of rivers is to cease building in the floodplains. One way to accomplish that, he contends, is to terminate the federal subsidy for repairing levees and make local governments pay the cost. In the meantime, however, many communities still have riparian areas that are important to understand and protect.

Riparian Areas

Riparian areas can be identified by the presence of vegetation that requires free or unbound water and conditions more moist than normal. These areas may vary considerably in size and the complexity of their vegetative cover because of the many combinations that can be created between the source of water and the physical characteristics of the site. Such characteristics include gradient, aspect of slope, topography, soil, type of stream bottom, quantity and quality of the water, elevation, and the kind of plant community.

Riparian areas have the following things in common: (1) they create well-defined habitats within much drier surrounding areas, (2) they make up a minor portion of the overall area, (3) they are generally more productive than the remainder of the area in terms of the biomass of plants and animals, (4) wildlife use riparian areas disproportionately more than any other type of habitat, and (5) they are a critical source of diversity within an ecosystem.

There are many reasons why riparian areas are so important to wildlife, but not all can be attributed to every area. Each combination of the source of water and the attributes of the site must be considered separately. Some of these reasons are as follows:

1. The presence of water lends importance to the area because habitat for wildlife is composed of food, cover, water, and space. Riparian areas offer one of these critical components and often all four.

2. The greater availability of water to plants, frequently in combination with deeper soils, increases the production of plant biomass and provides a suitable site for plants that are limited elsewhere by inadequate water. The combination of these factors leads to increased diversity in the species of plants and in the structural and functional diversity of the biotic community.

3. The dramatic contrast between the complex of plants in the riparian area and that of the general surrounding vegetation of the upland forest or grassland adds to the structural diversity of the area. For example, the bank of a stream that is lined with deciduous shrubs and trees provides an edge of stark contrast when surrounded by coniferous forest or grassland. Moreover, a riparian area dominated by deciduous vegetation provides one kind of habitat in the summer when in full leaf and another type of habitat in the winter following leaf fall.

4. The shape of many riparian areas, particularly the linear nature of streams and rivers, maximizes the development of edge effect, which is so productive in terms of wildlife.

5. Riparian areas, especially those in coniferous forests, frequently produce more edges within a small area than would otherwise be expected based solely on the structure of the plant communities. In addition, many strata of vegetation are exposed simultaneously in stair-step fashion. This stair-stepping of vegetation of contrasting form (deciduous versus coniferous, or otherwise evergreen, shrubs and trees) provides diverse opportunities for feeding and nesting, especially for birds and bats.

6. The microclimate in riparian areas is different from that of the surrounding area because of increased humidity, a higher rate of transpiration (loss of water) from the vegetation, more shade, and increased movement in the air. Some species of animals are particularly attracted to this microclimate.

7. Riparian areas along intermittent and permanent streams and rivers provide routes of migration for wildlife, such as birds, bats, deer, and elk. Deer and elk frequently use these areas as corridors of travel between high-elevation summer ranges and low-elevation winter ranges.

8. Riparian areas, particularly along streams and rivers, may serve as forested connectors between forested habitats or elevational habitats, such as grasslands. Wildlife may use such riparian areas for cover while traveling across otherwise open areas. Some species, especially birds and small mammals, may use such routes in dispersal from the original habitats. This may be caused by the pressures of overpopulation or by shortages of food, cover, or water. Riparian areas provide cover and often provide food and water during such movements.

In addition, riparian areas supply organic material in the form of leaves and twigs, which become an important component of the aquatic food chain. Riparian areas also supply large woody debris in the form of fallen trees, which form a critical part of the land/water interface, the stability of banks along streams and rivers, and instream habitat for a complex of aquatic plants as well as aquatic invertebrate and vertebrate organisms.[171]

Setting aside riparian areas as undeveloped open space or repairing them through ecological restoration[172] means saving the most diverse, and often the most heavily used, habitat for wildlife in proximity to a community. Riparian areas are also an important source of large woody debris for the stream or river whose banks they protect from erosion.[171] Furthermore, riparian areas are periodically flooded in winter, which, along with floodplains, is how a stream or river dissipates part of its energy. It is important that streams and rivers be allowed to dissipate their energy; otherwise, floodwaters would cause considerably more damage than they already do in settled areas.

Floodplains

A floodplain is a plain that borders a stream or river that is subject to flooding. Like riparian areas, floodplains are critical to maintain as open areas because, as the name implies, they frequently flood. These are areas where storm-swollen streams and rivers spread out, decentralizing the velocity of their flow by encountering friction caused by the increased surface area of their temporary bottoms, both of which dissipate much of the floodwater's energy.

It is wise to include floodplains within the matrix of open spaces for several other reasons: (1) they will inevitably flood, which puts any human development at risk, regardless of efforts to steal the floodplain from the stream or river for human use (witness the Mississippi River); (2) they are critical winter habitat for fish;[171] (3) they form important habitat in spring, summer, and autumn for a number of invertebrate and vertebrate wildlife that frequent the water's edge;[171] and (4) they can have important recreational value.

If all these kinds of areas are incorporated into a system of well-designed, well-connected open spaces, a community would be wealthy indeed. In addition, the community would have done much to maximize the quality of life (its cultural capacity), not only in the present but also for the future.

Consider, for example, that a well-implemented system of open spaces helps to ameliorate the cumulative effects of a concentrated human population on its immediate surroundings. It also ensures that some areas are protected from the intrusion of artificial structures to clutter and fragment the space, which allows the seeming "emptiness" to be filled with wildflowers, grasses, trees, butterflies, bird song, and glimpses of wildlife in an area where they need not compete with such human endeavors as agriculture and transportation. Open space also connects people with the land and its variety of habitats and life-forms. Most importantly, open space, as the nonnegotiable constraint around which a community plans and carries out its development, allows both roads and people to be placed in the best locations from a sustainable point of view, both environmental and socially.

TRANSPORTATION

When the system of transportation becomes the center of a community's vision for its future, the community is placing the primacy of its vision on the human relationship to mass movement from one place to another, which in turn determines where and how the population and open spaces will be situated. Here a fundamental question might be posed: Does building more and more roads really relieve congestion, which, after all, seems to be what drives the design of a transportation system?

According to Bill Bishop, editorial page columnist for the *Herald–Leader* in Lexington, Kentucky, building more roads does not relieve congestion—it *adds* to it.[173] I think he has a good point because I see a parallel in buying houses.

I have often heard people say they have so much stuff that they need a larger house. This statement seems reasonable enough on the surface, but in practice, most people I know who have actually bought a larger house begin immediately filling it to capacity. Why? I think our American compulsion to fill every nook and cranny is in part a product of not having been taught how to live with empty space, or at least space that is not crammed full all the time.

Is the same true with roads? If our cities' roads are congested and we build more roads to relieve the congestion, will we not just fill the new roads again to the point of congestion, like our houses? It seems to me that one could logically say: like our houses, so our roads. This is also the contention of columnist Bill Bishop.

"Trying to pave your way out of traffic congestion," writes Bishop, "is like trying to eat your way back into your high school jeans. Cars fill in the new pavement just like middle age created the market for Dockers." Although it seems counterintuitive, says Bishop, building more roads actually leads to more traffic. On the other hand, he continues, closing roads, or even narrowing streets, does not create more congestion—it tends to cut the volume of traffic, especially in cities.

"Lord knows," says Bishop, "the evidence of this phenomenon is stalled in full view of most citizens. As soon as roads are built, they're filled. And to relieve the new traffic, we build new roads. You'd think somebody would connect the dots." What dots? The dots pointing to the fact that the level of consciousness that caused the problem in the first place, such as the levees along the Snake River near Jackson, Wyoming, which largely destroyed the river, is not the level of consciousness that can solve it. A higher level of consciousness is required—recognizing, accepting, and acting on the evidence under our noses, which is connecting the dots.

Some people have connected the dots, quips Bishop. "Adding new roadways and widening older ones was seen as the way to solve the problem," observed the Texas Transportation Institute in a study of city traffic. "In most cities, this new roadway capacity was quickly filled with additional traffic, and the old problems of congestion returned." On the other hand, researchers at the University College of London, England, examined 60 cases from around the world in which roads had been closed. They found that a goodly portion of the traffic that once used the roads simply "evaporated." The cars and trucks were not simply rerouted on nearby streets, but disappeared altogether.

On average, one-fifth of the vehicular use, and in some cases as much as 60 percent, went away once a road was closed, and the full volume of vehicles did not reappear once a road was reopened. The Tower Bridge in London, for example, was temporarily closed in 1994, and the traffic dispersed. Three years after the bridge was reopened, traffic still had not returned to its former level.

Writer James Howard Kunstler argued in the online magazine *Slate* that "we have transformed the human ecology of America, from sea to shinning sea, into a national automobile slum." "...Do we get what we get," muses Bishop, "just because we can't remember any other way to live?"

That is a good question because while transportation may be the center of a community's vision for its future, which increases the artificial structures of urbanization, light and noise pollution, and simultaneously precludes much of Nature through fragmentation of habitats, a community has two options in planning its transportation system: ecological constraints (greater emphasis on cultural capacity) or economic constraints (greater emphasis on carrying capacity).

If a community chooses to design its transportation system around ecological constraints, it may still be able to have a relatively good system of open spaces, but the system will suffer far greater fragmentation than if the open-space system itself had driven the vision and its implementation. On the other hand, if a community chooses to design its transportation system around economic constraints, open space as a viable system is all but foregone because fragmentation of habitat is inevitably maximized, as are noise and light pollution. There is also a greater likelihood (as opposed to a community where a system of open spaces has primacy) that both exotic and naturalized species would take over remaining parts of the landscape as habitat fragmentation created by and growth in the human population accommodated by the transportation system put evermore outside pressure on the survival of indigenous species. All of these things operate synergistically as cumulative effects that exhibit a lag period before fully manifesting themselves.

POPULATION

When a community uses its human population as the primary nonnegotiable constraint around which development will revolve, it is most likely, in my experience, to view the size of the proposed population in terms of continual economic growth (carrying capacity) as opposed to ecological sustainability (cultural capacity), although it has the option of leaning more toward ecological sustainability. Thus, a vision based on the human population as the nonnegotiable constraint usually, but not always, places its primacy on pushing the biological carrying capacity to the perceived limit. In so doing, the placement of people as dictated by the desirability of available private property and individual tastes usually determines where the transportation system will be located, which together maximize the fragmentation of habitat, precluding a connected system of open spaces with any integrity of habitat.

Choosing the perceived biological carrying based first and foremost on the human population, which in my experience is usually based more on economics and politics than on sound ecological science, maximizes the cumulative effects of light and noise pollution, artificial structures, fragmentation of the habitat, and declines in and extinctions of local populations and species of indigenous plants and animals. Again, all these effects are not only hidden for some time in the ecological lag period but also work synergistically in shifting the landscape from the more natural end of the continuum to the more cultural end. Beyond some point, these effects upset the ecological integrity and ultimately affect the quality of life, almost inevitably in the negative. So, where do we go from here?

CONCLUSIONS

Nature has endowed us with a seemingly limitless array of physical and biological diversity, some of such beauty that it bedazzles the eye, some of such mystery that it teases the imagination, and some of such colossal magnitude that it causes us to ponder the presence of a Consciousness beyond our understanding.

At first, people were awed by diversity and erected gods to appease some of its more frightening aspects. Then people learned to harness diversity and used it to empower their lives. Today, people are trying to own diversity and through such ownership wield the power of control over their fellow human beings and life itself.

If humanity is to live sustainably on the Earth, we must learn to understand, accept, and once again respect the meaning of diversity as its dimensions are revealed to us through science, sociology, and spirituality. Understanding, accepting, and respecting diversity is not enough, however; we must also act on that knowledge and account for and protect diversity in the land-use plans that guide the implementation of our respective visions for sustainable community development.

Although we will never understand all of the dimensions of diversity because they are too complex, especially the functional dimensions, it is precisely *because* our understanding of Nature's diversity is so very limited that we must today protect as much diversity as is humanly possible. Diversity in all its dimensions is, after all, the foundation of sustainable community development and thus of social–environmental sustainability as a whole, and diversity is inexorably tied to those human values that drive our vision of the future and thus become embedded in land-use planning, the outworking of our vision, be it self-centered or other-centered, thoughtful or mindless, fragmentary or holistic, myopic or far-sighted.

Clearly, decisions about the current quality of life, such as those discussed in this book, belong to us, the adults of the world. But we must remember that with every decision we make we irrevocably bequeath the consequences to those silent generations we call "the future," who will be left twisting in the wind of growing ecological poverty and increasing social uncertainty—unless we speak and act for them now, today, while there is still time.

ENDNOTES

1. The discussion of chocolate is based on Carol Kaesuk Yoon. 1998. Chocoholics take note: beloved bean in peril. *The New York Times,* May 4.
2. Bill McKibben. 1998. A special moment in history. *The Atlantic Monthly,* May:55–60, 62–65, 68–73, 76–78.
3. Colin Greer. 1994. The well-being of the world is at stake. *Parade Magazine,* January 23:4–5.
4. The discussion of resource overexploitation is based in part on an article by Donald Ludwig, Ray Hilborn, and Carl Walters. 1993. Uncertainty, resource exploitation, and conservation: lesson from history. *Science,* 260:17, 36.
5. The discussion of the white abalone and the following comments on extinctions of species in the ocean are based on David Malakoff. 1997. Extinction on the high seas. *Science,* 277:486–488.
6. The discussion of the North Atlantic swordfish is based on an article by Katherine Roth. 1998. Chefs remove swordfish from menus. *Corvallis Gazette-Times* (Corvallis, OR), January 25.
7. Gretchen C. Daily, Susan Alexander, Paul R. Ehrlich, Larry Goulder, Jane Lubchenco, et al. 1997. Ecosystem services: benefits supplied to human societies by natural ecosystems. *Issues in Ecology,* 2:1–16.
8. *The Holy Bible, Authorized King James Version,* World Bible Publishers, Iowa Falls, IA, Genesis 1, Verse 2.
9. *Corvallis Gazette-Times* (Corvallis, OR). 1998. Bug attacks a boon for radish sprouts. May 1.
10. The following discussion of the southern Appalachian Mountains is based on Hazel R. Delcourt and Paul A. Delcourt. 1988. Quaternary landscape ecology: relevant scales in space and time. *Landscape Ecology,* 2:23–44, and Paul A. Delcourt and Hazel R. Delcourt. 1958. Dynamic landscapes of east Tennessee: an integration of paleoecology, geomorphology, and archaeology. *Studies in Geology,* 9:191–220.
11. The Associated Press. 1998. Logging-road problem bigger than thought. *Corvallis Gazette-Times* (Corvallis, OR), January 22.

12. John Lancaster. 1991. As Utah's Salt Flats disappear an unusual alliance emerges. *The Oregonian* (Portland, OR), June 16.

13. Discussion of the coelacanth is based on *Corvallis Gazette-Times* (Corvallis, OR). 1989. Rare fish faces extinction. October 4; Peter Forey. 1998. A home from home for coelacanths. *Nature,* 395(6700):319–320; and Mark V. Erdmann, Roy L. Caldwell, and M. Kasim Moosa. 1998. Indonesian "King of the Sea" discovered. *Nature,* 395(6700):335.

14. The discussion of elephant seals is based on Paul McHugh. 1998. Elephant seals returning in a big way. *Corvallis Gazette-Times* (Corvallis, OR), January 18.

15. Paul Stephen Corn and James C. Fogleman. 1984. Extinction of montane populations of the northern leopard frog (*Rana pipiens*) in Colorado. *Journal of Herpetology,* 18:147–152.

16. F. Stuart Chapin III, Brian H. Walker, Richard J. Hobbs, et al. 1997. Biotic control over the functioning of ecosystems. *Science,* 277:500–504.

17. Michael Kiefer. 1989. Fall of the Garden of Eden. *International Wildlife,* July–August:38–43.

18. The following discussion is based on G. William Fiero. 1988. *Nevada's Valley of Fire,* KC Publications, Las Vegas, 48 pp.

19. P.J. Spielmann. 1994. Jurassic pine tree found living in a "lost world" near Sydney. *Corvallis Gazette-Times* (Corvallis, OR), December 15.

20. The discussion about streams, rivers, and wood in oceans is drawn from Chris Maser and James R. Sedell. 1994. *From the Forest to the Sea: The Ecology of Wood in Streams, Rivers, Estuaries, and Oceans,* St. Lucie Press, Boca Raton, FL, 200 pp.

21. Sir Charles Lyell. 1866. *Principles of Geology; or the Modern Changes of the Earth and Its Inhabitants,* D. Appleton & Co., New York, 834 pp.

22. The discussion of tropical forests is based on Louise H. Emmons. 1989. Tropical rain forests: why they have so many species, and how we may lose this biodiversity without cutting a single tree. *Orion,* 8:8–14.

23. The Associated Press. 1998. 10 percent of tree species under threat of extinction. *Corvallis Gazette-Times* (Corvallis, OR), August 26.

24. The discussion of decomposing salmon is based on James R. Sedell, Joseph E. Yuska, and Robert W. Speaker. 1983. Study of Westside Fisheries in Olympic National Park, Washington, Final Report CX-9000-0-E 081, National Park Service, U.S. Department of the Interior, 74 pp, and The Associated Press. 1997. Fish carcasses bring new life to Northwest streams. *Corvallis Gazette-Times* (Corvallis, OR), November 24.

25. The discussion of the Shoshonean peoples and the Salt Creek pupfish is based in part on W.D. Clark. 1981. *Death Valley, The Story Behind the Scenery,* KC Publications, Las Vegas, 45 pp.

26. Discussion of the atlatl is based on Knight-Ridder Tribune New Service. 1996. One spear stops 10,000 pounds? *Corvallis Gazette-Times* (Corvallis, OR), March 28, and Dr. Rob Bonnichsen, Director for the Study of First

Americans, Department of Anthropology, Oregon State University, Corvallis, personal communication.

27. Stuart Piggott. 1991. *The Druids,* Thames and Hudson, New York, 214 pp.
28. The discussion of sugar maples is based in part on F.T. Ledig and D.R. Korbobo. 1983. Adaptation of sugar maple along altitudinal gradients: photosynthesis, respiration, and specific leaf weight. *American Journal of Botany,* 70:256–265.
29. Robert L. Park. 1998. Scientists and their political passions. *The New York Times,* May 2.
30. The discussion of steelhead is based on Ellen Morris Bishop. 1998. Years of adapting separate steelhead from hatchery cousins. *Corvallis Gazette-Times* (Corvallis, OR), March 5, and Jeff Barnard. 1998. Columbia steelhead listed as threatened. *Corvallis Gazette-Times* (Corvallis, OR), March 14.
31. Todd Lewan. 1997. Study: half of the Amazon is ready to go up in smoke. *Corvallis Gazette-Times* (Corvallis, OR), December 4.
32. Michael Astor. 1997. Scientist uncovers new species in Brazil. *Corvallis Gazette-Times* (Corvallis, OR), December 28.
33. The discussion of Lake Erie is based on Frank N. Egerton. 1987. Pollution and aquatic life in Lake Erie: early scientific studies. *Environmental Review,* 11:189–205, and Robert Cooke. 1991. Lake Erie has improved, but complete recovery is unlikely. *The Oregonian* (Portland, OR), June 16.
34. Ed Ayres. 1997. Outcompeting ourselves. *WorldWatch,* 10(5):3–4.
35. John Tuxill. 1997. Death in the family tree. *WorldWatch,* 10(5):13–21.
36. The following discussion of Zion National Park is based in part on A.J. Eardley and James W. Schaack. 1989. *Zion, The Story Behind the Scenery,* KC Publications, Las Vegas, 46 pp.
37. The discussion of how a change in arctic vegetation might have triggered an ice age is based on Knight-Ridder Tribune New Service. 1996. Ice age theory looks at plants. *Corvallis Gazette-Times* (Corvallis, OR), August 11.
38. Christopher Flavin. 1996. Facing up to the risks of climate change. pp. 21–39 in *State of the World 1996: A Worldwatch Institute Report on Progress Toward a Sustainable Society,* Lester R. Brown, Janet Abramovitz, Chris Bright, et al. (Eds.), W.W. Norton, New York.
39. The discussion of short-term climatic patterns is based on Carl Holcombe. 1997. Thinking globally. *Corvallis Gazette-Times* (Corvallis, OR), January 5; Brian Meehan. 1996. An ocean of trouble. *The Oregonian* (Portland, OR), December 8; OSU (Oregon State University) News Service. 1998. Biologist: it's not just El Niño. *Corvallis Gazette-Times* (Corvallis, OR), January 7; S. Stouder. 1997. Winds of change? *Corvallis Gazette-Times* (Corvallis, OR), October 23; Brad Cain. 1998. Ancient stumps rise from Oregon surf. *Corvallis Gazette-Times* (Corvallis, OR), March 12; Larissa Lùbomudrov. 1997. El Niño, Oregon State University Sea Grant Collage, Corvallis, 8 pp; *Corvallis Gazette-Times* (Corvallis, OR). 1998. Fire out of control. March 17; Michael Astor. 1998. Yanomami see apocalypse in Amazon forest wildfires. *Corvallis*

Gazette-Times (Corvallis, OR), March 19; Fred L. Nials, Eric E. Deeds, Michael Mosley, Shelia G. Prozorski, Thomas G. Prozorski, and Robert Feldman. 1979. El Niño: the catastrophic flooding of coastal Peru. *Field Museum of Natural History Bulletin*, 50(7):4–14; Fred L. Nials, Eric E. Deeds, Michael Mosley, Shelia G. Prozorski, Thomas G. Prozorski, and Robert Feldman. 1979. El Niño: the catastrophic flooding of coastal Peru. *Field Museum of Natural History Bulletin*, 50(8):4–10; William H. Quinn, Victor T. Neal, and Santiago E. Antunez de Mayolo. 1987. El Niño occurrences over the past four and a half centuries. *Journal of Geophysical Research*, 92:14,449–14,461.

40. John K. Wiley. 1998. Asian storm dusts part of West. *Corvallis Gazette-Times* (Corvallis, OR), May 1.

41. The following discussion of heat is based on Randolph E. Schmid. 1998. Heat: a common killer. *Corvallis Gazette-Times* (Corvallis, OR), July 24.

42. Joseph B. Verrengia. 1998. Study: global warming could result in spread of grasslands, wildfire. *Corvallis Gazette-Times* (Corvallis, OR), August 5.

43. Lester R. Brown. 1996. The acceleration of history. pp. 3–20 in *State of the World 1996: A Worldwatch Institute Report on Progress Toward a Sustainable Society*, Lester R. Brown, Janet Abramovitz, Chris Bright, et al. (Eds.), W.W. Norton, New York.

44. D.W. Schindler, K.G. Beaty, E.J. Fee, D.R. Cruikshank, et al. 1990. Effects of climatic warming on lakes of the central boreal forest. *Science*, 250:967–970.

45. Steve Newman. 1998. Earthweek: a diary of the planet. *Corvallis Gazette-Times* (Corvallis, OR), July 5.

46. Steve Newman. 1998. Earthweek: a diary of the planet. *Corvallis Gazette-Times* (Corvallis, OR), February 8.

47. M.J. Jarvis, B. Jenkins, and G.A. Rodgers. 1998. Southern hemisphere observations of a long-term decrease in F region altitude and thermospheric wind providing possible evidence for global thermosphere cooling. *Journal of Geophysical Research*, 103(A9):20,774–20,787.

48. The Associated Press. 1995. Experts call extinction rates "alarming." *Corvallis Gazette-Times* (Corvallis, OR), November 19.

49. The Associated Press. 1995. U.N. report sounds alarm on dying species. *Corvallis Gazette-Times* (Corvallis, OR), November 14.

50. The following discussion of the treaty formulated in Kyoto, Japan, is based on H. Josef Hebert. 1998. Opposition to global warming treaty try to bar talk about it. *Corvallis Gazette-Times* (Corvallis, OR), July 7.

51. The speech given by Theodore Roosevelt in 1908 was reprinted under the title "The First Environmental President" in the Forum section of *The Sunday Oregonian* (Portland, OR), July 22, 1990.

52. Richard Read. 1991. Turtle-shell artisans say craft endangered. *The Oregonian* (Portland, OR), June 16.

53. Victor Frankl. 1963. *Man's Search for Meaning*, Pocket Books, New York.

54. Sue Cross. 1987. Pair rescue legends as Tlingit tongue dies. *Corvallis Gazette-Times* (Corvallis, OR), November 15.
55. Eloise Salholz, David L. Gonzalez, Harry Hurt III, and Pat Wingert. 1989. Say it in English. *Newsweek,* February 20:22–23.
56. Richard Gallagher and Betsy Carpenter. 1997. Human-dominated ecosystems. *Science,* 277:485.
57. The discussion of the overuse of antibiotics is based on The Associated Press. 1998. Overuse of antibiotics threatens world health. *Corvallis Gazette-Times* (Corvallis, OR), May 15.
58. Lyric Wallwork Winik. 1998. Before the next epidemic strikes. *Parade Magazine,* February 8:6–9.
59. The following discussion is based on Oregon State University News Service. 1998. Lubchenco: environment deserves top priority. *Corvallis Gazette-Times* (Corvallis, OR), January 27, and Peter M. Vitousek, Harold A. Mooney, Jane Lubchenco, and Jerry M. Melillo. 1997. Human domination of earth's ecosystems. *Science,* 277:494–499.
60. The following discussion is based on I.G. Simmons. 1988. The earliest cultural landscapes of England. *Environmental Review,* 12:105–116.
61. F.F.H. Allen and Thomas W. Hoekstra. 1994. Toward a definition of sustainability. pp. 98–107 in Sustainable Ecological Systems: Implementing an Ecological Approach to Land Management, W. Wallace Covington and Leonard F. DeBano (Technical Coordinators), USDA Forest Service General Technical Report RM-247, Rocky Mountain Forest and Range Experiment Station, U.S. Department of Agriculture, Fort Collins, CO.
62. *The Holy Bible, Authorized King James Version,* World Bible Publishers, Iowa Falls, IA, Numbers 35:34.
63. The discussion about the importance of soil in this paragraph is based on G.C. Daily, P.A. Matson, and P.M. Vitousek. 1997. Ecosystem services supplied by soil. pp. 113–132 in *Nature's Services: Societal Dependence on Natural Ecosystems,* G. Daily (Ed.), Island Press, Washington, D.C., and Gretchen C. Daily, Susan Alexander, Paul R. Ehrlich, Larry Goulder, Jane Lubchenco, et al. 1997. Ecosystem services: benefits supplied to human societies by natural ecosystems. *Issues in Ecology,* 2:1–16.
64. L.R. Oldeman, V. van Engelen, and J. Pulles. 1990. The extent of human-induced soil degradation. Annex 5 in *World Map of the Status of Human-Induced Soil Degradation: An Explanatory Note,* rev. 2nd ed., L.R. Oldeman, R.T.A. Hakkeling, and W.G. Sombroek (Eds.), International Soil Reference and Information Centre, Wageningen.
65. The discussion of the formation of soil is taken from Mark Ferns. 1995. Geologic evolution of the Blue Mountains region, the role of geology in soil formation. *Natural Resource News,* 5:2–3, 17; Rob Marvin. 1991. The Earth churns, moans, breathes, and the "living rocks" keep rollin' on. *The Oregonian* (Portland, OR), April 18; James L. Clayton. 1995. Processes of soil

formation. *Natural Resource News,* 5:4–6; David D. Alt and Donald W. Hyndman. 1978. *Roadside Geology of Oregon,* Mountain Press, Missoula, MT, 268 pp; Dwight R. Crandell. 1965. The glacial history of western Washington and Oregon. pp. 341–353 in *The Quaternary of the United States,* J.E. Wright, Jr. and David G. Frey (Eds.), Princeton University Press, Princeton, NJ; S.N. Dicken and E.F. Dicken. 1979. *The Making of Oregon: A Study in Historical Geography,* Vol. 1, Oregon Historical Society, Portland, 207 pp; Alan E. Harvey. 1995. Soil and the forest floor: what it is, how it works, and how to treat it. *Natural Resource News,* 5:6–9; and Elaine R. Ingham. 1995. Organisms in the soil: the functions of bacteria, fungi, protozoa, nematodes, and arthropods. *Natural Resource News,* 5:10–12, 16–17.

66. The paragraph on agricultural pollution is based on Curt Anderson. 1998. Ag is biggest river polluter. *Corvallis Gazette-Times* (Corvallis, OR), May 17.

67. The following discussion of the indigenous peoples of the Americas is based on Martin A. Baumhoff and Robert F. Heizer. 1967. Postglacial climate and archaeology in the desert West. pp. 697–707 in *The Quaternary of the United States,* J.E. Wright, Jr. and D.G. Frey (Eds.), Princeton University Press, Princeton, NJ; James B. Griffin. 1967. Late Quaternary prehistory in the northeastern woodlands. pp. 655–667 in *The Quaternary of the United States,* J.E. Wright, Jr. and D.G. Frey (Eds.), Princeton University Press, Princeton, NJ; Clement W. Meighan. 1967. Pacific coast archaeology. pp. 709–720 in *The Quaternary of the United States,* J.E. Wright, Jr. and D.G. Frey (Eds.), Princeton University Press, Princeton, NJ; Robert L. Stephenson. 1967. Quaternary human occupation of the plains. pp. 685–696 in *The Quaternary of the United States,* J.E. Wright, Jr. and D.G. Frey (Eds.), Princeton University Press, Princeton, NJ; Stephen Williams and James B. Stoltman. 1967. An outline of southeastern United States prehistory with particular emphasis on the Paleo-Indian era. pp. 669–683 in *The Quaternary of the United States,* J.E. Wright, Jr. and D.G. Frey (Eds.), Princeton University Press, Princeton, NJ; Martyn J. Bowden. 1992. The invention of American tradition. *Journal of Historical Geography,* 18:3–26; Allan Chen. 1987. Unraveling another Mayan mystery. *Discover,* June:40, 44, 46, 48–49; K.A. Deagan. 1987. La Navidad, 1492: searching for Columbus's lost colony. *National Geographic,* 172:672–675; William M. Denevan. 1992. The pristine myth: the landscape of the Americas in 1492. *Annals of the Association of American Geographers,* 82:369–385; W. George Lovell. 1992. Heavy shadows and black night: disease and depopulation in colonial Spanish America. *Annals of the Association of American Geographers,* 82:426–443; Philadelphia. 1998. First Americans 30,000 years ago. *Corvallis Gazette-Times* (Corvallis, OR), February 17; Richard L. Hill. 1998. Digs in Peru and linguistics may prove humans lived in the Western Hemisphere 33,000 years ago. *The Oregonian* (Portland, OR), February 17; Kim A. McDonald. 1998. New evidence challenges traditional model of how the New World was settled. *The Chronicle of Higher Education,* March 13:A22–A23; S.M. Wilson. 1992. That unmanned

wild country: Native Americans both conserved and transformed New World environments. *Natural History,* May:16–17; The Associated Press. 1998. New evidence suggests ancient immigrants came by boat. *Corvallis Gazette-Times* (Corvallis, OR), August 24; and Dr. Rob Bonnichsen, Director for the Study of First Americans, Department of Anthropology, Oregon State University, Corvallis, personal communication.

68. Robert V. Hine. 1980. *Community on the American Frontier,* University of Oklahoma Press, Norman.

69. This discussion is based on Gerard Stropnicky. 1998. Naked history: 200 years of letters to the editor, excerpted from *Letters to the Editor: Two Hundred Years in the Life of an American Town,* Touchstone/Simon & Schuster, New York. The excerpt appeared in the *Corvallis Gazette-Times* (Corvallis, OR), July 21.

70. John G. Neihardt. 1961. *Black Elk Speaks,* University of Nebraska, Lincoln.

71. Wendell Berry. 1990. The road and the wheel. *Earth Ethics,* 1:8–9.

72. Clyde S. Martin. 1940. Forest resources, cutting practices, and utilization problems in the pine region of the Pacific Northwest. *Journal of Forestry,* 38:681–685.

73. Joseph Campbell. 1988. *The Power of Myth,* Doubleday, New York.

74. The following discussion of North Dakota is based on Robert V. Bartlett. 1988. Adapt or get out: the Garrison Diversion project and controversy. *Environmental Review,* 12:57–74.

75. Donald Worster. 1985. *Rivers of Empire: Water, Aridity, and the Growth of the American West,* Pantheon Books, New York.

76. Wallace Stegner. 1987. The function of aridity. *Wilderness,* Fall:17–18.

77. The following discussion is based on George Monbiot. 1997. Land reform in Britain. *Resurgence,* 181:4–8, and Rebecca Adamson. 1997. People who are indigenous to the Earth. *YES! A Journal of Positive Futures,* Winter:26–27.

78. The following discussion is based on Hanns J. Prem. 1992. Spanish colonization and indian property in central Mexico, 1521–1620. *Annals of the Association of American Geographers,* 82:444–459, and Susana Hayward. 1987. Land's wealth may doom remote tribe. *Corvallis Gazette-Times* (Corvallis, OR), December 27.

79. Steve Newman. 1998. Earthweek: a diary of the planet. *Corvallis Gazette-Times* (Corvallis, OR), February 22.

80. The discussion of the freedom of the market in this section is based on Noam Chomsky. 1995. How free is the free market? *Resurgence,* 173:6–9, and Samuel Huntington. 1997. Westernization of the world. *Resurgence,* 182:14–15.

81. Frances Hutchinson. 1995. We are all economists. *Resurgence,* 173:57.

82. George Monbiot. 1998. The gene debate. *Resurgence,* 188:7.

83. Alastair McIntosh. 1998. The cult of biotechnology. *Resurgence,* 188:8–11.

84. This and the next paragraph are based on Alan Simpson. 1998. Soul ownership. *Resurgence,* 188:12–14.

85. Helena Paul. 1998. Colonization of life. *Resurgence,* 188:14–15.

86. Seth Shulman. 1995. Patent medicine. *Technology Review,* 98:28–36.

87. Ashok Sharma. 1995. Poor countries want control over resources. *Corvallis Gazette-Times* (Corvallis, OR), October 22.

88. K.D. McCormick, M.A. Deyrup, E.S. Menges, S.R. Wallace, et al. 1993. Relevance of chemistry to conservation of isolated populations: the case of volatile leaf components of *Dicerandra* mints. *Proceedings of the National Academy of Sciences U.S.A.,* 90:7701–7705, and N. Myers. 1983. *A Wealth of Wild Species,* Westview Press, Boulder, CO.

89. Alan Ereira. 1995. Mayan medicine. *Resurgence,* 173:59.

90. *Corvallis Gazette-Times* (Corvallis, OR). 1996. Blood, sweat and science. April 21.

91. Scott Sonner. 1998. Lawsuit tries to block "bio-prospecting" at Yellowstone Park. *Corvallis Gazette-Times* (Corvallis, OR), March 8.

92. The following discussion of intellectual property is based on Vandana Shiva. 1997. The second coming of Columbus. *Resurgence,* 182:12–13.

93. The discussion of the new ethnobotany is based on Barbara Johnston. 1998. The new ethnobotany: sharing with those who shared: an interview with Michael Balick and Rosita Arvigo. *HerbalGram,* 42:60–63.

94. The following discussion of biopiracy is based on Lester R. Brown. 1997. Can we raise grain yields fast enough? *WorldWatch,* 10:8–17; Andrew Kimbrell. 1997. Breaking the law of life. *Resurgence,* 182:10–11; Malcolm Ritter. 1997. Scientists clone adult mammal for first time. *Corvallis Gazette-Times* (Corvallis, OR), February 24; James Webb. 1998. Scientist says he'll clone human. *Corvallis Gazette-Times* (Corvallis, OR), January 8; Kelly Wiseman. 1998. Get ready for bioengineered foods. *The Thymes,* February:7; Amy Knutson. 1998. Diminishing diversity. *The Growing Edge,* 3:32–35; The Washington Post. 1998. Scientist files for patent on way to make part-humans. *Corvallis Gazette-Times* (Corvallis, OR), April 3; Jennifer Nagorka. 1988. Clear policy needed on gene patents. *Corvallis Gazette-Times* (Corvallis, OR), April 10; and Jeremy Rifkin. 1998. God in a labcoat. *Unte Reader,* May–June:66–71.

95. Ricarda Steinbrecher. 1998. What is wrong with Nature? *Resurgence,* 188:16–19.

96. Malcolm Ritter. 1997. Scientists clone adult mammal for first time. *Corvallis Gazette-Times* (Corvallis, OR), February 24.

97. James Webb. 1998. Scientist says he'll clone human. *Corvallis Gazette-Times* (Corvallis, OR), January 8.

98. John Hendren. 1998. Cloning debate moves to states. *Corvallis Gazette-Times* (Corvallis, OR), March 18.

99. Boston Globe. 1998. Wife to carry clone. *Corvallis Gazette-Times* (Corvallis, OR), September 7.

100. Mark Harris. 1998. To be or not to be? *Vegetarian Times,* June:64–70.

101. David Suzuki and P. Knudtson. 1988. *Genethics, The Ethics of Engineering Life,* Stoddart Publishing, Toronto, Canada, 384 pp.

102. The discussion of superweeds is based on Jeff Barnard. 1998. Genetic engineering may spawn "super weed." *Corvallis Gazette-Times* (Corvallis, OR), September 3.

103. The discussion of farming is based on John Kinsman. 1995. Republican reforms threaten family farms. *Corvallis Gazette-Times* (Corvallis, OR), November 12.

104. *Corvallis Gazette-Times* (Corvallis, OR). 1997. Mass-produced salmonella. December 24.

105. The discussion of forest ownership is based on Tracy Loew. 1995. Coast Range's private forest land controlled by a few, study says. *Corvallis Gazette-Times* (Corvallis, OR), November 9.

106. Wendell Berry. 1995. Conserving communities. *Resurgence*, 170:6–11.

107. David Orr. 1995. Conservatives against conservation. *Resurgence*, 172:15–17.

108. Steve Newman. 1998. Earthweek: a diary of the planet. *Corvallis Gazette-Times* (Corvallis, OR), September 6.

109. Chris Maser, E. Wayne Hammer, and Murray L. Johnson. 1969. Abnormal coloration in *Microtus montanus*. *Murrelet,* 50:39.

110. The discussion of toxic wastes in fertilizer is based on Duff Wilson. 1998. Toxic wastes being used as fertilizers. *Corvallis Gazette-Times* (Corvallis, OR), March 27.

111. The discussion on animal wastes is based on H. Josef Hebert. 1998. Rules proposed for livestock waste. *Corvallis Gazette-Times* (Corvallis, OR), March 8.

112. The discussion of pollution in the waters of Dixon Creek is based on Scott MacWilliams. 1998. What's in the water? *Corvallis Gazette-Times* (Corvallis, OR), February 14.

113. The discussion of the Aswan High Dam is based on personal experience and C.J. George. 1972. The role of the Aswan Dam in changing fisheries of the south-western Mediterranean. in *The Careless Technology,* M.T. Farvar and J.P. Milton (Eds.), Natural History Press, New York.

114. R.G. Johnson. 1997. Climate control requires a dam at the Strait of Gibraltar. *EOS, Transactions, American Geophysical Union,* 78:277–281.

115. R.G. Johnson. 1997. Ice age initiation by an ocean–atmospheric circulation change in the Labrador Sea. *Earth Planetary Science Letters,* 148:367.

116. The following comments on risk are gleaned from B. John Garrick. 1997. Society must come to terms with risk. *Corvallis Gazette-Times* (Corvallis, OR), November 9.

117. The Associated Press. 1997. Ah-choo, Arizona no longer haven for allergy sufferers. *Corvallis Gazette-Times* (Corvallis, OR), March 25.

118. The Associated Press. 1998. Hair spray, lawn mowers blamed for dirtying air. *Corvallis Gazette-Times* (Corvallis, OR), March 7.

119. Steve Newman. 1998. Earthweek: a diary of the planet. *Corvallis Gazette-Times* (Corvallis, OR), April 17.

120. Aaron Corvin. 1998. Importing raw logs would be dangerous, forum panelists warn. *Corvallis Gazette-Times* (Corvallis, OR), July 8.

121. The Associated Press. 1998. Impact of salt on Mount Hood ski slopes still unknown. *Corvallis Gazette-Times* (Corvallis, OR), August 25.

122. Steve Newman. 1998. Earthweek: a diary of the planet. *Corvallis Gazette-Times* (Corvallis, OR), March 1.

123. The following discussion of the living soil crust is based on The Associated Press. 1998. "Skin" that shields range is disappearing. *Corvallis Gazette-Times* (Corvallis, OR), July 26.

124. The discussion of Owens Lake is based on The Associated Press. 1998. Historic deal to end Owens Lake dust. *Corvallis Gazette-Times* (Corvallis, OR), July 17.

125. The Associated Press. 1998. Four-wheelers damage meadow in national forest. *Corvallis Gazette-Times* (Corvallis, OR), July 24.

126. Jane Lubchenco. 1998. Entering the century of the environment: a new social contract for science. *Science,* 279:491–497.

127. Garrett Hardin. 1986. Cultural carrying capacity: a biological approach to human problems. *BioScience,* 36:599–606.

128. Leo Tumerman. 1986. *Corvallis Gazette-Times* (Corvallis, OR), April 29.

129. Greg Beacham. 1988. State attorneys question safety of nuclear waste facility and its dangerous neighbors. *Corvallis Gazette-Times* (Corvallis, OR), January 29.

130. Richard Cole. 1998. Feds agree to increase safety for nuke shipments. *Corvallis Gazette-Times* (Corvallis, OR), January 30.

131. The Associated Press. 1998. Professor to teach homelessness class based on experience. *Corvallis Gazette-Times* (Corvallis, OR), March 1.

132. The discussion of the extinction of domestic animals is based on The Associated Press. 1996. Should we save pandas and pigs? *Corvallis Gazette-Times* (Corvallis, OR), January 21.

133. The Associated Press. 1986. Nepal tree-planting fight provokes new scrutiny. *Corvallis Gazette-Times* (Corvallis, OR), June 6.

134. The following discussion of the town of Riddle, Douglas County, in southwestern Oregon is based on The Associated Press. 1998. Falling prices force Glenbrook Nickel to call it quits. *Corvallis Gazette-Times* (Corvallis, OR), January 31.

135. The following discussion of Charleston, Coos County, Oregon, is based on Joseph B. Frazier. 1998. Fishing limits hurting coastal communities. *Corvallis Gazette-Times* (Corvallis, OR), March 14.

136. Louis W. Botsford, Jean Carlos Castilla, and Charles H. Peterson. 1997. The management of fisheries and marine ecosystems. *Science,* 277:509–515.

137. The discussion of talents follows Laurence G. Boldt. 1993. *Zen and the Art of Making a Living,* Penguin/Arkana, New York.

138. John Addington Symonds. no date. *The Life of Michelangelo,* Carlton House, New York.

139. Sarah van Gelder. 1997. Beyond greed & scarcity. *YES! A Journal of Positive Futures,* Spring:34–39.

140. The following discussion of the difference between money and wealth is based on David C. Korten. 1997. Money versus wealth. *YES! A Journal of Positive Futures,* Spring:14–18.

141. The following discussion of water is based on Deborah Seward. 1998. 1 billion people lack access to clean water. *Corvallis Gazette-Times* (Corvallis, OR), March 22.

142. The discussion of people building along shores is based on Roberta Ulrich. 1991. Growth fuels coastal-protection laws. *The Oregonian* (Portland, OR), June 16.

143. The following discussion of the endangered homes at The Capes at Oceanside, a small town along the northern Oregon coast, is based on The Associated Press. 1998. Officials weigh action to save beach homes. *Corvallis Gazette-Times* (Corvallis, OR), February 10; Brad Cain. 1998. Neighbor turns against neighbor as homes hang on crumbling dune. *Corvallis Gazette-Times* (Corvallis, OR), February 11; The Associated Press. 1998. Local officials reject plan to save beach townhomes. *Corvallis Gazette-Times* (Corvallis, OR), February 12; Brad Cain. 1998. Governor to homeowners: no emergency help. *Corvallis Gazette-Times* (Corvallis, OR), February 13; The Associated Press. 1998. Homeowners warn of damage if houses fall onto beach. *Corvallis Gazette-Times* (Corvallis, OR), February 20; The Associated Press. 1998. Cliffside houses seemed like a good idea. *Corvallis Gazette-Times* (Corvallis, OR), February 23; The Associated Press. 1998. Owners of endangered homes look to new plan. *Corvallis Gazette-Times* (Corvallis, OR), March 9; The Associated Press. 1998. Erosion slows at The Capes. *Corvallis Gazette-Times* (Corvallis, OR), March 13; and The Associated Press. 1998. Plan to save homes gets tentative OK. *Corvallis Gazette-Times* (Corvallis, OR), March 17.

144. Lawrence L. Knutson. 1998. Americans sunward bound. *Corvallis Gazette-Times* (Corvallis, OR), March 18.

145. Laurence Arnold. 1998. White House tries to curb controversial sand pumping. *Corvallis Gazette-Times* (Corvallis, OR), March 8.

146. The discussion of the loss of biological diversity in Hawaii is based on Daniel B. Wood. 1991. Report details decline of Hawaiian paradise. *The Oregonian* (Portland, OR), November 7, a joint report that took a decade for the U.S. Fish and Wildlife Service, the Hawaii Department of Land and Natural Resources, and The Nature Conservancy of Hawaii to prepare, and Rocky Baker. 1995. Mending fences: lessons in island biodiversity protection from Hawai'i. *East–West Center Working Papers: Environmental Series,* 45:1–46.

147. The discussion on salmon and steelhead in the Columbia River is based on Scott Stouder. 1997. Coho need more than volunteers. *Corvallis Gazette-Times* (Corvallis, OR), March 27; Bob Baum. 1998. BPA urges barging fish.

Corvallis Gazette-Times (Corvallis, OR), January 24; The Associated Press. 1998. Feds to irrigation district: get rid of dam. *Corvallis Gazette-Times* (Corvallis, OR), February 14; Rocky Barker. 1998. Saving salmon. *Corvallis Gazette-Times* (Corvallis, OR), February 26; George Tibbits. 1998. Feds propose endangered listing for Puget Sound, California chinook. *Corvallis Gazette-Times* (Corvallis, OR), February 27; The Associated Press. 1998. Panel opposes federal salmon barging plan. *Corvallis Gazette-Times* (Corvallis, OR), March 6; The Associated Press. 1998. Breaching dams wouldn't bankrupt the BPA, study says. *Corvallis Gazette-Times* (Corvallis, OR), March 18; Cathy Kessinger. 1998. The cost of saving a species. *Corvallis Gazette-Times* (Corvallis, OR), March 29; C.J. Chivers. 1998. An old dam gives way to old man river. *USA Today*, May 6; and The Associated Press. 1998. Study: Willamette among nation's least healthy rivers. *Corvallis Gazette-Times* (Corvallis, OR), May 31.

148. The discussion of invasive plants and animals is based on Daniel Simberloff. 1998. New tactics could halt invasion of harmful species. *Corvallis Gazette-Times* (Corvallis, OR), March 1.

149. Lisa Marinelli. 1998. Hawaii lawmakers propose plan to protect exotic fish. *Corvallis Gazette-Times* (Corvallis, OR), February 15.

150. Karen F. Schmidt. 1997. "No-take" zones spark fisheries debate. *Science*, 277:489–491.

151. Kirk Talbott. 1993. *Central Africa's Forests: The Second Greatest Forest System on Earth*, World Resources Institute, Washington, D.C., January.

152. The discussion of purposefully, illegally destroying someone else's land for profit is based on The Associated Press. 1998. Dam protecting sensitive wetland destroyed. *Corvallis Gazette-Times* (Corvallis, OR), February 6.

153. The following story is based on The Associated Press. 1998. Mayor fights federal basin study. *Corvallis Gazette-Times* (Corvallis, OR), March 8.

154. C.J. De Loach. 1971. The effect of habitat diversity on predation. *Proceedings Tall Timber Conference on Ecological Animal Control by Habitat Management*, 2:223–241.

155. David Pimentel. 1971. Population control in crop systems: monocultures and plant spatial patterns. *Proceedings Tall Timber Conference on Ecological Animal Control by Habitat Management*, 2:209–220.

156. Jay Walljasper. 1977. Chairman X. *Resurgence*, 182:41.

157. N.W. Moore, M.D. Hooper, and B.N.K. Davis. 1967. Hedges. I. Introduction and reconnaissance studies. *Journal of Applied Ecology*, 4:201–220.

158. P.A. Matson, W.J. Parton, A.G. Power, and M.J. Swift. 1997. Agricultural intensification and ecosystem properties. *Science*, 277:504–509.

159. The Associated Press. 1998. Butterfly found in Polk County. *Corvallis Gazette-Times* (Corvallis, OR), March 9.

160. The following discussion of lost diversity in agricultural crops is based on Amy Knutson. 1998. Diminishing diversity. *The Growing Edge*, 3:32–35.

161. Geoff Mulgan. 1997. Connexity, how to live in a connected world. *Resurgence,* 184:6–7.

162. Chris Maser. 1999. *Vision and Leadership in Sustainable Development,* Lewis Publishers, Boca Raton, FL.

163. Geoffrey Hill. 1996. The sacredness of space. *Creation Spirituality,* 12:31–33.

164. The following discussion of forests in the area of Puget Sound, Washington, is based on J. Martin Mcomber. 1998. Study shows Puget Sound forests are slowly thinning. *Corvallis Gazette-Times* (Corvallis, OR), July 15.

165. Rick Patterson and Jan Aiels. 1998. Iowa restoration becomes a community project. *Land and Water,* 42:43–45.

166. The discussion of Bill McDonald is based on Arthur H. Rotstein. 1998. Genius at home on the range. *Corvallis Gazette-Times* (Corvallis, OR), June 22.

167. The brief discussion on the scarcity of water is drawn from my own experience; Roar Bjonnes. 1997. Sweet water and bitter. *Resurgence,* 181:32–34; and Paul Simon. 1998. From an excerpt of his new book, *Tapped Out,* which appeared in *Parade Magazine,* August 23:4–6.

168. Chris Maser. 1989. *Forest Primeval: The Natural History of an Ancient Forest,* Sierra Club Books, San Francisco, 282 pp.

169. Chris Maser. 1994. *Sustainable Forestry: Philosophy, Science, and Economics,* St. Lucie Press, Boca Raton, FL, 371 pp.

170. The following discussion about restoring part of the Snake River to a more natural condition is based on Jim Robbins. 1998. Engineers plan to send a river flowing back to nature. *The New York Times,* May 12.

171. Chris Maser and James R. Sedell. 1994. *From the Forest to the Sea: The Ecology of Wood in Streams, Rivers, Estuaries, and Oceans,* St. Lucie Press, Boca Raton, FL, 200 pp.

172. For good examples of how to repair riparian areas see Steve Apfelbaum and Jack Broughton. 1988. Applying an ecological systems approach in urban landscapes. *Land and Water,* 42:6–9, and David Lee and Jim Lovell. 1998. Urban trout stream gets a second chance. *Land and Water,* 42:16–19.

173. The discussion of congestion and transportation is based on Bill Bishop. 1998. To reduce congestion, don't build more roads—close 'em. *Corvallis Gazette-Times* (Corvallis, OR), May 20.

REFERENCES

Allison, Ira S. 1966. Fossil Lake, Oregon, its geology and fossil faunas. *Oregon State University Studies in Geology,* 9:1–48.

Bak, Per and Kan Chen. 1991. Self-organizing criticality. *Scientific American,* 267:46–53.

Bird, E.A.R. 1987. The social construction of nature: theoretical approaches to the history of environmental problems. *Environmental Review,* 11:255–264.

Botkin, D.B. 1979. A grandfather clock down the staircase: stability and disturbance in natural ecosystems. pp. 1–10 in *Forests: Fresh Perspectives from Ecosystem Analysis,* R.H. Waring (Ed.), Proc. 40th Annu. Biol. Colloquium, Oregon State University Press, Corvallis.

Broad, D. 1995. Globalization versus labor. *Monthly Review,* 47(7):20–31.

Carter, V.G. and T. Dale. 1974. *Topsoil and Civilization,* rev. ed., University of Oklahoma Press, Norman.

Davis, Margaret B. 1989. Lags in vegetation response to greenhouse warming. *Climatic Change,* 15:75–82.

DeAngelis, D.L., W.M. Post, and C.C. Travis. 1986. *Positive Feedback in Natural Systems,* Springer-Verlag, Berlin.

Dillon, L.S. 1956. Wisconsin climate and life zones in North America. *Science,* 123:167–176.

Dix, R.L. 1964. A history of biotic and climatic changes within the North American grassland. pp. 71–89 in *Grazing in Terrestrial and Marine Environments,* D.J. Crisp (Ed.), Blackwell Science Publishing, England.

Dobson, Andy, Alison Jolly, and Dan Rubenstein. 1989. The greenhouse effect and biological diversity. *Tree,* 4:64–68.

Dobzhansky, T. 1937. What is a species? *Scientia,* 61:280–286.

Dobzhansky, T. 1970. *Genetics of the Evolutionary Process,* Columbia University Press, New York.

Dorf, E. 1960. Climatic changes of the past and present. *American Scientist,* 48:341–346.

Fetcher, N. and G.R. Shaver. 1990. Environmental sensitivity of ecotypes as a potential influence on primary productivity. *American Naturalist,* 136:126–131.

397

Franklin, J.F. and R.T.T. Forman. 1987. Creating landscape patterns by forest cutting: ecological consequences and principles. *Landscape Ecology,* 1:5–18.

Fryer, J.H. and F.T. Ledig. 1972. Microevolution of the photosynthetic temperature optimum in relation to the elevational complex gradient. *Canadian Journal of Botany,* 50:1231–1235.

Gaiser, R.N. 1952. Root channels and roots in forest soils. *Soil Science Society of America Proceedings,* 16:62–65.

Gardner, G. 1996. Preserving agricultural resources. pp. 78–94 in *State of the World 1996: A Worldwatch Institute Report on Progress Toward a Sustainable Society,* Lester R. Brown, Janet Abramovitz, Chris Bright, et al. (Eds.), W.W. Norton, New York.

Ghiselin, M.R. 1974. A radical solution to the species problem. *Systematic Zoology,* 23:536–544.

Graham, A. and C. Heimsch. 1960. Pollen studies of some Texas peat deposits. *Ecology,* 41:751–763.

Grayson, Donald K. 1977. On the Holocene history of some northern Great Basin lagomorphs. *Journal of Mammalogy,* 58:507–513.

Grayson, Donald K. 1979. Mount Mazama, climatic change, and Fort Rock Basin archaeofaunas. pp. 427–457 in *Volcanic Activity and Human Ecology,* Academic Press, New York.

Grayson, Donald K. 1987. The biogeographic history of small mammals in the Great Basin: observations on the last 20,000 years. *Journal of Mammalogy,* 68:359–375.

Guilday, J.E., P.W. Parmalee, and H.W. Hamilton. 1977. The Clark's Cave bone deposits and the late Pleistocene paleoecology of the Central Appalachian Mountains of Virginia. *Carnegie Museum of Natural History Bulletin,* 2:1–87.

Hardin, G. 1984. An ecolate view of the human predicament. *The Environmental Fund, Monograph Series,* pp. 1–14.

Harmon, M.E., W.K. Ferrel, and J.F. Franklin. 1990. Effects on carbon storage of conversion for old-growth forests to young forests. *Science,* 247:699–702.

Harris, L.D. 1984. *The Fragmented Forest,* University of Chicago Press, Chicago, 211 pp.

Heichelheim, F.M. 1956. The effects of classical antiquity on the land. pp. 165–182 in *Man's Role in Changing the Face of the Earth,* W.L. Thomas (Ed.), University of Chicago Press, Chicago.

Hillinger, C. 1987. Russia's colony in America. *Corvallis Gazette-Times* (Corvallis, OR), December 27.

Hoekstra, T.W., T.F.H. Allen, and Curtis H. Flather. 1991. Implicit scaling in ecological research, on when to make studies of mice and men. *BioScience,* 41:148–154.

Holling, C.S. 1973. Resilience and stability of ecological systems. *Annual Review of Ecological Systems,* 4:1–24.

Hopkins, D.M. 1959. Cenozoic history of the Bering Land Bridge. *Science,* 129: 1519–1528.

Illich, I. 1990. The shadow our future throws. *Earth Ethics,* 1:3–5.

James, W. 1982. *The Varieties of Religious Experience,* Penguin Books, New York.

Jordan, W.R., III. 1986. Restoration and the reentry of nature. *Orion,* 5:14–25.

Jung, C.G. 1960. On the nature of the psyche. pp. 159–234 in *The Collected Works of C.G. Jung,* Vol. 8, H. Read et al. (Eds.), Pantheon, New York.

Kennedy, C.B., J.L. Sell, and E.H. Zube. 1988. Landscape aesthetics and geography. *Environmental Review,* 12:31–55.

Koopes, C.R. 1987. Efficiency/equity/esthetics: towards a reinterpretation of American conservation. *Environmental Review,* 11:127–146.

Kriebel, H.B. 1957. Patterns of Genetic Variation in Sugar Maple, Ohio Agricultural Experiment Station Research Bulletin 791, Wooster, OH.

Lancaster, J. 1991. Public land, private profit. *Journal of Forestry,* 89:20–22.

Laszlo, E. 1985. The crucial epoch. *Futures,* February:2–23.

Lowdermilk, W.C. 1975. Conquest of the Land Through Seven Thousand Years, Agricultural Information Bulletin No. 99, Soil Conservation Service, U.S. Department of Agriculture, U.S. Government Printing Office, Washington, D.C.

Magnuson, John J. 1990. Long-term ecological research and the invisible present. *BioScience,* 40:495–501.

Magnuson, J.J., C.J. Bowser, and A.L. Beckel. 1983. The invisible present: long term ecological research on lakes. *L&S Magazine* (University of Wisconsin, Madison), Fall:3–6.

Manley, S.A.M. and F.T. Ledig. 1979. Photosynthesis in black and red spruce and their hybrid derivatives: ecological isolation and hybrid inviability. *Canadian Journal of Botany,* 57:305–314.

Mayr, E. 1949. The species concept: semantics vs. semantics. *Evolution,* 3:371–372.

Mayr, E. 1953. Concepts of classification and nomenclature in higher organisms and microorganisms. *Annals, New York Academy of Science,* 56:391–397.

Mayr, E. 1963. *Animal Species and Evolution,* Belknap Press of Harvard University Press, Cambridge, MA.

Mayr, E. 1964. *Systematics and the Origin of Species from the Viewpoint of a Zoologist,* Dover Publications, New York.

Mayr, E., E.G. Linsley, and R.L. Usinger. 1953. *Methods and Principles of Systematic Zoology,* McGraw-Hill, New York.

Merchant, C. 1987. The theoretical structure of ecological revolutions. *Environmental Review,* 11:265–274.

Miller, J.Ann. 1991. Biosciences and ecological integrity. *BioScience,* 41:206–210.

Morrison, P.H. and F.J. Swanson. 1990. Fire History and Pattern in a Cascade Range Landscape, U.S. Department of Agriculture Forest Service General Technical Report PNW-GTR-254, Pacific Northwest Research Station, Portland, OR.

Olson, Sherry. 1988. Environments as shock absorbers, examples from Madagascar. *Environmental Review,* 12:61–80.

Payne, J.F. 1991. A viewpoint on endangered species. *Science and Technology,* 25:364–365.

Perlin, J. 1989. *A Forest Journey: The Role of Wood in the Development of Civilization*, W.W. Norton, New York.

Perry, David A. 1988. An overview of sustainable forestry. *Journal of Pesticide Reform*, 8:8–12.

Perry, D.A. 1988. Landscape pattern and forest pests. *Northwest Environmental Journal*, 4:213–228.

Perry, D.A. and J.G. Borchers. 1990. Climate change and ecosystem responses. *Northwest Environmental Journal*, 6:293–313.

Perry, D.A. and J. Maghembe. 1989. Ecosystem concepts and current trends in forest management: time for reappraisal. *Forest Ecology and Management*, 26:123–140.

Perry, D.A., M.P. Amaranthus, J.G. Borchers, S.L. Borchers, and R.E. Brainerd. 1989. Bootstrapping in ecosystems. *BioScience*, 39:230–237.

Perry, D.A., J.G. Borchers, S.L. Borchers, and M.P. Amaranthus. 1990. Species migrations and ecosystem stability during climate change: the belowground connection. *Conservation Biology*, 4:266–274.

Petts, G.E. 1984. *Impounded Rivers, Perspectives for Ecological Management*, John Wiley & Sons, New York.

Péwé, T.L., D.M. Hopkins, and J.L. Giddings. 1967. The Quaternary geology and archaeology of Alaska. pp. 355–374 in *The Quaternary of the United States*, J.E. Wright, Jr. and D.G. Frey (Eds.), Princeton University Press, Princeton, NJ.

Rapport, D.J., H.A. Regier, and T.C. Hutchinson. 1985. Ecosystem behavior under stress. *The American Naturalist*, 125:617–640.

Reid, W.V. and K.R. Miller. 1989. *Keeping Options Alive, The Scientific Basis for Conserving Biodiversity*, World Resources Institute, Washington, D.C.

Roberts, A. and K. Tregonning. 1980. The robustness of natural systems. *Nature*, 288:265–266.

Robinson, M.C. 1989. The relationship between the U.S. Army Corps of Engineers and the environmental community. *Environmental Review*, 13:1–41.

Routledge, R.D. 1987. The impact of soil degradation on the expected present net worth of future timber harvests. *Forest Science*, 33:823–834.

Savonen, C. 1990. Ashes in the Amazon. *Journal of Forestry*, 88:20–25.

Schowalter, T.D. 1985. Adaptations of insects to disturbance. pp. 235–386 in *The Ecology of Natural Disturbance and Patch Dynamics*, S.T.A. Pickett and P.S. White (Eds.), Academic Press, New York.

Sessions, G. 1987. The deep ecology movement: a review. *Environmental Review*, 11:105–125.

Seybold, P. 1995. The politics of free trade: the global marketplace as a closet dictator. *Monthly Review*, 47(7):43–48.

Shaffer, M.L. 1981. Minimum population sizes for species conservation. *BioScience*, 31:131–134.

Shannon, M.A. 1981. Sociology and public land management. *Western Wildlands*, 7:3–8.

Shearman, R. 1990. The meaning and ethics of sustainability. *Environmental Management,* 14:108.

Simon, H.A. 1962. The architecture of complexity. *Proceedings of the American Philosophical Society,* 106:467–482.

Simpson, G.G. 1952. The species concept. *Evolution,* 5:285–298.

Slocombe, D.S. 1989. History and environmental messes: a nonequilibrium systems view. *Environmental Review,* 13:1–13.

Sokal, R.R. 1973. The species problem reconsidered. *Systematic Zoology,* 22: 360–374.

Soroos, M.S. 1988. The international commons: a historical perspective. *Environmental Review,* 12:22.

Thomas, J.W., E.D. Forsman, J.B. Lint, E.C. Meslow, B.R. Noon, and J. Verner. 1990. A Conservation Strategy for the Northern Spotted Owl, Report of the Interagency Scientific Committee to Address the Conservation of the Northern Spotted Owl, U.S. Government Printing Office, Washington, D.C.

Tighem, K.V. 1996. From wilds to weeds. *Environment Views,* 19:5–8.

Turner, M.G. 1989. Landscape ecology: the effect of pattern on process. *Annual Review of Ecological Systems,* 20:171–197.

Turner, M.G., E.P Odum, R. Costanza, and T.M. Springer. 1988. Market and nonmarket values of the Georgia landscape. *Environmental Management,* 12:209–217.

Wells, P.V. 1970. Postglacial vegetational history of the Great Plains. *Science,* 167:1574–1582.

Whitaker, John O., Jr. 1970. The biological subspecies: an adjunct of the biological species. *Biologist,* 52:12–15.

Wilson, E.O. and W.L. Brown, Jr. 1953. The subspecies concept and its taxonomic application. *Systematic Zoology,* 2:97–111.

Worster, D. 1987. The vulnerable Earth: toward a planetary history. *Environmental Review,* 11:87–103.

Zedler, P.H., C.R. Gautier, and G.S. McMaster. 1983. Vegetation change in response to extreme events: the effect of a short interval between fires in California chaparral and coastal scrub. *Ecology,* 64:809–818.